MW01700244

JAVA™

SUN CERTIFIED PROGRAMMER®

Sun 认证 Java 2 程序员学习指南 (Exam 310-025) 第二版

(影印本)

[美] Syngress Media 公司 著

人民邮电出版社　　麦格劳-希尔国际公司 McGraw Hill

图书在版编目（CIP）数据

SJC 学习指南/美国 Syngress Media 公司编，—北京：人民邮电出版社，2001.9
ISBN 7-115-09579-5

I.S… II.美… III.JAVA 语言—程序设计—工程技术人员—资格考核—自学参考资料—英文
IV.TP312

中国版本图书馆 CIP 数据核字（2001）第 053416 号

Syngress Media,Inc.：Sun Certified Programmer for Java 2 Study Guide,Second Edition(Exam：310-025)
ISBN 0-07-213208-6

Sun 认证 Java 2 程序员学习指南
（Exam 310－025）第二版（影印本）

◆ 著　［美］ Syngress Media 公司
责任编辑　陈　昇

◆ 人民邮电出版社出版发行　北京市崇文区夕照寺街 14 号
邮编　100061　电子函件　315@pptph.com.cn
网址　http://www. pptph.com.cn
读者热线　010-67180876
北京汉魂图文设计有限公司制作
北京顺义振华印刷厂印刷
新华书店总店北京发行所经销

◆ 开本：800×1000　1/16
印张：41.75
字数：913 千字　2001 年 9 月第 1 版
印数：5 001-7 000 册　2002 年 4 月北京第 3 次印刷

著作权合同登记　图字：01-2001-3348 号
ISBN 7-115-09579-5/TP・2421

定价：70.00 元（附光盘）

本书如有印装质量问题，请与本社联系 电话：（010）67129223

INTRODUCTION

How to Take the Sun Certified Java Programmer Exam

by Bill Rossi
Sun Certified Java Programmer and Developer
Rossi Engineering

This chapter covers the importance of your Java Programmer certification and prepares you for taking the actual examination. It gives you a few pointers on methods of preparing for the exam, including how to study and register, what to expect, and what to do on exam day. The Java certification program was created in late 1996 to address the needs of IT managers trying to find qualified Java professionals. At the time the technology was very new and therefore developers did not have any long-term experience with it. Certification was created as a tool to separate the experts from the rest.

Today, Java has been on the IT scene for several years. It is now possible to distinguish Java professionals by their experience level in addition to certification. Experience, however, does not indicate the same solid understanding of the fundamentals of the language that the certification exams demand. In order to succeed on the Sun Certified Programmer Exam, a candidate must demonstrate a comprehensive understanding of the core language concepts.

Why Certification?

Certification helps identify you as a Java expert. It is a tool that IT managers can use to identify those who have a solid grasp of the core language concepts. This is not to say that there are not good Java professionals that aren't certified, but when taken into consideration with experience, certification can be a powerful tool to the IT manager.

Some people become certified as an aid to compete in the demanding IT marketplace. Some companies use the exam as the final phase of a Java training course. Others take it purely for the challenge. Whatever your reasons for tackling the exam, this book will help you prepare for it.

It would be nice to know some statistics about the exam such as the pass/fail ratio and the number of people certified. Sun however has decided to keep this information confidential. The actual questions on the exam are also kept confidential and are even copyrighted. The questions and materials in this book are therefore based largely upon the experience of those who have previously taken and passed the exam as well as on Sun's publicly stated objectives.

DILBERT® United Features Syndicate / Reprinted by Permission.

Over the years, technology vendors have created their own certification programs because of industry demand. This demand arises when the marketplace needs skilled professionals and an easy way to identify them. Vendors benefit because it promotes people skilled in their product. Professionals benefit because it boosts their career. Employers benefit because it helps them identify qualified people.

Technology changes too often and too quickly to rely on traditional means of certification, such as universities and trade associations. Because of the investment and effort required to keep certification programs current, vendors are the only organizations suited to keep pace with the changes. In general, such vendor certification programs are excellent, with most of them requiring a solid foundation in the essentials, as well as their particular product line.

Corporate America has come to appreciate these vendor certification programs and the value they provide. Employers recognize that certifications, like university degrees, do not guarantee a level of knowledge, experience, or performance; rather, they establish a baseline for comparison. By seeking to hire vendor-certified employees, a company can assure itself that it has also hired a person skilled in the specific products the company uses.

Technical professionals have also begun to realize the value of certification and the impact it can have on their careers. By completing a certification program, professionals gain an endorsement of their skills from a major industry source. This endorsement can boost their current position, and it makes finding the next job even easier. Often, a certification determines whether a first interview is even granted.

Today, a certification may place you ahead of the pack. Tomorrow, it may be a necessity to keep from being left in the dust.

Sun's Certification Program

Currently there are three Java certification exams. They are the *Programmer*, the *Developer*, and the *Architect* exams.

The Programmer Exam

The Programmer exam is designed to test your knowledge of the Java programming language itself. It requires detailed knowledge of language syntax, core concepts, and application programming interfaces (APIs). It does not test any issues related to program design or architecture, and it does not ask why one approach is better than another, but rather it asks whether the given approach works.

The Developer Exam

The Developer exam picks up where the Programmer exam leaves off. Passing the Programmer exam is required before you can start the Developer exam. The Developer exam requires you to develop an actual program and then defend your design decisions. It is designed to test your understanding of why certain approaches are better than others in certain circumstances.

The Architect Exam

The Architect exam operates at an even higher level of abstraction than the Developer exam. It asks whether one technology is better than another at solving a given business problem. The Architect exam has no prerequisites and does not require a detailed understanding of the Java language.

on the job

In addition to finding the technical objectives that are being tested for each exam, you will find much more useful information on Sun's Web site at http://www.suned.sun.com/usa/cert_test.html. You will find information on becoming certified, exam-specific information, sample test questions, and the latest news on Sun certification. This is the most important site you will find on your journey to becoming Sun certified.

Sun maintains a Web site for its certification programs at http://suned.sun.com. This Web site will give you instructions on how to register for the exam. It also has the e-mail addresses and phone numbers for the people at Sun who are responsible for the exam.

Don't hesitate to contact Sun if you have questions regarding the exam. They have always been very responsive to questions and appreciate candidate feedback.

Computer-Based Testing

In a perfect world, you would be assessed for your true knowledge of a subject, not simply how you respond to a series of test questions. But life isn't perfect, and it just isn't practical to evaluate everyone's knowledge on a one-to-one basis.

For the majority of its certifications, Sun evaluates candidates using a computer-based testing service operated by Sylvan Prometric. This service is quite popular in the industry, and it is used for a number of vendor certification programs, including Novell's CNE and Microsoft's MCSE. Thanks to Sylvan Prometric's large number of facilities, exams can be administered worldwide, generally in the same town as a prospective candidate.

For the most part, Sylvan Prometric exams work similarly from vendor to vendor. However, there is an important fact to know about Sun's exams: they use the traditional Sylvan Prometric test format, not the newer adaptive format. This gives the candidate an advantage, since the traditional format allows answers to be reviewed and revised during the test.

exam watch

Many experienced test takers do not go back and change answers unless they have a good reason to do so. Only change an answer when you feel you may have misread or misinterpreted the question the first time. Nervousness may make you second-guess every answer and talk yourself out of a correct one.

To discourage simple memorization, Sun exams present a different set of questions every time the exam is administered. In the development of the exam, hundreds of questions are compiled and refined using beta testers. From this large collection, a random sampling is drawn for each test.

Each Sun exam has a specific number of questions and test duration. Testing time is typically generous, and the time remaining is always displayed in the corner of the testing screen, along with the number of remaining questions. If time expires during an exam, the test terminates, and incomplete answers are counted as incorrect.

At the end of the exam, your test is immediately graded, and the results are displayed on the screen. Scores for each subject area are also provided, but the system will not indicate which specific questions were missed. A report is automatically printed at the proctor's desk for your files. The test score is electronically transmitted back to Sun.

In the end, this computer-based system of evaluation is reasonably fair. You might feel that one or two questions were poorly worded; this can certainly happen, but you shouldn't worry too much. Ultimately, it's all factored into the required passing score.

exam Watch

When you find yourself stumped answering multiple-choice questions, use your scratch paper to write down the two or three answers you consider the strongest, and then underline the answer you feel is most likely correct. Here is an example of what your scratch paper might look like when you've gone through the test once:

21. B or C

33. A or C

This is extremely helpful when you mark the question and continue on. You can then return to the question and immediately pick up your thought process where you left off. Use this technique to avoid having to re-read and re-think questions. You will also need to use your scratch paper during complex, text-based scenario questions to create visual images to better understand the question. This technique is especially helpful if you are a visual learner.

Exam Quality

Because the exam questions are held confidentially by Sun, it may happen that you will come across a question that doesn't seem to have a right answer. Sun does try to quality-check the exam thoroughly, but without an outside review, some badly formulated questions may occur.

Unfortunately, there isn't much you can do about this when you are taking the exam. You can't write the question down and take it with you, so I'd recommend trying to remember the question before you leave and check it out later. If you still believe the question to be in error, contact Sun as soon as possible and try to work out a solution. This at least helps to keep others from having the same problem in the future.

There aren't supposed to be any multiple-choice questions that don't have any right answers. There may be some that have multiple right answers, but they should all have at least one. If you find a question that you think has no correct answers, pick the answer that is the closest to being correct, and contact Sun about the question after the exam.

Question Types

Sun's Java exams pose questions in a variety of formats, most of which are discussed here. As candidates progress toward the more advanced certifications, the difficulty of the exams is intensified, both through the subject matter as well as the question formats.

exam Watch

To pass these challenging exams, you may want to talk with other test takers to determine what is being tested, and what to expect in terms of difficulty.

True/False

The classic true/false question format is not used in the Sun exams, for the obvious reason that a simple guess has a 50 percent chance of being correct. Instead, true/false questions are posed in multiple-choice format, requiring the candidate to identify the true or false statement from a group of selections.

Multiple Choice

Multiple choice is the primary format for questions in Sun exams. This is the classic multiple choice question where the candidate selects one, two, three, or possibly four answers from a list of about four choices. The exam now identifies exactly how many answers to choose: "Select One;" "Select Two" etc. Also, there will never be any questions where there are 0 correct answers.

exam Watch

Make it easy on yourself and find some "braindumps." These are notes about the exam from test takers, which indicate the most difficult concepts tested, what to look out for, and sometimes even what not to bother studying.

Fill in the Blank

Fill-in-the-blank questions are less common in Sun exams. They may be presented in multiple-choice or freeform response format.

Tips on Taking the Exam

There are 59 questions on the exam. You will need to get at least 36 of them correct to pass—just over 61 percent. You are given two hours to complete the exam. This information is subject to change. Always check with Sun before taking the exam.

You are allowed to answer questions in any order, and you can go back and check your answers after you've gone through the test. There are no penalties for wrong answers, so it's better to at least attempt an answer than to not give one at all.

A good strategy for taking the exam is to go through once and answer all the questions that come to you quickly. You can then go back and do the others. The code samples provided for some questions may help you with others. For example, if a short-answer question wants the name of the method for taking square roots, another multiple-choice question may contain that information.

Be very careful on the code examples. Check for syntax errors first, count curly braces and parenthesis and make sure there are as many left ones as right ones. Look for capitalization errors and other such syntax problems before trying to figure out what the code does.

Many of the questions on the exam will hinge on subtleties of syntax. You will need to have a thorough knowledge of the Java language in order to succeed.

Tips on Studying for the Exam

First and foremost, give yourself plenty of time to study. Java is a complex programming language, and you can't expect to cram what you need to know into a single study session. It is a field best learned over time, by studying a subject and then applying your knowledge. Build yourself a study schedule and stick to it, but be reasonable about the pressure you put on yourself, especially if you're studying in addition to your regular duties at work.

One easy technique to use in studying for certification exams is the 15-minutes per day effort. Simply study for a minimum of 15 minutes every day. It is a small, but significant commitment. If you have a day where you just can't focus, then give up at 15 minutes. If you have a day where it flows completely for you, study longer. As long as you have more of the "flow days," your chances of succeeding are extremely high.

Another excellent way to study is through case studies. Case studies are articles or interactive discussions that offer real-world examples of how technology is applied to meet a need. These examples can serve to cement your understanding of a technique or technology by seeing it put to use. Interactive discussions offer added value because you can also pose questions of your own. User groups are an excellent source of examples, since the purpose of these groups is to share information and learn from each other's experiences.

Scheduling Your Exam

The Sun exams are scheduled by calling Sylvan Prometric directly. For locations outside the United States, your local number can be found on Sylvan's Web site at http://www.2test.com. Sylvan representatives can schedule your exam, but they don't have information about the certification programs. Questions about certifications should be directed to Sun's training department.

These representatives are familiar enough with the exams to find them by name, but it's best if you have the specific exam number handy when you call. After all, you wouldn't want to be scheduled and charged for the wrong exam (for example, the instructor's version, which is significantly harder).

Exams can be scheduled up to a year in advance, although it's really not necessary. Generally, scheduling a week or two ahead is sufficient to reserve the day and time you prefer. When scheduling, operators will search for testing centers in your area. For convenience, they can also tell which testing centers you've used before.

Sylvan accepts a variety of payment methods, with credit cards being the most convenient. When paying by credit card, you can even take tests the same day you call—provided, of course, that the testing center has room. (Quick scheduling can be handy, especially if you want to re-take an exam immediately.) Sylvan will mail you a receipt and confirmation of your testing date, although this generally arrives after the test has been taken. If you need to cancel or reschedule an exam, remember to call at least one day before your exam, or you'll lose your test fee.

When registering for the exam, you will be asked for your ID number. This number is used to track your exam results back to Sun. It's important that you use the same ID number each time you register, so that Sun can follow your progress.

Address information provided when you first register is also used by Sun to ship certificates and other related material. In the United States, your Social Security Number is commonly used as your ID number. However, Sylvan can assign you a unique ID number if you prefer not to use your Social Security Number.

Arriving at the Exam

As with any test, you'll be tempted to cram the night before. Resist that temptation. You should know the material by this point, and if you're too groggy in the morning, you won't remember what you studied anyway. Instead, get a good night's sleep.

Arrive early for your exam; it gives you time to relax and review key facts. Take the opportunity to review your notes. If you get burned out on studying, you can usually start your exam a few minutes early. On the other hand, I don't recommend arriving late. Your test could be cancelled, or you may not be left with enough time to complete the exam.

When you arrive at the testing center, you'll need to sign in with the exam administrator. In order to sign in, you need to provide two forms of identification. Acceptable forms include government-issued IDs (for example, passport or driver's license), credit cards, and company ID badge. One form of ID must include a photograph.

Aside from a brain full of facts, you don't need to bring anything else to the exam. In fact, your brain is about all you're allowed to take into the exam! All the tests are "closed book," meaning you don't get to bring any reference materials with you. You're also not allowed to take any notes out of the exam room. The test administrator will provide you with paper and a pencil. Some testing centers may provide a small marker board instead.

Calculators are not allowed, so be prepared to do any necessary math in your head or on paper. Additional paper is available if you need it.

Leave your pager and telephone in the car, or turn them off. They only add stress to the situation, since they are not allowed in the exam room, and can sometimes still be heard if they ring outside of the room. Purses, books, and other materials must be left with the administrator before entering the exam. While in the exam room, it's important that you don't disturb other candidates; talking is not allowed during the exam.

Once in the testing room, the exam administrator logs onto your exam, and you have to verify that your ID number and the exam number are correct. If this is the first time you've taken a Sun test, you can select a brief tutorial of the exam software. Before the test begins, you will be provided with facts about the exam, including the duration, the number of questions, and the score required for passing. Then the clock starts ticking and the fun begins.

The testing software is Windows-based, but you won't have access to the main desktop or any of the accessories. The exam is presented in full screen, with a single question per screen. Navigation buttons allow you to move forward and backward between questions. In the upper-right corner of the screen, counters show the number of questions and time remaining. Most important, there is a 'Mark' checkbox in the upper-left corner of the screen—this will prove to be a critical tool in your testing technique.

Test-Taking Techniques

Without a plan of attack, candidates are overwhelmed by the exam or become side-tracked and run out of time. For the most part, if you are comfortable with the material, the allotted time is more than enough to complete the exam. The trick is to keep the time from slipping away during any one particular problem.

The obvious goal of an exam is to answer the questions effectively, although other aspects of the exam can distract from this goal. Here are some tips for taking the exam more efficiently.

Size Up the Challenge

First, take a quick pass through all the questions in the exam. "Cherry-pick" the easy questions, answering them on the spot. Briefly read each question, noticing the type of question and the subject. As a guideline, try to spend less than 25 percent of your testing time in this pass.

This step lets you assess the scope and complexity of the exam, and it helps you determine how to pace your time. It also gives you an idea of where to find potential answers to some of the questions. Often, the answer to one question is shown in the exhibit of another. Sometimes the wording of one question might lend clues or jog your thoughts for another question.

If you're not entirely confident with your answer to a question, answer it anyway, but check the Mark box to flag it for later review. In the event that you run out of time, at least you've provided a "first guess" answer, rather than leaving it blank.

Second, go back through the entire test, using the insight you gained from the first go-through. For example, if the entire test looks difficult, you'll know better than to spend more than a minute or so on each question. Break down the pacing into small milestones; for example, "I need to answer 10 questions every 15 minutes."

At this stage, it's probably a good idea to skip past the time-consuming questions, marking them for the next pass. Try to finish this phase before you're 50–60 percent through the testing time.

Third, go back through all the questions you marked for review, using the Review Marked button in the question review screen. This step includes taking a second look at all the questions you were unsure of in previous passes, as well as tackling the time-consuming ones you deferred until now. Chisel away at this group of questions until you've answered them all.

If you're more comfortable with a previously marked question, unmark it now. Otherwise, leave it marked. Work your way through the time-consuming questions now, especially those requiring manual calculations. Unmark them when you're satisfied with the answer.

By the end of this step, you've answered every question in the test, despite having reservations about some of your answers. If you run out of time in the next step, at least you won't lose points for lack of an answer. You're in great shape if you still have 10–20 percent of your time remaining.

Review Your Answers

Now you're cruising! You've answered all the questions, and you're ready to do a quality check. Take yet another pass (yes, one more) through the entire test, briefly re-reading each question and your answer.

Carefully look over the questions again to check for "trick" questions. Be particularly wary of those which include a choice of "Does not compile." Be alert for last-minute clues. You're pretty familiar with nearly every question at this point, and you may find a few clues that you missed before.

The Grand Finale

When you're confident with all your answers, finish the exam by submitting it for grading. After what will seem like the longest 10 seconds of your life, the testing software will respond with your score. This is usually displayed as a bar graph, showing the minimum passing score, your score, and a PASS/FAIL indicator.

If you're curious, you can review the statistics of your score at this time. Answers to specific questions are not presented; rather, questions are lumped into categories, and results are tallied for each category. This detail is also printed on a report that has been automatically printed at the exam administrator's desk.

As you leave the exam, you'll need to leave your scratch paper behind or return it to the administrator. (Some testing centers track the number of sheets you've been given, so be sure to return them all.) In exchange, you'll receive a copy of the test report.

This report will be embossed with the testing center's seal, and you should keep it in a safe place. Normally, the results are automatically transmitted to Sun, but occasionally you might need the paper report to prove that you passed the exam.

In a few days, Sun will send you a package in the mail containing a nice paper certificate, a lapel pin, and artwork for the "steaming coffee cup" logo. You will be given a license to use the logo on your personal stationary and business cards.

Re-Testing

If you don't pass the exam, don't be discouraged. Try to have a good attitude about the experience, and get ready to try again. Consider yourself a little more educated. You know the format of the test a little better, and the report shows which areas you need to strengthen.

If you bounce back quickly, you'll probably remember several of the questions you might have missed. This will help you focus your study efforts in the right area. Serious go-getters will re-schedule the exam for a couple of days after the previous attempt, while the study material is still fresh in their mind.

Ultimately, remember that Sun certifications are valuable because they're hard to get. After all, if anyone could get one, what value would it have? In the end, it takes a good attitude and a lot of studying, but you can do it!

ABOUT THE CONTRIBUTORS

About Syngress Media

Syngress Media creates books and software for Information Technology professionals seeking skill enhancement and career advancement. Its products are designed to comply with vendor and industry standard course curricula, and are optimized for certification exam preparation. You can contact Syngress via the Web at www.syngress.com.

Author

Brian Bagnall (Sun Certified Java Programmer and Developer) is co-author of the *Sun Certified Programmer for Java 2 Study Guide, Second Edition*, the *E-mail Virus Protection Handbook*, and *Hack Proofing Your Network Internet Tradecraft*. He is currently the lead programmer at IdleWorks, a company located in Western Canada. IdleWorks develops distributed processing solutions for large- and medium-sized businesses with supercomputing needs. His background includes working for IBM developing client-side applications. Brian is also a key developer of Lejos, a Java software development kit for Lego Mindstorms. Brian would like to thank his family for their support, and especially his father Herb.

Contributors

Eileen Sauer (Sun Certified Java Programmer, Developer and Architect) is President and CEO of Emprise Computing, Inc. She has more than 13 years of experience doing full software life cycle development, technical training, and mentoring in industries such as brokerage, banking, telecommunications, and insurance. Eileen works with Java, Visual Age, Rational Rose, EJB (Weblogic), Sybase/Oracle, etc., and has a Bachelor's in Math/CS from the University of Notre Dame. Eileen Sauer can be reached at http://www.geocities.com/emprise.

Frank Sauer (MSCS) has been developing object-oriented systems since 1986 using Smalltalk, C++ and Java. His expertise includes object-oriented design and analysis using UML, design and analysis patterns, and distributed object systems. He presently works as an infrastructure modeler for The Technical Resource

Connection Inc., a wholly owned subsidiary of Perot Systems Corporation. At TRC, he has been building enterprise distributed object systems using Java, CORBA and, most recently, Enterprise Java Beans (EJB). He has worked on medical information and imaging systems, customer support systems in the financial industry, and supply chain management systems in the food industry. He and his wife Eileen live in Tampa, Florida. When he is not programming in Java, he enjoys classical and new age music, ballroom dancing, and scuba diving.

Jay Foster (BSEE) has been an IT professional since 1989. His expertise includes object-oriented design and modeling, design documentation, software engineering, system testing, and N-tier application development. He presently works for The Technical Resource Connection, Inc., a wholly owned subsidiary of Perot Systems Corporation. Jay has extensive experience in the following technologies: Java Servlets, Enterprise JavaBeans (EJB), Java Server Pages (JSP), Java Database Connectivity (JDBC), Remote Method Invocation (RMI), Java Foundation Classes (JFC), Swing, object-oriented design using the Unified Modeling Language (UML), and CORBA. During the course of his career, Jay has worked on manufacturing process control systems in the automotive and food processing industries, electronic display control systems in the sign industry, and order entry/workflow systems in both the telecommunications and insurance industries. He has been developing object oriented systems in Java for 3 years and is a Sun Certified Java Programmer. Jay is married and currently resides in Tampa, Florida. His hobbies include motorcycles and basketball. Jay can be reached at jfoster@trcinc.com.

Jonathan Meeks (Sun Certified Java Programmer) is a Senior Engineer for DARC Corporation, in Chicago, Illinois, where he works on Enterprise Application Integration adapter technology. He has a wide area of experience, including Oracle RDBMS, XML for e-commerce, and distributed object computing. Mr. Meeks holds a B.A. in Cognitive Science from Northwestern University. He dedicates his work on this book to his wife, Wendy.

Bob Hablutzel has been working in computer technology for much longer than he likes to admit: nearly two decades. In that time, he has worked as an operator, programmer, modeler, analyst, consultant, and architect, and is currently Chief Technology Officer of WebCredit.com. He thanks his wife and his pets for their support and assistance.

Mike Keene (Sun Certified Java Programmer), during his professional career, has acquired a vast amount of experience using the Java 2 Enterprise Edition technologies. Currently, he is working as a consultant for Booz-Allen & Hamilton on a U.S. Customs Service project to locate high-risk vehicles coming into the country. The system is built using Java Server Pages as the front end and utilizing

Enterprise Java Beans and the Java Messaging Service in the middle tier with Oracle 8i as the database. He would like to thank his family for giving him the time to produce such an informational and useful book for people.

Rick R. Ratliff (Sun Certified Java Programmer) is the chief software architect for A.B. Watley Group in Allen, Texas. Rick has a Bachelor of Science in Computer Science from Southwest Texas State University and has worked in software development since 1985, specializing in object-oriented technology. He is currently studying for the Sun Certified Java Developer and Java Architect exams, and can be reached at either rick.ratliff@abwg.com or rick@ratliff.org

Tristan Yates (Sun Certified Java Programmer) is an independent Java/Oracle consultant in the Washington, D.C., area. Recent clients have included the Discovery Channel, Qwest, the Library of Congress, and Sallie Mae. He holds certifications in Java, Oracle, and Powerbuilder.

Diego Moriarty (Sun Certified Java Programmer and Developer) started programming as a hobby when he was twelve, and is one of the lucky people who has made a career out of his passion. He has developed software in areas such as telecommunications, e-commerce, banking, internet tools and medicine. He is currently between contracts, traveling around the world and doing some bungy jumping and paragliding.

Chad Tippin has been writing software professionally since 1992 and has been using Java for more than four years. His skills include object-oriented analysis and design, practical application of design patterns and the design of distributed enterprise applications using technologies such as CORBA, RMI, and Enterprise Java Beans (EJB). Chad is a Senior Designer/Developer for The Technical Resource Connection, Inc, a wholly owned subsidiary of Perot Systems Corporation. He currently resides in Tampa, Florida with his wife Tracy and son Ashton. He can be reached at ctippin@trcinc.com.

Trent Heintz has four years of IT experience as a Software Developer. He is currently part of a team of developers working on a new distributed-computing Java software package. Trent is fairly new to the IT industry, having only graduated as a client/server programmer three years ago. His course of study was in object-oriented technologies, Java, Visual Basic, Database theory, C++, and Web development. Trent has also just completed a Java 2 study guide for the Sun programmer exam, for a Web site designed for people who are about to take the exam. Trent's main interest is in Java and Internet programming, as well as Website design and development, where he has advanced his skills in HTML, CSS, JavaScript, and other new types of media such as Flash.

Series Editor

Bill Rossi (Sun Certified Java Programmer and Developer) is President of Rossi Engineering (http://www.rossi.com), an independent consulting firm specializing in Java and Internet-related projects. He has over a decade of software engineering experience, focusing the last four years on Java development and architecture.

Technical Editors

Harold Cabrera (Sun Certified Java Programmer) is a Software Engineer and co-founder of IdleWorks Inc. He is the lead architect for their software development team which has developed a distributed computing application called *Distco.* Harold is a recipient of the IEEE Best Thesis Award for his undergraduate thesis entitled "A Distributed Computing System: An Application Written in Java for Distributed Computing". Harold holds a bachelor's degree in Computer Engineering from the University of Manitoba and he is a Java Certified Programmer.

James W. Archer is a software consultant based in southern New England. With a B.A. from the University of Rhode Island, Jim has more than a decade of experience in object-oriented software design and development. He currently specializes in leveraging client-server, Intranet, and Internet technologies including XML, Java, and Enterprise Java Beans to build extensible, Internet accessible data systems that evolve quickly and easily with the needs of their owners. Jim can be reached at jim@archer.net.

FOREWORD

From Global Knowledge

At Global Knowledge we strive to support the multiplicity of learning styles required by our students to achieve success as technical professionals. In this book, it is our intention to offer the reader a valuable tool for successful completion of the Java 2 Programmer Certification Exam.

As the world's largest IT training company, Global Knowledge is uniquely positioned to offer these books. The expertise gained each year from providing instructor-led training to hundreds of thousands of students worldwide has been captured in book form to enhance your learning experience. We hope that the quality of these books demonstrates our commitment to your lifelong learning success. Whether you choose to learn through the written word, computer-based training, Web delivery, or instructor-led training, Global Knowledge is committed to providing you the very best in each of those categories. For those of you who know Global Knowledge, or those of you who have just found us for the first time, our goal is to be your lifelong competency partner.

Thank you for the opportunity to serve you. We look forward to serving your needs again in the future.

Warmest regards,

Duncan Anderson

Duncan Anderson
President and Chief Executive Officer, Global Knowledge

PREFACE

This book's primary objective is to help you prepare for and pass the Sun Certified Java 2 Programmer Exam (310-025). We believe that the only way to do this is to help you increase your knowledge and build your skills. After completing this book, you should feel confident that you have thoroughly reviewed all of the objectives that Sun has established for the exam.

In This Book

This book is organized around the topics covered within the Sun Certified Java 2 Programmer Exam administered at Sylvan Testing Centers. Sun has specific objectives for the Programmer's exam; we've followed their list carefully, so you can be assured you're not missing anything.

In Every Chapter

We've created a set of chapter components that call your attention to important items, reinforce important points, and provide helpful exam-taking hints. Take a look at what you'll find in the chapters:

- Each chapter begins with the **Certification Objectives**—what you need to know in order to pass the section on the exam dealing with the chapter topic. The Certification Objective headings identify the objectives within the chapter, so you'll always know an objective when you see it!
- **Certification Exercises** are interspersed throughout the chapters. These are step-by-step exercises. They help you master skills that are likely to be an area of focus on the exam. Don't just read through the exercises; they are hands-on practice that you should be comfortable completing. Learning by doing is an effective way to increase your competency with the language.
- **From the Classroom** sidebars describe the issues that come up most often in the training classroom setting. These sidebars give you a valuable perspective

into certification- and product-related topics. They point out common mistakes and address questions that have arisen from classroom discussions.

- S & S sections lay out specific problems and solutions in a quick-read format.
- The **Certification Summary** is a succinct review of the chapter and a re-statement of salient points regarding the exam.
- The **Two-Minute Drill** at the end of every chapter is a checklist of the main points of the chapter. It can be used for last-minute review.
- The **Self Test** offers questions similar to those found on the certification exam. The answers to these questions, as well as explanations of the answers, can be found at the end of the particular chapter. By taking the Self Test after completing each chapter, you'll reinforce what you've learned from that chapter, while becoming familiar with the structure of the exam questions.

Some Pointers

Once you've finished reading this book, set aside some time to do a thorough review. You might want to return to the book several times and make use of all the methods it offers for reviewing the material:

1. *Re-read all the Two-Minute Drills*, or have someone quiz you. You also can use the drills as a way to do a quick cram before the exam.
2. *Review all the Q & A scenarios* for quick problem solving.
3. *Re-take the Self Tests.* Taking the tests right after you've read the chapter is a good idea, because it helps reinforce what you've just learned. However, it's an even better idea to go back later and do all the questions in the book in one sitting. Pretend you're taking the exam. (For this reason, you should mark your answers on a separate piece of paper when you go through the questions the first time.)
4. *Complete the exercises.* Did you do the exercises when you read through each chapter? If not, do them! These exercises are designed to cover exam topics, and there's no better way to get to know this material than by practicing.

5. *Check out the Web site.* Global Knowledge invites you to become an active member of the Access Global Web site. This site is an online mall and an information repository that you'll find invaluable. You can access many types of products to assist you in your preparation for the exams, and you'll be able to participate in forums, on-line discussions, and threaded discussions. No other book brings you unlimited access to such a resource. You'll find more information about this site in Appendix B.

CONTENTS

1

Language Fundamentals

CERTIFICATION OBJECTIVES

- 1.01 Source Files
- 1.02 Package, Import, Class, Method, and Variable Declarations
- 1.03 Java Programming Language Keywords and Identifiers
- 1.04 Using a Variable or Array Element That Is Uninitialized and Unassigned
- 1.05 Ranges of All Primitive Data Types
- ✓ Two-Minute Drill
- Q&A Self Test

This chapter will familiarize you with the Java fundamentals that you need to know in order to pass the Java 2.0 Programmer exam. Because you are planning on becoming Sun certified, it is probably safe to assume that you know the basics of Java, so this chapter will focus on the details you might not be familiar with, but which are essential for passing the exam.

CERTIFICATION OBJECTIVE 1.01

Source Files

A *source file* is a plain text file containing your Java code. The Java compiler *javac* processes the source file to produce a byte code file, which ends with the suffix *class*.

exam watch

The exam is concerned with how the Java compiler deals with a source file. For this reason, it is a good idea to prepare for the exam using only the Java Development Kit (JDK) 1.2 or 1.3 supplied by Sun, a text editor, and a command prompt. This may be a little awkward at first for people used to working in an integrated development environment such as IBM's Visual Age for Java. You are roughing it a bit by using only the command line, but perhaps it will give you the same back-to-basics thrill as starting a fire with two sticks.

A Java source file must meet strict requirements; otherwise, the Java compiler will generate errors. A plain text file can be compiled using the JDK in the following manner, and will produce no screen output from the compiler if successful:

```
c:\Java Projects>javac Calculate.java
c:\Java Projects>
```

Now, if you look in the Java Projects directory, you will see a file named Calculate.class. The source file must be saved with the suffix *java*. If you try to compile a source file that does not have the java suffix, the compiler produces an error:

```
c:\Java Projects>javac Calculate.jav
Calculate.jav is an invalid option or argument.
```

Identifiers are names that we assign to classes, methods, and variables. Java is a *case-sensitive* language, which means identifiers must have consistent capitalization throughout. Identifiers can have letters and numbers, but a number may not begin the identifier name. Most symbols are not allowed, but the $ and _ (underscore) symbols are allowed because they provide support for preexisting names on earlier systems. Examine the following examples:

```
int 99year; // invalid
int year99; // valid
int hello#; // invalid
int $hello$; // valid
int MAX_VALUE; // valid
```

File names are also case sensitive. The file itself can contain as many spaces, tabs, and carriage returns as you wish, but they must not break up words within the file. For example, the following file will compile just fine:

```
          public
     class
MyClass { int
month
;}
```

At the very least, a source file must contain…nothing! That's right, the compiler will produce no errors when compiling a blank file. The minimum viable source file, which will produce a class, looks like this:

```
class MyClass {}
```

A source file may only have one public class or interface and an unlimited number of default classes or interfaces defined within it, and the filename must be the same as the public class name. For example, the following file is saved as MyClass.java:

```
// Will not work
public class YourClass {}
```

When we attempt to compile, we get the following error:

```
c:\Java Projects>javac MyClass.java
MyClass.java:1: Public class YourClass must be defined in
     a file called "YourClass.java".
```

It is not imperative for the filename to match the name of a class (or interface) in the source file. For example, a file could be called ChessPieces.java and contain classes such as Rook, Knight, and King. If there is a public class/interface in the source file, however, then the name of the source file must be the same as the name of the public class. The following file has the filename BobsClass.java, and it will compile fine because there are no public classes:

```
// This works
class YourClass {}
class MyClass {}
class JensClass {}
```

Exercise 1-1 demonstrates how to create a basic source file and compile it. Create a source file containing one public class and two default classes. The classes can be empty, with just curly braces after the class declaration. Save the file with a legal file name and compile it with the standard Sun 2.0 Java compiler.

EXERCISE 1-1

Creating and Compiling a Source File

1. Install Java 2.0 on your computer by following the documentation provided by Sun.
2. Open a text editor and type the class definitions.
3. Save the file with an appropriate filename. Make sure the file ends with .java and not .txt.
4. At a command prompt, type **javac (*filename*).java**.
5. If you receive no errors then you have done everything correctly.

CERTIFICATION OBJECTIVE 1.02

Package, Import, Class, Method, and Variable Declarations

A *declaration* is a statement that declares a package, import, class, interface, method, or variable in a source file. A typical example of a source file is as follows:

```
package trades;
import java.util.Math;
public class Quote extends Thread implements Tradable {
    // Code goes in here
}
```

It is not necessary to use each of these declarations, but the order in which you place your declarations in the source file is important. They must appear in the following order:

1. The package declaration (optional)
2. The import function (optional)
3. Any class definitions

Packages

A *package* is an entity that groups classes and interfaces together. Packages perform the following functions:

- Organize and group classes, normally by function. For example, the java.awt package contains the classes with graphical components.

- Help to define access to variables and methods. For example, by using the access modifier *protected* only classes in the same package will have access to it.
- Make it easy to import other programmers' classes into your code, while keeping the code separate from your own.

Placing the package declaration at the top of your source file includes these classes in a package with the name that you specify.

```
package trades.quotes;
```

If no package is explicitly declared, Java places your classes into a default package.

The name of the package must reflect the directory structure used to store the classes in your package. The subdirectory begins in any directory indicated by the *classpath* environment variable. Setting the classpath environment variable is specific to your operating system. The Readme file located in your main JDK directory contains information on how to set this up in UNIX and Windows environments. Exercise 1-2 will also explain how to set this up.

Now, with the classpath set, you can start dropping classes belonging to the package trades.quotes into the appropriate subdirectory:

```
c:\MyPackages\trades\quotes\
```

To avoid having different people trying to use the same package name, Sun recommends using the reverse of your Internet domain name to package your classes. For example, Sun would keep its classes in the following package:

```
package com.sun.java;
```

Once the classpath is set, any classes in the package can be run from any directory in the system; it is not necessary to be in the same directory as the classes. People commonly have a problem trying to run their class once they include it in a package. For example, if I place a class called Trade in a package called trades.quotes, then try to run it in the normal way, the following error will occur:

```
c:\MyPackages\trades\quotes>java Trade
Exception in thread "main" java.lang.NoClassDefFoundError:
     Trade (wrong name: trades/quotes/Trade)
```

To run this class, you must specify the entire package name after the java command. Again, because the class is in a package and the classpath environment variable has been set, it does not matter where the command prompt is.

```
c:\>java trades.quotes.Trade
```

Exercise 1-2 covers how to create a package and insert classes into the package. You will use the file you created in the previous exercise for this. Try to add this file to a package called com.syngress.

EXERCISE 1-2

Creating a Package and Inserting Classes

1. Create a directory called **Java Packages** or any other name you wish. Edit your environment variable classpath to include the directory you just created. For Linux, Solaris, and other UNIX-based systems, do the following:

   For UNIX:

   ```
   setenv CLASSPATH .:$HOME/cpsc120/classes:/pub/java/jdk/lib/classes.zip
   ```

   For Linux bash shell:

   ```
   export CLASSPATH=$CLASSPATH:/java/classes:/home/tchin/myclasses
   ```

   For Linux tcsh or csh:

   ```
   set CLASSPATH = ($CLASSPATH /java/classes /home/tchin/myclasses)
   ```

   Note the CLASSPATH variable on UNIX systems must be in all capitals, because UNIX environment variables are case sensitive. Additionally, all paths should be separated using a ':' (colon). For Windows users, at a DOS prompt, type the following command (assuming you keep the JDK 1.2 in the following directory):

   ```
   set classpath = c:\jdk1.2\lib;c:\Java Packages\;
   ```

   An even easier way to set the classpath is by using the -cp or -classpath argument when running java.exe:

   ```
   c:\java -cp Path1;Path2
   ```

   Note that this setting will not be permanent, and it will apply only to the current DOS window.

2. Create the directory structure **com\syngress** within the Java Packages directory.
3. Copy your class file to the Syngress directory.

4. Add the package statement to the top of the file:

```
package com.syngress;
```

5. Try compiling it. If you did everything properly, it should compile:

```
c:\>javac MyClass.java
```

6. Try running the class from the command prompt. For example:

```
c:\>java com.syngress.MyClass
```

on the Job

It is a good idea to become familiar with the java.util package. There are a lot of classes in this package that are frequently used. Among these classes you will find an Arrays class which helps in sorting and searching arrays, a Vector class for storing unsorted data types, and the Random class for generating random numbers. It takes under an hour to familiarize yourself with the classes and methods, and it will end up saving you a lot of time. Nothing is worse than creating a whole new class, then realizing you have just reinvented the wheel.

Classes

Let's briefly review some object-oriented terms. A *class* is a definition for a potential object. Think of a class as a skeleton or framework that contains the data and methods. Once the class is instantiated it becomes an *object* (sometimes referred to as an instance). The constructor method of a class is invoked when an object is instantiated. The constructor method contains code that generally performs *initialization* (assigns values to) of variables within the class.

It is important to declare your class with the keywords in the proper order. A typical, large class definition looks like this:

```
public abstract class MyClass extends Parent implements A, B {}
```

A *modifier* is a keyword in a class, method, or variable declaration that modifies the behavior of the element. An *access modifier* is a modifier that changes the protection of an element (Chapter 2 will explain further). The order of the modifiers and keywords is as follows:

1. "public" access modifier (optional, can be placed after final/abstract)
2. "final" modifier (optional, cannot be used with abstract)
3. "abstract" modifier (optional, cannot be used with final)
4. "class" keyword
5. name of the class
6. "extends" and the class it extends (optional)
7. "implements" and any interfaces it implements (optional)
8. curly braces {}

It is important to note number two and number three on the list. These cannot be used together when defining a class because the abstract modifier implies the class will be extended, yet the final modifier prevents the class from being extended. This will be further explained in Chapter 2.

Let's briefly review some object-oriented terminology. C++ programmers call a parent class a *base class* and the child class is called a *derived class* (as in the class is derived from a base class). In Java, the equivalent is a *subclass*, which extends a *superclass*.

All Java classes must extend a superclass. If you do not specify a class to extend, Java will derive your class from the class Object. Object is the highest-level Java class, and all classes are subclasses of the Object class.

Objects can also refer to themselves by using the keyword *this*. Observe the following code that shows two examples of the keyword *this*:

```
class Money {
     public double costs;
     public double revenue;
     public double profit;
     public Money (double costs) {
          this.costs = costs;  // Specifying a particular variable
          profit = Accounting.calculateProfit(this); // Passes itself
     }
}
```

In the sixth line of the program there are two variables with the name *costs*. The instance variable is defined at the top of the code, and the local variable is passed to the Money() constructor method as an argument. To differentiate the two, it is necessary to use the keyword *this*.

Sometimes it is necessary for an object to pass itself to another method, as in line six of this class. By using *this*, it passes a reference of itself to the method calculateProfit().

You can also use this() to invoke a constructor method for a class. The this() method may be invoked only from a constructor method, as in the following example:

```
class ThisSample{
      String screenTitle;
      public ThisSample() {
            this("Main Screen");
      }
      public ThisSample(String title) {
            screenTitle = title;
      }
}
```

Examine line four of the preceding class. It is calling a separate constructor using a string as an argument. It must call the this() method in the first line of a constructor, otherwise it will not compile.

Methods, variables, and inner classes always appear within the curly braces of the class definition. You might think you could create a class with only one line, for example a variable declaration, and not use the curly braces.

```
class Tiny
      int size; // Will not work!
```

This seems logical, because after an *if* statement if there is only one line, you do not have to create a block of code in curly brackets, so why would you need to with a class? This is not the case; all code belonging to a class must appear in the curly braces. This is just the sort of obscure question they might ask you on the exam.

Interfaces

An *interface* is a nonfunctional class that can contain constants and method declarations but no functional methods. It is really only necessary to know how to define an interface and how to use the Runnable interface for the exam. We will go slightly more in depth, however, because it is always better to know more, rather than less, when preparing for the exam.

An interface is declared in much the same way as a class, except we use the keyword *interface*:

```
interface Fabric {
     public Image getSample();
}
```

Notice we define a method within the interface, but instead of ending with curly braces we end with a semicolon. The Fabric interface ensures that any class that implements this interface will have a method called getSample(). Now let's try implementing our interface:

```
import java.awt.Image;
class Chair extends Furniture implements Fabric {
     Image sampleImage;
     public Image getSample() {
          return sampleImage;
     }
// Additional code goes here
}
```

In the preceding code, we actually created the method getSample() that was specified in the interface. If we had not declared this method, the compiler would have produced an error. Interfaces can also declare variables; however, they must be initialized with a value, as in the following example:

```
interface ServerCodes {
     public static final int MAXCONNECTIONS = 20;
     public static final int MAXUSERS= MAXCONNECTIONS * 5;
}
```

Interfaces may not, however, declare variables unless they are initialized. This is because variables in interfaces are implicitly public, static, and final (even though the keywords are not used). Examine the following interface:

```
interface Fabric {
     Image sampleImage;
     public Image getSample();
}
```

Now if we attempt to compile the preceding example, we will receive the following error:

```
c:\Java Projects\Server>javac Fabric.java
Fabric.java:2: This final variable must be initialized:
     Image sampleImage;
```

```
1 error
c:\Java Projects\Server>
```

An interface may also extend one or more interfaces:

```
interface MyInterface extends YourInterface, Runnable {}
```

Notice that we do not extend another interface by using the command *implements*. If we try to implement another interface, we will get a compiler error.

Java also allows classes to implement more than one interface, as in the following example:

```
class MyClass implements MyInterface, YourInterface {}
```

Implementation of an Interface

The only interface you will need to know for the exam is java.lang.Runnable. The Runnable interface is used to make a threaded class, about which we will go into greater detail in Chapter 9. For now, let's try making a threaded class using the Runnable interface.

```
public class ExponentialGrowth implements Runnable {}
```

If we try to compile the preceding code now, without any of the methods defined in the interface, we will get the following error:

```
c:\Java Projects\Exponential>javac ExponentialGrowth.java
ExponentialGrowth.java:1: class ExponentialGrowth must be declared
     abstract. It does not define void run() from interface
     java.lang.Runnable.
..
```

As we can see, the Java compiler expects us to implement the method run(), defined in the Runnable interface. Let's create a run() method in our class which shows us the value of our money compounding at an interest rate of 10 percent per year.

```
public class ExponentialGrowth implements Runnable {
     public final double INTEREST = 0.10;
     public void run () {
          double dollars = 1.0;
          int years = 0;
          while (true) {
               System.out.println("$" + dollars + " after " + years +
```

```
            " years");
          dollars *= (1 + INTEREST);
          years += 1;
          // pause for 1000 milliseconds:
          try {Thread.sleep(1000);
          } catch(InterruptedException e) {}
        }
      }
    }
```

For now, ignore the try-catch block; it is necessary only to pause the thread for one second. Also, notice there is no need to use an import statement to access the Runnable interface, because it is part of the java.lang package, which is automatically imported. Now, to see our wonderful investment compounding yearly at 10 percent interest, we must create an instance of the class in the main() method.

```
class ShowGrowth {
    public static void main (String [] args) {
        ExponentialGrowth growth = new ExponentialGrowth();
        Thread compoundThread = new Thread(growth);
        compoundThread.start();
    }
}
```

The code in the main method deserves further examination. The first line in the method creates an instance of the class ExponentialGrowth and assigns it to the variable *growth*. The next line creates a new thread, using the constructor which takes a Runnable object as the argument. The final line invokes the start() method to begin our thread. By the way, if you are wondering how to stop the thread, try pressing CTRL-C.

Methods

A *method* declares executable code that can be invoked, passing a fixed number of values as arguments. A large method definition can look like this:

```
public static final synchronized double getPrice(final int itemCode,
    Color itemColor) throws Exception {/* code here */}
```

Notice that the local variable *itemCode* is declared as final. Arguments that are passed to a method are treated as local variables, hence they can be declared final by the method. Of course, not all of these keywords must be used. The smallest method definition, which does absolutely nothing, looks like this:

```
void playSong() {}
```

Once again, it is important to use the keywords in the proper order:

1. Access modifiers—public, private, protected, or none (default)
2. Special modifiers—abstract, final, native, static, or synchronized (optional)
3. Return type—a variable or void
4. Name of method (identifier)
5. Arguments passed to the method within ( ) brackets (none or many)
6. Exceptions thrown (optional)
7. Curly braces enclosing the method code (not with abstract or interface methods)

The order of number one and number two is not important. For example, the following method definition is quite valid:

```
synchronized static final public double getSquare (double Number) {..}
```

As with class definitions, abstract and final may not be used in the same method definition. As noted in number seven, an abstract method, or a method defined in an interface, must end in a semicolon without curly braces:

```
public abstract void showImage();
```

exam Watch

Keep in mind how picky the exam will be about the order and combinations of keywords that make up a legal definition of a method. The exam will test you on every conceivable combination of keywords, and for each example, you must know whether it is valid.

Main Method and Command-Line Arguments

The main() method is used to start the ball rolling for a Java program. The main() method is defined like any other method, only it contains an array of strings passed from the command line when the class is started.

```
public class MainTest {
     public static void main (String [] args) {
```

```
            for (int i = 0;i < args.length;i++) {
                System.out.println("Argument " + i + ": " + args[i]);
            }
        }
}
```

In the preceding example, it is not necessary to name the command-line arguments array *args*, but by convention most programmers go this way. The preceding code will output any command-line arguments, as in the following example:

```
C:\Java Projects\Main>java MainTest Philip K Dick
Argument 0: Philip
Argument 1: K
Argument 2: Dick
```

It is important to note that the first argument, *Philip*, correlates to the index value of 0, and the second argument, *K*, correlates to the index value of 1, and so on.

The code will compile if you create a method named main() without modifying it as static; however, when you try to run the class from the command line it will say no main() method exists.

Constructor Method

When a class is first instantiated, the first method to be invoked is always the *constructor*.

```
class DataServer{
      public String serverName;
      public DataServer () {
            serverName = "Customer Service";
      }
}
```

The constructor is typically responsible for initializing variables. If no constructor method is present for a class, Java uses the default constructor from the superclass. (Remember, if no superclass is specified then the class Object is the superclass by default.)

Constructors are different from normal methods in some important ways:

- The method name is the same as the class name.
- There is no return type.
- Constructors can't be inherited as other superclass methods are.

FROM THE CLASSROOM

Static and Non-Static Members

Students of the Java language will often run into problems when they try to code within the main method. The compiler starts to say funny things such as, "Can't make a static reference to a non-static variable." This is because the main() method is static; therefore, any methods or variables used by the main() method must also be static. Any methods it tries to use that are not static will cause problems. For example, in the following example, the main() method will try to change the value of a variable defined outside of the main() method:

```
class DataClient {
    int users;
    public static void main(String [] args) {
        users += 1; // Non-static variable manipulated in static method
    }
}
```

When we try to compile the preceding code, we get the following:

```
c:\Java Projects\Client>javac DataClient.java
DataClient.java:4: Can't make a static reference to nonstatic
variable users in class DataClient.
         users += 1;
1 error
c:\Java Projects\Client>
```

The preferred solution is not to start making everything static (this works but is messy), but rather to create an instance of the class in which the main() method resides. For example, the following code shows a class that makes an instance of itself:

```
class DataClient {
     int users;
     public static void main(String [] args) {
          DataClient client = new DataClient();
          client.users += 1;
     }
}
```

—Brian Bagnall, Sun Certified Programmer and Developer

■ The constructor method can't be final, abstract, synchronized, native, or static.

There are times when you require the constructor of the superclass to initialize first, followed by the constructor of the subclass. This can be accomplished by using the keyword *super()*.

```
class DataServer extends Server{
     public String serverName;
     public DataServer (int startCode) {
          super(startCode);
          serverName = "Customer Service";
     }
}
```

The super() command must be the first line of your constructor method, otherwise the compiler will generate an error. It must also appear in a constructor method; only a constructor may invoke another constructor explicitly. Chapter 2 will discuss constructors in more depth.

Variable Declarations and Identifiers

A *reference variable* is an identifier that refers to a primitive type or an object (including an array). A variable declaration is used to assign a variable name to an object or primitive type. The following is an example of a variable declaration at class level and local level:

```
public class Variables {
     public static int users; // Declares an integer named 'users'
     public Variables() {
          int port; // Local variable
     }
}
```

The preceding code sets up a variable of primitive type integer, and assigns memory to store the integer number. Variables may be declared within the curly braces of a class or a method, as the variable *port* is in the example.

The following are the keywords that may be used in declaring a variable:

1. public, private, protected, or none (default)
2. final, static, transient, and volatile (optional)
3. variable type (int, Boolean, String, and so on)
4. an identifier name

A *local variable* is a variable declared within a method. These are also known as *automatic variables.* Local variables may include only variable type, identifier, and final from the preceding list. A declaration can also initialize the variable, although for class members this is normally done in the constructor method.

```
public int users = 10; // Declares and initializes an integer
```

Final variables can be initialized only once within Java code. If the code attempts to reinitialize a final variable with another value, the compiler will complain. The following code is legal, even though the final variable is not initialized within the same line on which it is declared:

```
public final int users; // Does not initialize a final variable
```

Several variables may be declared on the same line when they are of the same type. This is accomplished by placing a comma after each identifier. For example, Java code can define three integers: a, b, and c.

```
int a = 3, b, c = a;
```

Keep in mind that variables can not be synchronized, abstract, or native.

We can also declare an object variable. Objects can be declared without being initialized, or they can be initialized in the same line. The following example shows an object being initialized:

```
public Dimension = new Dimension(20,100);
```

The preceding code invokes the constructor method, Dimension (), which initializes an object of type Dimension using the arguments contained in the brackets.

String objects have a special place in the Java language. Strings can be declared in the normal way using *new,* or they can be declared without using a constructor, as in the following example:

```
private String name = "Robert A. Heinlein";
```

exam Watch

The Sun Certified Programmer for Java 2.0 exam is difficult to pass. It is possible for people who are excellent Java programmers with years of experience under their belts to fail the exam because they were not prepared for the level of detail that the exam requires. I can't emphasize how picky the exam can be with details. The difference between right and wrong is sometimes determined by whether or not a single letter is capitalized.

Import Statements

An *import statement* allows us to individually select classes within a package, or select an entire package of classes that we may use in our code. The import statement is used to make the classes in a package available. A typical import statement appears after any package statement and before any class definitions.

```
import java.util.Dictionary;
```

The preceding code allows us to access the class Dictionary. We can also import all the classes within a package in one statement.

```
import javax.swing.event.*;
```

You might think it is possible to import every core application programming interface (API) package with the following statement:

```
import java.*;
```

This example will compile, and it will try to import any classes within the directory Java. It will not, however, import any of the packages located in subdirectories of Java. In the preceding instance, there are no classes located directly in the Java package; therefore, nothing will be imported.

It is possible to use a class from a package without using the import statement, but you must specifically drill down through the packages each time you refer to it.

```
java.util.Date now = new java.util.Date();
```

It is also possible for two classes to belong to different packages but have the same name. For example, a Date class can be found in java.util.Date and java.sql.Date. In this case, it is necessary to discriminate between the two by drilling down with the exact package and class name, as shown earlier, otherwise Java will use the first class it comes upon in the classpath setting.

The java.lang package is imported automatically, making it unnecessary to add an import statement for this particular package.

CERTIFICATION OBJECTIVE 1.03

Java Programming Language Keywords and Identifiers

Keywords and *identifiers* are special reserved words in Java that cannot be used as identifiers for classes, methods, and variables. Table 1-1 contains all 48 of the reserved keywords.

You must memorize these for the test. Notice none of the reserved words have capital letters; this is a good first step when weeding out non-keywords on the exam. You are probably familiar with most of them, but we'll review them anyway. Learning them in their categories makes it easier to memorize them all.

TABLE 1-1 Complete List of Java Keywords

abstract	boolean	break	byte	case	catch
char	class	const	continue	default	do
double	else	extends	final	finally	float
for	goto	if	implements	import	instanceof
int	interface	long	native	new	package
private	protected	public	return	short	static
strictfp	super	switch	synchronized	this	throw
throws	transient	try	void	volatile	while

Access Modifiers

The following are access modifiers:

- **private** Makes a method or a variable accessible only from within its own class.
- **protected** Makes a method or a variable accessible only to classes in the same package or subclasses of the class.
- **public** Classes outside the package can access the class, methods, or variables.

Class, Method, and Variable Modifiers

The following are class, method, or variable modifiers:

- **abstract** A method or class that cannot be instantiated, and which may define methods to be overwritten.
- **class** Keyword used to specify a class.
- **extends** Used to indicate the superclass that a subclass is extending.
- **final** Makes it impossible to extend a class, override a method, or reinitialize a variable.
- **implements** Used to indicate the interfaces that a class will use.
- **interface** Keyword used to specify an interface.
- **native** Indicates a method is written in a platform-dependent language, such as C.
- **new** Used to instantiate an object by invoking the constructor method.
- **static** Makes a method or a variable belong to a class.
- **strictfp** Used in front of a method or class to indicate that floating point numbers will follow FP-strict rules in all expressions.
- **synchronized** Indicates that a method can be accessed by only one thread at a time.
- **transient** Prevents fields from ever being serialized. Transient fields are always skipped when objects are serialized.
- **volatile** Indicates a variable may change out of sync because it is used in threads.

Control Flow

The following are keywords used to control the flow through a block of code:

- **break** Exits from the block of code in which it resides.
- **case** Executes a block of code, dependent on what the switch tests for.
- **continue** Stops the rest of the code following this statement from executing in a loop and then begins the next iteration of the loop.
- **default** Executes this block of code if none of the switch-case statements match.
- **do** Performs a block of code one time, then, in conjunction with the *while* statement, it performs a test to determine whether the block should be executed again.
- **else** Executes an alternate block of code if an *if* test is false.
- **for** Used to perform a conditional loop for a block of code.
- **if** Used to compare two variables for true or false.
- **instanceof** Determines whether an object is an instance of a class or any superclass.
- **return** Returns from a method without executing any code that follows the statement (can optionally return a variable).
- **switch** Indicates the variable to be compared with the case statements.
- **while** Executes a block of code repeatedly while a certain condition is true.

Error Handling

The following are keywords used in error handling:

- **catch** Declares the block of code used to handle an exception.
- **finally** Block of code usually following a try-catch statement which is executed no matter what program flow occurs when dealing with an error.
- **throw** Used to pass an exception up to the method that called this method.
- **throws** Indicates the method will pass an exception to the method that called it.
- **try** Block of code that will be tried, but which may cause an exception.

Package Control

The following are keywords used for package control:

- **import** Statement to import packages or classes into code.
- **package** Specifies to which package all classes in a source file belong.

Primitives

The following keywords are primitives:

- **boolean** Boolean literals indicating true or false.
- **byte** 8-bit integer.
- **char** Stores one Unicode character.
- **double** 64-bit floating-point number.
- **float** 32-bit floating-point number.
- **int** 32-bit integer.
- **long** 64-bit integer.
- **short** 16-bit integer.

Variable Keywords

The following keywords are variables:

- **super** Reference variable referring to the immediate superclass.
- **this** Reference variable referring to the current instance of an object.
- **void** Indicates no return type for a method.

Unused Keywords

There are two keywords that are reserved in Java but which are not used. If you try to use one of these reserved keywords, the Java compiler will produce the following:

```
KeywordTest.java:4: 'goto' not supported.
             goto MyLabel;
1 error
```

- **const** Do not use to declare a constant; use public static final.
- **goto** Not implemented in the Java language.

exam Watch

Many of these keywords are only briefly introduced because it is not necessary to know much about them for the exam. You will not need to know much about strictfp, volatile, native, and transient other than that they are keywords.

You may notice *null*, *true*, and *false* do not appear anywhere on the list. According to the Java Language Specification, these are technically literal values and not keywords. A literal is much the same as a number or any other value. If we try to create an identifier with one of these literal values, we will receive errors.

```
class LiteralTest {
      public static void main (String [] args) {
            int true = 100; // this will cause error
      }
}
```

Compiling this code gives us the following error:

```
c:\Java Projects\LiteralTest>javac LiteralTest.java
LiteralTest.java:3: Invalid expression statement.
                        int true = 100;
..
```

In other words, trying to assign a value to *true* is much like saying:

```
int 200 = 100;
```

exam Watch

There are 51** reserved words **in Java. That is, words that you can't use for naming classes, variables, or methods. Of those, 48 are Java** keywords**. There are also null, true, and false which are** literal values**. On the exam, be careful to answer the question accordingly. You should answer the question differently, depending on whether the test asks to specify keywords or reserved words.

CERTIFICATION OBJECTIVE 1.04

Using a Variable or Array Element That Is Uninitialized and Unassigned

As noted previously, when declaring a variable, Java gives us the option of initializing the variable or leaving it uninitialized. If we attempt to use the uninitialized variable, we can get different behavior. This behavior depends on what type of variable or array we are dealing with (primitives or objects). The behavior also depends on the level at which we are declaring our variable. An *instance variable* is declared at class level, whereas a *local variable* is declared at method level. The Java compiler will produce an error if you try to use a local (automatic) variable without initializing it with a value, as we shall see.

Primitive and Object Type Class Members

Class members are variables defined at the class level. These include both instance variables and class (static) variables.

Primitive Type Class Members

In the following example, the integer *year* is defined as a class member because it is within the initial curly braces of the class and not within a method's curly braces.

```
public class BirthDate {
     int year;
     public static void main(String [] args) {
          BirthDate bd = new BirthDate();
          bd.showYear();
     }
     public void showYear() {
```

```
            System.out.println("The year is " + year);
        }
    }
```

When the program is started, it gives the variable *year* a value of zero. All class-level primitives are assigned a default value. Of the eight primitives, the six number primitives are given a value of zero; the Boolean primitive is given a value of false; and the char primitive is given the Unicode character of /u0000, which is a blank space by default.

on the job

It is a good idea to initialize all your variables, even if you are assigning them with the default value. It makes your code easier to read and it appears more logical to another programmer.

Object Class Members

Objects are a completely different story when they are not initialized (or instantiated). Let's look at the following code:

```
import java.util.Date;
public class BirthDate {
    static Date birthDay;
    public static void main(String [] args) {
        System.out.println("The year is " + birthDay.getYear());
    }
}
```

This code will compile fine. However, when we try to run the BirthDate class, the Java interpreter will produce the following error:

```
c:\Java Projects\BirthDate>java BirthDate
java.lang.NullPointerException
        at BirthDate.main(BirthDate.java:5)
```

The reason we get this error is because the reference variable birthDay does not point to any data. The constructor for the class BirthDate has not been executed; therefore, no object has been instantiated. We can check to see whether an object has been instantiated by using the keyword *null*, as the following revised code shows:

```
import java.util.Date;
public class BirthDate {
    static Date birthDay;
    public static void main(String [] args) {
        if (birthDay != null)
```

```
            System.out.println("The year is " + birthDay.getYear());
        }
    }
```

The preceding code checks to make sure the object birthDay is not null before trying to use it. It is often necessary to check this because methods can sometimes return null.

Array Class Members

The third type of entity we will examine is the array. An array is essentially an object. We initialize an array in a different manner from an object or a primitive, but in effect it is doing much the same work as the constructor for an object. Much like an object, it is possible to declare an array without initializing it, but this makes the array unusable.

```
public class BirthDate {
    static int [] year;
    public static void main(String [] args) {
        if(year == null)
            System.out.println("The array year[] is null.");
    }
}
```

When the preceding class is executed, we get the following:

```
c:\Java Projects\BirthDate>java BirthDate
The array year[] is null.
```

Much like a normal object, an uninitialized array object equals null. But if we initialize an array, what happens to the objects contained in the array? Objects will equal null if they are not initialized individually with values. If primitives are contained in an array, they will be given their respective default values. For example, in the following code, the array year[] will contain 100 integers that all equal zero by default.

```
public class BirthDays {
    static int [] year = new int[100];
    public static void main(String [] args) {
        for(int i=0;i<100;i++)
            System.out.println("year[" + i + "] = " + year[i]);
    }
}
```

If the preceding code is executed, it will produce output that indicates all 100 integers in the array equal zero.

Local (Automatic) Primitives and Objects

Local variables, otherwise known as automatic variables, are defined within a method.

exam Watch

Automatic is just another term for local variable. It does not mean the automatic variable is automatically assigned a value! The opposite is true; an automatic variable must be assigned a value in the code, otherwise the compiler will throw an error.

Local Primitives

In the following time travel simulator, the integer year is defined as an automatic variable because it is within the curly braces of a method.

```
public class TimeTravel {
     public static void main(String [] args) {
          int year = 2050;
          System.out.println("The year is " + year);
     }
}
```

Okay, so it's not much of a simulator. Local variables, including primitives, must be initialized before you attempt to use them (though not necessarily on the same line of code). Java does not supply primitives with a default value; therefore, you must explicitly initialize them with a value, as in the preceding example. If you try to use an uninitialized primitive in your code, the Java compiler will generate an error:

```
public class TimeTravel {
     public static void main(String [] args) {
          int year;
          System.out.println("The year is " + year);
     }
}
```

Compiling produces the following output:

```
c:\Java Projects\TimeTravel>javac TimeTravel.java
TimeTravel.java:4: Variable year may not have been initialized.
           System.out.println("The year is " + year);
1 error
```

To correct our code, we must give the integer year a value. In this updated example, we will declare it on a separate line, which is perfectly valid.

```
public class TimeTravel {
     public static void main(String [] args) {
          int year;
          int day; // Remains uninitialized
          System.out.println("You step into the portal.");
          year = 2050;
          System.out.println("Welcome to the year " + year);
     }
}
```

Notice in the preceding example I have declared an integer called *day* that is not initialized, yet the code compiled and ran fine. It is legal to declare a local variable without initializing it if you do not use the variable, but let's face it, if you declare an integer you are probably going to be using it. It could be important to know this for the exam, however.

Local Objects

Objects also behave differently when declared within a method. As we saw before, you can get away with leaving an object uninitialized if the code checks to determine if it is equal to null before using it. And even if it's not checked, the code will still compile. With local objects, however, any attempt to use the uninitialized object will result in a compiler error:

```
import java.util.Date;
public class TimeTravel {
     public static void main(String [] args) {
          Date date;
          if (date == null)
               System.out.println("date is null");
     }
}
```

Compiling the code results in the following error:

```
c:\Java Projects\TimeTravel>javac TimeTravel.java
TimeTravel.java:5: Variable date may not have been initialized.
          If (date == null)
1 error
```

If you don't wish to initialize a local object, you can actually initialize it to equal null by using the null keyword. The following local variable will compile properly:

```
Date date = null;
```

Local Arrays

Arrays behave differently from local variables. Once we define a local array, every primitive within the array will have a default value. Examine the following:

```
public class Century {
      public static void main(String [] args) {
            int [] year = new int[100];
            System.out.println("year[5] = " + year[5]);
      }
}
```

The preceding example compiles and runs just fine. When it runs it will output the value of 0 for year[5]. Notice none of the integers in the array year[] are explicitly initialized. Remember, normally a local variable must be initialized before it is used, but with an array this is not necessary.

CERTIFICATION OBJECTIVE 1.05

Ranges of All Primitive Data Types

You will be required to know the range of the various data types for the exam. This could be quite a task because the primitive *long* has a range of -9,223,372,036,854,775,808 to 9,223,372,036,854,775,807. The good news is you will not have to memorize such ridiculous numbers. There is an easier method to calculate the ranges. First, let's review the concepts involved.

All six number types in Java are signed, meaning they can be negative or positive. Table 1-2 shows the number types with their sizes and ranges. The range for float numbers is complicated to determine, but luckily you do not need to know this range for the exam. For a byte, there are 256 possible numbers (or 2^8). Half of these are negative, one is a zero, and half minus one are positive. We use the formula $-2^{(bits - 1)}$ to calculate the negative range, and we use $2^{(bits -1)} - 1$ for the positive range.

For Boolean types there is not a range. Boolean types are either true or false.

Character types contain a single Unicode character. There are only 256 characters in the ASCII set. Because there are more Unicode characters than ASCII characters, it is necessary to use 2 bytes of data to store a Unicode character. Characters run from \u0000 to \uffff, or 0 to 65535 (2^{16}).

TABLE 1-2 Ranges of Primitive Numbers

Type	Bits	Bytes	Minimum Range	Maximum Range
byte	8	1	-2^{7}	$2^{7} - 1$
short	16	2	-2^{15}	$2^{15} - 1$
int	32	4	-2^{31}	$2^{31} - 1$
long	64	8	-2^{63}	$2^{63} - 1$
float	32	4	not needed	not needed
double	64	8	not needed	not needed

Literal Values for Strings

A string literal is a source code representation of a value of a string. For example, the following is an example of a string literal:

```
"Johan Guttenberg"
"Johan" + " Guttenberg"
"Johan" + b // Not a string literal
```

The third example is not a string literal because it contains a variable, which will be computed at runtime.

Literal Values for All Primitive Types

A primitive literal is merely a source code representation of the primitive data types.

Integer Literals

There are three ways to represent integer numbers in the Java language: octal (base 8), decimal (base 10), and hexadecimal (base 16).

Octal Literals Octal integers use the digits 0 to 7. We can indicate that a number is represented in octal form by placing a zero in front of the number, as follows:

```
class Octal {
    public static void main(String [] args) {
```

```
        int five = 06; // Equal to decimal 6
        int seven = 07; // Equal to decimal 7
        int eight = 010; // Equal to decimal 8
        int nine = 011; // Equal to decimal 9
        System.out.println("Octal 010 = " + eight);
    }
}
```

Notice when we get past seven and are out of digits to use (we are only allowed the digits 0 to 7 for octal numbers), we revert back to zero, and one is added to the beginning of the number. You can have up to 21 digits in an octal number, not including the leading zero. If we run the preceding program, it displays the following:

```
Octal 010 = 8
```

Decimal Literals Decimal integers need no explanation; you have been using them since grade one or earlier and are quite familiar with the system. In the Java language, they are represented as is, with no prefix of any kind.

Hexadecimal Literals Hexadecimal numbers are constructed using 16 distinct symbols. Because no one has invented single digit symbols for the numbers 10 to 15, it is necessary to use alphabetic characters to represent these digits.

```
0 1 2 3 4 5 6 7 8 9 a b c d e f
```

Java will accept capital or lowercase letters for the extra digits. You are allowed up to 16 digits in a hexadecimal number, not including the prefix *0x* or the optional suffix extension *L* which will be explained later. In Table 1-3, let's do a little counting in hexadecimal format to make sure the concept is clear.

TABLE 1-3 A Practice Exercise for Counting in Hexadecimal Numbers

Decimal	Hexadecimal
0	0x0
9	0x9
10	0xa
11	0xb
15	0xf
16	0x10
17	0x11

The following hexadecimal numbers are all legal:

```
class LiteralTest {
     public static void main (String [] args) {
          int x = 0x0001;
          int y = 0x7fffffff;
          int z = 0xDeadCafe;
          System.out.println("x = " + x + " y = " + y + " z = " + z);
     }
}
```

All three integer literals (octal, decimal, and hexadecimal) are defined as *int* by default, but they may also be specified as *long* by placing a suffix of *L* after the number:

```
long l = 110599L;
```

Floating-Point Literals

Floating-point numbers are defined as a number, a decimal symbol, and more numbers representing the fraction.

```
float f = 11301874.9881024;
```

In the preceding example, the number 11301874.9881024 is the literal value. The rest (*float f* = and ;) have nothing to do with the literal value, but are included to show how it looks in Java code.

Floating-point literals are defined as *double* by default, but if you want to specify in your code a number as *float*, you may attach the suffix *F* to the number. You may also optionally attach a *D* to double literals, but it is not necessary because this is the default behavior.

```
float f = 221194.491122F;
double d = 110599.995011D;
```

Boolean Literals

Boolean literals are the source code representation for Boolean values. Boolean values can only be defined as either true or false. In C it is common to use numbers to represent true or false, but this will not work in Java.

```
boolean t = true;
```

Character Literals

A character literal is represented by a single character in single quotes.

```
char a = 'a';
char b = '@';
```

Optionally, we can use a hexadecimal value by using the escape code \u to represent a character:

```
char question = '\uFFFF'; // A question mark
```

You can also use the escape code \" if you wish to represent quotes.

```
char c = '\"'
```

Now that you are familiar with the basic data types and their ranges, you will be able to identify the proper data type to use in a given situation. Here are some examples of real life quantities. Try to pick the primitive type that best represents the quantity.

Arrays

Arrays are objects in Java that store multiple variables of the same type. As objects, they must first be initialized, otherwise they will equal null. Arrays can also store different types of objects if they are derived from the same superclass. Because all objects derive from the class Object, it is possible to create an array that will store many different types of objects by using casting, which will be discussed in Chapter 3.

SCENARIO & SOLUTION	
Which primitive type would be best to represent the number of stars in the universe?	long
Which primitive type would be best to represent a single multiple choice question on a test, with only one answer allowed?	char
Which primitive type would be best to represent a single multiple choice question on a test, with more than one answer allowed?	char []
Which primitive type would be best to represent the number of dependents in a household?	byte
Which primitive type would be best to represent the amount of money (in dollars and cents) you plan on having at retirement?	float (or double if you are a CEO of a software company)

Declaration

Arrays are declared by stating the type, which can be an object or a primitive, followed by square brackets to the left or right of the identifier.

```
int [] key; // Square brackets before name
int key []; // Square brackets after name
```

We can also declare multidimensional arrays, which are in fact arrays of arrays. This can be done in the following manner:

```
String [][][]occupantName;
String [] occupantName [];
```

The first example is a three-dimensional array and the second is a two-dimensional array. Notice in the second example we have one square bracket before the variable name and one after. This is perfectly legal to the compiler.

Initialization

The most common way to initialize (allocate) an array is by using the *new* keyword, followed by the type, then in square brackets the number of elements in the array.

```
Date [] famousYear = new Date [5];
```

An important fact to remember is the constructor for Date is in no way being executed when the keyword new is used here. All of the Date variables within famousYear are not initialized or instantiated, and therefore equal null.

Once an array is initialized, the size of the array can't be changed without some extra code. If I try to reinitialize famousYear to an array of five elements instead of 10, the variable famousYear becomes a brand-new empty array.

The individual elements in the array can be accessed with an index number. The index number always begins with zero, so for an array of ten objects the index numbers will run from 0 to 9. Observe the following code:

```
class Counting {
     public static void main (String [] args) {
          int [] number = new int[10];
          for (int i = 0;i<10;i++)
               number[i] = i + 1;
          System.out.println("number[5] = " + number[5]);
     }
}
```

The preceding code fills an array with the numbers 1 to 10. Study it carefully and try to determine what the output will look like. Let's execute the class to find out what happens:

```
c:\Java Projects\Counting>java Counting
number[5] = 6
```

Java also allows us to initialize the array size and initialize the values in the array in one line, as the following demonstrates:

```
int [] famousYear = {1912, 1942, 1969, 1984, 2001};
```

This creates an array with five elements, all initialized with values. Notice there is a semicolon after the final curly brace. You can also initialize an array of objects in the same way:

```
Button [] button = {new Button("Open"), new Button("Close")};
```

Length

An array object has an integer variable named *length* that we can access to determine the size of an array. This tells us the dimension of the array, not the number of initialized variables within the array.

```
class ArrayTest {
      public static void main (String [] args) {
            Object [][] any = new Object[20][10];
            System.out.println("any.length = " + any.length);
            System.out.println("any[0].length = " + any[0].length);
            System.out.println("any[1].length = " + any[1].length);
      }
}
```

Notice how we reference the main array without using any square brackets. The output from this class indicates the size of **any** is 20, and the size of each of the 20 arrays is 10.

EXERCISE 1-3

Creating a Program That Outputs Command-Line Arguments

1. Create a program that outputs every command-line argument, then displays the number of arguments.
2. You should use the array variable *length* to retrieve the length of the array.
3. Your completed program should look something like this:

```
public class MainTest {
     public static void main (String [] args) {
          for (int i = 0;i < args.length;i++) {
               System.out.println(args[i]);
          }
          System.out.println("Total words: " + args.length);
     }
}
```

CERTIFICATION SUMMARY

The information in this chapter lays the groundwork for learning more about the Java language. After absorbing the material in this chapter, you should be familiar with some of the nuances of the Java language. Let's briefly review what you will need to know for the exam.

Source files contain package declarations, import statements, class definitions, and interface definitions. Classes can be public or default, not private or protected. For the exam you should know how to define an interface, and the only interface you will need to be able to implement is the java.lang.Runnable interface. Also, you must be able to state the correspondence between an array index value and the corresponding command-line argument passed to main().

There will be at least one question dealing with keywords, so be sure you can identify which are keywords and which aren't. Make sure you are familiar with primitives and the ranges of integer primitives. And, although this isn't Java language specific, you must be able to convert between octal, decimal, and hexadecimal literals. You have also learned about arrays, and how they behave when declared in a class or a method.

For the exam, knowing what you can't do with the Java language is just as important as knowing what you can do. Give the sample questions a try. It should be an eye opener for how difficult the exam can be. Don't worry if you get a lot of them wrong. If you find a topic that you are weak in, it would be well worth your time to target those areas for extra study.

✓ TWO-MINUTE DRILL

Source Files

- ❑ A source file declares a package, imports packages, and defines classes (in this order).
- ❑ Only one public class can exist in a single source file.
- ❑ Additional default classes may also be contained in the source file.

Package, Import, Class, Method, and Variable Declarations

- ❑ Packages must be contained in the same directory structure as the package name.
- ❑ A class implementing an interface must define all methods in the interface.
- ❑ Methods can be public, private, protected, or default (none). They may also be abstract, final, native, static, and/or synchronized.
- ❑ The first argument from a command line passed to main() is index 0 in the array.
- ❑ There is no return type for a constructor method (not even void).
- ❑ Local (automatic) variables can only have the modifier of final. They cannot be public, private, protected, static, transient, or volatile.
- ❑ The "*" symbol can be used to import all classes in a specific package.

Java Programming Language Keywords and Identifiers

- ❑ Memorize all reserved words and keywords, and remember: true, false, and null are reserved words but not keywords. There is a difference in terminology.
- ❑ *Keywords* and *identifiers* are special reserved words in Java that cannot be used as identifiers for classes, methods, and variables.

Using a Variable or Array Element That Is Uninitialized and Unassigned

- ❑ When an array is initialized, objects within the array are not instantiated and therefore equal null. Primitive class variables are given a default value.

- ❑ Primitive class members are initialized with a default value, but not automatic variables.
- ❑ (3)Ranges of All Primitive Data Types The range of integral numbers is from $-2^{(bits - 1)}$ to $2^{(bits - 1)} - 1$.
- ❑ You must understand octal, decimal, and hexadecimal numbering systems.

SELF TEST

The following questions will help you measure your understanding of the material presented in this chapter. Read all the choices carefully because there might be more than one correct answer. Choose all correct answers for each question.

Source Files

1. Given the file FirstClass.java:

```
import java.*;
public class FirstClass {}
public interface Second {}
abstract class SecondClass {}
```

What error will the compiler likely generate?

A. Package java not found in import.

B. Public class FirstClass must be defined in a file called "FirstClass.java."

C. Public interface Second must be defined in a file called "Second.java."

D. Class SecondClass may not be defined as abstract.

E. None. The file will compile fine.

2. Assume you have just entered some Java code into a source file *with no public classes.* You now wish to save and compile it. Which of the following will work? (Choose all that apply.)

A. Save it in a file called MyClass.jav and compile with javac MyClass.jav.

B. Save it in a file called 1999Work.java and compile with javac 1999Work.java.

C. Save it in a file called MyClass.java and compile with javac MyClass.

D. Save it in a file called MyClass.java and compile with javac MyClass.java.

Package, Import, Class, Method, and Variable Declarations

3. Given:

```
import java.util.Vector;
public Vector v = new Vector();
class Test {
   public static void main (String [] args) {
      System.out.println("Good luck");
   }
}
```

What will happen if we try to compile and run this code?

A. The code will compile and run fine.

B. The code will compile fine, but an error will occur when the class is instantiated.

C. The code won't compile.

4. You have just created a few classes in a source file called Server.java. There is a main class called Server, which begins the program. The top of this file has the line:

```
package com.syngress;
```

The classpath environment setting is properly set so it will look in c:\Java Packages for packages, and there is a subdirectory structure of c:\Java Packages\com\syngress\Server. Which of the following procedures will work?

A. You place the classes in the directory Server, and type the following:

```
c:\Java Packages\com\syngress\Server>java Server
```

B. You place the classes in the directory syngress, and type the following:

```
c:\Java Packages\com\syngress\Server>java com.syngress.Server
```

C. You place the classes in the directory syngress, and type the following:

```
c:\Java Packages\com\syngress>java Server
```

D. You place the classes in the directory Server, and type the following:

```
c:\>java com.syngress.Server
```

E. None of the above.

5. Which of the following class definitions are legal? (Choose all that apply.)

A. private class A {}

B. class B {}

C. public class C {}

D. final class Class {}

E. abstract class E;

F. final abstract class F {}

6. Which of the following interface definitions are legal? (Choose all that apply.)

A. public interface A {int a();}

B. public interface B implements A {}

C. interface C {int a;}

D. private interface D {}

E. abstract interface E {}

7. Given:

```
1.  public class Century implements Runnable {
2.     public void run () {
3.        for (int year = 1900;year < 2000;year++) {
4.           System.out.println(year);
5.           try {Thread.sleep(1000);
6.           } catch(InterruptedException e) {}
7.        }
8.        System.out.println("Happy new millenium!");
9.     }
10. }
11. class CountUp {
12.       public static void main (String [] args) {
13.            Century ourCentury = new Century();
14.
15.       }
16. }
```

You now wish to begin the thread from another class. Which is the proper code, placed in the second class at line 14, to begin the thread?

A. Thread t = new Thread(this);
   t.start();

B. Thread t = new Thread(ourCentury);
   ourCentury.start();

C. Thread t = new Thread(this);
   t.start(ourCentury);

D. Thread t = new Thread(this);
   ourCentury.run();

E. Thread t = new Thread(ourCentury);
   t.start();

8. Which of the following methods will compile properly when inserted into a class? (Choose all that apply.)

A. public static final synchronized getPrice() {}

B. public abstract int getPrice();

C. public static final int getPrice() {}

D. public final static int getPrice(int unit) {return unit;}

E. protected volatile int getPrice() {}

F. protected int static getPrice(int unit) {}

9. We would like to create a valid main() method that we can use to start a class from the command line. Which of these candidates will work? (Choose all that apply.)

A. static public void main(String [] args) {}

B. public static int main(String [] args) {}

C. public static void main(String args []) {}

D. public static void main(String [] argh) {}

10. Which of these methods, when inserted into a legal class, will compile properly? Only one method will be inserted into the class at a time. (Choose all that apply.)

A. public void main(String [] args) {}

B. public int main(String [] args) {return 2;}

C. public static void main() {}

D. void public static main(String [] args) {}

11. Given:

```
1.  class DataServer extends Server{
2.     public String serverName;
3.     public DataServer () {
4.         serverName = "Customer Service";
5.         super(serverName);
6.     }
7.  }
```

Which of these statements about the above code is true?

A. The code will compile and run fine.

B. The code will compile fine, but an error will occur when the class is instantiated.

C. The code won't compile because of line 2.

D. The code won't compile because of line 5.

12. Given:

```
1.  strictfp class Main {
2.      public Main() {
3.      }
4.      public void Main() {
5.      }
6.      strictfp public void Main(double x) {
7.      }
8.  }
```

Which of these statements about the above code is true? (Choose all that apply.)

A. The code will compile and run fine.

B. The code won't compile because of line 1.

C. The code won't compile because of line 2.

D. The code won't compile because of line 4.

E. The code won't compile because of line 6.

13. Which of the following variable definitions are legitimate if it is defined at the class level? (Choose all that apply.)

A. protected int a;

B. transient int b = 3;

C. public static final int c;

D. volatile int d;

E. private synchronized int d;

Java Programming Language Keywords and Identifiers

14. Which one of these contains only Java keywords?

A. class, Thread, void, long, if, continue, strictfp

B. goto, instanceof, native, finally, default, throws

C. try, redo, throw, final, volatile, transient

D. true, throws, super, implements, do

E. null, byte, break, switch

15. Given:

```
public class Test {
    public int t = 4;
    public static void main (String [] args) {
        new Test().NumberPlay();
    }
    public void NumberPlay() {
        int t = 2;
        t = t + 5;
        this.t = this.t - 2;
        t = t - this.t;
        System.out.print(t + “ ”);
        System.out.println(this.t);
    }
}
```

What is the output of this code?

A. 2 5

B. -9 0

C. 0 -9

D. 5 2

E. 7 2

F. 2 7

Using a Variable or Array Element That is Uninitialized and Unassigned

16. Given:

```
import java.util.Date;
public class Y2K {
    public static void main(String [] args) {
        Date date;
        if (date == null)
            System.out.println(“date is null”);
    }
}
```

What will happen when we try to compile and run this class?

A. It will compile, but will produce an interpreter error when executed.

B. It will compile and output *date is null* to the screen.

C. It will not compile and will give a compiler error.

D. None of the above.

17. Given:

```
public class CheckDefault {
   private static boolean test;
   public static void showTest() {
      System.out.println(test);
   }
}
```

If we invoke the static method showTest(), what will the output be?

A. true

B. false

C. None, the class will not compile.

18. Given:

```
public class LocalTest {
   public static void main(String [] args) {
      int i;
      System.out.print("int i = " + i);
      i = 20;
   }
}
```

If you try to compile and run this class, what will happen?

A. It will compile, but will produce an interpreter error when executed.

B. It will compile and output '0' to the screen.

C. It will not compile and will give a compiler error.

D. None of the above.

19. Assuming the array is declared as a class member, which of the following will declare an array and initialize it with five numbers?

A. Array a = new Array(5);

B. int [] a = {23, 22, 21, 20, 19}

C. int [] array;

D. int array [] = new int[5];

E. int a [] = new int(5);

20. We are given a two-dimensional array named *a* with the hypothetical dimensions *x* by *y*. In this example, *x* represents the size of the first array, and *y* represents the size of the second dimension of arrays. The value of *x* is 10. Which of the following can we use to determine the value of *y*?

A. a.length();

B. a.size();

C. a[0].length;

D. a.length(10);

E. a[].length;

Ranges of All Primitive Data Types

21. Your manager has given you some estimates of insect populations in your area.
Bees: 2^{17}
Ants: 2^{31}
Spiders: 2^{8}
Mosquitoes: 2^{56}

You are thinking of using the *int* data type to store these figures. Determine which of these insect populations can be stored in an *int* type. (Choose all that apply.)

A. Spiders

B. Bees

C. Ants

D. Mosquitoes

22. Given two literal numbers: 0x001B and 033. What are these numbers equal to in decimal?

A. 21 and 33

B. 21 and 27

C. 27 and 33

D. 33 and 33

E. 27 and 27

SELF TEST ANSWERS

Source Files

1. ☑ C. There can be only one public class or interface per source file.
☒ A is incorrect because, although it does not end up importing any classes, it still compiles fine. B is incorrect because the filename matches the class name. D is incorrect because an abstract class is perfectly legal.

2. ☑ B and D. These both work because you must save it with the extension and specify the java extension when compiling. B works because numbers are allowed for the filename; however, if there were a public class this would not work because classes can not be named with numbers.
☒ A is incorrect because it ends with *jav.* C is incorrect because the suffix *java* must be included when compiling.

Package, Import, Class, Method, and Variable Declarations

3. ☑ C. The Vector variable is declared outside of a class, which is illegal.
☒ A and B are incorrect because the code will not compile.

4. ☑ B. B works just fine, because you can run the class from any directory location, as long as the package name is specified.
☒ A is incorrect because the classes must be in the directory syngress. C will not work because you must specify com.syngress.Server. D will not work for the same reason that A does not work. E is incorrect because there is a correct answer choice.

5. ☑ B, C, and D. B is correct because there is a legal class name with a legal declaration statement. No modifiers are necessary. C is correct for the same reason B is correct, only the access modifier public is included. D is correct, even though it uses the word Class. Class is capitalized, and since Java is a case-sensitive language, it does not confuse this with lower-case class. Also, final is a legal class modifier.
☒ A is incorrect because a class can not be private. E is incorrect because there must be curly braces instead of the semicolon, even for an abstract class. F is not legal because a final class can't be extended.

6. ☑ A and E. A contains a legal method definition for an interface. E is correct because just like a class, an interface can be declared abstract (even though it is redundant).
☒ B will not work because interfaces can only extend interfaces. C will not work because integers must be initialized in an interface. D will not work because an interface can't be private.

7. ☑ E. A thread object must be made, using the Thread() constructor, which accepts a Runnable interface as an argument. The next line starts the thread running.
☒ A is incorrect because the constructor Thread() only accepts a Runnable type in the constructor. B is incorrect because the start() method should be called on the Thread object t, not the **ourCentury** object. C is incorrect for the same reason A is incorrect. Also, the start() method accepts no arguments. D is incorrect for the same reason A is incorrect. Also, the method run() is not used to start a thread. The run() method includes the code for the thread, however.

8. ☑ B and D. B is correct because it is proper to end an abstract method with a semi-colon. D is correct because public, static, and final are all legal modifiers for a method. Also, it returns an int as specified by the return type modifier. If this method failed to return an int value it would be illegal.
☒ A is incorrect because it has no return type specified. C is incorrect because it has no return value. E is illegal because only variables can use the keyword *volatile*. F is incorrect because the return type *int* must come directly before the identifier.

9. ☑ A, C, and D. A works even though the keywords are in an unusual order. C works even though the array is defined in a different manner. D works even though the array is not identified as *args*.
☒ B does not work because it has a return type of *int*.

10. ☑ A, B, and C. None of these methods will allow the program to start from the command line, however they will compile fine. There is nothing sacred about the main() method that forbids you from overloading it. A works even though static is missing. B works even though it returns an int. C works even though there is no array for command line arguments.
☒ D does not work because void must come directly in front of the method name.

11. ☑ D. The super() method must be located at the first line of code in the constructor method.
☒ A and B are incorrect because it won't compile at all. C is incorrect because the DataServer() method is not static; therefore, the String serverName may be manipulated within the method.

12. ☑ A. This is a legally defined class with legal methods.
☒ B is incorrect because strictfp can occur in front of a class definition and Main is a legal class name (as is lower case main) since it is not a reserved word. C is incorrect because this is a legal

constructor. D is incorrect because you can declare a method with the same name as the class name. E is incorrect because you can use strictfp in front of a method as well.

13. ☑ A, B, C, and D. A and B are correct because protected and transient are legal variable modifiers. C is correct because when a variable is declared final it does not have to be initialized with a value in the same line. D is correct because volatile is a proper modifier for a variable.
☒ E is incorrect because synchronized is a method keyword only.

Java Programming Language Keywords and Identifiers

14. ☑ B. This is correct because all of these are legal keywords.
☒ In A, thread is a class and not a keyword. In C, redo is completely made up. In D, true is not a keyword but rather a literal, as is null in E.

15. ☑ D. In the code, *this.t* refers to the class member, and *t* refers to the local variable. The class-level variable this.t starts off as 4, then 2 is subtracted for a final value of 2. The automatic variable t starts off as 2, then 5 is added, then this.t (2) is subtracted for a final value of 5.
☒ A, B, C, E, and F are incorrect because the sequence of additions and subtractions does not produce any of these combinations.

Using a Variable or Array Element That Is Uninitialized and Unassigned

16. ☑ C. The variable *date* is not initialized, so if we attempt to use the local variable *date* in any way, this will not compile.
☒ A and B are both incorrect because the code will not compile. D is incorrect because there is a correct answer choice.

17. ☑ B. A Boolean variable is given a default of false.
☒ A is incorrect because true is not the default value for a Boolean. C is incorrect because the class will compile fine.

18. ☑ C. The compiler will not compile this, and will recognize that the code is attempting to use variable **i** before it is initialized. All automatic variables must be initialized.
☒ A does not work because the compiler will recognize that a local variable is being used before it is initialized. B does not work because local variables are not given default values. D is incorrect because there is a correct answer choice.

19. ☑ D. This is correct because class variables are initialized with default values of 0. The syntax for this declaration is correct.
☒ A does not work because there is not an object called Array. B does not work because there

is no semicolon after the statement. **C** will declare an array but it does not initialize it with five integers. **E** does not work because the size of the array must be declared in square brackets.

20. ☑ **C**. The correct way to check the length of an array is with the variable **length**. Since this is a two-dimensional array, in order to find the length of the second-array we must refer to an object. In this case we used a[0], although we could have used any integer from 0 to 9.
☒ **A** does not work because length is a variable and not a method. **B** does not work because there is no such size method. **D** does not work for the same reason that **A** does not work. **E** does not work because you must refer to the length of a specific array index.

Ranges of All Primitive Data Types

21. ☑ **A** and **B**. An integer has a maximum value of 2^{31} - 1 (or 2147483647).
☒ **C** is incorrect because int can only store 2^{31} - 1. The number 2^{31} is too large by a value of one. **D** is incorrect because only a long type could store this number.

22. ☑ **E**. The first is a hexadecimal number. The digit 1 is equal to 16, the digit B is equal to 11. These sum to 27 (16 + 11). The second number is octal. The digit 003 is equal to 3, and the digit 030 is equal to 3 x 8 (or 24). These sum to 27 as well (3 + 24).
☒ **A**, **B**, **C**, and **D** are all incorrect because they do not equate to the respective values.

2

Declarations and Access Control

CERTIFICATION OBJECTIVES

2.01	Class Modifiers and Access Control
2.02	Method and Variable Access Control
2.03	Default Constructors
2.04	Legal Return Types
✓	Two-Minute Drill
Q&A	Self Test

After wading through the material thus far, you should have a good understanding of what kind of knowledge is required to pass the exam. We touched briefly on declaring classes, methods, and variables and their modifiers in Chapter 1. In this chapter, we will go into depth on how these modifiers affect access control, and their relationships with packages. We will also examine default constructors and legal return types in methods.

CERTIFICATION OBJECTIVE 2.01

Class Modifiers and Access Control

What does it mean to access a class? When we say a class has access to another class, it means it has the ability to do one of three things:

- Create an instance of another class.
- Extend a class.
- Access certain methods and variables within the class.

In effect, to have access means the class is visible. Within each class, access control determines individually which methods and variables may be accessed. *Access control* is important because it controls visibility of a class, a method, or a variable. This means that you can control the external appearance or interface for a class, a method, or a variable. Controlling the visible application programming interface (API) of a class is called *encapsulation*, which is an important feature of object-oriented design (Chapter 7 deals with this).

Default Access

A class with default access needs no modifier preceding it in the declaration. Default access allows other classes within the same package to have visibility to this class, but a class member or constructor is not accessible in any other package. Examine the following source file:

```
import certification.SuperClass;
class SubClass extends SuperClass{
```

```
   static public void main(String [] args) {
      System.out.println("SubClass.");
   }
}
```

Examine the second source file:

```
package certification;
class SuperClass{
   static public void main(String [] args) {
      System.out.println("SuperClass!");
   }
}
```

As you can see, we have a superclass that resides in a different package from the subclass. The subclass has no package declaration; therefore, it is placed into an unnamed default package. The import statement at the top of the SubClass file is attempting to import the SuperClass class. The superclass belongs to the certification package, and it compiles fine. Watch what happens when we try to compile the SubClass file:

```
c:\Java Projects\Package>javac Package.java
Package.java:1: Can't access class certification.SuperClass.
Class or
interface must be public, in same package, or an accessible
member
class.
import certification.SuperClass;
..
```

This example does not work because the superclass is in a different package from the subclass. There are two ways to make this work. We could leave both classes as default access and add SubClass to the package certification. The other way is to declare SuperClass as public, as the next section describes.

Public Access

The *public* keyword placed in front of a class allows all classes from all packages to have access to a class. In other words, all classes in the Java Universe have access to a public class. It is still necessary to import the class with the import statement if it belongs to another package, but otherwise it is completely usable by all other classes.

In the example from the preceding section, we may not want to place the subclass in the same package as the superclass. To make the code work, we need to add the keyword *public* in front of the SuperClass declaration, as follows:

```
package certification;
public class SuperClass{
   static public void main(String [] args) {
      System.out.println("SuperClass!");
   }
}
```

This changes the SuperClass class so it will be visible to all classes in all packages. The class can now be instantiated and extended from all other classes.

Final Classes

The *final* keyword restricts a class from being extended by another class. Using the keyword final serves two purposes. First, it prevents inheritance from other classes. If you try to extend a final class, the Java compiler will give an error. Second, final classes are more efficient when run through the Java interpreter. The java.lang.Math class, for example, is final for primarily this reason. Let's modify our SuperClass example by placing the keyword final in the declaration:

```
package certification;
public final class SuperClass{
   static public void main(String [] args) {
      System.out.println("SuperClass!");
   }
}
```

Now, if we try to compile the SubClass code as it appeared earlier, we receive the following:

```
c:\Java Projects\Access>javac SubClass.java
SubClass.java:3: Can't subclass final classes: class
certification.SuperClass class SubClass extends SuperClass{
1 error
```

As we can see, the compiler will not allow a final class to be extended.

Abstract Classes

An *abstract class* is a type of class that is not allowed to be instantiated. The only reason it exists is to be extended. Abstract classes generally contain methods and variables common to all the subclasses, but the abstract class itself is of a type that will not be used. For example, we can make an abstract class called Furniture and a subclass of Furniture called Chair. Examine the following abstract class:

```
abstract class Furniture {
   private double price;
   public static final double TAX = 0.14;
   public double getCost() {
      double cost = price + (price * TAX);
      return cost;
   }
   // Additional code goes here
}
```

The preceding code will compile fine. However, if you try to initialize the class Furniture in another body of code, you will receive a compiler error, as follows:

```
AnotherClass.java:7: class certification.Furniture is an abstract
class. It can't be instantiated.
      Furniture f = new Furniture();
1 error
```

You may also create functional methods within an abstract class, or specify certain methods as abstract, which we will see later in this chapter. Abstract classes cannot be declared as final, because an abstract class exists only to be extended (the final keyword would prevent the class from being extended).

EXERCISE 2-1

Creating an Abstract Superclass and Subclass

The following exercise will test your knowledge of public, default, final, and abstract classes. Create an abstract superclass named Fruit and a subclass named Apple. The superclass should belong to a package called *food* and the subclass can belong to the default package. Make the superclass public and give the subclass default protection.

1. Create the superclass as follows:

```
package food;
public abstract class Fruit{ /* any code you want */}
```

2. Create the subclass in a separate file as follows:

```
import food.Fruit;
class Apple extends Fruit{ /* any code you want */}
```

3. Create a directory called *food* off the directory in your class-path setting.
4. Attempt to compile the two files. If you want to use the Apple class, make sure you place the Fruit.class file in the food subdirectory.

CERTIFICATION OBJECTIVE 2.02

Method and Variable Access Control

Access control can be a difficult concept to learn because there are many factors and combinations of factors that can make a difference in which members can be accessed. These concepts are essential to know for the certification exam.

Methods and variables are collectively known as *members*. Because method and variable members are given access control in exactly the same way, I will explain them in the same section.

There are four types of member access control:

- Public
- Private
- Protected
- Default

Default protection is achieved by using no access modifier in the member declaration. The default and protected access control types have almost identical behavior, except for one difference, which will be mentioned later.

exam Watch

It is very important to know access control inside and out for the exam. There are at least five questions that will deal specifically with this topic. Each question will test several concepts of access control at the same time, so not knowing one small part of access control could blow an entire question.

What does it mean for a class to have access to members of another class? For now, ignore any differences between methods and variables. If a class has access to another member, it means it is visible to it. When a class has no access to another member, the compiler will behave as though the member you are attempting to reference does not exist (even though it is only hidden).

There are two types of access that we must look at. The first type of access is when a method tries to access a method or a variable of a class or object. The second type of access that we are concerned with is when a class extends another class. In this case, the subclass can access certain members of the superclass, depending on what the access is on those members.

Keep in mind that different modifiers can control access to a class member based on whether the class belongs to the same package or a different package. It is also important to note that, as mentioned earlier, if the class itself can't be accessed then no members within it can be accessed either. We will now discuss public, private, protected, and default access in depth.

exam Watch

Often, new students of Java wonder what the effects are of different combinations of class and member access (such as a default class with a public variable). To figure this out, first look at the access level of the class. If the class itself will not be visible to another class, then none of the members will be either, even if the member is declared public. Once it is confirmed that the class is visible, then it is prudent to look at access levels on individual members.

Public Members

When a method or a variable member is declared public, it means all other classes, regardless of the package that they belong to, can access the member (assuming the class itself is visible). Examine the following source file:

```
import certification.OtherClass;
class AccessClass {
    static public void main(String [] args) {
        OtherClass o = new OtherClass();
        o.testIt();
    }
}
```

Examine the second file:

```
package certification;
public class OtherClass {
    public void testIt() {
        System.out.println("OtherClass");
    }
}
```

As you can see, these classes are in different packages. However, the first class can invoke the method without any problems because OtherClass is public and the method testIt() is declared public.

When a member is declared public, it can of course be accessed directly from a subclass as though it belonged to the class itself. Examine the following code:

```
package certification;
public class SuperClass {
    public int x = 9;
}
```

This code declares the integer member *x* as public. Now we can use this member in any subclass, even if it is in a different package.

```
package other;
import certification.SuperClass;
class SubClass extends SuperClass {
    public void testIt() {
        System.out.println("Variable x is " + x);
    }
}
```

Notice that in the preceding code the variable *x* is used without having to preface it with the keyword super.

Private Members

A private member cannot be accessed by any other class, except for members within the same class in which it is declared. This includes inner classes, which we will discuss more in Chapter 8. The *private* keyword essentially makes the variable or method invisible to all classes but itself. Let's make a small change to OtherClass from an earlier example.

```
package certification;
public class OtherClass {
   private void testIt() { // Changed access to private
      System.out.println("OtherClass");
   }
}
```

Line three now declares the method testIt() as private, so no other class may use it. AccessClass will remain the same:

```
import certification.OtherClass;
class AccessClass {
   static public void main(String [] args) {
      OtherClass o = new OtherClass();
      o.testIt();
   }
}
```

If we try to compile the first source file, we now get the following compiler error:

```
c:\Java Projects\Access>javac AccessClass.java
AccessClass.java:5: No method matching testIt() found in class
certification.OtherClass.
      o.testIt();
1 error
```

As you can see, it is as though the method testIt() does not exist.

What about a subclass that tries to access a private member? When a member is declared private, it can't be accessed from a subclass.

```
package certification;
public class SuperClass {
   private int x = 9; // Declared private
}
```

The altered code declares the integer *x* as private. The variable is now off limits to all other subclasses, even those in the same package:

```
package certification; // Same package
import certification.SuperClass;

class SubClass extends SuperClass {
   public void testIt() {
      System.out.println("Variable x is " + x); // Won't work
   }
}
```

If we attempt to compile the class SubClass, we will get the following error:

```
c:\Java Projects\certification>javac SubClass.java
SubClass.java:4: Undefined variable: x
      System.out.println("Variable x is " + x);
1 error
```

on the job

Java allows variables to be public, but in practice it is often best to keep all variables private except for constants. If variables need to be changed or set, programmers generally use what is known as accessor methods to modify the variable. The accessor method has the added benefit of having the ability to check the new value to ensure that it is indeed legal. You will find that all JavaBeans use accessor methods to change values. Chapter 7 will discuss encapsulation in more detail.

Protected and Default Members

The protected and default types give almost identical access. A protected member may be accessed only if the class accessing the member belongs to the same package. Examine the following class:

```
import certification.OtherClass;
class AccessClass {
   static public void main(String [] args) {
      OtherClass o = new OtherClass();
      o.testIt();
   }
}
```

Examine the second file:

```
package certification;
public class OtherClass {
   protected void testIt() {
      System.out.println("OtherClass");
   }
}
```

As you can see, the testIt() method in the second file is protected. Also, the first class belongs to a different package from the second class. Will AccessClass be able to use the method testIt()? Let's find out.

```
c:\Java Projects\Access>javac AccessClass.java
AccessClass.java:5: No method matching testIt() found in class
certification.OtherClass.
      o.testIt();
1 error
```

From the results, you can see that AccessClass has no visibility to the method testIt() because testIt() is declared with the protected keyword.

Default and protected behavior differs when it comes to subclasses in packages. This difference is rarely used in actual practice, but this does not mean it will be absent from the exam! You will very likely be asked this. Now let's examine the difference between the two.

If the protected keyword is used to define a member, the subclass will be able to access it. It does not matter if the classes are in different packages, it will still be visible. This is in contrast to the default behavior, which will not allow a subclass to access members from the superclass if they are in different packages. Let's first look at a protected variable with superclass members.

```
package certification;
public class SuperClass {
   protected int x = 9; // protected access
}
```

The preceding code now declares the integer *x* as protected. This makes the variable accessible to other classes in the certification package, as well as any subclasses of the SuperClass. Now let's create a subclass and attempt to access the variable *x* from a different package.

```
package other; // Different package
import certification.SuperClass;
class SubClass extends SuperClass {
```

```
    public void testIt() {
        System.out.println("Variable x is " + x); // Will work
    }
}
```

The preceding code compiles fine. Now let's take a look at the default behavior of a member with a subclass. We will modify the SuperClass member *x* to make it default.

```
package certification;
public class SuperClass {
    int x = 9; // No access modifier
}
```

Notice we did not place an access modifier in front of the variable *x*. We will now attempt to access it from the SubClass class that we saw earlier. When we compile the SubClass file, we receive the following error:

```
c:\Java Projects\certification>javac SubClass.java
SubClass.java:4: Undefined variable: x
        System.out.println("Variable x is " + x);
1 error
```

The compiler gives the same error when a member is declared as private. This is because SubClass has no visibility to *x* in the superclass. Now what about the default behavior with two classes in the same package?

```
package certification;
public class SuperClass{
    int x = 9;
}
```

And the second class:

```
package certification;
class SubClass extends SuperClass{
    static public void main(String [] args) {
        SuperClass sc = new SuperClass();
        sc.testIt();
    }
    public void testIt() {
        System.out.println("Variable x is " + x);
    }
}
```

The preceding source file compiles fine, and the class SubClass runs and displays the value of *x*. This proves that default members are visible only to the subclasses that are in the same package.

That about does it for our discussion on public, private, protected, and default modifiers. If this information is still not clear, perhaps Table 2-1 will help. It contains all the combinations of access and visibility, and should serve to solidify the concepts.

Methods

We have already discussed method access, which refers to the ability of one class to invoke a method from another class. Let's review the other modifiers that apply to methods.

Method Arguments

Method arguments are the variable declarations that appear in between the brackets in a method declaration. A typical method declaration with multiple arguments looks like this:

```
public Record getRecord(int fileNumber, int recordNumber) {}
```

These arguments are actually exactly the same as local variables. In the preceding example, the variables *fileNumber* and *recordNumber* will both follow all the rules applied to local variables. This means they can also have the modifier *final*. Examine the following code:

```
public Record getRecord(final int recordNumber) {}
```

TABLE 2-1 Determining Access to Class Members

Visibility	Public	Protected	Default	Private
From the same class	Yes	Yes	Yes	Yes
From any class in the same package	Yes	Yes	Yes	No
From any class outside the package	Yes	No	No	No
From a subclass in the same package	Yes	Yes	Yes	No
From a subclass outside the same package	Yes	Yes	No	No

In this example, the variable *recordNumber* is declared as final, which of course means it cannot be modified within the method. If you recall from Chapter 1, local variables cannot be modified as public, private, protected, static, transient, or volatile.

Abstract Methods

An *abstract method* is a method declaration that is not implemented, and therefore contains no functional code. The reason for using an abstract method is to ensure that subclasses of this class will include this method. Any class that is not abstract, and therefore capable of being instantiated, must override this method. (Chapter 7 will explore overriding.) A typical abstract method declaration is as follows:

```
public abstract void showSample();
```

Notice that the abstract method ends with a semicolon instead of curly braces. It is illegal to have an abstract method in a class that is not declared abstract. Examine the following illegal class:

```
public class IllegalClass{
   public abstract void doIt();
}
```

The preceding class will produce the following error if you attempt to compile it:

```
C:\Java Projects\abstract>javac IllegalClass.java
IllegalClass.java:1: class IllegalClass must be declared abstract.
It does not define void doIt() from class IllegalClass.
public class IllegalClass{
1 error
```

You can, however, have an abstract class with no abstract methods. The following example will compile fine:

```
public abstract class LegalClass{ }
```

Final Methods

The final keyword prevents a method from being overridden in a subclass. For this reason, final and abstract may not be used together in a method declaration. Final methods are often used to enforce the API functionality of a method. For example, the Thread class has a method called isAlive() that checks whether a thread is still active. If someone extends the Thread class, there is really no reason to override this method, so the designers have made it final. A typical final declaration looks like this:

```
class SuperClass{
   public final void showSample() {
      System.out.println("One thing.");
   }
}
```

It is legal to extend SuperClass; however, we will not be allowed to override the method showSample() in our subclass, as the following code attempts to do:

```
class SubClass extends SuperClass{
   public void showSample() {
      System.out.println("Another thing.");
   }
}
```

Attempting to compile the preceding code gives us the following:

```
c:\Java Projects\final>javac FinalTest.java
FinalTest.java:5: The method void showSample() declared in class
SubClass cannot override the final method of the same signature
declared in class SuperClass. Final methods cannot be overridden.
    public void showSample() { }
1 error
```

Static Methods

A method that is declared static is called a *class method.* A class method is always invoked without reference to a particular object. A method that is not declared static is called an *instance method,* and sometimes called a *nonstatic method.* An example of static methods in action can be found in the Math class (see Chapter 10). Let's look at a class with two methods. One of the methods is static and one is not.

```
class TestStatic {
   public static void greetUser(String name) {
      System.out.println("Good day, " + name);
   }
   public void greetUser2(String name) {
      System.out.println("Good day, " + name);
   }
}
```

The first method is static, and therefore it can be accessed without instantiating the class TestStatic. The second is a normal instance method and can only be invoked on an instance of the class. We also need a class to test this with:

```
public class Greetings {
   public static void main(String [] args) {
      TestStatic.greetUser("Arthur"); // will work
      TestStatic.greetUser2("Agatha"); // will not work
      new TestStatic().greetUser(" Arthur "); // will work
      new TestStatic().greetUser2("Agatha"); // will work
   }
}
```

If we attempt to compile the second class, we receive the following error:

```
c:\Java Proejcts\StaticTest>javac Greetings.java
Greetings.java:4: Can't make a static reference to method void
greetUser2(java.lang.String) in class TestStatic.
         TestStatic.greetUser2("Agatha");
1 error
```

Note that in line five of the Greetings class, the static method can be called from an instance as well. Line six shows the proper usage of the greetUser2() method. This time the nonstatic method greetUser2() works because we have made an instance of the class to call the method from.

Synchronized Methods

The synchronized keyword indicates that a method may be accessed by only one thread at a time. This topic will be discussed more in Chapter 9. For now, all we are concerned with is creating a viable declaration. A typical synchronized declaration looks like this:

```
public synchronized Record retrieveUserInfo(int id) { }
```

Native Methods

Native indicates that a method is written in a platform-dependant language, such as C. You will not need to know how to use native methods for the exam, other than knowing that *native* is a reserved keyword.

Variables

We have already discussed variable access, which refers to the ability of one class to read or alter (if it is not final) a variable in another class. Let's look at the other keywords that apply to variable declarations.

Static Variables

A *static variable* can be accessed from a class directly, even though the class has not been instantiated. Examine the following code:

```
class TestServer {
   static int users = 0;
   public void logIn() {
      users += 1;
   }
}
```

This class demonstrates the declaration of a static variable. Notice that *users* can be modified from within the class using a nonstatic method. The variable *users* is modified in the instance method logIn() without any problems. We can also access the variable *users* from outside the class, as follows: `TestServer.users`

Instance Variables

Instance variables are defined at the class level and are only initialized when the class is instantiated. Instance variables may not be accessed from static methods because a static method can be invoked when no instances of the class exist. If no instances exist, then the instance variable has not been initialized and therefore would cause an error. The following illegal code demonstrates a static method attempting to access an instance variable. If you attempt to compile this code, you will receive a compile error.

```
class IllegalAccess {
   int totalHits;
   public static void main(String [] args) {
      ++totalHits; // Illegal
   }
}
```

Automatic (Method Local) Variables

Automatic or *local variables* are variables that are declared within a method and discarded when the method has completed. Automatic variable declarations do not include modifiers such as public and static, but they can be final. Before an automatic variable can be used, it must be initialized with a value.

```
class TestServer {
   public void logIn() {
      int count = 10;
   }
}
```

Typically, the variable is initialized in the same line in which the variable is declared, although there can be good reasons for initializing it later in the method. It is important to remember that an automatic variable must be initialized before it is used. The compiler will reject any code that attempts to use a local variable that has not been initialized.

An automatic variable may not be referenced anywhere in the code except for within the method in which it is declared. In the preceding code, it would be impossible to refer to the variable *count* anywhere else in the class except within the scope of the method logIn().

It is possible to declare a local variable with the same name as an instance variable or class variable. The following code demonstrates this in action:

```
class TestServer {
   int count = 9;
   public void logIn() {
      int count = 10;
      System.out.println("local variable count is " + count);
   }
   public void count() {
      System.out.println("instance variable count is " + count);
   }
   public static void main(String[] args) {
      new TestServer().logIn();
      new TestServer().count();
   }
}
```

Final Variables

The final keyword makes it impossible to reinitialize a variable once it has been initialized. For primitives, this means the value cannot be altered once it is initialized.

For objects, the data within the object can be modified, but the reference variable cannot be changed. Final variables do not have to be initialized in the same line in which they are declared. Keep in mind that a final instance variable will not take the default value of zero. Examine the following code:

```
class FinalTest{
   final int x; // Will not work
   public void showFinal() {
      System.out.println("Final x = " + x);
   }
}
```

Attempting to compile the preceding code gives us the following:

```
c:\Java Projects\final>javac FinalTest.java
FinalTest.java:2: Blank final variable 'x' may not have been
initialized. It must be assigned a value in an initializer, or in
every constructor.
   final int x;
1 error
```

We can assign a value to the variable *x*, even though it is not in the same line in which it was declared. This must be done in the constructor method or it will not work:

```
class FinalTest{
   final int x; // Will work
   public FinalTest() {
      x = 28;
      System.out.println("Final x = " + x);
   }
}
```

It is illegal to change a variable once it is initialized. Let's look at declaring an object variable as final. We will create a class that creates an instance of a date, manipulate data in it, and then try to reinitialize it.

```
import java.util.Date;
class TestClass {
   final Date d = new Date();
   public void showSample() {
      d.setYear(2001); // Altering data in instance
   }
}
```

In line five in the preceding class, the year is modified within the instance. This is perfectly legal, and the class will compile fine because an instance can have its data modified even though it is final. Now let's see what happens when we reinitialize an object.

```
import java.util.Date;
class FinalTest {
   final Date d = new Date();
   public void showSample() {
      d.setYear(2001);
      d = new Date(); // Will not work
   }
}
```

Line seven now tries to reinitialize the variable *d.* If we attempt to compile the preceding class, we receive the following error:

```
c:\Java Projects\final>javac FinalTest.java
FinalTest.java:6: Can't assign a value to a final variable: d
         d = new Date();
1 error
```

As we can see, with final variables, the reference variable cannot be changed after it is assigned to an instance.

Transient Variables

The *transient* keyword indicates which variables are not to have their data written to an ObjectStream. You will not be required to know how to use transient for the exam, other than the keyword.

Volatile Variables

The *volatile* keyword indicates that a variable may change out of sync due to its usage in threads. You will not be required to know anything about volatile for the exam, other than the keyword. See Chapter 9 for more on using the volatile keyword.

CERTIFICATION OBJECTIVE 2.03

Default Constructors

When an object is instantiated, a constructor is always invoked. If you do not specify a constructor for the class, Java creates a *default constructor* that contains no arguments. When we say it creates a constructor, it does not actually place it in the source code. Examine the following code:

```
class Fruit {
   public static void main(String [] args) {
      Fruit f = new Fruit();
   }
}
```

In the preceding code example we are creating an instance of the Fruit class. The main method clearly calls a constructor method called Fruit(), which we did not create anywhere in the code. Java actually created the no-arguments constructor.

This begs the question, what does the default constructor do? This constructor will call the no-arguments constructor for the superclass. In the preceding example, it calls the constructor for the Object class, because all classes extend the Object class. If any other constructor is created, Java will no longer create a default no-arguments constructor for you:

```
class Constructor {
   public static void main(String [] args) {
      System.out.println("Initializing a new Constructor...");
      Constructor c = new Constructor();
   }
   public Constructor(int i) {
      System.out.println("The Constructor(int i) constructor ran.");
   }
}
```

Notice that in the preceding example we are trying to initialize a constructor with the default Constructor() method. If we try to compile this, the following error occurs:

```
c:\Java Projects\Constructor>javac Constructor.java
Constructor.java:4: No constructor matching Constructor() found in
class Constructor.
                    Constructor c = new Constructor();
1 error
```

This is because we have created another constructor—in this case, one that uses an int argument. As soon as Java sees that there is another constructor, it no longer creates a default constructor for you.

There is one other instance in which Java will not create a constructor for you. If the superclass contains a constructor that has arguments, Java will not create a default constructor for any subclasses that are created.

```
class Fruit{
    public Fruit(String color) {
        System.out.print("Color = " + color);
    }
}
class Apple extends Fruit{
    public static void main(String [] args) {
        Apple m = new Apple();
    }
}
```

Notice in the preceding code that Fruit contains a constructor with an argument. The class Apple extends Fruit and attempts to create an instance of Apple using the default constructor. When we try to compile this code, we receive the following:

```
Fruit.java:6: No constructor matching Fruit() found in class Fruit.
class Apple extends Fruit{
1 error
```

For now, this is all you need to know about default constructors. Chapter 7 will discuss invoking superclass constructors and overloading constructors.

exam Watch

The only time that a default constructor is supplied for a class is when the programmer has not supplied a constructor. As soon as you supply any constructor, either with arguments or without, Java will no longer create a no-arguments default constructor. Also, if the superclass contains a constructor that uses anything other than a no-arguments constructor, then no default constructor will be created.

EXERCISE 2-2

Creating a Superclass and a Subclass

This exercise will familiarize you with constructor methods. The object of this exercise is to create a superclass and a subclass. One of the class' constructors will display the words *Hello* and one will display the word *flipper* to make a coherent greeting.

1. Create the superclass as follows:

```
class Mammal{
   public Mammal() {
      System.out.print("Hello");
   }
}
```

2. Create the subclass as follows:

```
class Dolphin extends Mammal{
   public Dolphin() {
      System.out.println(" flipper.");
   }
   public static void main(String [] args) {
      Dolphin d = new Dolphin();
   }
}
```

3. Compile and run the subclass to see if it works. It is important to note that even though we did not use super() to invoke the superclass constructor, the no-arguments superclass constructor is still executed.

CERTIFICATION OBJECTIVE 2.04

Legal Return Types

For the exam, you will need to be able to state the legal return types for any given method. A *return type* is the variable that a method may return when the method is finished executing. A *declared type* is the variable type stated in the method declaration. The return type may actually be different from the declared type due to inheritance. A return type is legal if it can be implicitly converted to the declared type. This concept will become clear when we start looking at integer return types. To introduce the concept, we'll start with the boolean primitive.

boolean

If you create a method that returns a type of *boolean,* the only type of value that can be returned is a Boolean literal such as *true* or *false.* Java will not accept a Boolean object, null, an integer value such as 0 or 1, or any other type. The following example will return true:

```
public boolean bool {
   return (1 < 2); // returns true
}
```

char

A method with a declared type of *char* can return a char literal. This includes a character enclosed in single quotes, or an escape sequence in single quotes. It is not legal to return a String object containing only one character. The following examples demonstrate legal and illegal lines of code:

```
char x = 'd'; // legal
char y = '\u0023'; // legal
char z = "d"; // not legal
```

It is also legal to return an integral value. As we learned in Chapter 1, a char is a 16-bit value that ranges from 0 to 65535. This means some (but not all) integral types are legal return types for char. A negative integral number, or an integral larger than 65535 is not legal. Examine the following examples of legal and illegal lines of code:

```
char a = 23; // legal
char b = -22; // not legal
char c = 66000; // not legal
int d = 23;
char e = d; // not legal
char f = (char)d; // legal
```

As we can see in the preceding code, the compiler knows an *int* primitive may be larger than 65535, so it will not allow it unless the value is cast into a *char* type.

Integer Primitive Types

A method that declares an integral return type (int, byte, short, or long) can return only an integral value, or sometimes a char value. This includes returning the result of an expression that evaluates to an integral value. Examine the following method:

```
public int getValue() {
   int a = 200;
   return a + 50;
}
```

This is a very simple method that declares the return type as an *int* type. If we look in the method, we can see it is returning the value of an int variable named *a* plus 50. This is all very normal, but we can also return other integral types. Examine the following revised code:

```
public int getValue() {
   byte a = 100;
   return a;
}
```

This method will work just fine in a class. The reason it works is because an int value is larger than a byte; therefore, int is able to store a byte value. Both a short type and a long type can also store a byte, because they too are larger than a byte. In general, an integral type can hold a place value for a smaller integral type. For example, a long can hold an int, but an int can't hold a long.

We discussed char types earlier. A char ranges from 0 to 65535, so this means int and long are the only two integral types that can legally return a type of char. The following code demonstrates this in action:

```
public int getValue() {
   char a = 'd';
```

```
    return a; // legal
}
```

When a method has a declared integral type (byte, short, int, or long), it cannot return a floating-point number (float or double), even if the floating-point number has no fraction after the decimal. Examine the following code:

```
public int getValue() {
    float a = 100;
    return a;
}
```

If we insert this method into a class and attempt to compile the code, it will result in the following error:

```
c:\Java Projects\BookTest>javac Return.java
Return.java:4: Incompatible type for return. Explicit cast
needed to
convert float to int.
    return a;
1 error
```

Table 2-2 shows the integer types that other integer variables can store legally.

exam Watch ***A good way to determine whether an integral return type is legal is to think of the number of bits that a primitive can hold. If the bits value of the return type is less than the declared return type, it is legal.***

Float Primitive Types

Floating-point return types are slightly more complicated than integer types. A method with a return type of a floating-point number can return integers as well as

TABLE 2-2 Legal Return Types for Integer Numbers

Declared Type	Legal Return Types
byte	byte
short	byte, short
int	byte, short, int, char
long	byte, short, int, long, char

float types. In other words, a floating-point number can return integral numbers, but integrals can't return floating-point numbers. This also applies to the char type. As discussed earlier, a char is well within the range of floating-point number types (0 to 65535). Examine the following method:

```
public double getValue() {
   long a = 100;
   return a;
}
```

The preceding method declares a return type of double. If we look within the method, however, we see it is actually returning an integer type of long. This works because a double is capable of storing numbers with or without fractions after the decimal. Table 2-3 shows the legal return types for floating-point numbers. Notice that a 32-bit float can actually return a 64-bit long.

It is also worth mentioning that a method with a *double* return type can also return a type of *float*. This is because a 64-bit double has enough space to hold a 32-bit float.

```
public double getValue() {
   float a = 8920.12518f;
   return a;
}
```

exam Watch

It is illegal for a primitive to be assigned to null. In other words, if a method declares a primitive return type, then the method may not attempt to return null.

TABLE 2-3

Legal Return Types for Floating-Point Numbers

Declared Type	Legal Return Types
float	byte, short, int, long, float, char
double	byte, short, int, long, float, double, char

FROM THE CLASSROOM

The Mystery of Floating Point Numbers

You may have noticed in this chapter that a 32-bit float is capable of storing a 64-bit integer. If you are at all familiar with computer memory and bits, this seems like quite a mystery. It is like someone claiming to have a 2-gallon bucket that can hold 4 gallons of water. So how does Java manage to pull this trick off?

When float numbers get very large they begin to use exponential numbers. In other words, if there are 19 individual digits in single number, it will give you a number x10^{18}. So for the number 1,234,567,890, it will be represented as 1.23456789 x 10^{9}. No accuracy is lost with this small of a number, however. But what about larger numbers? Examine the following sample code:

```
class AccuracyTest {
   public static void main(String [] args) {
      long salary = Long.MAX_VALUE - 443322112233L;
      System.out.println("long is " + salary);

      float taxes = salary;
      System.out.println("float is " + taxes);

      long net = (long)taxes;
      System.out.println("New long is " + net);
   }
}
```

In this example, the long is arbitrarily assigned a very large number. It then gets converted to a float, then back to a long again. Let's examine the output to see what happens:

```
long is 9223371593532663574
float is 9.2233715E18
New long is 9223371487098961920
```

As you can see, the large float loses some accuracy. In the above example, it is off by the not so insignificant value of `106,433,701,654.` So float can handle

FROM THE CLASSROOM

large numbers, but as a banker or mathematician you would have to doubt these results. A better solution would be to use java.math.BigInteger or java.math.BigDecimal. These classes are slower to use, but they have no upper limit on numbers, and they provide most of the methods contained in the java.lang.Math class.

—*Trent Heintz*

Object Return Types

A method with an object return type can return the same object type, or subclasses of the object. For example, the Component class is a base class for the various Abstract Window Toolkit (AWT) components, such as Button, Label, and TextField. We can write a method that declares a return type of Component, as follows:

```
public Component getComponent() {
   Button b = new Button("Close");
   return b;
}
```

As you can see, this method is returning a Button object. You could also create a method that returns any object by using a return type of Object, because every Java class extends the Object class.

It is also legal to have a return type that is an interface. This may seem inexplicable, because an interface is not a real object, but it fits in with Java's object-oriented design. For example, a method can use Runnable as its return type even though a Thread object is being returned. This is because Thread implements the Runnable interface. Keep in mind, however, that if the return type is a Thread, you will not be able to return an object just because it implements the Runnable interface. Let's take a look at a legal method with a declared return type of Runnable:

```
public Runnable getRunnable() {
   Thread myThread = new Thread(this);
   return myThread;
}
```

SCENARIO & SOLUTION	
What are the possible legal return types for the primitive byte?	A byte is the only one.
What are the possible legal return types for an Object?	Absolutely any Object (that is, any subclass of Object), but not a primitive.
What are the possible legal return types for a float?	byte, short, int, long, float, char
What are the possible legal return types for an object of type Component?	Component, Checkbox, Panel, Button, and so on. (Refer to the Java Core API specification.)

String objects operate as any other type of object. You might think that a method with a return type of String could return an array of chars, but in fact it does not. The only objects that a method with a String return type can return are String types. You will learn more about Strings in Chapter 11.

Finally, we must mention that when the declared return type is an object, it is perfectly legal to return a null value. It is also legal to initialize an object using null.

Now that you have a better understanding of return types, refer to the following Scenario & Solution for possible declared types and their legal return types.

CERTIFICATION SUMMARY

You now have a good understanding of access control as it relates to classes, methods, and variables. You can also determine which constructor will be invoked for a given class, as well as which return types are legal for a method definition. Let's review what you have learned from this chapter.

Access control for classes is limited to default or public access, whereas variables and methods can be private, default, protected, or public. For classes and members, it is important to recognize the package relationships in order to determine if an entity will be visible. Classes, methods, and variables use a unique set of modifier keywords. For the test, be sure that you know which keywords apply to these elements. There is some overlap, but some keywords (such as synchronized) are for one type of entity only.

Almost every type of class uses a constructor to become instantiated (except for abstract classes and anonymous inner classes). The default constructor is the no-arguments constructor that Java creates if a constructor is not implicitly created in the code. If you create a constructor, then Java will not create a default constructor.

Finally, make sure you are comfortable with legal return types for a given method declaration. For integer types, if the declared return type is larger than the actual return type then it is legal. Declared integer types may not return floating-point values; however, declared floating-point values may return integer types. With objects, a declared superclass type may return any valid subclass.

TWO-MINUTE DRILL

Here are some of the key points from each certification objective in Chapter 2.

Class Modifiers and Access Control

- ❑ Default class access allows access only to classes in the same package.
- ❑ Public class access opens the class to all other classes.
- ❑ Final classes and methods may not be extended or overwritten.
- ❑ Abstract classes may not be instantiated.

Method and Variable Access Control

- ❑ Public members may be accessed from all other methods.
- ❑ Private members may be accessed only by the class in which the member is declared.
- ❑ Instances of protected and default members may be accessed only by classes in the same package.
- ❑ Subclasses may access members of the superclass that are public or protected; default members can only be accessed if the classes belong to the same package, private members can't be accessed by subclasses.
- ❑ Static methods may not access instance members.

Default Constructors

- ❑ If no constructor is created, Java will supply a no-arguments default constructor.
- ❑ If the superclass contains a constructor with any number of arguments, Java will not create a default constructor for subclasses.

Legal Return Types

- ❑ Methods with declared floating-point return types can return any integer type.
- ❑ Methods with declared integral return types can return any type of integer that is smaller than or equal to the declared type.
- ❑ Methods may return subclasses of the declared class type.

SELF TEST

The following questions will help you measure your understanding of the material presented in this chapter. Read all of the choices carefully, as there may be more than one correct answer. Choose all correct answers for each question.

Class Modifiers and Access Control

1. One or both of the following files will not compile:

```
1.  package payroll;
2.  class EmployeeNames{
3.      public static String [] names ={"Ian","Paul","Adam","Jansky"};
4.      public static String [] getNames() {
5.          return names;
6.      }
7.  }
```

This is the second file:

```
 8.  package client;
 9.  import payroll.EmployeeNames;
10.  class TraderNames extends EmployeeNames{
11.       public String [] traders = {"Marty", "Niko", "Kris"};
12.  }
```

There are several ways to make this code work. Which of the following line changes, on their own, will make this code work? (Choose all that apply.)

A. `1.  package client;`

B. `2.  protected class EmployeeNames {`

C. `8.  package payroll;`

D. `10.  public class TraderNames extends EmployeeNames{`

2. Given:

```
1.  package payroll;
2.  final public class EmployeeNames{
3.     public static final String [] names = {"Paul","Adam","Jansky"};
4.     public static String [] getNames() {
5.        return names;
6.     }
7.  }
```

And the following:

```
package client;
class TraderNames extends EmployeeNames{
    public static String [] Traders = {"Ziggy", "Niko", "Chris"};
}
```

Which of the following statements is true?

A. The file with class EmployeeNames will not compile.

B. The file with class TraderNames will not compile.

C. The files will both compile, but an error will occur when the class TraderNames is instantiated.

D. The files will compile, and when either class is instantiated, it will work fine.

3. Given:

```
1.  class A{
2.      abstract int getNum();
3.  }
```

And the following:

```
4.
5.      public static int pi = 3;
6.      int getNum(){
7.          return 3;
8.      }
9.  }
```

The second file can be compiled successfully by inserting a line of code on line 4. Which of the following lines will allow compilation to succeed? (Choose all that apply.)

A. class B extends A {

B. abstract class B extends A{

C. final abstract class B extends A{

D. final class B extends A{

E. abstract class B{

Method and Variable Access Control

4. Given:

```
package payroll;
class EmployeeNames{
   private static String[] names = {"Ian","Paul","Adam","Jansky"};
   public static String[] getNames() {
      return names;
   }
}
```

And the following:

```
package payroll;
class TraderNames extends EmployeeNames{
   public static String [] Traders =names;
}
```

Which of the following statements are correct?

A. The file with class EmployeeNames will not compile.

B. The file with class TraderNames will not compile.

C. The files will both compile, but an error will occur when the class TraderNames is instantiated.

D. The files will compile, and when either class is instantiated, it will work fine.

5. Given:

```
package payroll;
public class UserConnection{
   final int MAXUSERS = 20;
   public static String getServerName() {
      return "Main Server";
   }
}
```

And the following:

```
package client;
import payroll.UserConnection;
```

```
10.  class ServerConnection extends UserConnection{
11.      public final int MAXCONNECTIONS = MAXUSERS * 10;
12.  }
```

What will happen when these classes are compiled and run?

A. The file with class UserConnection will not compile.

B. The file with class ServerConnection will not compile.

C. The files will both compile, but an error will occur when the class ServerConnection is instantiated.

D. The files will compile, and when either class is instantiated, it will work fine.

6. Given:

```
1.  package payroll;
2.  public class UserConnection{
3.
4.        public static String getServerName() {
5.              return "Main Server";
6.        }
7.  }
```

And the following:

```
8.  package client;
9.  import payroll.UserConnection;
10. class ServerConnection extends UserConnection{
11.       public final int MAXCONNECTIONS = MAXUSERS * 10;
12. }
```

Which line, inserted at line 3, will allow both of these files to compile properly? (Choose all that apply.)

A. protected int MAXUSERS = 20;

B. private int MAXUSERS = 20;

C. protected final int MAXUSERS;

D. protected static int MAXUSERS = 20;

7. Given:

```
1.  package payroll;
2.  public class UserConnection{
3.      protected int users = 0;
4.      public static String getServerName() {
```

```
        return "Main Server";
    }
}
```

And the following:

```
package client;
import payroll.UserConnection;
class ServerConnection {
    public UserConnection getUserConnection() {
        UserConnection u = new UserConnection();
        u.users += 1;
        return u;
    }
}
```

Which of the following statements are true?

A. The file with class UserConnection will not compile.

B. The file with class ServerConnection will not compile.

C. The files will both compile, but an error will occur when the class ServerConnection is instantiated.

D. The files will compile, and when either class is instantiated, it will work fine.

8. Given:

```
package server;
public class ServerNames{
    abstract public static String sendName();
}
```

What will happen when the class is compiled and run?

A. The file will not compile.

B. The file will compile, but an error will occur when the class ServerNames is instantiated.

C. The file will compile, and when the class is instantiated, it will work fine.

9. Given:

```
package server;
public class ServerNames{
    protected final int MAXUSERS = 20;
    public final static String sendName() {
        return "Main Server";
```

```
6.      }
7.  }
```

And the following:

```
8.  package client;
9.  import server.ServerNames;
10. class Retrieve extends ServerNames{
11.     public final int MAXCONNECTIONS = MAXUSERS * 10;
12.     public static String sendName(String s) {
13.         return s;
14.     }
15. }
```

What is the result?

A. Compilation succeeds.

B. Compilation fails due to line 3.

C. Compilation fails due to line 8.

D. Compilation fails due to line 11.

E. Compilation fails due to line 12.

10. Given:

```
class TestServer {
    static int users = 0;
    public void logIn() {
        users += 1;
    }
    public static void main(String [] args) {
        new TestServer().logIn();
    }
}
```

What is the result?

A. The file will not compile.

B. The file will compile, but an error will occur when the class is instantiated.

C. The files will compile, and when either class is instantiated, it will work fine.

11. Given:

```
class TestServer {

    static public void logIn() {
```

```
4.          users += 1;
5.      }
6.  }
```

Which line of code, when inserted at line 2, will cause a compilation error? (Choose all that apply.)

A. int users = 0;

B. float users = 0;

C. static int users;

D. static float users = 1;

12. Given:

```
class TestServer {
   public TestServer() {
      int users = 1;
   }
   public void increment() {
      users = users + 1;
   }
   public static void main(String [] args){
      TestServer ts = new TestServer();
      ts.increment();
      System.out.println("Variable users = " + ts.users);
   }
}
```

What will the output of this class be?

A. Variable users = 1.

B. Variable users = 2.

C. The file will compile, but will give an error when run.

D. The file will not compile.

13. Given:

```
class TestServer {
   static final int users = 20;
   public TestServer() {
      int users;
      users = this.users * 10;
   }
   public static void main(String [] args){

```

```
9.      }
10.  }
```

Which of the following lines of code, when inserted at line 8, will output a value of 200 to the system output?

A. System.out.println(" " + this.users);

B. System.out.println(" " + users);

C. System.out.println(" " + users + 180);

D. None of the above.

Default Constructors

14. Given:

```
class TestVariable {
    static int objs = -1;
    public TestVariable() {
        objs++;
        System.out.println("Total Objects = " + objs);
    }
}
class SubTest extends TestVariable {}
```

The class is instantiated with the following line of code:

```
SubTest t = new SubTest();
```

Which of the following statements are true the first time we try to instantiate SubTest? Assume no other instances of these two classes have been instantiated.

A. Total Objects = 0

B. Total Objects = 1

C. Total Objects = 2

D. Nothing will output to the screen.

E. These classes will not compile.

15. Given:

```
class SuperServer {
    public SuperServer() {
        System.out.print(35);
    }
```

```
}
class TestServer extends SuperServer{
   public TestServer(int y) {
      y = y * 10;
      System.out.print(y);
   }

   public static void main(String [] args){
      TestServer ts = new TestServer(10);
   }
}
```

What will be the output of this class?

A. 12100

B. 10012

C. 1224

D. 35100

16. Given:

```
class SuperServer {
   public SuperServer() {
      System.out.print(" all ");
   }
   public SuperServer(int y){
      this();
      System.out.println (" good ");
   }
}
class TestServer extends SuperServer{
   public TestServer(int y) {
      System.out.print(" things ");
   }
   public TestServer() {
      super(10);
      System.out.print(" come ");
   }
   public static void main(String [] args){
      TestServer ts = new TestServer(10);
   }
}
```

What will be the output of this class?

A. good things

B. all things come

C. all things

D. all good things

Legal Return Types

17. Given:

```
class Force {
    public short Jerec() {
        byte Kyle = 20;
        return Kyle;
    }
    public int Pic() {
        long Gorc = 200;
        return Gorc;
    }
    public Boolean Sariss() {
        boolean Boc = true;
        return Boc;
    }
    public long Maw() {
        float Yun = 2000F;
        return Yun;
    }
}
```

Which of the following methods are legal?

A. Jarec()

B. Pic()

C. Sariss()

D. Maw()

18. Given:

```
class A {
    public float airbag() {
        long airbag = 1980;
        return airbag;
    }
    public float android() {
```

```
            double paranoidAndroid = 2056;
            return paranoidAndroid;
        }
        public double alien() {
            float homesickAlien = 2623.12F;
            return homesickAlien;
        }
        public double asteroid() {
            byte asteroids = 2000;
            return asteroids;
        }
        public double army() {
            char army = '\u03b9';
            return army;
        }
    }
```

Which of the following methods are legal? (Choose all that apply.)

A. airbag()

B. android()

C. alien()

D. asteroid()

E. army()

19. Given the following four class definitions:

```
class Food implements Eatable{}
class Vegetable extends Food {}
class GreenPeas extends Vegetable {}
class Meat extends Food {}
```

And the following method:

```
1.  public Vegetable getSomething() {
2.
3.  }
```

Choose all of the legal lines of code that could be inserted into the method getSomething() at line 2. (Choose all that apply.)

A. return new Vegetable();

B. return new Food();

C. return new Meat();

D. return new GreenPeas();

20. Given the following four class definitions:

```
class Food{}
class Vegetable extends Food {}
class GreenPeas extends Meat {}
class Meat extends Food implements Eatable{}
```

And the following method:

```
1.  public Eatable getSomething() {
2.
3.  }
```

Choose all of the legal lines of code that could be inserted into the method getSomething() at line 3. (Choose all that apply.)

A. return new Vegetable();

B. return new Food();

C. return new Meat();

D. return new GreenPeas();

SELF TEST ANSWERS

Class Modifiers and Access Control

1. ☑ A and C. The second file containing TraderNames will not compile because it does not have access to the class EmployeeNames. Default protection does not allow classes outside the package to access the class. A is correct because both classes will be in the same package; client. C is correct because this will make both classes in the same package: payroll.
☒ B is incorrect because the modifier protected may not be used on a class. D is incorrect because the visibility of TraderNames is not important. If we made EmployeeNames public, this would make the code valid.

2. ☑ B. This file will not compile because EmployeeNames is a final class; therefore, no other class can attempt to subclass it.
☒ A is incorrect because EmployeeNames is a valid class definition. C and D are incorrect because TraderNames will not compile.

3. ☑ A, B, D, and E. A is correct because class B extends class A, which is legal. B is correct because a class can be abstract, even though it has no abstract methods. D is legal because it is subclassing A and declaring itself final. E is correct because it can declare itself abstract without subclassing A.
☒ C is incorrect because an abstract class may not be final. An abstract class exists to be extended, and the final keyword would prevent this.

Method and Variable Access Control

4. ☑ B. This file will not compile because it does not have access to the array *names.* Private protection does not allow variables outside the class to access the variable.
☒ A is incorrect because EmployeeNames will compile fine. C and D are incorrect because TraderNames does not compile.

5. ☑ B. This file will not compile because it does not have access to the variable MAXUSERS. Default access does not allow a subclass outside the package to access the variable.
☒ A is incorrect because UserConnection is properly defined. C and D are incorrect because ServerConnection will not compile.

6. ☑ **A** and **D**. **A** is correct because protected access allows the subclass ServerConnection to access the variable MAXUSERS. **D** is correct for the same reason, and it can also be used in ServerConnection even though it is static.
☒ **B** is incorrect because private variables cannot be accessed by subclasses. **C** is incorrect because final variables must be initialized with a value.

7. ☑ **B**. This file will not compile because it does not have access to the variable *users*. Protected access does not allow variables outside the package to access the variable.
☒ **A** is incorrect because UserConnection will compile properly. **C** and **D** are incorrect because ServerConnection will not compile.

8. ☑ **A**. This file will not compile because this class contains an abstract method, but the class itself is not declared as abstract.
☒ **B** and **C** are both incorrect because the file compiles.

9. ☑ **A**. This is correct because this file will compile successfully.
☒ **B** is incorrect because it has access to the protected variable MAXUSERS. Protected access allows subclasses outside the package to access the variable. **C** is incorrect because the packages do not make a difference when using protected with subclasses. **D** is incorrect because it has access to MAXUSERS, and this is a legal line of code. **E** is incorrect because it is okay to overload a final method *if* it has a different signature (arguments) from the method declared as final.

10. ☑ **C**. This class works because a static variable may be modified in an instance method.
☒ **A** and **B** are incorrect because the file compiles and executes successfully.

11. ☑ **A** and **B**. **A** and **B** cause compiler errors because the static method logIn() may not modify an instance variable.
☒ **C** is incorrect because it does not cause a compilation error. This static variable is declared at the class level and will receive a default value of 0. **D** is incorrect for the same reason, and a float may be initialized with an integral value.

12. ☑ **D**. This class does not work because the variable users is declared only as an automatic variable. It should be declared as an instance or static variable.
☒ **A**, **B**, and **C** are all incorrect because this file will not compile.

13. ☑ **D**. None of these lines will output 200 to the screen.
☒ **A** is incorrect because this line will output 20 to the screen. The instance variable *this.users* is not modified anywhere in the program. **B** is incorrect for the same reason. The variable users still refers to *this.users*, not the local variable in the constructor. **C** is incorrect because it will

output 20180 to the screen, rather than actually adding the variable users to 180. The operator + is actually a concatenate function when used with a string.

Default Constructors

14. ☑ A. The static variable objs starts with a value of -1. When the default constructor SubTest() is first called, it will invoke the TestVariable() constructor, which increments the instance variable objs by 1.
☒ B and C are both incorrect because of the program flow described previously. D is incorrect because the prototype constructor for the default constructor of SubTest is the no-arguments constructor for TestVariable. E is incorrect because this file will compile.

15. ☑ D. The default SuperServer constructor at line 2 is executed first, which prints 35 to the screen (using the print() method which doesn't use a line return). Next, the TestServer constructor is executed using an argument of 10. Within the constructor the variable y (10) is multiplied by the argument (10), then printed to the screen.
☒ A, B, and C are all incorrect because of the program flow described previously.

16. ☑ C. The default SuperServer constructor at line 2 is run first, followed by the code in the TestServer(int y) constructor. (More about overloading and overriding constructors can be found in Chapter 7.)
☒ A, B, and C are all incorrect because of the program flow described previously.

Legal Return Types

17. ☑ A. A method with a declared return type of short may return a byte.
☒ B is incorrect because a long is larger than an int; therefore, long is not a legal return type ssfor int. C is incorrect because the declared return type is a Boolean object, but the attempted return type is a Boolean literal. D is incorrect because the declared return type of long is an integral number, whereas the attempted return type is a floating-point number.

18. ☑ A and E. A is correct because a method with a declared return type of short may return a byte. E is correct because a method with a declared return type of float may return a char value. It will be automatically cast into a float number.
☒ B is incorrect because a long is larger than an int; therefore, long is an illegal return type. C is incorrect because a Boolean object is the declared return type, but the method tries to return a primitive Boolean. D is incorrect because a long cannot store a float type; therefore, float is illegal as a return value.

19. ☑ A and D. A is correct because Vegetable is a legal return type, as it is declared as the return type for the method getSomething(). D is correct because GreenPeas is also a Vegetable type, as it is a subclass of Vegetable.
☒ B is incorrect because Food is not of type Vegetable. C is incorrect because meat is not of type Vegetable.

20. ☑ C and D. Meat and GreenPeas are of type Eatable. GreenPeas inherits the Eatable methods and variables from Meat, which directly implements Eatable.
☒ A and B are incorrect because Eatable is nowhere in the object hierarchy of these classes.

JAVA™

SUN CERTIFIED PROGRAMMER®

3

Operators and Assignments

CERTIFICATION OBJECTIVES

3.01 Java Operators

3.02 The equals() Method

3.03 Passing Variables into Methods

✓ Two-Minute Drill

Q&A Self Test

This chapter thoroughly examines the various operations and comparisons that can be performed on primitives and objects. We will cover the basic mathematical operations that are used on a day-to-day basis, but more importantly we will be reviewing (or more likely introducing) several obscure operations that are guaranteed to be tested on the exam. The Boolean equals() method is a method that all objects contain, so we will be looking at the behavior of this method. We will also examine what happens to primitives and objects when they are passed into a method as arguments.

CERTIFICATION OBJECTIVE 3.01

Java Operators

Operators are functions built into the Java language that produce new values from one or more operands. The result of performing a Java operator is a *Boolean* or numeric value. There is one operator (+) that is overloaded to handle String objects.

Assignment Operators

The equal (=) sign is used for assigning a value to a variable; hence, it is called an *assignment operator*. There are actually 12 assignment operators, but the rest are just amalgams of the equal sign and other arithmetic operators, as shown in Table 3-1.

The equal sign can be used with both primitive values and objects, but there are differences between how it affects objects and primitives. It is important to remember that variables are merely pointers to the actual object itself. If we assign an existing

TABLE 3-1 All 12 Assignment Operators of the Java Language

=	*=	/=	%=
+=	-=	<<=	>>=
>>>=	&=	^=	|=

instance of an object to a new reference variable, then two reference variables will point to the same object. Examine the following code:

```
import java.awt.Dimension;
class ReferenceTest {
  public static void main (String [] args) {
    Dimension a = new Dimension(5,10);
    System.out.println("a.height = " + a.height);
    Dimension b = a;
    b.height = 30;
    System.out.println("a.height = " + a.height +
      "after change to b");
  }
}
```

In the preceding example, a Dimension object *a* is declared and initialized with a width of 5 and a height of 10. Next, Dimension *b* is declared as a reference to *a.* Finally, the height property is changed using the *b* reference. Now think for a minute: Is this going to change the height property of *a* as well? Keep in mind that variables for objects are merely pointers to the actual object itself. Let's see what the output will be:

```
c:\Java Projects\Reference>java ReferenceTest
a.height = 10
a.height = 30 after change to b
```

From this output, we can conclude that both variables point to the same instance of the Dimension object. When we made a change to *b*, the height property was also changed for *a.*

String objects are given special treatment by the Java language. It is also important to differentiate how String objects behave when compared to regular objects. Examine the following code:

```
class Strings {
    public static void main(String [] args) {
        String x = "Java";
        String y = x;
        System.out.println("y string = " + y);
```

```
        x = x + " Bean";
        System.out.println("y string = " + y);
    }
}
```

You might think String *y* will contain the characters *Java Bean* after the variable *x* is changed, because strings are objects. Let's examine the output to find out:

```
C:\Java Projects\BookTest>java String
y string = Java
y string = Java
```

As you can see, even though *y* is a reference variable to the same object that *x* refers to, when we change *x* it does not change *y*. This is because a brand new String object is created every time we use the + operator to concatenate two strings. Chapter 11 will go into more detail on this important certification objective.

In contrast to objects, primitive number assignments are stored as values. In other words, primitive variables are assigned to unique values. Let's look at some code for an explanation of this:

```
class ValueTest {
    public static void main (String [] args) {
        int a = 10;
        System.out.println("a = " + a);
        int b = a;
        b = 30;
        System.out.println("a = " + a + "after change to b");
    }
}
```

This code is very similar to the previous example using objects, except we are using primitive values instead of objects. The output from this program is the following:

```
c:\Java Projects\Reference>java ValueTest
a = 10
a = 10 after change to b
```

Notice this time the value of *a* stayed at 10. This is because primitive types are assigned by value and not by reference.

Comparison Operators

Comparison operators always result in a Boolean value. This Boolean value is most often used in an *if* statement, but it can also be assigned directly to a Boolean primitive:

```
class CompareTest {
    public static void main(String [] args) {
        boolean b = 100 > 99;
        System.out.println("The value of b is " + b);
    }
}
```

There are four comparison operators that can be used to compare any combination of integral numbers, floating-point numbers, or characters:

- > greater than
- >= greater than or equal to
- < less than
- <= less than or equal to

Let's examine some legal comparisons:

```
class GuessAnimal {
    public static void main(String [] args) {
        String animal = "unknown";
        int weight = 700;
        char sex = 'm';
        double colorWaveLength = 1.630;
        if (weight >= 500) animal = "elephant";
        if (colorWaveLength > 1.621) animal = "gray " + animal;
        if (sex <= 'f') animal = "female " + animal;
        System.out.println("The animal is a " + animal);
    }
}
```

In the preceding code, we are using a comparison between characters. It is also legal to compare a character primitive with any number, as the code shows (though this isn't great programming style). Running the preceding class will output the following:

```
C:\Java Projects\BookTest>java GuessAnimal
The animal is a gray elephant
```

We mentioned that characters can be used in comparison operators. When comparing a character with a character, or a character with a number, Java will take the ASCII or Unicode value of the character as the numerical value.

instanceof Comparison

The *instanceof* comparison operator is used for object variables only. The purpose of this operator is to determine whether an object belongs to a given class (or any of the superclasses). The instanceof operator is one of Java's mechanisms that allow *reflection*; the ability to examine its own code. This comparison may not be made on primitive types and will result in a compile-time error if it is attempted. Let's examine a typical example of instanceof:

```
import java.awt.*;
class CompareTest {
    public static void main(String [] args) {
        Button b = new Button("Exit");
        boolean compare1 = b instanceof Button;
        boolean compare2 = b instanceof Component;
        System.out.println("Is b a Button? " + compare1);
        System.out.println("Is b a Component? " + compare2);
    }
}
```

This class creates an instance of a Button, and then uses instanceof to see if it is of type Button and Component. Running the preceding program produces the following:

```
C:\Java Projects\CompareTest>java CompareTest
Is b a Button? true
Is b a Component? true
```

There is a very important rule when using instanceof. It is not legal to attempt to compare an instance to a class if the instance is not in the same object hierarchy as the class. If we attempt to compare an instance with a class that is not part of the hierarchy, the compiler will produce an error. Examine the following code:

```
import java.awt.*;
class CompareTest {
   public static void main(String [] args) {
      Button b = new Button("Exit");
      boolean compare = b instanceof String;
      System.out.println("Is b a String? " + compare);
   }
}
```

The code simply creates a Button object, then tests to see if it is a String object. The String type is not in the hierarchy of Button; therefore, this will not work. If we attempt to compile this code, we receive the following:

```
C:\Java Projects\CompareTest>javac CompareTest.java
BookTest.java:5: Impossible for java.awt.Button to be instance
of java.lang.String.
      boolean compare = b instanceof String;
1 error
```

The Java compiler knows it is impossible for Button *b* to be a String because it is explicitly declared as a Button, and String is nowhere in the object hierarchy of Button. One small change to our code will allow this to compile:

```
import java.awt.*;
class CompareTest {
   public static void main(String [] args) {
      Object b = new Button("Exit");
      boolean compare = b instanceof String;
      System.out.println("Is b a String? " + compare);
   }
}
```

We have changed the declaration type of *b* to Object, so *b* is not explicitly declared as a Button at compile time. Theoretically, when the program is run, *b* could become a String, a Date, or any other class type. In this case, it is initialized on the same line as a Button, but it still could become anything else, so Java allows this to be tested with instanceof.

In addition, it is legal to test whether a null object (or *null* itself) is an instance of a class. This will always result in false, of course. The following code demonstrates this:

```
class InstanceTest {
   public static void main(String [] args) {
      String a = null;
```

```
        boolean b = null instanceof String;
        boolean c = a instanceof String;
        System.out.println(b + " " + c);
    }
}
```

When this code is run we get the following output:

```
false false
```

So even though variable *a* was defined as a String, the underlying object is null; therefore, instanceof returns a value of false when compared to the String class.

Equality Operators

Equality can be tested with the operators equals and not equals:

- == equals
- != not equals

Equality operators compare two entities and return a Boolean value. Each individual comparison is allowed to use either two numbers (including char), two Boolean values, or two object/null variables. Two differing types are not allowed to be compared—such as a Boolean and a number. There are four different types of entities that can be tested:

- Numbers
- Characters
- Boolean primitives
- Reference variables to objects

Equality for Primitives

Most programmers are familiar with comparing primitive values. The following code shows some primitives being compared for equality:

```
class ComparePrimitives {
    public static void main(String [] args) {
        System.out.println("character 'a' == 'a'? " + ('a' == 'a'));
        System.out.println("character 'a' == 'b'? " + ('a' == 'b'));
```

```
        System.out.println("5 != 6? " + (5 != 6));
        System.out.println("5.0 == 5L? " + (5.0 == 5L));
        System.out.println("true == false? " + (true == false));
    }
}
```

Notice that in line six we are comparing an integer to a float number. This program produces the following output:

```
c:\Java Projects\Equality>java ComparePrimitives
character 'a' == 'a'? true
character 'a' == 'b'? false
5 != 6? true
5.0 == 5L? true
true == false? false
```

As we can see, if a float is compared with an integer and the values are the same, the == operator returns true as expected.

Equality for Reference Variables

A *reference variable* is a name that is used in Java to reference an instance of a class. As was previously stated, two reference variables can point to the same object, as the following code snippet demonstrates:

```
Button a = new Button("Exit");
Button b = a;
```

After running this code, both variable *a* and variable *b* will refer to the same object (a button with the label Exit). Reference variables can be tested to see if they point to the same object by using the == operator. Examine the following code:

```
import java.awt.Button;
class CompareReference {
   public static void main(String [] args) {
       Button a = new Button("Exit");
       Button b = new Button("Exit");
       Button c = a;
       System.out.println("Is reference a == b? " + (a == b));
       System.out.println("Is reference a == c? " + (a == c));
   }
}
```

This code creates three reference variables. The first two, *a* and *b*, are separate Buttons which happen to have the same label. The third reference variable, *c*, is initialized to point to the same instance that *a* refers to. When this program runs, the following output is produced:

```
Is reference a == b? false
Is reference a == c? true
```

As we can see by this result, both *a* and *c* reference the same instance of a Button. Because strings are also objects and not primitives, strings with the same characters may not be equal when we test them using the == operator. This will be discussed in detail later in this chapter, as well as in Chapter 11.

Arithmetic Operators

Most people are familiar with the basic arithmetic operators:

- \+ addition
- – subtraction
- × multiplication
- / division
- % remainder (modulo)

These can be used in the standard way:

```
class MathTest {
    public static void main (String [] args) {
        int x = 5 * 3;
        int y = x % 4;
        System.out.println("The remainder of " + x + " % 4 is " + y);
    }
}
```

It is possible to abbreviate each of these operators if the operation is being done to a single variable, as shown in Table 3-1. These assignment operators can be used as follows:

```
class MathTest {
   public static void main (String [] args) {
      int x = 15;
      x %= 4; // same as x = x % 4;
      System.out.println("The remainder of 15 % 4 is " + x);
   }
}
```

Note that the plus sign and the minus sign are used as prefixes on numbers to denote a positive or negative value:

```
int y = -20;
```

String Concatenation Operator

The plus sign can also be used to concatenate two strings together, as you have witnessed previously in this book:

```
String animal = "Grey " + "elephant";
```

Increment and Decrement

There are two operations that will increment or decrement a variable by exactly one. These operators are composed of either two plus or minus signs:

- ++ increment (prefix and postfix)
- -- decrement (prefix and postfix)

The operator is placed either before (prefix) or after (postfix) a variable to change the value. There is an important difference in the behavior of the operator, depending on whether it is before or after the operand. Examine the following:

```
class MathTest {
   static int users = 0;
   public static void main (String [] args) {
      System.out.println("Users online: " + users++);
      System.out.println("The value of users is " + users);
      System.out.println("The value of users is now " + ++users);
   }
}
```

Notice that in the fourth line of the program the increment operator is after the variable *users.* This will cause the variable *users* to be incremented by one after the value is used in the expression. When we run this program, it will output the following:

```
c:\Java Projects\Increment>java MathTest
Users online: 0
The value of users is 1
The value of users is now 2
```

Notice when the variable is written to the screen, at first it says the value is zero. This is because the postfix incremental operator occurs after the line of code executes. The next line does not increment *users;* it just outputs it to the screen, so the value displayed is one. The next line increments by one before the variable, so the output is two.

The postfix operator increments the value by one, but returns the current value. There is also a precedence of operators, which will be discussed later. Postfix has a precedence over prefix operators. Examine the following code:

```
class MathTest {
   public static void main (String [] args) {
      int x = 10;
      x = ++x + x++;
      System.out.println(x);
   }
}
```

You might think the output will be 21, but let's break this down. The postfix ++ has precedence, so the right side will increment x to 11, but return 10. The left side will then increment x from 11 to 12. So the equation actually looks like x = 12 + 10, and the result is 22. The exam will likely include a few simple precedence questions like this.

Shift Operators

The following are shift operators:

- >> right shift
- << left shift
- >>> right shift including negative bit

exam Watch

The more obscure the topic, the more likely it will appear on the exam. Operators such as +, -, *, and / will probably not be on the exam because they are commonly used. Shift operators are rarely or never used; therefore, they will most definitely be tested.

The shift operators shift the bits of a number to the right or left, producing a new number. Shift operators are used on integral numbers only (not float numbers). To determine the result of a shift, it is necessary to convert the number into bits. Let's look at an example of a bit shift, without using code.

We'll start with a simple example. Let's use the right-shift operator on the integer 8. First, we must convert this number to a bit representation:

```
0000 0000 0000 0000 0000 0000 0000 1000
```

An *int* is a 32-bit integer, so all 32 bits must be displayed. If we apply a bit shift of one to the right, using the >> operator, the new bit number is:

```
0000 0000 0000 0000 0000 0000 0000 0100
```

We can now convert this back to a decimal number (base 10), to get 4. Now let's examine how to do the exact same thing with code:

```
class BitShift {
   public static void main(String [] args) {
      int x = 8;
      System.out.println("Before shift x equals " + x);
      x = x >> 1;
      System.out.println("After shift x equals " + x);
   }
}
```

When we compile and run this program we get the following output:

```
c:\Java Projects\BitShift>java BitShift
Before shift x equals 8
After shift x equals 4
```

As you can see, the results are exactly what we expected them to be. Shift operations can take place on all integral numbers, regardless of the base they are displayed in (octal, decimal, or hexadecimal). The left shift works in exactly the same way, except all bits are shifted in the opposite direction. The following code uses a hexadecimal number to shift:

```
class BitShift {
    public static void main(String [] args) {
        int x = 0x80000000;
        System.out.println("Before shift x equals " + x);
        x = x << 1;
        System.out.println("After shift x equals " + x);
    }
}
```

To understand the preceding example, it is necessary to convert the hexadecimal number to a bit number. Fortunately, it is very easy to convert from hexadecimal to bits. Each hex-digit converts to a four-bit representation, as we can see:

```
8    0    0    0    0    0    0    0
1000 0000 0000 0000 0000 0000 0000 0000
```

In the preceding example, the very leftmost bit represents the sign (positive or negative). When the leftmost bit is 1 the number is negative, and when it is 0 the number is positive. Running our program gives us the following:

```
c:\Java Projects\BitShift>java BitShift
Before shift x equals -2147483648
After shift x equals 0
```

As we can see, shifting the bits one to the left moves the bit right out of the number, leaving us with all 0 bits.

When there is a negative bit and we shift to the right, the operator shifts the bit to the right but also keeps the negative bit. For example, let's use the hex number 0x80000000 again:

```
1000 0000 0000 0000 0000 0000 0000 0000
```

Now we will shift the bits, using >>, one to the right:

```
1100 0000 0000 0000 0000 0000 0000 0000
```

As we can see, the bit is shifted to the right but (and this is important) the negative bit remains behind. Let's try some code that shifts it four to the right:

```
class BitShift {
   public static void main(String [] args) {
      int x = 0x80000000;
      System.out.println("Before shift x equals " + x);
      x = x >> 4;
      System.out.println("After shift x equals " + x);
   }
}
```

In line five of this program, the number will be bit shifted four to the right. Running this program gives us the following output:

```
C:\Java Projects\BookTest>java BitShift
Before shift x equals -2147483648
After shift x equals -134217728
```

The number now equals the following in bit representation:

```
1111 1000 0000 0000 0000 0000 0000 0000
```

We can use a special shift operator if we do not want to keep the negative bit. This is the operator >>>. Let's change the code slightly to use this operator:

```
class BitShift {
   public static void main(String [] args) {
      int x = 0x80000000;
      System.out.println("Before shift x equals " + x);
      x >>>= 4; //Assignment operator
      System.out.println("After shift x equals " + x);
   }
}
```

The output for this program is now the following:

```
C:\Java Projects\BookTest>java BitShift
Before shift x equals -2147483648
After shift x equals 134217728
```

As we can see, the new number is positive because the negative bit was not kept. In bit representation, the new number is:

```
0000 1000 0000 0000 0000 0000 0000 0000
```

Notice the preceding code uses an assignment operator to accomplish the bit shift. The assignment operators (shown in Table 3-1) are as follows:

- <<=
- >>=
- >>>=

EXERCISE 3-1

Using Shift Operators

1. Try writing a class that takes an integer of 1, shifts the bit 31 to the left, then 31 to the right.
2. What number does this now represent?
3. What is the bit representation of the new number?

The program should look something like the following:

```
class BitShift {
   public static void main(String [] args) {
      int x = 0x00000001; // or simply 1
      x <<= 31;
      x >>= 31;
      System.out.println("After shift x equals " + x);
   }
}
```

The number should now equal -1. In bits, this number is:

```
1111 1111 1111 1111 1111 1111 1111 1111
```

FROM THE CLASSROOM

Converting Binary Numbers to Decimal in Java

Converting numbers from binary to decimal and vice versa is pretty easy to do for positive numbers, as long as you have a pencil and paper handy (which will be supplied for the exam). But what about negative numbers? These are a little more complicated to convert, and for this reason the exam adheres to using simple positive binary numbers. But for your own knowledge, let's examine how Java handles number conversions.

You might be wondering why the number -1 is stored as 1111 1111 1111 1111 1111 1111 1111 1111 in binary. In Java and in most systems, negative numbers are stored using the 2's complement of the number. To take the 2's complement for a number, first you look at the most significant bit (MSB). The MSB is the leftmost bit in a binary representation of a number (see the following example). If the MSB is 0 then the number is positive, and if it's 1 then the number is negative. If the number is positive, then the other 31 bits are the binary representation of the positive number. If the number is negative then to get its value, you have to take the rest of the bits and take their complement by "flipping" each bit and then adding 1. So if you look at the signed binary number :

```
1111 1111 1111 1111 1111 1111 1111 1111
^ most significant bit (MSB)
```

The most significant bit is 1, so you know it's a negative number. To figure out the actual number, you complement the other 31 bits by flipping them. So you get the following:

```
1000 0000 0000 0000 0000 0000 0000 0000
```

You then add 1 to get the 2's complement, so your final number is 1.

```
1000 0000 0000 0000 0000 0000 0000 0001
```

Now you know why the bit pattern 1111 1111 1111 1111 1111 1111 1111 1111 represents -1. You might ask why go through so much trouble representing negative numbers? The reason for this is that most logic circuits can readily add two binary numbers. The subtraction operation is equivalent to adding a binary number and the 2's complement of the other number. Therefore, 2's complement not only enables storage of positive and negative integers but also enables both addition and subtraction.

—Harold Cabrera, B.Sc. Comp. Eng., Java Certified Programmer

Bitwise Operators

The bitwise operators take two individual bit numbers, then use AND/OR to determine the result on a bit-by-bit basis. There are three bitwise operators:

- & AND
- | inclusive OR
- ^ exclusive OR

The & operator compares corresponding bits between two numbers or it can compare two Boolean values, treating them as bits. If both bits are 1, then the final bit is also 1. If only one of the bits is 1, then the resulting bit is 0. Once again, for bitwise operations we must convert numbers to bit representations. Table 3-2 displays the truth table for each of these operators. The left side of the table displays the x and y values, and the right side shows the result of the operator on these two values.

Let's compare two numbers, 10 and 9, with the & operator:

```
1010 & 1001 = 1000
```

As we can see, only the first bit (8) is a 1 in both locations, hence the final number is 1000 in bit representation (or 8 in decimal). Let's see this in some code:

```
class Bitwise {
    public static void main(String [] args) {
        int x = 10 & 9; // 1010 and 1001
        System.out.println("1010 & 1001 = " + x);
    }
}
```

TABLE 3-2 Calculating Values from a Truth Table

X	Y	& (AND)	| (OR)	^ (XOR)
0	0	0	0	1
0	1	0	1	0
1	0	0	1	0
1	1	1	1	1

When we run this code, the following output is produced:

```
c:\Java Projects\Bitwise>java Bitwise
1010 & 1001 = 8
```

The | (OR) operator is different from the & (AND) operator; when it compares corresponding bits, a 1 is the result if either bit is a 1. So, for the numbers 10 and 9, we get the following:

```
1010 | 1001 = 1011
```

In this case, because we have 1s in the 1, 2, and 8 bit slots, those bits are carried forth. It produces the number 11 (in decimal). Let's examine this in some code:

```
class Bitwise {
   public static void main(String [] args) {
      int x = 10 | 9; // 1010 and 1001
      System.out.println("1010 & 1001 = " + x);
   }
}
```

When we run the preceding code, we receive the following:

```
C:\Java Projects\BookTest>java Bitwise
1010 & 1001 = 11
```

on the job

The ^ operator is not tested on the exam, but you should be aware of its existence for programming, especially with graphics applications. The ^ operator compares two bits to see if they are different. If they are, the result is a 1. Examine the numbers 10 and 5 in bit representation:

```
1010 ^ 0101 = 1111
```

As we can see, the result is 15 in decimal form. Let's examine 8 and 13 in this example:

```
1000 ^ 1101 = 0101
```

The result is 5 in decimal form.

Logical Operators

There are two logical operators:

- && conditional AND
- || conditional OR

The && operator is similar to the & operator, except it evaluates only Boolean values. The && operator evaluates the left side of the equation first, to see if a false exists. If it does, it does not bother looking at the right side of the equation, because it already knows that no matter what the value of the right bit is, the result is still false.

```
class Logical {
    public static void main(String [] args) {
        boolean b = true && false;
        System.out.println("boolean b = " + b);
    }
}
```

When we run the preceding code, we receive the following:

```
C:\Java Projects\BookTest>java Logical
boolean b = false
```

The || operator is similar to the && operator, except it evaluates the left side to see if a true is present. If it is, it knows the result will be true, so it does not bother looking at the right side of the equation.

exam Watch

The || and && operators only work with Boolean operands. The exam may try to fool you by using integers with these operators, so be on guard for this.

Bitwise Complement Operator

The ~ operator is the reverse-bits operator. This operator will not be tested on the Java exam, but it is a good idea to be familiar with it. It will change all 1s to 0s and vice versa. Examine the following code:

```
class Bitwise {
    public static void main(String [] args) {
```

```
        int x = 5; // 000..0101
        System.out.println("x is initially " + x);
        x = ~x;
        System.out.println("~x is equal to " + x);
    }
}
```

This program is changing every bit into its complement, thus the output from this program is the following:

```
C:\Java Projects\Bitwise>java Bitwise
x is initially 5
~x is equal to -6
```

In bit representation, the conversion looks like this:

```
~0000 0000 0000 0000 0000 0000 0000 0101
```

Converts to:

```
1111 1111 1111 1111 1111 1111 1111 1010
```

Conditional Operators

Conditional operators (also known as ternary operators) are used to evaluate Boolean expressions, much like *if* statements, except instead of executing a block of code, a conditional operator will assign a value to a variable. A conditional operator is constructed using the following characters:

- ?
- :

Let's take a look at a conditional operator in some code:

```
class Salary {
    public static void main(String [] args) {
        int salary = 30000;
        String status = (salary<15000)?"poor":"not poor";
        System.out.println("This salary is classified as " + status);
    }
}
```

A conditional operator starts with a Boolean operation, followed by two possible values for the variable. The left value is assigned if the Boolean is true, the right if it is false. You can also apply many conditional operators in one statement.

```
class AssignmentOps {
    public static void main(String [] args) {
        int salary = 50000;
        String status = (salary<15000)?"poor":(salary<40000)?
            "middle class":(salary<70000)?"upper middle class":
            "upper class";
System.out.println("This salary is classified as " + status);
    }
}
```

As you can see, we can stack these operators into one long statement.

Casting

Casting can be used on primitives or instances to convert the current type. There are two types of casts, implicit and explicit. An *implicit cast* is legal at runtime, because the subclass value is converted to that of its superclass. In general, you can have an implicit cast when a widening conversion is done. An implicit cast requires no additional syntax within the code, as the following examples demonstrate:

```
TextField tf = new TextField("127.0.0.1");
Component text1 = tf; // implicit cast
int a = 100;
float b = a; // implicit cast
```

An explicit cast, on the other hand, is when a superclass value is converted to a subclass type. In general, an explicit cast is when a narrowing conversion is done. For primitives, narrowing means loss of precision, and for objects it means loss of generality. The following are examples of explicit casts:

```
Component tf;
tf = new TextField("127.0.0.1");
TextField text1;
text1 = (TextField)tf; // explicit cast from Component to
TextField
float a = 100.001;
int b = (int)a; // explicit cast of primitive
```

The following sections go into more detail on casting primitives and objects.

Primitive Casting

Integral values may be assigned to a double variable without explicitly casting the integral value. The following line demonstrates this:

```
double d = 100L; // implicit cast
```

In the preceding statement, a double is being initialized with a long value (as denoted by the L after the numeric value). No cast is needed in this case because a double can hold every piece of information that a *long* can store. If, however, we want to assign a double value to an integral type, we will run into problems:

```
class Casting {
   public static void main(String [] args) {
      int x = 3957.229; // illegal
   }
}
```

If we try to compile the preceding code, the following error is produced:

```
C:\Java Projects\Cast>javac Casting.java
Casting.java:3: Incompatible type for declaration. Explicit cast

needed to convert double to int.
      int x = 3957.229; // illegal
1 error
```

In the preceding code, a floating-point value is being assigned to an integer variable. Because an integer is not capable of storing decimal places, an error occurs. To make this work, we will cast the floating-point number into an integer:

```
class Casting {
   public static void main(String [] args) {
      int x = (int)3957.229; // legal cast
      System.out.println("int x = " + x);
   }
}
```

When we perform a cast on a floating-point number, it causes the value to lose all the digits after the decimal. Running the preceding code will produce the following output:

```
c:\Java Projects\Cast>java Casting
int x = 3957
```

We can also cast a larger number type, such as a long, into a smaller number type, such as a byte. Examine the following:

```
class Casting {
   public static void main(String [] args) {
      long l = 56L;
      byte b = (byte)l;
      System.out.println("The byte is " + b);
   }
}
```

The preceding code will compile and run fine. But what happens if the long value is larger than 127? Let's modify the code and find out:

```
class Casting {
   public static void main(String [] args) {
      long l = 130L;
      byte b = (byte)l;
      System.out.println("The byte is " + b);
   }
}
```

The code compiles fine, and when we run it we get the following:

```
c:\Java Projects\Cast>java Casting
The byte is -126
```

Java does not produce a runtime error, as you might expect. It actually starts counting up from -128 when we go over 127. Runtime errors can occur when casting objects, as we shall see in the next section.

EXERCISE 3-2

Casting Primitives

Create a float number type of any value, and assign it to a short using casting.

1. Declare a float variable: float f = 234.56F;
2. Assign the float to a short: short s = (short)f;

Your completed program should look something like this:

```
class Cast {
   public static void main(String [] args) {
```

```
        float f = 234.56F;
        short s = (short)f;
    }
}
```

Casting Objects

Objects may also be cast. When an object is cast, the subclass is implicitly stated. For example, the Button class is a subclass of Component. We can create an object of type Component and assign it to a Button variable without any additional syntax. If we want to assign our Component to a Button variable, however, we must cast our Component to a Button. The following illegal code will clarify this:

```
import java.awt.*;
class Casting {
    public static void main(String [] args) {
        Component c;
        c = new Button("Close");
        Button b = c; // Does not work
    }
}
```

As we can see in the preceding code, it is trying to assign our Component to a Button variable, *b*. If we attempt to compile this class, we will receive the following error from the compiler:

```
c:\Java Projects\Cast>javac Casting.java
Casting.java:6: Incompatible type for declaration. Explicit cast
needed to convert java.awt.Component to java.awt.Button.
        Button b = c; // Does not work
1 error
```

This generates an error, as we can see. To correct this, we must cast the variable *c* into a Button:

```
import java.awt.*;
class Casting {
    public static void main(String [] args) {
        Component c;
        c = new Button("Close");
        Button b = (Button)c;
    }
}
```

This brings us to an interesting point. What if we were attempting to cast *c* into a Button, but in fact *c* was a different Component, such as a Label?

```
import java.awt.*;
class Casting {
   public static void main(String [] args) {
      Component c;
      c = new Label("Close");
      Button b = (Button)c;
   }
}
```

This code will actually compile fine, but an error is generated at runtime. When there is a problem with casting at runtime, the Java virtual machine (JVM) will throw a ClassCastException, as the following shows:

```
C:\Java Projects\Cast>java Casting
Exception in thread "main" java.lang.ClassCastException:
java.awt.Label at Casting.main(Casting.java:6)
```

exam Watch

For the exam, it will be important to note when a runtime error will occur, and when a compile time error will occur. Make sure you know the difference between these two behaviors when it comes to casting.

Now that you have a better idea of operators and how they function, here are some operators in action and their results.

SCENARIO & SOLUTION	
What is the result of (1 & 3)?	1
What is the result of (1 | 3)?	3
What is the result of (5++)?	6
What is the result of (1 << 2)?	4
What is the resulting value of (new Button("Lock") instanceof Component)?	True

CERTIFICATION OBJECTIVE 3.02

The equals() Method

The equals() method is a special method contained in the Object class that compares properties between two objects. The properties that the method tests are determined by the type of object being tested. This is in contrast to the == operator, which tests whether two reference variables are the same, as described earlier in the chapter.

The equals() method is typically overridden in a subclass. When this method is not overridden, it is identical to the == operator (it compares two reference variables). For the Java exam, you will need to know the behavior of String, Boolean, and Object types.

java.lang.String

The String.equals() method compares the characters within a string to determine whether they are equal. Let's examine this in some code:

```
class Equals {
   public static void main(String [] args) {
      String ja = "Ja";
      String va = "va";
      String java1 = ja + va;
      String java = "Java";
      System.out.println("java.equals(java1)? " + java.equals(java1));
      System.out.println("java == java1? " + (java == java1));
   }
}
```

The preceding code creates two strings that contain the same string characters. Notice that the program goes to great lengths to create the variable java1 by concatenating two strings together at runtime. The reason for this will be explained later, but for now this shows the difference between equals() and the == operator. When we run this code we receive the following:

```
c:\Java Projects\Equals>java Equals
java.equals(java1)? true
java == java1? false
```

Notice that the equals() method shows the strings as equal, but the == operator does not indicate they are equal. To contrast this with the == operator, it will be beneficial to see how the == operator works. The following code tests various strings to see whether they are referring to the same object. This may seem to go against what you previously thought when comparing two strings. Normally when comparing two strings you use the String method equals(); however, there are instances in which Java references the same String object. This will be clarified in a moment. For now, examine the following code and try to guess which statements are true.

```
class StringLiteral {
   public static void main(String[] args) {
      String java = "Java", va = "va";
      System.out.println(java == "Java");
      System.out.println(Other.java == java);
      System.out.println(java == ("Ja"+"va"));
      System.out.println(java == ("Ja"+va));
   }
}
class Other { static String java = "Java"; }
```

Let's examine the output of this program to see if you were correct.

```
c:\Java Projects\StringLiteral>java StringLiteral
true
true
true
false
```

The first true value demonstrates that the variable *java* equals the literal value "Java." The reason for this is because the variable java is calculated as an instance at compile time, as are any variables that are assigned a literal. The Java language shares unique instances of strings if they are calculated at compile time, referencing them to the same object instead of creating unique objects.

The second true value shows us that strings in other classes can refer to the same string object. This applies to classes in other packages as well.

The third true is basically a reiteration of the first point. Ja + va is a literal value that is exactly the same as Java, and is assigned at compile time.

The false value shows what happens when we compare a string computed at runtime, and not compile time. Because it is computed at runtime, a new string object is created that is brand new and therefore not equal to our other string object.

This is the same as comparing two separate, nonstatic strings that contain the same series of characters.

So, as you can see, when strings are assigned to literal values, if the literal values are the same then the Java compiler assigns them to the same object. This concept will be expanded upon further in Chapter 11.

java.lang.Boolean

The Boolean.equals() method is similar to the String.equals() method. Examine the following code:

```
class Equals {
   public static void main(String [] args) {
      Boolean a = new Boolean(true);
      Boolean b = new Boolean(true);
      System.out.println("a.equals(b)? " + a.equals(b));
      System.out.println("a == b? " + (a == b));
   }
}
```

The preceding code creates two Boolean objects, both with a value of true. When we use the Boolean.equals() value, it compares the Boolean property, but when we use the == operator it compares reference variables, which of course are not equal because there are two separate objects. The output is as follows:

```
a.equals(b)? true
a == b? false
```

java.lang.Object

As we mentioned earlier, the Object.equals() method is contained in the Object class that compares properties between two objects. The Object.equals() method itself works in the same way that the == operator does when it is not overridden in a subclass; it compares the reference variables. Examine the following code:

```
public class Test extends Object {
   public static void main(String [] args) {
      Test a = new Test();
      Test b = new Test();
      Test c = b;
      System.out.println("a.equals(b)? " + a.equals(b));
```

```
            System.out.println("a == b? " + (a == b));
            System.out.println("b.equals(c)? " + b.equals(c));
            System.out.println("b == c? " + (b == c));
        }
    }
```

Notice the preceding code specifies that Object is being extended, even though it is not necessary to implicitly state this. The code demonstrates what happens when the Object.equals() method is not overridden in the subclass. When we run the code, we get the following:

```
c:\Java Projects\Equals>java Equals
a.equals(b)? false
a == b? false
b.equals(c)? true
b == c? true
```

This is clearly comparing reference variables and not some other property. The method Test.equals() compares the reference variables of two objects. In effect, Object.equals() and == are both doing the same thing.

Evaluation Order

There is a certain evaluation order when dealing with operators. The exam will likely include a few simple questions just to make sure you are aware of this order. The order, from high precedence to low precedence, is as follows:

1. ++ postfix, —postfix
2. ++ prefix, — prefix, + unary, - unary, ~, !
3. (type) casting
4. *, /, %
5. =, + (binary), - (binary)
6. <<, >>, >>>
7. <, >, <=, >=, instanceof
8. ==, !=
9. &

10. ^

11. |

12. &&

13. ||

14. ?: (ternary operator)

15. =, +=, -=, *=, /=, %=, >>=, <<=, >>>=, &=, ^=, |=

This seems a little overwhelming at first, but each part of the list contains a group that is more or less easy to remember. Also, each group at the same level in the list has equal precedence, so if they appear together in a line of code they are evaluated left to right.

I find a good way to evaluate an expression is to keep reducing it one operator at a time. Examine the following code:

```
class MathTest {
   public static void main (String [] args) {
      int x = 5;
      x = 3 << 1 / 2 & ++x;
      System.out.println(x);
   }
}
```

The first thing that will happen here is that x is incremented by one, so the equation reduces to:

```
x = 3 << 1 / 2 & 6
```

Next, the division operator is used. 1 divided by 2 is 0 for integers, so the equation reduces to:

```
x = 3 << 0 & 6
```

Now we use the bitshift operator. Because we are shifting by 0, there is no change:

```
x = 3 & 6
```

Finally, we AND these two numbers (0011 AND 0110 = 0010) to get:

```
x = 2
```

CERTIFICATION OBJECTIVE 3.03

Passing Variables into Methods

When passing object arguments to a method, you must keep in mind it is a reference variable that is being passed, and not the actual object itself. A *reference variable* is a name that points to a location in the computer's memory where the object is stored. This leads to two different types of behavior when an object or a primitive is passed to a method. First, let's look at what happens when a primitive is passed to a method:

```
class ReferenceTest {
   public static void main (String [] args) {
      int a = 1;
      ReferenceTest rt = new ReferenceTest();
      System.out.println("Before modify() a = " + a);
      rt.modify(a);
      System.out.println("After modify() a = " + a);
   }
   void modify(int number) {
      number = number + 1;
      System.out.println("number = " + number);
   }
}
```

In this simple program, the variable *a* is passed to a method called modify() which increments the variable by 1. The resulting output looks like this:

```
C:\Java Projects\Reference>java ReferenceTest
Before modify() a = 1
number = 2
After modify() a = 1
```

Notice that *a* did not change after it was passed to the method. It is as though a copy of *a* is passed to the method. When a primitive is passed to a method, it is *passed by value.* Passing by value means that the numeric value, and not a reference to a variable, is passed to the method.

Now let's see how the preceding performs when we use an object instead of a primitive. For this example, we will import the Dimension class from the java.awt package:

```
import java.awt.Dimension;
class ReferenceTest {
    public static void main (String [] args) {
        Dimension d = new Dimension(5,10);
        ReferenceTest rt = new ReferenceTest();
        System.out.println("Before modify() d.height = " + d.height);
        rt.modify(d);
        System.out.println("After modify() d.height = " + d.height);
    }
    void modify(Dimension dim) {
        dim.height = dim.height + 1;
        System.out.println("dim = " + dim.height);
    }
}
```

When we run this class, we get different behavior than we did by using a primitive.

```
C:\Java Projects\Reference>java ReferenceTest
Before modify() d.height = 10
dim = 11
After modify() d.height = 11
```

Notice when an object is passed to a method, any changes that occur inside the method also occur to the object outside the method. This is because the reference variables *d* and *dim* both point to the same object. Hence, a change made within the method changes the data in the same object. The object was *passed by reference.*

exam Watch

The exam will show some pretty tricky code examples. Make sure you have practiced looking at enough code to quickly analyze a program. You must be able to understand a program and determine values of variables and output.

CERTIFICATION SUMMARY

If you have studied this chapter diligently, you should have a firm understanding of all operations that can be used in the Java language. You should also understand the difference between the == operator and the equals() method, and you know how primitives and objects behave when passed to a method. Let's review what you have learned in this chapter.

Bit-shifting operators must be studied at the bit level of a number in order to be understood. The left shift (<<) shifts all bits to the left and the signed right shift (>>) shifts all bits right *leaving the signed bit untouched.* To shift the signed bit, the unsigned right shift (>>>) must be used.

The conditional operators (&& and ||) can be used only to evaluate two Boolean expressions. The bitwise operators (& and |) can be used on integral numbers to produce a resulting numeric value, or on Boolean values to produce a resulting Boolean value.

The == operator can be used to compare values of primitives, but it can also be used to determine whether two reference variables point to the same object. The Object.equals() method is identical to the == operator when it is not overridden.

There are differences between passing objects and primitive values to methods. Objects are passed *by reference*, but primitives are passed *by value.* This means that sif an object is modified within a method, it will affect the same object referred to outside the method.

Most of the operators in this chapter will be covered by at least one question on the exam. For example, the bit shift operator probably will be one whole question that will test every aspect of bit shift operators. Common operators such as arithmetic and comparison operators probably will not be explicitly tested because it is assumed you will know this already. Behavior of variables passed into methods will be thoroughly tested, so be prepared!

✓ TWO-MINUTE DRILL

Here are some of the key points from each certification objective in Chapter 3.

Java Operators

- ❑ The instanceof operator can be used only to test objects (or null) with class types that are in the same class hierarchy.
- ❑ The equality operators (== and !=) compare reference variables when used on objects, and values when used on primitives.
- ❑ The >> operator shifts bits to the right while keeping the sign bit. The >>> operator moves all bits to the right, including the sign bit.
- ❑ The & and | operator are used for integer or Boolean values only.
- ❑ The && and || operators are used for Boolean types only.
- ❑ Floating-point numbers may be cast to integral types.
- ❑ Larger number values may be cast to smaller types explicitly, and smaller types to large ones implicitly.
- ❑ Superclass object references may be cast to subclass types explicitly.

The equals() Method

- ❑ The equals() method compares properties in objects when overridden.
- ❑ When not overridden, the equals() method is identical to the == operator.

Passing Variables into Methods

- ❑ Instances of objects are accessed using reference variables.
- ❑ Primitive variables are stored as values.
- ❑ Primitive types are passed by value to methods, object types are passed by reference.

SELF TEST

The following questions will help you measure your understanding of the material presented in this chapter. Read all of the choices carefully, as there may be more than one correct answer. Choose all correct answers for each question.

Java Operators

1. Given:

```
1.  import java.awt.*;
2.  class CompareTest {
3.      static public void main(String [] args) {
4.          Component b = new Button("Exit");
5.          boolean compare = b.instanceof(Button);
6.      }
7.  }
```

Which line contains errors?

A. Line 2

B. Line 3

C. Line 4

D. Line 5

E. Nothing is wrong with this code.

2. Given:

```
1.  import java.awt.*;
2.  class Ticker extends Component {
3.      public static void main (String [] args) {
4.          Ticker t = new Ticker();
5.
6.      }
7.  }
```

Which of the following statements could legally be inserted into line 5 of this code? (Choose all that apply.)

A. boolean test = (Component instanceof t);

B. boolean test = (t instanceof Ticker);

C. boolean test = t.instanceof(Ticker);

D. boolean test = (t instanceof Component);

E. boolean test = t.instanceof(Object);

F. boolean test = (t instanceof String);

3. Given:

```
class Equals {
    public static void main(String [] args) {
        int x = 100;
        double y = 100.1;
        boolean b = (x = y);
        System.out.println(b);
    }
}
```

What is the output when the code is compiled and executed?

A. true

B. false

C. Nothing, the code will not compile.

D. Nothing, the code will compile but not execute.

4. Which of the following comparisons are legal to use in code? (Choose all that apply.)

A. 'a' == 'b'

B. 12.1 == 12L

C. 'a' == true

D. 'a' == 12

E. 1 == true

5. Given:

```
class Test {
    public static void main (String [] args) {
        String x = null;
        String y = "test";
        System.out.print((x instanceof String) + " ");
        System.out.println((Object)y instanceof String);
    }
}
```

What is the output?

A. true true

B. false true

C. true false

D. false false

E. Nothing. This will not compile.

6. Given:

```
import java.awt.Button;
class CompareReference {
    public static void main(String [] args) {
        Button a = new Button("Exit");
        Button b = new Button("Exit");
        Button c = a;
        System.out.println((a == b) + "  " + (a == c));
    }
}
```

What is the output from this code?

A. true false

B. true true

C. false true

D. false false

E. Nothing, this will not compile.

7. Which of the following lines of code are illegal? (Choose all that apply.)

A. x =% 3;

B. x++;

C. String animal = "Gray Elephant" – "Gray ";

D. --y;

E. String animal = "White " + "elephant";

8. Given:

```
class Logins {
    static int users = 0;
    public static void main (String [] args) {
```

```
        System.out.print(++users);
        System.out.println(users++);
    }
}
```

What is the output of this program?

A. 01

B. 02

C. 12

D. 11

E. None of the above.

9. Given:

```
class BitShift {
    public static void main(String [] args) {
        int x = 0x80000000;
        System.out.print(Integer.toBinaryString(x) + " and ");
        x = x >> 31;
        System.out.println(Integer.toBinaryString(x));
    }
}
```

The static Integer method toBinaryString() will convert a number into binary format. What is the output from this program?

A. 10000000000000000000000000000000 and 00000000000000000000000000000001

B. 0x80000000 and 0xffffffff

C. 10000000000000000000000000000000 and 11111111111111111111111111111111

D. 11111111111111111111111111111111 and 10000000000000000000000000000000

E. None of the above.

10. Given:

```
class BitShift {
    public static void main(String [] args) {
        int x = 0x80000000;
        System.out.print(x + " and  ");
```

```
        x = x >>> 31;
        System.out.println(x);
    }
}
```

What is the output from this program?

A. -2147483648 and 1

B. 0x8000000 and 0x00000001

C. -214783648 and -1

D. 1 and -214783648

E. None of the above.

11. Given:

```
class Bitwise {
    public static void main(String [] args) {
        int x = 11 & 9;
        System.out.println(x);
    }
}
```

What is the output from this program?

A. 20

B. 9

C. 11

D. 2

12. Given:

```
class Bitwise {
    public static void main(String [] args) {
        int x = 10 | 5;
        System.out.println(x);
    }
}
```

What is the output from this program?

A. 15

B. 0

C. 9

D. 2

E. None of the above.

13. Given:

```
class AssignmentOps {
   public static void main(String [] args) {
      int x=2;
      String sup = (>15000)?"Pencil":(>=5)?"Eraser":"Pen";
      System.out.println(sup);
   }
}
```

What is the result of compiling and running this code?

A. Pencil

B. Eraser

C. Pen

D. This code will not compile.

14. Which of the following are legal lines of code? (Choose all that apply.)

A. int w = (int)888.8;

B. byte x = (byte)1000L;

C. long y = (byte)100;

D. byte z = (byte)100L;

15. Given:

```
class Hardware {}
class Monitor extends Hardware{}
class HardDrive extends Hardware{
   public void test() {
      Monitor a = new Monitor();
      Hardware b = new Monitor();
      HardDrive c = (HardDrive)a;
      Monitor d = b;
   }
}
```

Which of the preceding lines are illegal? (Choose all that apply.)

A. Line 5

B. Line 6

C. Line 7

D. Line 8

The equals() Method

16. Examine the following code:

```
class StringLiteral {
    public static void main(String[] args) {
        String java = "Java", va = "va";
        System.out.println(java == "Java");
        System.out.println(java == ("Ja"+"va"));
        System.out.println(java == ("Ja"+va));
        System.out.println(java.equals("Ja"+va));
    }
}
```

What is the output produced by this program?

A. true true true true

B. true false false true

C. true true false true

D. true false false false

17. Given:

```
class Test {
    public static void main (String [] args) {
        String x = null;
        System.out.println("null".equals(x));
    }
}
```

What is the output from this program?

A. true

B. false

C. Nothing, this class will not compile.

18. Given:

```
class Equals {
    public static void main(String [] args) {
        Boolean a = new Boolean(true);
        Boolean b = new Boolean(true);
        System.out.println(a.equals(b));
        System.out.println(a == b);
    }
}
```

What is the output from this program?

A. true true

B. true false

C. false true

D. false false

Passing Variables into Methods

19. Given:

```
class  Inventory{
    public static void main (String [] args) {
        int code = 237;
        convertCode(code);
    }
    public static void convertCode(int inv) {
        inv = inv + 100000;
    }
}
```

What is the value of the variable *code* after the method convertCode() is run?

A. 237

B. 100237

C. Nothing, this class will not compile.

20. Given:

```
import java.awt.Dimension;
class ReferenceTest {
    public static void main (String [] args) {
        Dimension d = new Dimension(5,5);
```

```
        ReferenceTest rt = new ReferenceTest();
        System.out.print(d.height);
        rt.modify(d);
        System.out.println(d.height);
    }
    void modify(Dimension dim) {
        dim.height = dim.height + 1;
    }
}
```

What is the output from this code?

A. 55

B. 56

C. 01

D. 00

E. Nothing, this class will not compile.

SELF TEST ANSWERS

Java Operators

1. ☑ D. instanceof is an operator, not a method. The correct usage is (b instanceof Button), which equates to a Boolean value.
☒ A, B, and C are incorrect answers because they are properly defined lines of code.

2. ☑ B and D. B is correct because class type Ticker is part of the class hierarchy of *t*, therefore it is a legal use of the *instanceof* operator. D is also correct because Component is part of the hierarchy of *t*, because Ticker extends Component in line 2.
☒ A is incorrect because the syntax is wrong. A variable (or null) always appears before the *instanceof* operator, and a class appears after it. C and E are incorrect because the statement is used as a method, which is illegal. F is incorrect because the String class is not in the hierarchy of the *t* object.

3. ☑ C. The code will not compile because in line 5 the line will work only if we use (x == y) in the line. The == operator compares values to produce a Boolean, whereas the = operator assigns a value to variables.
☒ A, B, and D are incorrect because the code does not get as far as compiling. If we corrected this code, the output would be *false*.

4. ☑ A, B, and D. A is correct because any two primitives of the same type are legal to compare. B is correct because any number primitives may be compared for equality, even float and integer types. D is correct because char primitives may be compared to numbers.
☒ C and E are incorrect because Boolean values can be compared only with each other. It is illegal to compare a Boolean with anything but a Boolean.

5. ☑ B. The variable *x* is null, and comparing null to any class using *instanceof* always produces the Boolean value false. The instanceof operator always tests the type of the *underlying* object, which is a String. Therefore, line 6 will output true.
☒ A, C, and D are all incorrect. The variable *x* was never initialized as a String object, therefore it is null and produces an output of false. Even though the String *y* is cast into an Object, the underlying object is still a String. E is incorrect because this code compiles fine.

6. ☑ C. Button *a* and *b* are separate objects; therefore, the reference variables are not equal (false). Button *c* refers to the same object as Button *a*, so the reference variables are equal (true).
☒ A, B, and D are incorrect for the reasons described previously. E is incorrect because this is a properly defined class.

7. ☑ A and C. A is illegal because the shorthand assignment operator should be %= (not =%). C is illegal because the – operator may not be used with strings.
☒ B and D are incorrect. They are legal because the increment and decrement operators may be used before or after the variable. E is legal, and therefore incorrect, because the + operator may be used to concatenate two strings together.

8. ☑ D. The first line increments the variable users by one, then outputs it as 1. The second line outputs the variable, then increments it; hence the value sent to output is 1.
☒ A, B, and C are incorrect for the reasons stated previously. E is incorrect because the println() method adds a line-return at the end of the output string.

9. ☑ C. The >> operator moves bits to the right, keeping the sign bit. The bit transformation looks like this:
Before: 1000 0000 0000 0000 0000 0000 0000 0000
After: 1111 1111 1111 1111 1111 1111 1111 1111
☒ A is incorrect because the >> operator keeps the bit, so it fills up with 1s, as shown in C. B is incorrect because the method mentioned always displays integers in binary format. D is incorrect because this is the reverse order of the two output numbers. E is incorrect because there is a correct answer.

10. ☑ A. The >>> operator moves all bits to the right, including the sign bit. The bit transformation looks like this:
Before: 1000 0000 0000 0000 0000 0000 0000 0000
After: 0000 0000 0000 0000 0000 0000 0000 0001
☒ C is incorrect because the >>> operator moves the sign bit, so it travels right, as shown. B is incorrect because the output method print always displays integers in base 10. D is incorrect because this is the reverse order of the two output numbers. E is incorrect because there was a correct answer.

11. ☑ B. The & operator produces a 1 bit when both bits are 1. The equation is as follows:
1011 & 1001 = 1001 (or 9 in decimal)
☒ A is incorrect because we are not adding two decimal numbers together. C is incorrect because we are not using | (OR) on the two numbers. D is incorrect because we are not using ^ (exclusive OR).

12. ☑ A. The | operator produces a 1 bit when either bit is a 1. The equation is as follows:
1010 & 0101 = 1111 (or 15 in decimal).
☒ B is incorrect because the equation is not using the & operator. C and D are both incorrect results.

13. ☑ **D.** Assignment operators must use a Boolean test. The brackets in the code should contain the variable *x*, as follows (x>1500).
☒ **A, B,** and **C** are incorrect because this will not compile.

14. ☑ **A, B, C,** and **D. A** is correct because when a floating-point number (a double in this case) is casted to an int, it simply loses the digits after the decimal. **B** and **D** are correct because a long can be cast into a byte. If the long is over 127, it reverts back to -128. **C** actually works, even though a cast is not necessary, because a long can store a byte.
☒ There are no incorrect answer choices.

15. ☑ **C** and **D. C** is illegal because the *a* variable is of type Monitor, which is not in the same hierarchy as HardDrive. **D** is illegal because a cast must be used to assign the Monitor variable *d* to Hardware type *b*.
☒ **A** and **B** are both legal object declarations, therefore they are incorrect answers.

The equals() Method

16. ☑ **C.** Lines 4 and 5 compare two strings that are created at compile time with the same string, and are therefore equal. Line 6 compares a string created at runtime; therefore, *java* and the new variable refer to different objects in memory. Line 7 uses the equals() method, which compares the character contents of two strings.
☒ **A, B,** and **D** are incorrect for the reasons stated previously.

17. ☑ **B.** The equals() method compares the String "null" with the null value. They are not equal, therefore it returns null.
☒ **A** is incorrect because the String "null" and the keyword null are in no way equal within Java. **C** is incorrect. The equals() method is capable of dealing with null for all Objects, including String. Also, it is legal to call methods directly from a string such as "null."

18. ☑ **B.** When the equals() method is used on Boolean objects, it compares the Boolean property of the objects (true), but when we compare the reference variables using == it returns false because they are distinct objects.
☒ **A, C,** and **D** are incorrect for the reasons stated previously.

Passing Variables into Methods

19. ☑ **A.** The variable code is passed by value to the method convertCode(), so any changes made within the method will not change the original variable.

☒ B is incorrect because the variable inv behaves like a copy of code. C is incorrect because there is nothing wrong with this code.

20. ☑ B. When objects such as *d* are passed to a method they are passed by reference, which means any changes to the object within the method change the same object outside the method as well.
☒ A is incorrect because, unlike primitives, objects are passed by reference. C and D are incorrect because the width and height are initialized as five. E is incorrect because this class is properly defined.

4

Flow Control

CERTIFICATION OBJECTIVES

- 4.01 Writing Code Using if and switch Statements
- 4.02 Writing Code Using Loops
- 4.03 Using break and continue
- ✓ Two-Minute Drill
- Q&A Self Test

The true power of any programming language is to convince the computer to perform mathematical or relational computations on data rapidly to produce results. These results are obtained using flow control statements. Java is no different in that it also has its own version of these flow control statements. These statement types are conditional/decision, looping, and jumping statements. With these necessary language constructs, the programmer is able to control the logical direction of the program.

The *if* statement and the *switch* statement are types of conditional/decision controls that allow your program to perform differently at a proverbial "fork in the road." Java provides three different looping constructs, which allow you to perform the same code over and over again. Java's versions of jumping statements are found in *break* and *continue.* With these tools, you can produce an extremely powerful program that can handle any logical situation with ease. Let's delve into the usage of these constructs.

CERTIFICATION OBJECTIVE 4.01

Writing Code Using if and switch Statements

The *if* and *switch* statements are commonly referred to as *decision statements.* When you use decision statements in your program, you are asking the program to calculate a given expression to determine which course of action is required. Let's examine the if statement first.

exam Watch

Be prepared for some difficult questions on flow control for the exam. Keep in mind that the exam is less likely to ask about common forms of flow control and more likely to ask about obscure forms of flow control.

The basic format of an if statement is as follows:+

```
if (expression) { //expression that returns a boolean result
   System.out.println("Inside if statement");
}
```

The expression in parentheses must evaluate to a Boolean true or false result. If a compound expression is used, you must have all the expressions surrounded by parentheses. If you are only performing one line of code in the body of the if statement, you do not need to have the curly braces encompassing the body of the decision statement. The following code example illustrates this point.

```
if ( x > 3 )
   System.out.println("x is equal to three");
```

There might be a need to perform one block of code if the condition is true and another block of code if the condition is false. To do this, Java provides the keyword *else,* which labels one line of code or a block of code that will be performed if the condition is false. The following two code examples are variations of the if statement using the keyword else. The first example shows the use of one condition, and the second shows the use of two conditions. You can set up an if-else statement to test for numerous conditions.

```
if (hours > 40) {
   System.out.println("Calculating overtime.");
   hoursOvertime = (hours - 40) * 1.5;
   amount = (40 + hoursOvertime) * rate;
}
else {
   System.out.println("No overtime detected.");
   amount = hours * rate;
}
```

The following example uses two conditions. Notice there is no need to enclose the block of code after the else statement in curly braces. This is because the compiler implicitly understands that an if statement is a discreet block of code. To execute more than one statement, however, it is necessary to enclose the block of code in curly braces.

```
if (price < 300) {
   buyProduct();
}
else
   if (price < 400) {
      getApproval();
   }
   else {
      dontBuyProduct();
   }
```

There is sometimes a problem with a dangling else statement. Examine the following piece of code:

```
if (exam.done())
if (exam.getScore() < 0.61)
System.out.println("Try again.");
else System.out.println("Java master!"); // A "dangling else"
```

There is intentionally no indenting in this piece of code so it does not give clues as to which if statement the else belongs to. So, to which if statement does the else belong? The Java language decrees that an else clause belongs to the innermost if statement to which it might possibly belong. In the case of the preceding statement, it belongs to the second if statement in the listing. With proper indenting, it would look like this:

```
if (exam.done())
    if (exam.getScore() < 0.61)
        System.out.println("Try again.");
    else
        System.out.println("Java master!"); // A "dangling else"
```

The exam is very unlikely to be so kind as to indent the code properly, however, so you should prepare yourself for this. The following example shows just how tricky this can be with strange indenting:

```
if (exam.done())
    if (exam.getScore() < 0.61)
        System.out.println("Try again.");
else
    System.out.println("Java master!"); // A "dangling else"
```

Another way to simulate the use of multiple if statements is with the *switch* statement. I will first show you the syntax of a switch statement; then I will show a comparison between an if statement and a switch statement.

The basic switch statement:

```
switch (integral primitive) {
    case value1: {
        System.out.println("The value is " + value1);
    }
    default: {
        System.out.println("It did not match the other case
values");
```

```
    }
}
```

The only values that the switch can evaluate are the following: byte, short, int, and char. If another primitive data type or an object reference is used, you will not be able to compile the program. It is important to note that long cannot be used. Only types that can be implicitly cast into the int primitive are allowed. The values with the case label also have to be one of these types, and they must be constants. The default keyword is used to denote what will happen if none of the case values match the variable that is being used in the expression. You should also note that the variable must be enclosed in a pair of parentheses or you will not be able to compile the code.

The following code shows a comparison between an if statement and a switch statement:

```
int x = 3;

if(x == 1) {
   System.out.println("x equals 1");
}
else
   if(x == 2) {
      System.out.println("x equals 2");
   }
   else
      if(x == 3) {
         System.out.println("x equals 3");
      }
      else {
         System.out.println("No idea what x is");
      }
```

exam Watch ***The exam will not format the if-else statements using the easy-to-understand indenting you see in the preceding code. Quite the opposite; the exam will use bizarre indenting styles in an attempt to throw you off. Make sure you can identify the underlying program flow.***

The preceding statement is the same as

```
int x = 3;
switch (x) {
   case 1:
```

```
        System.out.println("x is equal to 1");
        break;
    case 2:
        System.out.println("x is equal to 2");
        break;
    case 3:
        System.out.println("x is equal to 3");
        break;
    default:
        System.out.println("The program doesn't know what x is");
}
```

It is illegal to have more than one default label per switch statement. It is also illegal to have more than one case label using the same value. For example, the following block of code is not legal because it uses two cases with the same value of 80:

```
int temp = 90;
switch(temp) {
    case 80 : {
        System.out.println("80");
        break;
    }
    case 80 : {
        System.out.println("80");
        break;
    }
    case 90:
        System.out.println("90");
        break;
    default:
        System.out.println("default");
}
```

You will learn more about why the break command is used here later in this chapter. You should also be aware that the default keyword is not needed in the switch statement. If it is left out and there is no corresponding case value to the expression used, then none of the code of any of the case values will be performed. Additionally, a programmer could place curly braces around the blocks of code for each case statement.

on the job

An if-then-else statement can be rewritten as a switch statement. You might wonder, for efficiency, which is faster at runtime? The switch statement tends to be faster because it evaluates the expression only once, whereas the if statement evaluates it every time the execution cycle comes into contact with the expression.

EXERCISE 4-1

Creating a switch-case Statement

Try creating a *switch-case* statement using a char value as the case. Include a default behavior if none of the char values match.

1. Make sure a char variable is declared before the switch statement.
2. Each case statement should be followed by a break.
3. The default value can be located at the end, middle, or top.
4. The code containing the switch-case block should look something like this:

```
char temp = 'c';
switch(temp) {
   case 'a': {
      System.out.println("A");
      break;
   }
   case 'b': {
      System.out.println("B");
      break;
   }
   case 'c':
      System.out.println("C");
      break;
   default:
      System.out.println("default");
}
```

Legal Argument Types for if and switch Statements

If and switch statements can accept only a certain set of argument types. This was briefly mentioned before; however, it is very important that you understand this to be successful on the exam. if statements are limited to expressions that yield a Boolean result. This is achieved by using one or more of Java's relational operators inside the parentheses of the statement to compare two or more variables. In addition, you can simply use the reserved word *true* as the expression to force execution of the block of code. What you cannot do is use an assignment or a number as the expression. For example, an old C language convention is to use the number 1 to force execution of the conditional. This is not valid Java syntax and will cause compilation failure.

It is possible to evaluate two or more Boolean statements in an if statement. The following code illustrates how this can be used. Notice we are using the object reference *gender* to evaluate the expression:

```
int age = 18;
String gender = "Male";

if ((age >= 18) && (gender.equals("Male"))) {
    register4SelectiveService();
}
```

The expression in the switch statement can only evaluate to an integral primitive type that can be implicitly cast to an int. As mentioned before, these types are byte, short, char, and int. Also, the switch can only check for equality. This means that the other relational operators such as *greater than* are rendered unusable. The following is an example of a valid expression using an object reference in a switch statement.

```
String s = "xyz";
switch (s.length()) {
    case 1:
        System.out.println("length is one");
        break;
    case 2:
        System.out.println("length is two");
        break;
    case 3:
        System.out.println("length is three");
        break;
    default:
}
```

There are rules that govern the types that can be associated to the case label. Like the switch statement, the primitive data types byte, short, int, and char can be used as valid expressions for the case label. Also, variable constants (that is, final variables) can be used in a case label. This allows you to set constant variables equal to other variables that you want tested in a switch statement. The following example shows the usage of variable constants in a case statement. Note that if the final keyword is omitted, the code will not compile.

```
final int one = 1;
final int two = 2;
int x = 1;
switch (x) {
```

```
    case one:  System.out.println("one");
               break;
    case two:  System.out.println("two");
               break;
}
```

CERTIFICATION OBJECTIVE 4.02

Writing Code Using Loops

Looping constructs are very important for useful program execution and are required knowledge on the Certification Exam. Java provides three flavors of loops (or iterations) consisting of the *while*, *do-while*, and *for* loops. The *while* loop is usually used in a situation where the program needs to execute certain Java statements an unspecified number of times while a given condition equates to true. The syntax for a while statement is as follows:

```
int x = 2;
while(x == 2) {
   System.out.println(x);
   ++x;
}
```

In this case, as in all loops, the expression must evaluate to a Boolean result. Any variables used in the expression of a while loop must be declared before the expression is evaluated. The program's execution cycle will only enter the loop if the condition results in a true value. If the body of the loop is only one line, then the brackets are not needed. Once inside the loop, the program will remain inside until the condition is no longer met and evaluates to false. In the previous example, program control will enter the loop because *x* is equal to 2. However, *x* is incremented in the loop, so when the condition is checked again it will evaluate to false and exit the loop.

The *do-while* loop is slightly different from the while statement in that the program execution cycle will always perform the commands in the body of a do-while at least once. It also adheres to the rule that you do not need brackets around the body if it is just one line of code. The following is an illustration of the syntax used in a do-while statement to print an arbitrary phrase:

```
do {
   System.out.println("Inside loop");
} while(false);
```

The phrase in the System.out.println statement will print once, even though the expression evaluates to false. The do-while loop will always perform what is in the loop at least once. The expression is not checked until after the code block is executed. Please note the use of the semicolon at the end of the while expression. The same syntax is used in C/C++ for the do-while; however, none of the other Java looping controls use a semicolon in this manner.

The *for* loop is an especially useful flow control statement when you already know how many times you need to execute the statements in the loop's block. There are three main parts used in the *for* statement. They are the declaration and initialization of variables, the expression, and incrementing or modifying variables. Each part is separated by semicolons. The following two examples demonstrate the for loop. The first example shows the parts of a for loop in a pseudo-code form, and the second shows the actual syntax of the loop.

```
for (/*Initialization*/ ; /*Condition*/ ;  /* Iterator */) {
    /* loop body */
}

for (int i = 0; i<10; i++) {
 System.out.println("i is " + i);
}
```

The for loop is very flexible. It allows you to declare and initialize zero, one, or multiple variables inside the parenthesis after the *for* keyword. If you declare more than one variable of the same type, then they need to be separated by a comma. This is the first part that gets executed when the program encounters a for loop. The next section that executes is the expression, which must evaluate to a Boolean value like the other looping statements. Like other looping constructs, you can have multiple expressions in a for loop but they all must be enclosed in at least one pair of parentheses. Next, the code block of the for loop is executed. Finally, the iterator expression is executed. It is important to note that none of these sections are required for the code to compile. The following example is perfectly legal:

```
for( ; ; ) {
    System.out.println("Inside an endless loop");
}
```

In the preceding example, all the parts are left out so it will act like an endless loop. For the exam, it is important to know that with the absence of the initialization and increment sections, the loop will act in the same manner as a *while* statement. The following example demonstrates how this is accomplished:

```
int i = 0;

for (;i<10;) {
    i++;
    //do some other work
}
```

The next example demonstrates a for loop with multiple variables in play. A comma separates the variables, and they must be of the same type. Note that these variables that are declared in the for statement are all local to the for loop.

```
for (int i = 0,j = 0; (i<10) && (j<10); i++, j++) {
    System.out.println("i is " + i + "j is " +j);
}
```

The last thing to note is that all the sections of the for loop are independent of each other. The three expressions in the for statement do not need to operate on the same variables. In fact, the iterator expression does not even need to iterate a variable; it could be a separate Java command. The following is an example of this.

```
int b = 3;
for (int a = 1;  b != 1; System.out.println("iterate")) {
    b = b - a;
}
```

exam Watch

The Java certification test changed format in October 2000. The old test allowed for questions with multiple answers, or even no answers. Sometimes the correct solution for a question was to not answer it at all! This has now been changed, and the exam tells you exactly how many correct answers there are for each question.

CERTIFICATION OBJECTIVE 4.03

Using break and continue

The *break* and *continue* keywords are used in conjunction with Java's looping and conditional features. These two statements allow a program to exit out of a loop. The need to exit out might be caused by a problem encountered by the program, a correct value being found in a switch statement, or by program design. For whatever reason they are used, the program will "jump" to a different section of the program.

exam Watch

The break and continue statements must be inside a loop; otherwise you will get a compile error. The break statement must be used in a switch, while, do, or for statement. The continue statement must be used only in a while, do, or for statement.

The break statement causes the program to stop execution of the innermost looping construct or switch statement and start processing the next line of code after the block. As mentioned earlier in the chapter, the break statement is usually used in switch statements as well. When the program encounters the word *break* during the execution of a switch statement, the next command after the switch statement will be performed. If break is omitted, then the program keeps executing the different case blocks until the break command is found or the switch statement ends. Examine the following code:

```
int x = 1;

switch(x) {
   case 1:  System.out.println("x is one");
   case 2:  System.out.println("x is two");
            break;
}
```

The code will print the following:

```
x is one
x is two
```

This combination occurs because the code did not encounter a break statement. Another way to set up this logic is shown in the following code. You might find this example to be a little more applicable in a real-world environment.

```
int x = someNumberBetweenOneAndTen;

switch (x) {
   case 2:
   case 4:
   case 6:
   case 8:
   case 10: {
      System.out.println("x is an even number");
      break;
   }
   default:  System.out.println("x is an odd number");
}
```

This switch statement will print the correct phrase, depending on whether the number is between one and ten and is odd or even.

The continue statement causes the current iteration of the innermost loop to cease and the next iteration of the same loop to start if the condition of the loop is met. In the case of using a continue statement with a for loop, you need to consider the effects that the continue has on the loop iterator. Examine the following code, which will be explained afterward.

```
for (int i = 0; i < 10; i++) {
   System.out.println("Inside loop");
   continue;
   // Compiler won't accept code here
}
```

The question: is this an endless loop? The answer is no. When the continue statement is encountered, *i* will increment before the condition is checked again. The continue statement should be used only when the need to check the condition of the loop and possibly reenter the loop arises. If the condition can't be met, then a break statement is probably more appropriate for the situation.

Unlabeled Statements

Both the break statement and the continue statement can be unlabeled or labeled. In most cases the use of the two commands is unlabeled, except when necessary to achieve correct program execution. As stated before, when unlabeled, the break statement will exit out of the innermost looping construct and proceed with the next line of code. This will happen even if the break statement is located inside an if statement that is embedded in a loop. An example of this concept is as follows:

```
boolean problem = true;
while (true) {
```

```
    if (problem) {
        System.out.println("There was a problem");
        break;
    }
}
//next line of code
```

In this example, even though the break is encompassed by the if statement, the program execution will proceed to the first command after the while loop. The concept you need to gain from this is to realize that the break statement has no effect on the exiting of an if statement. It only applies to loops and switches.

In the previous example, the use of the break statement is unlabeled. The following is an example of a continue statement that is unlabeled:

```
while (!EOF) {
    //read a field from a file
    if (there was a problem) {
        //move to the next field in the file
        continue;
    }
}
```

In this example there is a file being read from one field at a time. When an error is encountered, it moves to the next field in the file and uses the continue statement to go back into the loop (if it is not at the end of the file) and keeps reading the various fields. If the break command were used instead, the code would stop reading the file once the error occurred and move on to the next line of code.

Labeled Statements

The use of the break statement and the continue statement when they are labeled and when they are unlabeled is completely different. It is important that you understand the difference for the exam. A break statement will exit out of the labeled loop, as opposed to the innermost loop, if the break keyword is combined with a label. An example of what a label looks like is in the following code:

```
labelName:
    for (expression) {
        //...
    }
```

FROM THE CLASSROOM

Rules for the break and continue Statements When Combined with Labels

It is important to note that a label does not necessarily need to precede a looping construct. A label can be found almost anywhere in a program; however, there are certain rules that the break and continue statements must adhere to when they are combined with labels. First of all, a continue statement must be found in a loop. This is actually true whether or not it is combined with a label. In addition, the continue statement's label must refer to a loop within the same method (nonlocal jumps are not allowed).

The break statement is slightly different. The use of a labeled break will work in any situation where a label is defined as encompassing any block of code. The following code shows you in detail how this works.

```
Outer:
   if (true) {
      if (true) {
         System.out.println("Inside second if statement");
         break outer;
      }
      System.out.println("Last statement of first if");
   }
```

This code is perfectly legal and will compile. If the continue statement was used instead of the break statement, it would not compile. In this case the break statement is not used in a loop or a switch statement, but it will cause the program to exit out of the first if statement. The phrase "Inside second if statement" will be the only thing that prints out of this code example before execution is stopped. This is very unusual to see, and most programmers don't use it because there is usually no reason to use it. Also, it is not on the exam! However, I did want to give you a complete explanation of what will work and what won't. It can be confusing the first time it is encountered.

—Michael Keene, Sun Certified Programmer for Java

The label must adhere to the rules for a valid variable name and should adhere to the Java naming convention. The syntax for the use of a label name in conjunction with a break statement is the break keyword, then the label name, followed by a semicolon. A more complete example of the use of a labeled break statement is as follows:

```
outer:
   for(int i=0; i<10; i++) {
      for (int j=0; j<5; j++) {
         System.out.println("Hello");
         break outer;
      }
      System.out.println("Outer loop."); // Won't print
   }
System.out.println("Good-Bye");
```

In this example the word *Hello* will be printed one time. Then, the labeled break statement will be executed, and the flow will exit out of the loop labeled *outer.* The next line of code will then print out *Good-Bye.* Let's see what will happen if the continue statement is used instead of the break statement. The following code example is the same as the preceding one, with the exception of the two keywords being switched. The break statement is simply replaced by the continue statement.

```
outer:
   for (int i=0; i<10; i++) {
      for (int j=0; j<5; j++) {
         System.out.println("Hello");
         continue outer;
      }
   }
System.out.println("Good-Bye");
```

In this example, *Hello* will be printed ten times. After the continue statement is executed, the flow continues with the next iteration of the loop identified with the label. Finally, when the condition in the outer loop evaluates to false, the *i* loop will finish and *Good-Bye* will be printed.

Note: Those who noticed that *goto* is a Java reserved keyword might wonder why it wasn't mentioned in a chapter called flow control. Java does reserve the word goto for possible future use; however, there is not a current implementation of the statement.

EXERCISE 4-2

Creating a Labeled while Loop

Try creating a labeled *while* loop. Make the label *outer* and provide a condition to check whether a variable age is less than or equal to 21. Within the loop it should increment the age by one. Every time it goes through the loop, it checks whether the age is 16. If it is, it will print a message to get your driver's license and continue to the outer loop. If not, it just prints "Another year."

1. The outer label should appear just before the while loop begins. It does not matter if it is on the same line or not.
2. Make sure age is declared outside of the while loop.
3. The finished code should look similar to this:

```
class LoopTest {
   public static void main(String [] args) {
      int age = 12;
      outer:
      while(age < 21) {
         age += 2;
         if(age == 16) {
            System.out.println("Obtain driver's license");
            continue outer;
         }
         System.out.println("Another year.");
      }
   }
}
```

exam Watch

The labeled continue statement must be inside the loop that has the same label name; otherwise the code will not compile. This is true for a break statement as well.

Now that you have a better idea of flow control techniques, here are some possible scenario questions and their answers.

SCENARIO & SOLUTION	
What variable types can be evaluated by switch and case statements?	byte, short, int, and char.
What types of variables can be evaluated by if statements and loops?	The Boolean literal. This includes any operation that evaluates to a Boolean, such as > (greater than).
Name the three arguments in a for loop in the order they should appear.	Initialization, condition, and iterator. It is not necessary to know these names for the exam, but you must know the proper order if you see it in code.
Which flow-control keywords can use the continue statement?	while, do, and for.
Which flow-control keywords can use the break statement?	if, while, do, for, and switch/case.

CERTIFICATION SUMMARY

This chapter has covered a lot of information about various ways to control the flow of a program in Java. Hopefully it didn't seem like an endless loop to you! First you learned about *if* and *switch* statements. The if statement evaluates one or more expressions to a boolean result. If the result is true, the program will execute the code in the block that is encompassed by the if. If an else statement is used and the expression evaluates to false, then the code following the else will be performed. If the else is not used, then none of the code associated with the if statement will execute.

The switch statement is used to replace multiple if-else statements. The switch statement can evaluate only integral primitive types that can be implicitly cast to an int. Those types are byte, short, int, and char. At runtime, the Java virtual machine will try to find a match between the argument and the switch statement with an argument in a corresponding case statement. If a match is found, it will execute the statements in the following brackets until a break statement is found or the end of the switch statement occurs. If there is no match, then the default will execute if it is used.

You have learned about the three looping constructs available in the Java language. These constructs are the *for* loop, the *while* loop, and the *do-while* loop. In general, the for loop is used when you know how many times you need to go through the loop. The while loop is used when you do not know how many times you want to go through, whereas the do-while is used when you need to go through at least once. In the for loop and the while loop, the expression will have to evaluate to true to get inside the block and will check after every iteration of the loop. The do-while loop does not check the condition until after it has gone through the loop once. The major benefit of the for loop is the ability to initialize one or more variables and increment or decrement those variables in the for loop definition.

The *break* and *continue* statements can be used in either a labeled or unlabeled fashion. When unlabeled, the break statement will force the program to stop processing the innermost looping construct and start with the line of code following the loop. Using an unlabeled continue command will cause the program to stop execution of the current iteration of the innermost loop and proceed with the next iteration. When a break or a continue statement is used in a labeled manner, it will perform in the same way, with one exception. The statement will not apply to the innermost loop; instead it will apply to the loop with the label. The break statement is used most often in conjunction with the switch statement. When there is a match between the switch expression and the case value, the code following the case value will be performed. To stop the execution of the code, the break statement is needed.

This entire chapter is fair game for the exam, but you should pay close attention to the combination of the break and continue statements with the looping constructs.

✓ TWO-MINUTE DRILL

Here are some of the key points from each certification objective in Chapter 4.

Writing Code Using if and switch Statements

- ❑ The if statement must have all expressions enclosed by at least one pair of parentheses.
- ❑ Switch statements can evaluate only the byte, short, int, and char data types.
- ❑ If the condition in a switch statement matches a case value, it will perform all code in the switch following the matching case statement until a break or the end of the switch statement is encountered.
- ❑ The default keyword should be used in a switch statement if you want to perform some code when none of the case values match the conditional value.

Writing Code Using Loops

- ❑ A for statement does not require any arguments in the declaration.
- ❑ If a variable is incremented or evaluated in a for loop, it must be declared before or at the for loop declaration.
- ❑ All loops and if statements can use the keyword true to automatically enter the loop.
- ❑ You cannot use a number (old C-style language construct) or anything that does not evaluate to a Boolean value as a condition for an if statement or looping construct.
- ❑ The do-while loop will enter the body of the loop at least once, even if the condition is not met.

Using break and continue

- ❑ An unlabeled break statement will cause the current iteration of the innermost looping construct to stop and the next line of code following the loop to be executed.
- ❑ An unlabeled continue statement will cause the current iteration of the innermost loop to stop, the condition of that loop to be checked, and if the condition is met, perform the loop again.
- ❑ If the break statement or the continue statement is labeled, it will cause similar action to occur on the labeled loop, not the innermost loop.
- ❑ If a continue statement is used in a for loop, the variable is incremented (that is, the iteration statement is executed), and the condition is checked.

SELF TEST

The following questions will help you measure your understanding of the material presented in this chapter. Read all of the choices carefully, as there may be more than one correct answer. Choose all correct answers for each question.

Writing Code Using if and switch Statements

1. Given:

```
1.  class First {
2.      public static void prcam() {
3.          double x = 1;
4.          if(x < 0.34) then {
5.              x = x - 0.1;
6.          }
7.      }
8.  }
```

What will be the outcome?

A. Compilation succeeds.

B. Compilation fails because of an error in line 2.

C. Compilation fails because of an error in line 3.

D. Compilation fails because of an error in line 4.

2. Given:

```
1.  public class Second {
2.      public void loop() {
3.          byte i = -1;
4.          long j = 2;
5.          if (i == 1) && (j == 2) {
6.              j = j - j + j;
7.          }
8.      }
9.  }
```

What is the outcome?

A. Compilation succeeds.

B. Compilation fails because of an error in line 3.

C. Compilation fails because of an error in line 5.

D. Compilation fails because of an error in line 6.

3. What are the valid types for the expression in a switch statement? (Choose all that apply.)

A. int

B. long

C. byte

D. String

4. You are writing a program that uses a switch statement. You need to have the switch statement do something if there are no matches found for the condition. What Java keyword should you use? (Fill in the blank.)

The correct Java keyword is ____________.

Writing Code Using Loops

5. Which parts of a for loop are required? (Choose all that apply.)

A. Initialization

B. Condition

C. Increment

D. None of the above

6. Examine the following block of code. Assume it is enclosed properly in a class:

```
for (int i = 0; i < 10;) {
    if(i = 0)
        System.out.print("i equals 1");
    ++i;
}
```

There may be an error in this loop. Which of these statements are true?

A. If *i* is initialized in the for loop, it must be incremented in the for loop.

B. In Java, there must be brackets after an if statement.

C. There is something else wrong with the code.

D. There is nothing wrong with the code.

7. Of the following looping constructs, which is the code guaranteed to enter?

A. while

B. do-while

C. for

D. None of the above

8. Given:

```
1.  public class While {
2.      public void loop() {
3.          int I = 0;
4.          while ( 1 ) {
5.              System.out.print("I plus one is " + (I + 1));
6.          }
7.      }
8.  }
```

What is the result?

A. Compilation succeeds.

B. Compilation fails because of an error in line 1.

C. Compilation fails because of an error in line 4.

D. Compilation fails because of an error in line 5.

9. Given the following loop:

```
for (int I = 0; I < 2; I++) {
    switch (I) {
        case 0:  {
            System.out.println("I is " + I);
            break;
        }
        case 1:  {
            System.out.println("I is " + I);
            break;
        }
    }
}
System.out.println("Out of for loop");
```

What is the output of the following code block?

A. I is 0
I is 1
Out of for loop

B. I is 0
Out of for loop

C. I is 0
I is 1
I is 1
Out of for loop

D. Out of for loop

10. Given:

```
1.  public class For {
2.      public void test() {
3.          for ( ; ; I++) {
4.              int I = 0;
5.              System.out.println("I is " + I);
6.          }
7.      }
8.  }
```

What is the result?

A. Compilation succeeds.

B. Compilation fails because of an error in line 3.

C. Compilation fails because of an error in line 4.

D. Compilation fails because of an error in line 5.

11. Given:

```
public class For {
    public void test() {
        for ( ; ; ) {
            System.out.println("Inside the loop");
        }
    }
}
```

Will the following code block compile?

A. Yes

B. No

12. Given:

```
public class For {
    public void test() {
```

```
4.              System.out.println("I is " + I);
5.          }
6.      }
7.  }
```

And the following output:

```
I is 0
I is 1
```

Which of the following lines of code, inserted at line 3, will cause this output?

A. for (int I = –1; I < 2; ++I) {

B. for (int I = 1; I < 3; ++I){

C. for (int I = 0; I > 2; ++I){

D. for (int I = 0; I < 2; I++){

13. Given:

```
class Test {
    public static void main(String [] args) {
        int I = 1;
        do while (I < 1)
            System.out.println("I is " + I);
        while (I > 1);
    }
}
```

What is the result?

A. The code will not compile.

B. *I is 1* is printed once.

C. Nothing is printed.

D. *I is 1* is printed twice.

E. *I is 1* is printed infinitely.

Using break and continue

14. What happens if a labeled continue statement is used in a for loop?

A. The next line of code after the continue keyword is executed.

B. The current iteration of the loop stops and the next iteration of the innermost loop starts.

C. The current iteration of the outermost loop stops.

D. If a variable is incremented in the labeled for loop, it is incremented.

15. The use of the break statement causes what to happen when it is unlabeled? (Choose all that apply.)

A. The current iteration of a loop to stop and the next line of code to start after the loop block.

B. The current iteration of a loop to stop and the next iteration to start.

C. An exit from all loops.

D. An exit from a switch statement.

16. Given:

```
int I = 0;
outer:
    while (true) {
        I++;
        inner:
            for (int j = 0; j < 10; j++) {
                I += j;
                if (j == 3)
                    continue inner;
                break outer;
            }
            continue outer;
    }
System.out.println("I is " + I);
```

What will be the value of *I* when it is printed?

A. 1

B. 2

C. 3

D. 4

17. Given:

```
do{
    System.out.println("Inside do-while loop");
    break;
}  while (false);
```

What will be printed after this loop has executed?

A. Nothing; it will not compile.

B. Inside do-while loop will print once.

C. Nothing; the condition is false.

D. Inside do-while loop will print an infinite number of times.

18. Given:

```
for (int x; ; ) {
    x = 5;
    if (x == 5)
        System.out.println("x is equal to " + x);
    break;
}
```

What is wrong with this piece of code?

A. The value of *x* must be assigned in the for loop declaration.

B. The if statement needs to have brackets around its body.

C. If *x* is declared in the for statement, then it must be incremented in the for statement.

D. None of the above.

19. Given:

```
for (int I = 0; I < 2; I++) {
    switch (I) {
        case 0:  {
            System.out.println("I is 0");
            continue;
        }
        case 1:  {
            System.out.println("I is 1");
            break;
        }
    }
}
```

What will be printed from this code?

A. I is 0
   I is 1

B. I is 0
   I is 1
   I is 1

C. I is 0

D. Nothing; it will not compile.

20. Given:

```
int I = 0;
label:
    if (I < 2) {
        System.out.println("I is " + I);
        I++;
        continue label;
    }
```

Will this code compile, and if so, what will be printed?

A. It will not compile.

B. I is 1 will be printed;

C. I is 0
   I is 1 will be printed.

D. None of the above.

SELF TEST ANSWERS

Writing Code Using if and switch Statements

1. ☑ D. If statements are not followed by a then statement (as they sometimes are in other programming languages).
☒ A is incorrect because compilation will fail. **B** is incorrect because this is a valid static definition. C is incorrect because a float may be initialized with an integer value, so there are no problems with this line of code.

2. ☑ C. The code will not compile because the compiler will not realize that line 5 contains a compound expression. In order for it to work, you need to put a set of parentheses around all the conditions that are applicable to the if statement. It would be correct only if the statement was as follows:

```
if ((i == 1) && (j == 2)) {
```

☒ A is incorrect because compilation fails due to the preceding error. **B** is incorrect because a byte may be assigned a negative value. **D** is incorrect because this is a valid mathematical expression in Java.

3. ☑ A and C. The only valid values for a switch statement are byte, short, int, and char. No objects, floating-point numbers, or Boolean values are acceptable in this statement.
☒ **B** and **D** are incorrect because they are not one of the four acceptable types.

4. ☑ Default. If you need to simulate the else from an if-else statement, you need to use the *default* keyword in a switch statement.

Writing Code Using Loops

5. ☑ D. D is correct because even though these are the possible sections of the for statement, none of them are required. If all three are left out, the program execution will enter the loop and will not exit unless a break statement is used.
☒ A, B, and C are all incorrect because if any or all are left out it is still a valid statement.

6. ☑ C. The problem with the code is that in line 2 there is an assignment in the if statement, as opposed to a relational expression. In other words, there must be two equal signs, as opposed to just the single one. You should expect questions like this one on the exam.
☒ A is incorrect because it is perfectly legal to increment the variable that is initialized in a for

loop. B is incorrect because you do not need to use brackets if the body of the if statement is only one line. D is incorrect because there is something wrong with the code.

7. ☑ B. Because the condition of the do-while is not checked until after the execution of the loop, you are guaranteed to have it execute at least once.
☒ A, C, and D are incorrect because both while and for loops check the condition before entering the loop, and if the condition is false, the loop body may not be entered.

8. ☑ C. Using the integer 1 in the while statement, or any other looping or conditional construct for that matter, will result in a compiler error. This is old C terminology and is not valid Java syntax.
☒ A is incorrect because this file will not compile due to the preceding error. B is incorrect because Java is a case-sensitive language, so While is a legal class name. D is incorrect because an equation may be placed in a String operation as shown.

9. ☑ A. Program control enters the loop with *I* being set to zero. After the first pass at the switch statement, *I is 0* is printed. At this point, the break statement sends control out of the switch statement, but not out of the loop. The second time through the loop I is 1 and *I is 1* is printed. Again, the break statement sends control out of the switch, but not out of the for statement. I is incremented but the condition is no longer met. Finally, *Out of for loop* is printed.
☒ B, C, and D are all incorrect because the program flow will not output this sequence.

10. ☑ B. A variable that is incremented or evaluated in a for loop must be declared before or at the for loop declaration.
☒ A is incorrect because compilation will fail, as described in the preceding answer. C is incorrect because this is a legal declaration of a variable. This is not the reason the file fails to compile. D is incorrect because this is a legal statement.

11. ☑ A. This is a valid for loop declaration. It is considered an endless loop and would be equivalent to using the keyword true as the expression.
☒ B is incorrect because the code compiles and runs as described previously.

12. ☑ D. It doesn't matter whether you preincrement or postincrement the variable in a for loop. It is always incremented after the loop executes and before the expression is evaluated.
☒ A and B are incorrect because the first iteration of the loop I needs to be zero. C is incorrect because the loop would terminate immediately because the condition I > 2 is false before the increment section of the loop executes.

13. ☑ C. This is correct because the program flow produces no output. There are two different looping constructs in this problem. One is a do-while loop and the other is a while loop. The

body of the do-while is only a while loop, so you do not need brackets. You are assured that the while loop will be checked at least once. The first time it is checked, I is not less than 1 so nothing is printed. Then, the do-while condition is checked and it too evaluates to false, so the do-while loop ends, and nothing is ever printed out.
☒ B, D, and E are incorrect because of the preceding explanation. The code will compile, so A is incorrect. The loop is a little easier to understand if curly braces are added:

```
int I = 1;
do {
  while (I < 1)
        System.out.println("I is " + I);
} while (I > 1);
```

Using break and continue

14. ☑ D. If a for loop is designed to have a variable incremented in a normal situation, it will have that variable incremented even if a continue statement is used.
☒ A, B, and C are incorrect because a labeled continue statement stops the current iteration of all loops up to and including the labeled loop. In the case of a for statement, it performs any predefined calculations on the variables and starts the next iteration of the labeled loop. The labeled loop is not necessarily the outermost loop. A is incorrect because the continue statement always causes the next iteration of the loop. B would be correct for an unlabeled continue, but incorrect for a labeled continue. Remember the labeled loop may not be the innermost one. C is incorrect because the labeled continue stops the current iteration of the labeled loop, which may not be the outermost one.

15. ☑ A and D. When a break statement is used in an unlabeled manner, it has the ability of causing both A and D to happen.
☒ B is incorrect because this is what the continue statement does. C is incorrect because the unlabeled break statement only affects the innermost loop or switch.

16. ☑ A. A is correct because the following program flow occurs: I will be incremented by 1 after it enters the first loop. Then, I will be incremented by zero. The if statement evaluates to false, and the continue statement never gets executed. The next line of code tells the program to break out of the outer loop. At the time when I is printed, the value is still 1.
☒ B, C, and D are all incorrect because the program flow does not produce any of these results.

17. ☑ B. The code compiles fine.
☒ A is incorrect and the condition is not checked until after the first time the phrase is printed, so C is incorrect. It is not an endless loop as answer D infers; the break statement is encountered and the condition is false.

18. ☑ D. All of the code in this block is correct.
☒ A is incorrect because it is not necessary for the value of x to be assigned at this point. The value of x only needs to be assigned before the first time it is used, and this is done just before the if statement where it is first used. B is incorrect because the body of this if statement is only one line. C is incorrect because the three parts of a for statement are independent of each other.

19. ☑ A. The first time through the loop, I is 0. When the switch statement is entered, it goes to the case 0 block and prints I is 0. When the program encounters the continue statement, it stops the current iteration of the loop and starts the next iteration which makes **B** incorrect. Upon the second iteration, I is now 1 so it executes the case 1 block. I is 1 is printed and the program breaks out of the loop, making **C** incorrect.
☒ B, C, and D are incorrect. **B** is incorrect because when the program encounters the continue statement, it stops the current iteration of the loop and starts the next iteration. **C** is incorrect because upon the second iteration, I is now 1 so it executes the case 1 block. I is 1 is printed and the program breaks out of the loop. The code will compile, so **D** is incorrect.

20. ☑ A. The code will not compile because a continue statement has to be in a looping construct.
☒ B, C, and D are incorrect because it won't compile.

JAVA™

SUN CERTIFIED PROGRAMMER®

5

Exception Handling

CERTIFICATION OBJECTIVES

5.01	Catching an Exception Using try and catch
5.02	Using finally
5.03	Propagating Uncaught Exceptions
5.04	Defining Exceptions
5.05	Runtime Exceptions and Checked Exceptions
5.06	Overriding Methods
5.07	Writing and Throwing Your Own Exceptions
✓	Two-Minute Drill
Q&A	Self Test

There is an old maxim in software development that says 80 percent of the work is used 20 percent of the time. The 80 percent refers to the effort required to check and handle errors. In many languages, writing program code that checks for and deals with errors is tedious and bloats the application source into confusing spaghetti. Still, error detection and handling may be the most important ingredient of any robust application. Java arms developers with an elegant mechanism for handling errors that produces efficient and organized error handling code: *exception handling*.

Exception handling allows developers to detect errors easily without writing special code to test return values. Even better, it lets us handle these errors in code that is nicely separated from the code that generated them. It also allows us to handle an entire class of errors with the same code, and lets a method defer the handling of its errors to the method that called it. We will discuss each of these concepts and others in detail. We will also look at examples that demonstrate not only how to properly use exception handling but how not to use it as well.

CERTIFICATION OBJECTIVE 5.01

Catching an Exception Using try and catch

Before we begin, let's introduce some terminology. The term *exception* means "exceptional condition" and is an occurrence that alters the normal program flow. Exceptions are caused by a variety of happenings, including hardware failures, resource exhaustion, and good old bugs. When an exceptional event occurs, an exception is said to be *thrown.* The code that is responsible for doing something about the error is called an *exception handler,* and it *catches* the exception.

Exception handling works by transferring the execution of a program to an exception handler when an exception occurs. For example, if you call a method that opens a file but the file cannot be opened, execution of that method will stop, and code that you wrote to deal with this situation will be run. Therefore, we need a way of telling the compiler where to look for errors and what code to execute when a certain error happens. To do this, we use the *try* and *catch* keywords. Try is used to define a block of code in which errors may occur. This block of code is called a *guarded region* and the try keyword is said to *govern* this region. One or more catch clauses match a specific error (or class of errors—more on that later) to a block of code that handles it. Here is how it looks in pseudocode:

```
1: try {
2:     // This is the first line of the "guarded region"
3:     // that is governed by the try keyword.
4:     // Put code here that might cause some kind of exception.
5:     // We may have many code lines here or just one.
6: }
7: catch(MyFirstError) {
8:     // Put code here that handles this error.
9:     // This is the next line of the exception handler.
10:    // This is the last line of the exception handler.
11: }
12: catch(MySecondError) {
13:    // Put code here that handles this error.
14: }
15:
16: // Some other unguarded code begins here
```

In this pseudocode example, lines 2 through 5 constitute the guarded region that is governed by the try clause. Line seven is an exception handler for an exception of type MyFirstError. Line 12 is an exception handler for an exception of type MySecondError. Notice that the catch blocks immediately follow the try block. This is a requirement; if you have one or more catch blocks, they must immediately follow the try block. Additionally, the catch blocks must all follow each other.

Execution starts at line 2. If the program executes all the way to line 5 with no exceptions being thrown, then execution will transfer to line 15 and continue downward. However, if at any time in lines 2 through 5, the governed region inside the try block, an exception is thrown of type MyFirstError, execution will immediately transfer to line eight. Lines 8 through 10 will be executed so that the entire catch block is executed, and then execution will transfer to line 15 and continue.

This example demonstrates one of the benefits of using exception handling to remedy errors. Code to handle any particular error that may occur in the governed region needs to be written only once. There may be three different places in our try block that can generate a MyFirstError, but wherever it occurs, it will be handled by line 7. We'll discuss the primary benefits of exception handling near the end of this chapter.

CERTIFICATION OBJECTIVE 5.02

Using finally

Try and catch provide a terrific mechanism for trapping and handling exceptions, but we are left with the problem of how to clean up after ourselves. Because execution transfers out of the try block as soon as an exception is thrown, we can't put our cleanup code at the bottom of the try block and expect it to be executed if an error occurs. Almost as bad an idea is placing our cleanup code in the catch blocks. Exception handlers are a poor place to clean up after the code in the try block because each handler requires its own copy of the cleanup code. If, for example, you allocated a network socket or opened a file somewhere in the guarded region, each exception handler would have to close the file or release the socket. This design produces many opportunities to forget to do cleanup and a lot of redundant code. To address this problem, Java offers the *finally* block.

A finally block encloses code that is always executed at some point after the try block, whether an exception was thrown or not. Even if there is a return statement in the try block, the finally block executes right after the return statement. This is the right place to close your files, release your network sockets, and perform any other cleanup your code requires. If the try block executes with no exceptions, the finally block is executed immediately after the try block completes. If there was an exception thrown, the finally block executes immediately after the proper catch block completes.

Let's look at another pseudocode example.

```
try {
   // This is the first line of the "guarded region".
}
catch(MyFirstError) {
   // Put code here that handles this error.
}
catch(MySecondError) {
   // Put code here that handles this error.
}
finally {
   // Put code here to release any resource we
   // allocated in the try clause.
```

```
13: }
14:
15: // More code here
```

As before, execution starts at the first line of the try block, line two. If there are no exceptions thrown in the try block, execution transfers to line 11, the first line of the finally block. On the other hand, if a MySecondError exception is thrown while the code in the try block is executing, execution transfers to the first line of that exception handler, line 8 in the catch clause. After all the code in the catch clause is executed, the program moves to line 11, the first line of the finally clause.

Finally clauses are not required. If you don't write one, your code will compile and run just fine. In fact, if you have no resources to clean up after your try block completes, then you probably don't need a finally clause. Also, the compiler does not require catch clauses. Sometimes you will run across code that has a try block immediately followed by a finally block. Such code is useful when the exception is going to be passed to the calling method, as explained in the next section. This allows the cleanup code to execute in that case as well.

exam Watch

It is illegal to use a try clause without either a catch clause or a finally clause. A try clause by itself will result in a compiler error. Any catch clauses must immediately follow the try block. Any finally clauses must immediately follow the last catch clause. It is legal to omit either the catch clause or the finally clause, but not both.

CERTIFICATION OBJECTIVE 5.03

Propagating Uncaught Exceptions

Why aren't catch clauses required? What happens to an exception that's thrown in a try block when there is no catch clause waiting for it? Actually, there is no requirement that you code a catch clause for every possible exception that could be thrown from the corresponding try block. In fact, it's doubtful that you could accomplish such a feat! If a method does not provide a catch clause for a particular exception, that method is said to be "ducking" the exception.

So what happens to a ducked exception? Before we discuss that, we need to briefly introduce the concept of a *call stack*. Most languages have the concept of a method stack or a call stack. Simply put, the call stack is the chain of methods that your program executes to get to the current method. If your program starts in method Main and main calls method A, which calls method B that in turn calls method C, the call stack consists of the following:

```
Main
 A
 B
 C
```

A stack is said to grow downward. As you can see, the last method called is at the bottom of the stack. If you could print out the state of the stack at any given time, you would produce a *stack trace*. The method at the very bottom of the stack trace would be the method you were currently executing. If we move up the call stack, we are moving from the current method to the previously called method.

Now let's examine what happens to ducked exceptions. Exceptions are like bubbles in an aquarium. They start right where they are thrown, at the bottom of the stack, and if they are not caught by the current method, they float up the call stack to the previous method. If not caught there, they again float up to the previous method, and so on until they are caught or until they reach the top of the call stack. This is called *exception propagation*.

If they reach the top of the call stack, it's like reaching the surface of the water; they burst, and so does your program. Any exception that is never caught will cause your application to stop running. A description, if one is available, of the exception will be displayed, and the call stack will be dumped. This helps you debug your application by telling you what exception was thrown from what method and what the stack looked like at the time.

on the job

As you know, you can keep throwing an exception up through the methods. But what about when you get to the main() method at the top? It is actually possible to throw the exception out of main() as well. This results in the Java virtual machine (JVM) halting, and the stack trace will be printed to the output.

EXERCISE 5-1

Propagating and Catching An Exception

So far you have only seen exceptions displayed in this chapter with pseudocode. In this exercise we attempt to create two methods that deal with exceptions. One of the methods is the main() method, which will call another method. If an exception is thrown in the other method, it must deal with it. A finally statement will be included to indicate it is all done. The method it will call will be named reverse(), and it will reverse the order of the characters in the string. If the String contains no characters it will propagate an Exception up to the main() method.

1. Create an enclosing class called *Propogate* and a main() method, which will remain empty for now.
2. Create a method called reverse(). It takes an argument of a string and returns a string.
3. Check if the string has a length of 0 by using the String.length() method. If the length is 0, then it will throw a new Exception.
4. Now let's include the code to reverse the order of the string. Because this isn't the main topic of this chapter, the code has been provided, but feel free to try it on your own.

```
String reverseStr = "";
for(int i=s.length()-1;i>=0;--i) {
   reverseStr += s.charAt(i);
}
return reverseStr;
```

5. Now in the main() method we will attempt to call this method and deal with any potential exceptions. Additionally, we will include a finally statement that tells us it has finished.

The final code should look something like this:

```
class Propogate {
   public static void main(String [] args) {
      try {
         System.out.println(reverse("Hello"));
      }
      catch (Exception e) {
         System.out.println("The string was blank");
      }
      finally {
         System.out.println("All done!");
      }
   }
   public static String reverse(String s) throws Exception {
      if (s.length() == 0 ) {
         throw new Exception();
      }
      String reverseStr = "";
      for(int i=s.length()-1;i>=0;--i) {
         reverseStr += s.charAt(i);
      }
      return reverseStr;
   }
}
```

CERTIFICATION OBJECTIVE 5.04

Defining Exceptions

We have been discussing exceptions as a concept. We know that they are thrown when a problem of some type happens, and we know what effect they have on the flow of our program. In this section we will develop the concepts further and use exceptions in functional Java code. Earlier, I said that an exception is an occurrence that alters the normal program flow. There is another way to describe an exception and that is as an instance of a class derived from class Exception. When an exception is thrown, an object of a particular type is instantiated and handed to the exception handler as an argument to the catch clause. An actual catch clause looks like this:

```
try {
    // some code here
}
catch (ArrayIndexOutOfBoundsException e) {
    e.printStackTrace();
}
```

In this example, *e* is an instance of a class called ArrayIndexOutOfBoundsException. Like any other object, its methods, including those of its superclasses, may be called.

Exception Hierarchy

All exception classes derive from the class Exception. This class derives from the class Throwable (which derives from the class Object). Figure 5-1 shows the hierarchy for the exception classes.

As you can see, there are two subclasses that derive from Throwable: Exception and Error. Classes that derive from Error represent unusual situations that are not caused by program errors or by anything that would normally happen during program execution, such as the JVM running out of memory. Generally, your application won't be able to recover from an Error, so you're not required to handle these conditions. If your code does not handle them (and it usually won't) it will still compile with no trouble. Although often thought of as exceptional conditions, Errors are technically not exceptions because they do not derive from class Exception.

FIGURE 5-1

Hierarchy chart for the exception classes

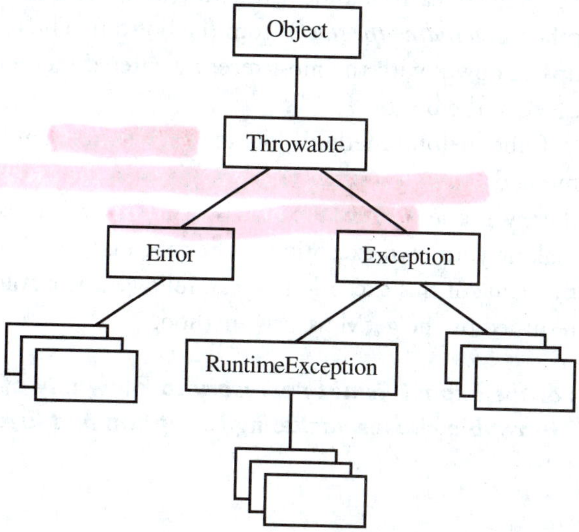

All of Java's exception types derive from class Exception. In general, an exception represents something that happens not as a result of a programming error, but rather because some resource is not available or some other condition required for correct execution is not present. For example, if your application is supposed to communicate with another application or computer that is not answering, this is an exception that is not caused by a bug. Figure 5-1 also shows a subtype of Exception called RuntimeException. These exceptions are a special case because they actually do indicate program errors when they occur. They can also represent rare, difficult to handle exceptional conditions. Runtime exceptions are discussed in greater detail later in this chapter.

Java provides many exception classes, most of which have quite descriptive names. There are two ways to get information about an exception. The first is from the type of the exception itself. The next is from information that you can get from the exception object. Class Throwable provides its descendants with some methods that are useful in exception handlers. One of these is printStackTrace(). As expected, if you call an exception object's printStackTrace() method, as in the earlier example, a stack trace from where the exception occurred will be printed. This method is overloaded to accept either no arguments, in which case the output is directed to the standard error; to accept a printStream object, in which case the output is directed to the printStream; or to accept a printWriter object. We discussed that a call stack grows downward with the most recently called method at the bottom. You will notice that this method prints the most recent method first and continues printing the name of each method as the function works its way up the call stack (this is called *unwinding the stack*) from the bottom. The result is that the stack is printed upside down, with the most recently entered method at the top and the first method called at the bottom.

Other helpful methods include getMessage() and toString(). The getMessage() method retrieves a string that was given to the exception when it was instantiated, if there was one. Otherwise, null is returned. We'll discuss this further when we cover making your own exceptions. The toString() method returns a string composed of the name of this exception's class, followed by a colon and the same string that is returned by the getMessage() method.

exam watch

For the exam it is not necessary to know any of the methods contained in the Throwable classes, including Exception and Error.

Handling an Entire Class Hierarchy of Exceptions

We have discussed that Java's catch keyword allows you to specify a particular type of exception to catch. You can actually catch more than one type of exception in a single catch clause. If the exception class that you specify in the catch clause has no subclasses, then only the specified class of exception will be caught. However, if the class specified in the catch clause does have subclasses, any exception object that subclasses the specified class will be caught as well.

For example, class IndexOutOfBoundsException has two subclasses, ArrayIndexOutOfBoundsException and StringIndexOutOfBoundsException. You may want to write one exception handler that deals with exceptions produced by either type of boundary error, but you might not be concerned with which exception you actually have. In this case you could write a catch clause like the following:

```
try {
   // Some code here that can throw a boundary exception
}
catch (IndexOutOfBoundsException e) {
   e.printStackTrace();
}
```

If any code in the try block throws ArrayIndexOutOfBoundsException or StringIndexOutOfBoundsException, the exception will be caught and handled. This can be a great convenience but it should be used sparingly. By specifying an exception class' superclass in your catch clause, you are discarding valuable information about the exception. You can, of course, find out exactly what exception class you have, but if you're going to do that, you are better off writing a separate catch clause for each exception type of interest.

Additionally, resist the temptation to write a single catchall exception handler such as the following:

```
try {
   // some code
}
catch (Exception e) {
   e.printStackTrace();
}
```

This code will catch every exception generated. Of course, no single exception handler can properly handle every exception, and programming in this way defeats the design objective. Exception handlers that trap many errors at once will probably reduce the reliability of your program because it's likely that an exception will be caught that the handler does not know how to handle.

Exception Matching

If you have an exception hierarchy composed of a base type exception and a number of subtypes, and you are interested in handling only one of the subtypes in a special way but want to handle the rest together, you need only write two catch clauses. When an exception is thrown, Java will try to find a catch clause for the exception type. If it does not find one, it will search for a handler for a supertype of the exception. If it does not find a catch clause that matches a supertype for the exception, then the exception is propagated up the call stack. This process is called *exception matching.*

Let's look at an example.

```
import java.io.*;
public class ReadData {
    public static void main(String args[]) {
        try {
            RandomAccessFile raf =
                new RandomAccessFile("myfile.txt", "r");
            byte b[] = new byte[1000];
            raf.readFully(b, 0, 1000);
        }
        catch(FileNotFoundException e) {
            System.err.println("File not found");
            System.err.println(e.getMessage());
            e.printStackTrace();
        }
        catch(IOException e) {
            System.err.println("IO Error");
            System.err.println(e.toString());
            e.printStackTrace();
        }
    }
}
```

This short program attempts to open a file and to read some data from it. Opening and reading files can generate many exceptions, most of which are

IOExceptions. For whatever reason, in this program we are only interested in knowing if the exact exception is a FileNotFoundException. Otherwise, we don't care exactly what the problem is.

FileNotFoundException is a subclass of IOException. Therefore, we could handle it in the catch clause that catches all IOExceptions, but then we would have to test the exception to determine whether it was a FileNotFoundException. Instead, we coded a special exception handler for the FileNotFoundException and a separate exception handler for all other IOExceptions.

Notice that the catch clause for the FileNotFoundException was placed above the handler for the IOException. This is very important. If this is done the opposite way, the program will not compile. The handlers for the most specific exceptions must always be placed above those for more general exceptions.

If this code generates a FileNotFoundException, it will be handled by the catch clause that begins at line 10. If it generates another IOException, perhaps EOFException, which is a subclass of IOException, it will be handled by the catch clause that begins at line 15. If some other exception is generated, such as a runtime exception of some type, neither catch clause will be executed, and the exception will be propagated up the call stack.

exam Watch

Be sure that if you catch both a subtype and a supertype of the same exception that the most specific type is caught first. If you don't, your program will not compile. When looking at exam questions, be sure to check that the question follows this rule.

Exception Specification and the Public Interface

So, how do we know that some method throws an exception that we have to catch? Just as a method must specify what type and how many arguments it accepts and what is returned, the exceptions that a method can throw must be specified. The list of thrown exceptions is part of a method's public interface. The *throws* keyword is used as follows to list the exceptions that a method can throw:

```
void myFunction() throws MyException1, MyException2 {
   // code for the method here
}
```

This method returns void, accepts no arguments, and throws two exceptions of type MyException1 and MyException2.

If you wish, you may specify that an exception is thrown by a method, but then not actually throw it. Also, your method may specify an exception that is thrown by some other method that your method calls. If you do this, you will not need to handle the exception. Instead, it will propagate up and be handled by a method further up the stack. Each method must either handle all checked exceptions by supplying a catch clause or list each unhandled checked exception as a thrown exception. This rule is referred to as Java's *catch or specify requirement.*

Again, there are some exceptions that are exempt from this rule. An object of type RuntimeException or Error, or any of their subclasses, may be thrown from any method without being specified as part of the method's public interface (and a handler need not be present). RuntimeException, Error, and their subtypes are unchecked exceptions and unchecked exceptions do not have to be specified or handled.

Here is an example:

```
import java.io.*;
class Test {
   public int myMethod1() throws EOFException {
      return myMethod2();
   }
   public int myMethod2() throws EOFException {
      // Some code that actually throws the exception goes here
      return 1;
   }
}
```

Let's look at myMethod1. Because EOFException subclasses IOException and IOException subclasses Exception, it is a checked exception and must be declared as an exception that may be thrown by this method. But where will the exception actually come from? The public interface for method myMethod2 called here specifies that an exception of this type can be thrown. Whether that method actually throws the exception itself, or calls another method that throws it is unimportant to us; we simply know that we have to either catch the exception or specify that we throw it. The method myMethod1 does not catch the exception, so it specifies that it throws it.

Now let's look at another example, myMethod3.

```
public void myMethod3() {
   // Some code that throws a NullPointerException goes here
}
```

According to the comment, this method can throw a NullPointerException. Because RuntimeException is the immediate base class of NullPointerException, it is an unchecked exception and need not be specified. We can see that myMethod3 does not specify any exceptions.

FROM THE CLASSROOM

How Does Exception Handling Improve My Application?

Students sometimes wonder exactly how exceptions are helpful to a Java programmer. There are three primary benefits of exception handling:

- **Exception Handlers Are Separated From A Method's Primary Logic** Checking each method return code right after the method is called tends to add several extra code lines for each method. Worse, they are added right in the middle of your method, adding significant clutter that obfuscates the logic of the method. Usually, you end up with spaghetti code that is very hard to debug and maintain. By moving all the error handling code into its own special location, the readability and maintainability of the source is increased, which increases the code's reliability.
- **Similar Errors Can Be Handled Together** Another important benefit provided by Java's exception handling is that it allows us to handle related errors together if we choose to. This is implemented when we place a supertype into a catch clause so that it will handle any subtype exception.

  For example, when conducting file operations, we can catch all exceptions of type IOException in a single catch clause. We won't need to test an error code and say if the error is this type or that type or the other type then do this or that or the other thing. We can use one exception handler for all the exception subtypes. If any of the subtypes need to be handled differently, we can easily provide a catch clause for each of them and allow the more generic catch for the supertype to handle the rest.
- **Exception Propagation** The exception propagation mechanism is another significant benefit provided by exception handling. By allowing the methods that called the method we wrote to handle errors that we report by throwing exceptions, we increase the number of situations in which our code can be used. Very often, we won't know what corrective action to take when an exception is generated, so being able to defer to our caller is a valuable capability.

Imagine that we are writing a class library that we intend to distribute widely. Perhaps one of the methods in our library will do something as

FROM THE CLASSROOM

simple as connect to another computer across a network. Our method is passed the name of the other computer, but we are unable to connect to it. We don't know why we were trying to connect and we certainly don't know what to do about it. Do we try again? Do we try another address? There is no way to know, and we should avoid making any assumptions about how our library is being used. The only good solution is to allow the developer of the application to decide what to do. To do this, we simply throw an exception from our method.

—Chad Tippin

CERTIFICATION OBJECTIVE 5.05

Runtime Exceptions and Checked Exceptions

Runtime exceptions are a special case in Java. Because they have a special purpose of signaling events that happen at runtime, usually as the result of a programming error, or bug, they do not have to be caught and typically are not. When they appear and are not caught, they stop your application and print the name of the exception and a stack trace, as discussed earlier. Some of the most common causes of a RuntimeException are the use of a null reference, incorrect array indices, and so on.

Runtime exceptions are referred to as *unchecked exceptions.* All other exceptions, meaning all those that do not derive from java.lang.RuntimeException, are *checked exceptions.* A checked exception must be caught somewhere in your code. If you use a method that throws a checked exception but you do not catch the checked exception somewhere, your code will not compile. That's why they are checked exceptions; the compiler checks them to make sure they are handled. Many of the methods supplied in Java's runtime classes throw checked exceptions, so you will often write exception handlers to cope with exceptions generated by methods you didn't write.

exam Watch

When an object of type Exception is thrown, it must be caught. These objects are called checked exceptions. This does not include RuntimeException, which is an unchecked exception.

Remember, objects of type Error are not exception objects, although they do represent exceptional conditions. When an object of type Error or a subclass of type Error is thrown, it is unchecked. You are not required to catch Error objects or Error subtypes.

exam Watch

All runtime exceptions derive from class RuntimeException and are unchecked exceptions. If an exception object does not subclass RuntimeException, it is a checked exception and must be either handled or specified.

on the Job

Because Java has checked exceptions, it is commonly said that Java forces developers to handle errors. This is not true. Yes, Java forces us to write exception handlers for each exception that can occur during normal operation, but it's up to us to make the exception handlers do something useful. A catch clause can contain anything from an empty block of code to a complete solution to the problem. Don't make the mistake of believing that just because a program is written in Java all the potential exceptional conditions are handled correctly.

CERTIFICATION OBJECTIVE 5.06

Overriding Methods

When you override a method, you may not declare an exception type that is different from one declared by the base method. You may, however, specify that the overridden method throws exception types that are subclasses of those thrown by the base method. The overriding method may throw the same exceptions as the overridden method, it may throw as many exceptions as it wants as long as they are subclasses of the base-class exception, or it may throw no exceptions at all.

Here is an example:

```
public class MyBaseClass {
    public void myMethod() throws java.io.IOException { }
}

class OkSubClass0 extends MyBaseClass {
    public void myMethod() throws java.io.IOException {}
}

```

```
 9: class OkSubClass1 extends MyBaseClass {
10:     public void myMethod() throws java.io.FileNotFoundException {}
11: }
12:
13: class OkSubClass2 extends MyBaseClass {
14:     public void myMethod() {}
15: }
16:
17: class OkSubClass3 extends MyBaseClass {
18:     public void myMethod() throws java.io.EOFException,
19:         java.io.FileNotFoundException, java.util.zip.ZipException {}
20: }
21:
22: class NotOkSubClass extends MyBaseClass {
23:     public void myMethod() throws java.awt.AWTException {} //Illegal
24: }
```

The code in this example declares a base class called MyBaseClass that is subclassed five times. The base class has only one method called myMethod() that declares that it throws an exception of type IOException.

The first subclass, OkSubClass0, overrides the method correctly because it specifies the same exception type to be thrown. The second subclass also overrides myMethod() correctly at line 10 because it declares that it throws a subclass of IOException (FileNotFoundException). The third subclass, OkSubClass2 also correctly overrides myMethod() at line 14, because it specifies no thrown exceptions. A method that overrides another need not throw the same exceptions that the base method throws. The fourth subclass, OkSubClass3, throws more methods than the parent, but they are all subclasses of the base-class exception, so this is legal.

The last subclass, NotOkSubClass, is incorrect at line 18. Here, myMethod() attempts to specify an AWTException. AWTException is not a subtype of IOException; therefore, this method will generate a compiler error.

CERTIFICATION OBJECTIVE 5.07

Writing and Throwing Your Own Exceptions

We have seen that the Java language has lots of prefabricated exceptions that it can throw, but Java developers can also throw exceptions from their own methods. Additionally, a developer can write custom exception classes.

Throwing an exception is quite easy. Just use the *throw* keyword with an instance of an exception object to throw:

```
throw new RuntimeException();
```

That's all there is to it. This code instantiates an object of type RuntimeException and then generates an exception by throwing the object. Whenever an instance of an exception is created, a stack trace is saved in the object with the current method at the bottom of that trace. If the catch clause that catches this exception prints out the call stack, the method from which this exception was thrown will be at the bottom.

Each exception has two constructors: a no-arguments default constructor, and one that accepts a string as a parameter. If you instantiate an Exception object with a string in its constructor, this string will be returned when the exception object's getMessage() and toString() methods are called.

You can throw an exception from any place in a method where you want to signal an error. One interesting place to throw an exception from is in an exception handler. Throwing an exception from within a catch clause is no different from throwing one from anywhere else. As you would expect, if you instantiate and throw a new exception from a catch clause, the stack trace information will indicate that the exception was thrown from the method that contained the throw keyword, not the location from which the original exception was thrown.

Rethrowing the Same Exception

Just as you can throw a new exception from a catch clause, you can also throw the same exception you just caught. Here is a catch clause that does this:

```
catch(NullPointerException e) {
    e.printStackTrace();
    throw e;
}
```

When the throw executes here, the exception is handed to the next method up. All additional catch clauses associated with the same try block are ignored. In addition, the stack trace information does not change. If the next exception handler to catch this exception prints the stack trace, the output will be identical to that generated by the call to printStackTrace() in the original catch clause.

It is possible to reset the stack trace of an exception so it properly reflects the current method as the base of the stack trace. This can be accomplished by the fillInStackTrace() method of the exception, as follows:

```
catch(NullPointerException e) {
    e.printStackTrace();
    Throwable changedE = e.fillInStackTrace();
    throw changedE;
}
```

What's interesting here is that the fillInStackTrace() method returned an object of type Throwable, which is the superclass of Exception. It was that returned object that was actually thrown. The fillInStackTrace() method is used primarily to hide the original location where the exception was created. The stack information placed in the exception object when it was created is replaced with the stack trace to the current location when this method is called.

If you do throw an object of type Throwable, your method needs to specify that. Here is an example that generates an IOException, changes its origin, and rethrows it.

```
 1: import java.io.*;
 2: public class Test {
 4:     public void foo() throws Throwable {
 6:         try {
 7:             new FileInputStream("nonexistent-file");
 9:         }
10:         catch (IOException e) {
11:             throw e.fillInStackTrace();
12:         }
13:     }
14: }
```

In line 4, method foo() specifies that it throws a Throwable. Line 10 catches an IOException. Line 11 modifies the stack trace and throws an object of type Throwable.

Catching a Throwable is just like catching an Exception. Here is a fragment that shows how to catch a Throwable:

```
catch(Throwable t) {
    // Handler code here
}
```

Rather than actually throwing the object returned by fillInStackTrace() as a Throwable, it's usually a better idea to cast it down to the Throwable subtype that it was when it was caught. Here is the earlier example again, modified to cast the Throwable to an IOException:

```
import java.io.*;
public class Test {
    public void foo() throws IOException {
        try {
            new FileInputStream("nonexistent-file");
        }
        catch (IOException e) {
            throw (IOException) e.fillInStackTrace();
        }
    }
}
```

on the job

If you want to handle an exception in more than one handler, you can re-throw the exception. If you want to hide the details of the exception's true origin from the additional handlers, call the exception's fillInStackTrace() method. This will change the stack trace information in the exception so that the bottom of the trace is the current method.

Creating New Exceptions

It's easy to create your own exception classes. All you need to do is to inherit from an existing exception. Here is a complete exception class:

```
class MySpecialException extends Exception {
    public MySpecialException() {}
    public MySpecialException(String s) { super(s); }
}
```

This simple class inherits all the functionality of its base class, Exception, and adds no functionality. If you subclass RuntimeException, Error, or any of their subclasses, you are creating an unchecked exception. Likewise, if you subclass Exception or any Exception subtype other than RuntimeException, you are creating a checked exception.

It is possible to add additional functionality, just like any other class. However, developers don't generally expect to find extra behaviors in their exception objects. If you're writing a library for other developers, especially one that will be distributed outside your own organization, it's best not to add anything new to exceptions.

exam watch

For the exam it is not necessary to know how to create a new exception.

EXERCISE 5-2

Creating an Exception

In this exercise we attempt to create a custom exception. We will not put any methods in this exception, and it will be a checked exception.

1. Let's first create our exception. We will call it BadWordException. This exception is a runtime exception and will be thrown when a bad word is encountered.
2. Create an enclosing class called *MyException* and a main() method, which will remain empty for now.
3. Create a method called checkWord(). It takes an argument of a string and will throw our Runtime exception if it doesn't like the word it was given. Otherwise, it tells us it likes the word. You can add any words you aren't particularly fond of to the list.
4. Now in the main() method we will attempt to call this method. Because it is a runtime exception there is no need to handle it. If a bad word is encountered it will just bring the JVM to a halt and print out the runtime stack.

The final code should look something like this:

```
class BadWordException extends RuntimeException {}
class MyException {
   public static void main(String [] args) {
      checkWord("Visual Age for Java");
      checkWord("mud");
   }
   public static void checkWord(String s) {
      String [] badWord = {"mud","snow","rain"};
      for(int i=0;i<badWord.length;++i) {
         if (s.equals(badWord[i]))
            throw new BadWordException();
      }
      System.out.println(s + " is ok with me.");
   }
}
```

As good as exception handling is, it's still up to the developer to make proper use of it. Exception handling makes organizing our code and signaling problems easy, but the exception handlers still have to be written. You will find that even the most complex situations can be handled, and after they are, your code is still reusable, readable, and maintainable.

CERTIFICATION SUMMARY

Error handling is one very important requirement for any application. Java provides an elegant mechanism in exception handling. Exception handling allows developers to isolate their error correction code into separate blocks so that the main code does not become cluttered by error checking code. Another elegant feature allows similar errors to be handled together. Also, the error handling can be deferred to methods that were previously called. Now let's review the main points you will need to know for the exam.

Java's try keyword is used to specify a guarded region, which is a block of code in which errors will be detected. The try clause is said to govern the region. An exception handler is the code that is executed when an exception occurs. The handler is defined by using Java's catch keyword. All catch clauses must immediately follow the related try block. Java also provides the finally keyword. This is used to define a block of code that is always executed, either immediately after a catch clause completes or immediately after the associated try block in the case that no exception was thrown. Use finally blocks to release system resources and to perform any cleanup required by the code in the try block. finally blocks follow the catch clauses and are not required.

An exception object is an instance of class Exception or one of its subclasses. The catch clause takes, as a parameter, an instance of an object of a type derived from the Exception class. Java requires that each method either catch any exception it can throw or else specify that it throws the exception. The exception specification is part of the method's public interface. To declare an exception may be thrown, the throws keyword is used in a method definition, along with a list of all thrown exceptions.

Runtime exceptions are exceptions that are of type RuntimeException or are derived from that type. These exceptions are a special case because they do not need to be handled or declared. Errors are of type java.lang.Error or its subclasses, and they also do not need to be handled or declared. Checked exceptions are exception types that are not RuntimeExceptions or Errors. If your code fails to either handle a checked exception or declare that it is thrown, it will not compile.

In the Java programming world, exceptions tend to be relegated to sideshow status because they are not considered a part of the functionality of an application. However, if programmers do not put much thought into the handling of exceptions it can make for a very nonrobust program. For this reason, Sun wants to make sure that Certified Programmers understand exception handling. Expect several questions on the exam to deal with exceptions.

✓ TWO-MINUTE DRILL

Here are some of the key points from each certification objective in Chapter 5.

Catching an Exception Using try and catch

- ❑ A section of code enclosed in braces and started with the keyword try is referred to as a guarded region. The try keyword governs this region. This is the code that will be watched for exceptions.
- ❑ The catch keyword is used to define an exception handler for a particular type of exception object and its subclasses, if any.
- ❑ catch blocks must always immediately follow the try block they pertain to and the other catch clauses for the same try block. Catch blocks are not required.
- ❑ The appropriate catch clause is executed immediately after an exception is thrown. The remaining code in the try block is not executed.
- ❑ Either a catch clause or a finally block must be specified with a try block.
- ❑ Any method from which an exception can be thrown must either handle this exception by providing a try block or else specify that the exception can be thrown. This rule is referred to as the *catch or specify requirement.*

Using finally

- ❑ The finally keyword is used to define a block of code that is always executed after the catch clause or after the try clause if no exceptions occurred. This block is typically used to release resources and to perform any needed cleanup for the try clause. finally blocks are not required.

Propagating Uncaught Exceptions

- ❑ Exceptions can be propagated up the call stack to be handled by a previously called method by throwing the exception out of the method.
- ❑ Specifying a thrown exception is done by using the throws keyword after a method's parameter list and following it with a list of exception types.

Defining Exceptions

- ❑ An exception, or exceptional condition, is an occurrence during your program execution that alters the normal flow.
- ❑ An Exception object is an instance of the class Exception or one of its subclasses.
- ❑ An Error object is an instance of the class Error or one of its subclasses.

Runtime Exceptions and Checked Exceptions

- ❑ A runtime exception is an instance of the class RuntimeException or any of its subclasses.
- ❑ Runtime exceptions and Errors are exceptions to the catch or specify requirement. Runtime exceptions may be thrown from any method without being handled or specified.
- ❑ A checked exception is any exception that is neither a RuntimeException nor an Error. Checked exceptions are subject to the catch or specify requirement. If checked exceptions are neither handled nor specified, the Java compiler will produce an error, and the application will not be compiled.

Overriding Methods

- ❑ When overriding a method, it is not legal to declare an exception type that is different from one declared by the base method.
- ❑ It is legal to specify that the overridden method throws exception types that are subclasses of those thrown by the base method.
- ❑ The overriding method may choose to throw no exceptions at all.

Writing and Throwing Your Own Exceptions

- ❑ Exceptions are thrown by instantiating an Exception class and using the throw keyword, like this:

```
throw new RuntimeException("MyException");
```

- ❑ You can create your own exceptions by subclassing any existing Exception class or any of its subclasses.
- ❑ Once caught, an exception may be rethrown. A rethrown exception will contain the same stack trace information as it did when it was originally thrown. You can modify the stack trace by calling an Exception object's fillInStackTrace method. This method returns an object of type Throwable.

SELF TEST

The following questions will help you measure your understanding of the material presented in this chapter. Read all of the choices carefully, as there may be more than one correct answer. Choose all correct answers for each question.

Catching an Exception Using try and catch

1. Given:

```
1.  public class MyProgram {
2.     public void main(){
3.        try {
4.           System.out.println("Hello World ");
5.        }
6.     }
7.  }
```

Which statement is correct?

A. The program will compile correctly.

B. This program will not compile because of something in line 2.

C. The program will not compile because there is no catch clause and/or finally clause after line 5.

D. The program will not compile because at line 2 main() does not specify any exceptions, but there is a try block.

2. Given:

```
System.out.print("Start ");
try {
   System.out.print("Hello world");
   throw new FileNotFoundException();
}
System.out.print(" Catch Here ");
catch(EOFException e) {
   System.out.print("End of file exception");
}
catch(FileNotFoundException e) {
   System.out.print("File not found");
}
```

EOFException and FileNotFoundException are both subclasses of IOException. Assuming this block of code is placed into a class, which statement is most true concerning this code?

A. The code will not compile.

B. The code will print Start Hello world File Not Found.

C. The code will print Start Hello world End of file exception.

D. The code will print Start Hello world Catch Here File not found.

Using finally

3. Given:

```
public class MyProgram {
    public static void main(String args[]){
        try {
            System.out.print("Hello world ");
        }
        finally {
            System.out.println("Finally executing ");
        }
    }
}
```

What will the output of this program be?

A. Nothing. The program will not compile because no exceptions are specified.

B. Nothing. The program will not compile because no catch clauses are specified.

C. Hello world.

D. Hello world Finally executing.

4. Given:

```
import java.io.*;
class MyProgram {
    public static void main(String args[]){
        FileOutputStream out;
        try {
            out = new FileOutputStream("test.txt");
            out.write(122);
        }
        catch(IOException io) {
            System.out.println("IO Error.");
        }
```

```
12.         finally {
13.            out.close();
14.         }
15.     }
16.  }
```

Given that all methods of FileOutputStream, including close(), throw an IOException, which of these statements are true?

A. This program will compile fine.

B. This program fails to compile due to an error at line 4.

C. This program fails to compile due to an error at line 6.

D. This program fails to compile due to an error at line 9.

E. This program fails to compile due to an error at line 13.

5. Complete the following sentence.
finally clauses ______________________________________.

A. Are executed only after a try block executes with no exceptions

B. Are only executed if an exception is thrown but no matching catch clause is found

C. Are always executed after try and catch blocks

D. Are only executed if a catch clause is executed in the current method

Propagating Uncaught Exceptions

6. Given:

```
public class MyProgram {
   public static void throwit() {
     throw new RuntimeException();
   }
   public static void main(String args[]){
      try {
         System.out.println("Hello world ");
         throwit();
         System.out.println("Done with try block ");
      }
      finally {
         System.out.println("Finally executing ");
      }
   }
}
```

Which answer most closely indicates the behavior of the program?

A. The program will not compile.

B. The program will print "Hello world," then will print that a RuntimeException has occurred, then will print "Done with try block," and then it will print "Finally executing."

C. The program will print "Hello world," then will print that a RuntimeException has occurred, and then it will print "Finally executing."

D. The program will print "Hello world," then will print "Finally executing," then it will print that a RuntimeException has occurred.

7. Given:

```
class MyException throws NullPointerException {
   public static void main(String [] args) {
      String s = null;
      System.out.println("String is " + s);
   }
}
```

Which of these statements is true?

A. The code will not compile.

B. The code will run and then throw a NullPointerException.

C. This code will run and output *String is.*

8. Given:

```
import java.awt.*;
class Simulate {
   public void check() throws AWTException {
      try {
         System.out.print("Check-1-2-3");
      }

      finally {
         System.out.println(" OK");
      }
   }
   public static void main(String [] args) {
      try {
         new Simulate().check();
      } catch(Exception e) {}
   }
}
```

Assume this method is called from another class. What is the result of this program?

A. Compilation fails due to line 3.

B. Compilation fails due to something missing at line 7.

C. Check-1-2-3 OK.

D. Check-1-2-3.

Defining Exceptions

9. Given:

```
try {
   throw new EOFException();
}
catch(IOException e) {
   System.out.println("IO Exception caught ");
}
```

EOFException is a subtype of IOException. Assuming this block of code is placed in a class, which of the following statements are true?

A. The code will not compile.

B. The code will run and print "IO Exception Caught."

C. The thrown exception will be ignored because there is no catch clause for it.

D. The thrown error will propagate up the call stack, and the program will terminate.

10. The superclass for Exception is ______________. (Fill in the blank.)

11. Given:

```
try {
   throw new FileNotFoundException();
}
catch(IOException e) {
   System.out.println("IO Exception caught");
}
catch(EOFException e) {
   System.out.println("EOF Exception caught");
}
```

EOFException and FileNotFoundException are subtypes of IOException. Assuming this block of code is contained in a class, which of the following statements are true?

A. The code will not compile.
B. The code will print "IO Exception Caught."
C. The thrown exception will propagate up the call stack.
D. The code will print "EOF Exception caught."

12. Complete the following sentence.
Exceptions that are not RuntimeExceptions or Errors ________________.

A. Must be either caught or specified
B. Need not be caught or specified
C. Must not be caught
D. Must not be specified

Runtime Exceptions and Checked Exceptions

13. Unhandled checked exceptions ________________.

A. Terminate the application
B. Are ignored at runtime
C. Cause the program to not compile
D. Are handled automatically by the JVM

14. Unhandled unchecked exceptions ________________.

A. Terminate the application
B. Are ignored
C. Cause the program to not compile
D. Are handled automatically by the JVM

15. Complete the following sentence.
RuntimeExceptions ________________.

A. Must be either caught or specified
B. Need not be caught or specified
C. Must not be caught
D. Must not be specified

16. Complete the following sentence.
RuntimeExceptions usually______________________________.

A. Cannot be caught

B. Are just like other exceptions

C. Represent program bugs

D. Must be specified

Overriding Methods

17. Complete the following sentence.
Overridden methods____.

A. May add exceptions from new hierarchies to the method's exception specification

B. May not add exceptions from new hierarchies to the method's exception specification

C. May not throw exceptions

D. May only throw RuntimeExceptions

Writing and Throwing Your Own Exceptions

18. Given:

```
class MySpecialRunException extends RuntimeException {
   public MySpecialRunException() {}
   public MySpecialRunException(String s) { super(s); }
}
```

Which of the following statements are correct?

A. This will not compile.

B. This code creates a type of checked exception.

C. This code creates a type of unchecked exception.

D. This will compile but can never be used in any class.

19. Given:

```
class MySpecialException extends Exception {
   public MySpecialException() {}
   public MySpecialException(String s) { super(s); }
}
```

Which of the following statements is correct?

A. This code will not compile.

B. This creates a type of checked exception.

C. This creates a type of unchecked exception.

D. This will compile but can never be used in any class.

20. Which of the following is not an advantage of exception handling?

A. Exception handling improves code organization by separating a method's error handling code from the body of the method.

B. Exception handling allows a method to defer the handling of its errors to a previously called method.

C. Exception handling improves an application's performance.

D. Exception handling allows similar errors to be handled by a single handler.

SELF TEST ANSWERS

Catching an Exception Using try and catch

1. ☑ C. Although neither catch nor finally is required, you are required to provide at least one of them with a try clause.
☒ A is incorrect because of the reason given above. B is incorrect because the main() method can be overloaded just like any other method. D is incorrect because there is no need to declare which exception may be thrown because no exceptions are thrown in the code.

2. ☑ A. Line 6 causes this code to produce a compile error. catch clauses must immediately follow try blocks. If they do not, a compile error will result.
☒ B, C, and D are all incorrect because the program cannot run if it does not compile. B would be correct if this code was fixed by removing line 6.

Using finally

3. ☑ D. The program will first execute the try block, printing *Hello world* and will then execute the finally block, printing *Finally executing.*
☒ A is incorrect because this program compiles fine. B is incorrect because a catch clause is not required when a finally block is present. C is incorrect because it does not account for the execution of the finally block.

4. ☑ E. Any method that throws a checked exception must be called within a try clause, or the method must declare that it throws the exception. The finally clause does not count.
☒ A is incorrect because this program does not compile. B, C, and D are all incorrect because these are valid lines of code.

5. ☑ C. Finally clauses are always executed. If a try block executes with no exceptions, the finally clause is executed immediately after the try block. If the try block generates an exception, the finally block executes after the catch clause completes, if there is a catch clause available in the current method. If there is no catch clause, the finally block is executed, and the exception is propagated up the call stack.
☒ A, B, and D are all incorrect because a finally block always executes at some point.

Propagating Uncaught Exceptions

6. ☑ D. Once the program throws a RuntimeException that is not caught, the finally block will be executed, and the program will be terminated. If a method does not handle an exception, the finally block is executed before the exception is propagated.
☒ A is incorrect because this program compiles fine. In line 2, runtime exceptions do not have to be caught or declared in the method. B is incorrect because no part of the try block is executed after an exception is thrown from within it. C is incorrect because nothing will execute after a program is terminated by a runtime exception.

7. ☑ A. The error is in line 1. A class may not declare that it throws an exception, only methods (including constructor methods) can do this.
☒ B and C are both incorrect because this will not even compile correctly.

8. ☑ C. The program will first execute the try block, printing *Check-1-2-3* and will then execute the finally block, printing *OK*.
☒ A is incorrect because it is legal to declare an exception will be thrown, even though it isn't. B is incorrect because a catch clause is not required when a finally block is present. D is incorrect because it does not account for the execution of the finally block.

Defining Exceptions

9. ☑ B. Because the catch clause is coded to catch a supertype of the thrown exception, it will catch the exception and execute the catch clause.
☒ A is incorrect because this will compile correctly. C is incorrect because thrown exceptions are never ignored; if they are checked exceptions they must be handled and if they are unchecked they will terminate the program. D is incorrect because, as stated in answer *B*, the catch clause will catch the exception because the exception is a subtype of the type in the catch clause.

10. ☑ Throwable. All Exception types derive from class Throwable.

11. ☑ A. Catch clauses for the most specific classes must be listed before those of their supertype. Lines 4–6 must be swapped with lines 7–9.
☒ B, C, and D are all incorrect because the code cannot run if it does not compile, so there can be no runtime behavior.

12. ☑ A. Nonruntime exceptions are checked exceptions and checked exceptions must be either caught or specified.
☒ B, C, and D all contradict Java's catch or specify requirement and are therefore incorrect.

Runtime Exceptions and Checked Exceptions

13. ☑ C. Java programs must provide handlers for all checked exceptions in order to compile.
☒ A and D are incorrect because the program cannot run if it does not compile. A is true for an Error or a Runtime exception. B is incorrect because checked exceptions must be handled at some point.

14. ☑ A. If not handled, unchecked exceptions terminate the application.
☒ B is incorrect because exceptions must be handled at some point. C is incorrect because a program need not provide handlers for unchecked exceptions to compile. D is incorrect because no exceptions are automatically handled by the JVM.

15. ☑ B. Runtime exceptions are an exception to Java's catch or specify rule. They may be caught or declared, but it is not necessary.
☒ A, C, and D are all incorrect because the question asked about unchecked exceptions, not checked ones.

16. ☑ C. Runtime errors usually occur because of bugs in your program. Typically, your code does not catch a runtime error. Runtime errors are an exception to Java's catch or specify rule, so they need not be caught or specified.
☒ A is incorrect because any exception can be caught with a catch clause. B is incorrect because RuntimeExceptions are special, in that they are exempt from the catch or specify requirement. D is incorrect because RuntimeExceptions need not be specified.

Overriding Methods

17. ☑ B. When you override a method, you may specify no exceptions or you may specify subtypes of exceptions thrown by the overridden method. You cannot specify any exceptions that are not the same type as, or a subtype of, exceptions specified by the overridden method.
☒ A is incorrect because it contradicts this rule. C is incorrect because overridden methods may throw exceptions. D is incorrect because there is no requirement that overridden methods, in general, may only throw RuntimeExceptions.

Writing and Throwing Your Own Exceptions

18. ☑ C. By subclassing Java's RuntimeException class, you are creating a special type of unchecked exception for your application.
☒ A is incorrect, as there are no mistakes that would prevent a successful compile.

B is incorrect because we are subclassing an unchecked exception, not just a regular Exception. D is incorrect because there is nothing that will prevent this code from executing.

19. ☑ B. By subclassing Java's Exception class, or any of its subclasses other than RuntimeException, you are creating a special type of checked exception for your application.
☒ A is incorrect, as there are no mistakes that would prevent a successful compile. C is incorrect because we are subclassing a checked exception, so that's what this new type will be. D is incorrect, as there is nothing that will prevent this code from executing.

20. ☑ C. Error handling does not improve an application's performance.
☒ A, B, and D represent the three primary benefits of exception handling.

JAVA™

SUN CERTIFIED PROGRAMMER®

6

Garbage Collection

CERTIFICATION OBJECTIVES

- 6.01 The Behavior of the Garbage Collection System
- 6.02 Writing Code That Explicitly Makes Objects Eligible for Collection
- ✓ Two-Minute Drill
- Q&A Self Test

This chapter introduces you to garbage collection, the process that Java uses for managing unused memory. Every object created in Java uses memory. Garbage collection ensures that when your program is finished using an object, the memory is freed. This decreases the chance of creating an unwanted memory leak in Java code, although memory leaks can still occur in some situations. It also greatly simplifies the design and implementation of code, as opposed to C and C++, in which programmers spend precious time manually programming memory management.

Although the Java specification doesn't require it, most implementations of the Java Virtual Machine (JVM) use a *mark-sweep* garbage collection system. In this system, objects become eligible for deletion as soon as the last reference to them drops, but they aren't actually deleted until free memory is exhausted. When the system determines that it needs memory, it deletes any object that it determines is no longer in use. This takes the deletion control out of the hands of the programmer. The object's finalizer is called to alert the programmer that an object is about to be deleted. The finalizer of the object is simply a method of an object that is called just before the object is deleted; the finalizer for an object isn't required and is often omitted.

The Java language provides some built-in routines for controlling garbage collection: the methods System.gc() and System.runFinalization(). System.gc() requests that garbage collection be run. System.runFinalizers() asks that finalizers be executed, but that memory not necessarily freed. We'll discuss the difference later in the chapter. We'll also talk about the new classes in java.lang.ref that you can use for more advanced memory management.

Although garbage collection simplifies the writing of Java code, it is not an excuse to become lazy. Garbage collection imposes some trade-offs, and you still have to make decisions so the system works efficiently. After you read this chapter, you'll be able to make those decisions with certainty.

Garbage Collection

Garbage collection is nothing new; it has been used in languages such as Lisp and Smalltalk for many years. When an application runs, it uses memory. Memory is one of the most basic computer resources and tends to be one of the most limited. The action of creating a new object is the biggest use of memory in a Java application. Because it is difficult to tell how many objects are going to be created when a program runs, it is difficult to tell how much memory a program will need.

Java manages memory in a structure called a *heap*. Every object that Java creates is allocated in the heap, which is created when the application begins and is managed automatically by the JVM. Java attempts to ensure that there is always enough memory in the heap to create a new object through a process called *garbage collection*.

The basic idea behind a garbage collection system is simple: if memory is allocated, it eventually has to be freed. There is only so much memory on a computer—even today's modern machines with huge amounts of memory have an upper limit. If a program repeatedly allocates memory without freeing it, the system will eventually run out of memory and the program will fail.

The problem with freeing memory is that it can be very difficult to determine when memory should be freed. It is always clear when memory is allocated; each object can be tracked down to the single new statement that created it. It is not as clear when an object is no longer being used. An object may be in use by many different parts of a program at once; determining which of these parts is the last one to use the object can be impossible to figure out before the program runs.

Consider a class that represents a company with employees. Each employee has a reference to the company. There are an unknown number of employees in the system. If all the employees for the company are freed, the company is no longer being used and should be freed. However, the company should not be freed until all the employees have been freed.

Now you have a problem: How do you know when to free the Company object? If you free the Company object too soon while there are still employees referring to the company, then those employee objects may fail when they attempt to reference the nonexistent company. If you never free the Company object, although there are no employees referring to the company, then we are unnecessarily using up valuable memory.

on the Job

Can a Java application run out of memory? Yes, if there are too many strong references. The garbage collection system attempts to remove objects from memory when they are not used. However, if you maintain too many live objects (strongly referenced from other live objects,) the system can run out of memory. Garbage collection cannot ensure that there is enough memory, only that the memory that is available will be managed as efficiently as possible.

It takes a great deal of work and diligence on behalf of a programmer to do this manually. Java relieves the programmer of having to do this by moving the determination of which objects are in use into the Java runtime system. The runtime system can look behind the scenes to determine which objects are in use and automatically free those that are not.

This may sound like a trivial advance in programming languages, but studies have shown that up to 90 percent of all programming errors are related to poorly written memory management. By automatically managing memory, Java automatically removes up to 90 percent of the possible bugs in your programs!

Although garbage collection does a nice job of making sure that objects are freed once they are no longer used, it cannot give you an infinite amount of memory, and it cannot make your program use less memory. If you continuously add objects in a Java program without dropping references to them, the program can still run out of memory. Garbage collection makes sure that well-behaved programs have enough memory; it doesn't ensure that poorly programmed ones do.

CERTIFICATION OBJECTIVE 6.01

The Behavior of the Garbage Collection System

The first part of this chapter deals with classic garbage collection: garbage collection as it was introduced in the first Java releases. This is what will be tested on the Java 2 exam. With the release of Java 2, Sun added functionality on top of the existing system that allows for more programmer control of how and when objects are collected. This is only briefly covered in this chapter, because it is not tested on the exam.

In classic garbage collection, the JVM has the responsibility for making sure that unused objects are deleted from memory, or *collected*. It does this by checking to see if other objects refer to an object; an object that is not referenced is considered unused and can be collected.

Java manages these objects through *references*. A reference is what is returned from the *new* statement; it allows one object to refer to another. An object can have any number of references pointing to it; once the last of these references is dropped, the object can be collected. Java manages this for you, so you never have to delete an object explicitly.

Mark-Sweep

The JVM that Sun distributes is not the only one around; other companies such as Symantec, Borland, Netscape, IBM, and Microsoft have created them as well. The Java language specification gives these implementers a great deal of flexibility in how garbage collection is implemented. The specification describes how the system works from the programmer's point of view and not from an internal point of view. As long as the programmer experience is the same, the internal implementations of a JVM can be very different.

exam Watch

You will need to know what type of behavior is guaranteed by any JVM that follows the Java language specification. This means that you must acquire in-depth knowledge of the garbage collection model if you want to answer these questions accurately. The exam will not ask for terms such as **mark-sweep*****, but it will make sure that you understand what is happening during runtime.***

Having said that, most JVMs implement garbage collection using a variant of the *mark-sweep* algorithm. This algorithm gets its name from the two passes that it makes over the memory. The first pass marks those objects that are no longer used, and the second pass removes (sweeps) those objects from memory.

When discussing a garbage collection algorithm, the term *reachable* is used to describe objects that are in use. The idea is that active objects in memory find a huge interconnected web; any object that is on that web can be reached by traversing from another object that is in use. If no objects refer to an object, then that object is unreachable, and can therefore be removed from memory.

Mark-sweep starts with the assumption that some objects are always reachable. The main application object, for example, will be in use as long as the program is executing. The run() methods of threads, which are discussed in Chapter 9, are always reachable for similar reasons. Objects that are always reachable by definition are considered *root* objects, and are used to start traversing the web of objects. If an object can be reached from a root object, then it is in use. If an object can be reached from an object that can be reached from a root object, then it is in use. If an object can be reached from an object that can be…well, you get the idea. In general, if an object can be traced back to a root object, then it is in use.

Figure 6-1 shows a typical program containing several objects. All Java programs start from a main() method, which is the main thread of the program. The main() method can create several objects and hold references to them. In this example, it has created three objects: two Employee objects and a Timer thread. In our example, let's imagine that it only holds reference variables to the Employee objects. The thread was created with the *new* keyword, but no reference variable name was stored.

In this example, the Employee objects each have a reference to the same Company object. If the main() thread drops its variable reference to the Employee A object, then Employee A is eligible for collection, as is the String object and any other objects that Employee A contains. The Company object will still have a live variable reference from the Employee B object, so it is not eligible for collection. If the main() thread loses its variable references to both Employee objects, then Company would be eligible.

The mark phase of the mark-sweep garbage collection starts with the root objects and looks at all of the objects to which each root object refers. If the object is already marked as being in use, nothing more happens. If not, the object is marked as in use and all the objects to which it refers are considered. The algorithm repeats until all the objects that can be reached from the root objects have been marked as in use.

When the mark phase completes, the sweep phase begins. The sweep phase looks at each object in memory and sees if it was marked as in use by the mark phase. If it was, the sweep phase clears the in-use flag and does nothing more to the object. If, however, the object was not marked as in use, then the sweep phase knows that that object can be safely freed. The sweep phase then removes that object from memory.

Garbage Collection and Performance

As you can imagine, it can take a considerable amount of time to walk through all of the associations in memory. While the garbage collector is walking through these

FIGURE 6-1

Viewing some objects in a typical program

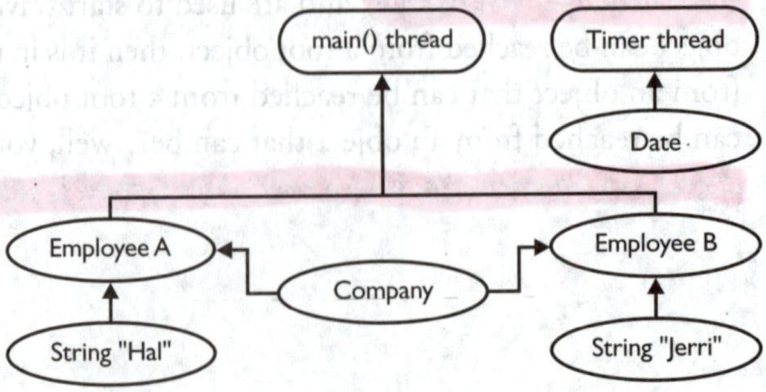

associations, it has to make sure that none of the associations changes. As a practical matter, this means that all other processing in the virtual machine stops while the garbage collector runs. This is one of the big disadvantages of garbage collection: the pause while the garbage collector runs.

One way that garbage collectors attempt to alleviate this overhead is by running the garbage collection only when needed. If there is plenty of free memory still available in the system, then there is no need to run a garbage collection. Unused objects are allowed to remain in memory because they do not affect the performance of the system; they are merely objects that sit in unused memory space.

The garbage collector is activated when Java attempts to allocate more memory than it has available. The garbage collector suspends the normal functioning of the virtual machine and executes a mark-sweep pass. After the garbage collector executes, the JVM attempts again to allocate memory. Ideally, the mark-sweep pass frees enough memory to satisfy the request . If the mark-sweep pass did not free enough memory, the request fails, and java.lang.OutOfMemoryError is thrown.

Let's look at the garbage collection system with some real Java code. We can't directly detect when it is called, but by monitoring the free memory, we can see when the JVM called for garbage collection. To monitor this, we will use the Runtime.freeMemory() method (Runtime is discussed later in this chapter). We'll make an endless loop that creates objects and then removes any reference to them:

```
1.  import java.util.Date;
2.  class GarbageFactory {
3.     public static void main(String [] args) {
4.        Runtime rt = Runtime.getRuntime();
5.        System.out.println("Total JVM memory: " + rt.totalMemory());
6.        Date d = null;
7.        int total = 0;
8.        while(true) {
9.           d = new Date();
10.          ++total;
11.          if(total % 500 == 0) {
12.             System.out.print("Objects: " + total);
13.             System.out.println(" Memory: " + rt.freeMemory());
14.          }
15.       }
16.    }
17. }
```

The code is pretty easy to follow. Line 8 creates an endless loop that keeps creating more objects. Line 11 uses modulus to print the status of our experiment every 500 objects. When I ran this on my computer, the memory started at about

800,000 bytes and slowly reduced to about 200,000 to 300,000 bytes before the free memory suddenly jumped back up to 800,000 bytes. From this, we can conclude that the garbage collection is being activated when there are about 200,000 bytes free to the JVM.

Therefore, the good news is that the JVM delays the running of the garbage collector as long as possible. The bad news is that garbage collection can run at any time. You don't receive prior notice that the garbage collector is about to run. Consequently, any request for more memory could result in the garbage collector running and making your program wait. This is one of the big problems with using Java for a real-time system—in a real-time system, you have to know when the pauses will be.

This is also the reason that garbage collection systems have the (undeserved) reputation for being slow. The total time that a garbage collection system takes to manage memory is only slightly more than the total time it takes to manage memory by hand. The difference is that a hand-written memory management scheme will rarely wait until memory is exhausted and then delete many objects at once. The action of deleting many objects at once causes the system to pause. Therefore, a garbage collected system might be only slightly slower overall, but may appear to be jerkier—performing a lot of work and then pausing—than a hand-written memory management scheme.

CERTIFICATION OBJECTIVE 6.02

Writing Code That Explicitly Makes Objects Eligible for Collection

In the previous section, we learned the theories behind Java garbage collection. This included a look behind the scenes on how the JVM deals with removing unused objects from memory. In this section, we show how to make objects available for garbage collection using actual code. We also discuss how to attempt to force garbage collection if it is necessary, and how you can perform additional cleanup on objects before they are removed from memory.

exam Watch

You will need to be able to state, for any given situation, the guaranteed behavior of the garbage collection system. This will mean looking at a body of code and stating whether hypothetical objects have been cleared from memory.

Making Objects Available for Garbage Collection

As we discussed earlier, an object becomes eligible for garbage collection when there are no more references to it. Obviously, if there are no references, it doesn't matter what happens to the object. For our purposes it is just floating in space, unused and no longer needed.

We can easily remove an object reference from a variable by setting the variable to null. Examine the following code:

```
class GarbageTruck {
   public static void main(String [] args) {
      String s = "hello";
      System.out.println(s);
      // At this point "hello" is not eligible for collection
      s = null;
      // Now the String "hello" is eligible for collection
   }
}
```

The String object "hello" is given the reference variable *s* in the third line. The String is used in line 4, but after that it is not really used anywhere. Although the rest of the code does not use the String "hello," it is not yet eligible for garbage collection. To do that, we set the variable *s* to null, which frees the String object "hello" from any reference variables. Our happy little hello string is now doomed.

We can also free up an object from a reference variable by setting the variable to point to another object. Examine the following code, which has been slightly altered:

```
class GarbageTruck {
   public static void main(String [] args) {
      String s1 = "hello";
      String s2 = "goodbye";
      System.out.println(s1);
      // At this point the String "hello" is not eligible
      s1 = s2; // Releases "hello" from s1 variable
      // Now the String "hello" is eligible for collection
   }
}
```

We know that threads are the main points at which the garbage collection starts looking for used objects. Therefore, any active thread is not eligible for collection. Once the thread has terminated, and if no other objects reference the Thread object, then it, too, is eligible for collection. Examine the following:

```
class GarbageDump extends Thread {
   public static void main(String [] args) {
      GarbageDump gd = new GarbageDump();
      gd.start();
      gd = null;
      // Eligible for collection?
   }

   public void run() {
      int i = 0;
      while(true) ++i;
   }
}
```

As you can see, this program creates an instance of a Thread object and then starts the thread looping by using Thread.start(). In the next line, the variable *gd* is set to null. Does this mean that our GarbageDump object is now eligible for collection? As mentioned previously, threads are the root of all object execution, so this cannot be collected until the thread terminates. Because it is a never-ending loop, this Thread object will never be collected—until you press CTRL-C, that is.

Objects that are created in a method also need to be considered. When a method is invoked, there are often local variables created that only have a usefulness for the duration of the method. Once the method has returned, the objects created in the method are ready for garbage collection. There is an obvious exception, however. If an object is returned from the method, it will be transferred to a reference variable in the method that called it; hence, it will not be eligible for collection. Examine the following code:

```
import java.util.Date;
class GarbageFactory {
   public static void main(String [] args) {
      Date d = getDate();
   }

   public static Date getDate() {
```

```
        Date d = new Date();
        String now = d.toString();
        System.out.println(now);
        return d;
    }
}
```

In the preceding example, we created a method called getDate() that returns a Date object. This method creates two objects: a Date and a String containing the date information. Since the method returns the Date object, it will not be eligible for collection once the method has executed. The String object will be eligible, even though we did not explicitly set the *now* variable to null. This covers everything you will need to know about making objects eligible for garbage collection. Now let's look at controlling garbage collection.

Forcing Garbage Collection

The first thing that should be mentioned here is, contrary to the section header, *garbage collection cannot be forced.* Java provides some routines that can help you control when the JVM pauses to perform garbage collection, however. For example, if you are about to perform some time-sensitive operations, you probably want to minimize the chances of a delay caused by garbage collection. The routines that Java provides are requests, and not demands; the virtual machine will do its best to do what you ask, but there is no guarantee that it will comply.

exam Watch

In reality, it is only possible to suggest to the JVM to perform garbage collection. However, there are no guarantees the JVM will actually remove all of the unused objects from memory. It is essential that you understand this concept for the exam.

The routines that Java provides are members of the Runtime class. The Runtime class is a special class that has a single object (a singleton) for each main program. The Runtime object provides a mechanism for communicating directly with the virtual machine. In order to get the Runtime instance, you can use the method Runtime.getRuntime(), which returns the singleton. Alternatively, for the methods we are going to discuss, you can use the same methods on the System class, which are static methods that do the work of obtaining the singleton for you. It is important to note that there is no constructor for Runtime! The following code demonstrates legal and illegal ways to get an instance of Runtime:

```
Runtime rt1 = Runtime.getRuntime(); // legal
Runtime rt2 = new Runtime(); // Will not compile
```

The first method is Runtime.gc(), which can be called using System.gc(). This method asks the virtual machine to perform a garbage collection pass. Theoretically, after calling Runtime.gc(), you will have as much free memory as possible and should be able to perform several allocations without having an unexpected garbage collection.

on the job

I tend to use System.gc() rather than Runtime.gc() (if I call these routines at all) to avoid calling Runtime.getInstance(), but that is a personal choice.

I say "theoretically" because this routine does not always work that way. First, the JVM you are using may not have implemented this routine; the language specification allows this routine to do nothing at all. Second, another thread (again, see Chapter 9) may perform a substantial memory allocation right after you run the garbage collection. You also have no idea how much memory was really freed by performing this garbage collection—it might not have been enough memory for the work that you wanted to do in the first place.

This is not to say that Runtime.gc() is a useless method—it's better than nothing. You just can't rely on Runtime.gc() to free up enough memory so that you don't have to worry about the garbage collector being run. The certification exam is interested in guaranteed behavior, not probable behavior.

The Runtime.gc() method does not take any arguments; it is simply a request to trigger a garbage collection. Keep in mind that this is not a static method, so you can't call it directly from the Runtime class. The following example demonstrates the use of garbage collection:

```
class GarbageMan {
   public static void main(String [] args) {

      Runtime rt = Runtime.getRuntime();
      rt.gc(); // legal
      Runtime.getRuntime().gc(); // legal
      System.gc(); // legal

      Runtime.gc(); // not legal
      new Runtime().gc(); // not legal
   }
}
```

If we attempt to compile this, we receive the following errors:

```
GarbageMan.java:11: Can't make static reference to method void gc() in
class java.lang.Runtime.
      Runtime.gc(); // not legal
GarbageMan.java:12: No constructor matching Runtime() found in class
java.lang.Runtime.
      new Runtime().gc(); // not legal
```

Now that we are somewhat familiar with how this works, let's do a little experiment to see if we can force garbage collection. The following program lets us know how much total memory the JVM has available to it and how much free memory it has. It then creates 10,000 Date objects. After this, it tells us how much memory is left and then calls the garbage collection (which, if it decides to run, should halt the program until all unused objects are removed). The final free memory result should indicate whether it has run. Let's look at the program:

```
import java.util.Date;
class CheckGC {
   public static void main(String [] args) {
      Runtime rt = Runtime.getRuntime();
      System.out.println("Total JVM memory: " + rt.totalMemory());
      System.out.println("Before Memory = " + rt.freeMemory());
      Date d = null;
      for(int i = 0;i<10000;i++) {
         d = new Date();
         d = null;
      }
      System.out.println("After Memory = " + rt.freeMemory());
      rt.gc();
      System.out.println("After GC Memory = " + rt.freeMemory());
   }
}
```

Now, let's run the program and check the results:

```
Total JVM memory: 1048568
Before Memory = 703008
After Memory = 458048
After GC Memory = 818272
```

As we can see, it actually did decide to collect the unused objects. If you recall from earlier in the chapter, the collection of unused objects usually occurred at about 200,000 to 300,000 bytes remaining. In the preceding example, we suggested to the JVM to collect at 458,048 bytes and it complied. This program has only one thread running, so there was nothing else going on when we called Runtime.gc(). Perhaps if there were other threads going it would not have done a collection. Moreover, this was done with the Sun JVM. Keep in mind that the behavior when gc() is called may be different for other JVMs, so there is no guarantee that the unused objects will be removed from memory.

EXERCISE 6-1

Collecting Garbage

At this point, you should be able to make objects eligible for collection and make a call to the garbage collection system. Since writing code to make objects eligible for collection is one of the certification objectives, let's go ahead and try this. To make things interesting, let's make a program that searches for prime numbers. We'll fill an array object with them, and then set the array to null and call Runtime.gc() to see if we can figure out exactly how much memory our array used. Don't be surprised if the results are not as expected!

1. Create a method that can identify if a number is prime. If you are not interested in figuring this out, you can use the following:

```
public static boolean isPrime(int number) {
    boolean isPrime = true;
    for(int i=number-1;i>1;--i) {
        if(number % i == 0)
            isPrime = false;
    }
    return isPrime;
}
```

2. Fill the array with prime numbers—let's use 100. Again, this isn't crucial to the topic of the chapter, so if you want to, you can use the following in the main() method:

```
int [] primes = new int[100];
int current = 0;
for(int i=0;i<primes.length;i++) {
    ++current;
    while (!isPrime(current))
        ++current;
    primes[i] = current;
    System.out.println("Prime: " + primes[i]);
}
```

3. Now we want to determine how much memory the *primes* array uses. First, perform a gc() to clean up the memory. Then, set *primes* to null, and call gc() again. The final code should look something like this:

```
class Prime {
   public static void main(String [] args) {
      int [] primes = new int[100];
      int current = 0;
      for(int i=0;i<primes.length;i++) {
         ++current;
         while (!isPrime(current))
            ++current;
         primes[i] = current;
         System.out.println("Prime: " + primes[i]);
      }

      Runtime rt = Runtime.getRuntime();
      rt.gc();
      System.out.println("Memory Before = " + rt.freeMemory());
      primes = null;
      rt.gc();
      System.out.println("Memory After GC = " + rt.freeMemory());
   }

   public static boolean isPrime(int number) {
      boolean isPrime = true;
      for(int i=number-1;i>1;--i) {
         if(number % i == 0)
            isPrime = false;
      }
      return isPrime;
   }
}
```

The (partial) results on my system are as follows:

```
Prime: 509
Prime: 521
Prime: 523
Memory Before = 819120
Memory After GC = 818536
```

This is a little surprising, since the memory went down instead of up after clearing the object array. This just goes to show that there is no guarantee as to what goes on behind the scenes with any given JVM.

Discovering Whether an Object Was Collected

There are some good reasons for knowing when an object is collected. You might be keeping a count of live objects or even attempting to debug an application. Additionally, if the object owns resources that are not a part of the Java garbage collection scheme (such as database connections, resources allocated in Java Native Interface (JNI) code, and so forth), then you still have the responsibility of making sure that those resources are cleaned up.

To allow for these contingencies, Java provides a notification mechanism that tells you that an object is about to be collected. Every class has a special method called a *finalizer* that is called just before an object is collected. The JVM calls the finalizer for you as appropriate; you never call a finalizer directly.

Think of the finalizer as a friendly warning from the virtual machine. Your finalizer should perform two tasks: performing whatever cleanup is appropriate to the object, and calling the superclass finalizer. If you don't have any cleanup to perform for an object, you're better off not adding a finalizer to the class.

The finalizer method is called Object.finalize(). It returns void and takes no arguments. Since all Java classes are derived from *Object* (which defines the finalize() method), all classes in the Java language have the finalize() method. Not all of them have overridden it, however.

The virtual machine invokes the finalize() method as the first step in collecting an object. The virtual machine reserves the right *not* to immediately collect the memory associated with an object after calling the finalizer! This allows the garbage collector to limit its own execution time. Garbage collectors may decide to run only for so long and may run a set of finalizers and go back later to actually collect the memory. They are free to do this; you cannot rely on the internal behavior of the garbage collector.

You can ask the garbage collector to run finalizers for you by invoking the Runtime.runFinalization() or System.runFinalization() method. This method is a request to the garbage collector to run finalizers for any objects that are currently unreachable, but that have not had finalizers run yet. The garbage collector may or may not decide to actually honor this request and may or may not decide to deallocate the memory for those objects for which it does run finalizers. A program could call finalize() directly, and the code in the finalize() method would execute, but this is the incorrect way to use finalize(), and it would not lead to garbage collection. In fact, it would likely lead to errors.

Now that we are familiar with how finalization occurs, let's examine this concept with some code. The following class is an experiment to see just how often finalization actually runs in the JVM. We will not perform runFinalization() at any time, so the JVM will choose when object finalization will occur.

```
 1.  class ObjectWatch {
 2.     public static int totalCreated;
 3.     public static int totalFinalized;
 4.
 5.     public ObjectWatch() {
 6.        ++totalCreated;
 7.     }
 8.
 9.     public static void main(String [] args) {
10.        for(int i=0;i<20000;i++) {
11.           ObjectWatch ow = new ObjectWatch();
12.           System.out.print("Created: " + totalCreated);
13.           System.out.println(" Finalized: " + totalFinalized);
14.        }
15.     }
16.
17.     protected void finalize() {
18.        ++totalFinalized;
19.     }
20.  }
```

This code is pretty easy to decipher. Line 6 adds one to the tally of objects it has created (totalCreated), and line 18 adds one to the tally of objects finalized (totalFinalized). Within the main() method, we are creating objects in a for loop. After each loop, the object that was created as *ow* loses its reference variable, and is therefore eligible for finalization and garbage collection. Let's run this example and see if we can find out how the JVM performs:

```
Created: 1388 Finalized: 0
```

```
Created: 1389 Finalized: 0
Created: 1390 Finalized: 0
Created: 1391 Finalized: 0
Created: 1392 Finalized: 1390
Created: 1393 Finalized: 1390
Created: 1394 Finalized: 1390
Created: 1395 Finalized: 1390
(...)
```

This is just a small snippet from the output. As you can see, none of the unused objects was finalized until there were at least 1390. At that point, the JVM decided to run finalization on all unused objects. I should also note that the JVM was sporadic as to when it ran the finalization. Sometimes it ran it after only a few hundred objects became unused, and other times it waited until it built up several thousand. There are two main points to take away from this: first, you can't rely on the JVM to finalize unused objects with any precision; and second, the finalization of objects takes place automatically without additional code from the programmer.

EXERCISE 6-2

Overriding the Finalize Method

In this exercise, we are going to try to create an object that overrides the finalize() method. As we learned, finalize() is normally used to clean up other system resources that the object might have used, but in our case, we are just going to make the finalize() method keep track of the number of objects finalized. We will also keep track of the number of objects created using the constructor method. This is very similar to the code presented previously, but the twist is that we will call runFinalization() for every 250 objects that are unused. By the way, don't be surprised if the program doesn't finalize methods when you want it to.

1. Create two static integer values to keep track of the objects that are created and destroyed.

2. The constructor for your class should increment the first integer each time an object is created and increment the other each time it is finalized.
3. In the main() method, try creating 1000 of these objects in a for loop.
4. In order to perform the runFinalization(), take your objects created modulus 250:

```
if (totalCreated % 250 == 0) System.runFinalization();
```

5. Add output to the screen to keep track of objects created and destroyed. The final code should look something like this:

```
class Exercise {
   public static int totalCreated;
   public static int totalFinalized;

   public Exercise() {
      ++totalCreated;
   }

   public static void main(String [] args) {
      for(int i=0;i<1000;i++) {
         Exercise e = new Exercise();
         System.out.print("Created: " + totalCreated);
         System.out.println(" Finalized: " + totalFinalized);
         if (totalCreated % 250 == 0) {
            System.out.println("About to run finalization...");
            System.runFinalization();
            try {Thread.sleep(1000);}
               catch(InterruptedException ie){}
         }
      }
   }

   protected void finalize() {
      ++totalFinalized;
   }
}
```

FROM THE CLASSROOM

Advanced Garbage Collection in Java 2

Up to this point, we have been discussing the original Java memory management model. With Java 2, the original model was augmented with *reference classes*. Reference classes, which derive from the abstract class *Reference*, are used for more sophisticated memory management. (You will not need to know the advanced management model for the exam.) The Reference class is the superclass for the *WeakReference*, *SoftReference*, and *PhantomReference* classes found in the java.lang.ref package.

By default, you as a programmer work with strong references. When you hear people talking about references (at parties, on the bus), they are usually talking about *strong references*. This was the classic Java way of doing things, and is what you have unless you go out of your way to use the Reference classes. Strong references are used to prevent objects from being garbage collected; a strong reference from a reachable object is enough to keep the referred-to object in memory.

Let's look at the other three types of references:

- **Soft references** The Java language specification states that soft references can be used to create memory-sensitive caches. For example, in an image program, when you make a change to the image (say, an Image object), the old Image object can stick around in case the user wants to undo the change. This old object is an example of a cache.
- **Weak references** These are similar to soft references in that they allow you to refer to an object without forcing the object to remain in memory. Weak references are different from soft references, however, in that they do not request that the garbage collector attempt to keep the object in memory. Unlike soft references, which may stick around for a while even after their strong references drop, weak references go away pretty quickly.
- **Phantom references** These provide a means of delaying the reuse of memory occupied by an object, even if the object itself is finalized. A *phantom* object is one that has been finalized, but whose memory has not yet been made available for another object.

Objects are placed into one of several categories, depending on what types of references can be used to get to the object. References are ordered as follows: strong,

FROM THE CLASSROOM

soft, weak, and phantom. Objects are then known as *strongly reachable*, *softly reachable*, *weakly reachable*, *phantom reachable*, or *unreachable*.

- **Strongly reachable** If an object has a strong reference, a soft reference, a weak reference, and a phantom reference all pointing to it, then the object is considered strongly reachable and will not be collected.
- **Softly reachable** An object without a strong reference, but with a soft reference, a weak reference, and a phantom reference will be considered softly reachable, and will only be collected when memory gets low.
- **Weakly reachable** An object without strong or soft references, but with weak and phantom references, is considered weakly reachable and will be collected at the next garbage collection cycle.
- **Phantom reachable** An object without strong, soft, or weak references, but with a phantom reference, is considered phantom reachable and will be finalized, but the memory for that object will not be collected.
- **Unreachable** What about an object without strong, soft, weak, or phantom references? Well, that object is considered unreachable and will already have been collected, or will be collected as soon as the next garbage collection cycle is run.

— *Bob Hablutzel*

At this point, we've covered most of the basics of garbage collection. When you write Java programs, you will mainly be using what we have already discussed. So, let's review what we've covered so far with some scenario questions and their answers.

SCENARIO & SOLUTION	
I want to allocate an object and make sure that it never is deallocated. Can I tell the garbage collector to ignore an object?	No. There isn't a mechanism for marking an object as undeletable. You can instead create a static member of a class, and store a reference to the object in that. Static members are considered live objects.
My program is not performing as well as I would expect. I think the garbage collector is taking too much time. What can I do?	First, if it really is the garbage collector (and it probably isn't), then the code is creating and dropping many references to many temporary objects. Try to redesign the program to reuse objects or require fewer temporary objects.
I am creating an object in a method and passing it out as the method result. How do I make sure the object isn't deleted before the method returns?	The object won't be deleted until the last reference to the object is dropped. If you return the object as a method return value, the method that called it will contain a reference to the object.
How do I drop a reference to an object if that object is referred to in a member of my class?	Set the member to *null.* Alternatively, if you set a reference to a new object, the old object loses one reference. If that is the last reference, the object becomes eligible for deletion.
I want to keep objects around as long as they don't interfere with memory allocation. Is there any way I can ask Java to warn me if memory is getting low?	Prior to Java 1.2, you would have to check the amount of free memory yourself and guess. Java 1.2 introduced soft references for just this situation. This is not part of the Java 2 exam, however.

CERTIFICATION SUMMARY

Garbage collection is one of the most popular and powerful features of the Java language, but is also one that requires the least programmer interaction. For most applications, the garbage collection system simply manages memory for you. Garbage collection ensures that objects are automatically removed when they are no longer required, while objects that are still in use stay alive. Most important, garbage collection determines automatically which objects are in use, relieving the programmer of having to do this.

You don't have to do anything special for basic garbage collection; it is automatic. When you create an object using *new*, you obtain a reference to the object. When there are no more references to an object, the *finalize()* method is called and the object is collected. There is no need for a delete method, so the language does not provide one.

Although for most applications the basic memory management model is enough, some programs can benefit from more advanced memory management. The Java 1.2 specification adds this advanced memory management in the form of reference objects; however, you will not be expected to know this API for the Java 2 certification exam.

Overall, the Java 1.2 garbage collection mechanism is a powerful addition to the language. The basic functionality is simple to use and adequate for most applications. The language mechanism also supports more powerful interactions with the garbage collector, at a slight price in complexity. Either way, the code will be simpler to understand and more reliable because the language itself is involved in the management of memory.

✓ TWO-MINUTE DRILL

Here are some of the key points from each certification objective in Chapter 6.

The Behavior of the Garbage Collection System

- Java memory management is generally automatic with no programmer interaction.
- The Java Virtual Machine (JVM) has the responsibility of finding unused objects and making sure that the memory they occupy is freed.
- *Garbage collection* is the automatic detection and deletion of unused objects.
- Most JVM implementations use mark-sweep garbage collection.
- Mark-sweep collection can delete objects, even if two unused objects refer to each other.
- Java applications can still run out of memory. The amount of memory on your computer and the amount of memory your application needs determine whether the application will run out of memory.

Writing Code That Explicitly Makes Objects Eligible for Collection

- To make an object eligible for collection, you must remove all reference variables to it.
- Reference variables can be removed from objects by setting a variable to *null*.
- When a reference variable is set to another object, the connection to the existing object is severed, and if no other variables point to it, then it is eligible for collection.
- Objects created in methods are only alive for the duration of the method, and then they become eligible for collection (unless they are returned by the method).
- The Runtime object is a singleton; therefore, there is no constructor for it. Use the Runtime.getRuntime() method to get an instance of this object.

- You can suggest to the JVM to do a garbage collection sweep using the Runtime.gc() method. This can also be called directly from the static System.gc() method.
- All objects in Java can include code in the Object.finalize() method by overriding this method. This allows for cleanup to occur before the object is removed from memory.
- The Runtime.runFinalization() method can be called to finalize all unused objects. This forces the JVM to finalize all objects that are pending finalization. This can also be called directly from the static System.runFinalization() method.

SELF TEST

The following questions will help you measure your understanding of the material presented in this chapter. Read all of the choices carefully, as there may be more than one correct answer. Choose all correct answers for each question.

The Behavior of the Garbage Collection System

1. What does a Java programmer have to do in order to release an object that is no longer needed?
   A. Use the delete statement.
   B. Call the finalize() method for the object.
   C. Call System.gc().
   D. Nothing.

2. Complete the following sentence. Garbage collection ______________________.
   A. Is faster than most programmer-coded memory management
   B. Is only available in the Java language
   C. Is more reliable than most programmer-coded memory management
   D. Uses less memory than most programmer-coded memory management

3. Complete the following sentence. Calling Runtime.gc() ______________________.
   A. Guarantees enough memory for the next memory allocation request
   B. Always frees up some memory, but may not free enough for the next allocation request
   C. May have no effect, based on the virtual machine implementation
   D. Should be performed before every memory allocation request

4. Complete the following sentence. The Java Virtual Machine specification ______________________.
   A. Requires mark-sweep garbage collection
   B. Requires some form of garbage collection, but not necessarily mark-sweep
   C. Allows for manual memory management
   D. Does not address memory management

5. Complete the following sentence. Mark-sweep garbage collection ______________________.

   A. Can identify unused objects, even if they refer to each other

   B. Cannot collect objects that refer to each other cyclically

   C. Is the fastest garbage collection system

   D. Runs every three seconds, in a separate system-level thread

Writing Code That Explicitly Makes Objects Eligible for Collection

6. Given:

```
1.  import java.util.Date;
2.  class TimeMonitor {
3.     public static void main(String [] args) {
4.        Date d = null;
5.        for(int i = 0;i<1000;i++) {
6.           d = new Date();
7.           System.out.println(d.toString());
8.        }
9.
10.       // Rest of program...
11.    }
12. }
```

   Which of the following statements inserted at line 9 calls the garbage collector?

   A. It is impossible to make a call for collection.

   B. System.out.gc();

   C. System.runFinalizer();

   D. Runtime.gc();

   E. new Runtime().gc();

   F. None of the above.

7. Name the method That is contained by all objects that can contain code to clean up an object before it is garbage-collected: ______________________. (Fill in the blank.)

8. Given:

```
class Counter extends Thread {
   public void run() {
      for(int i=0;i<100;i++) {
         System.out.println(i);
      }
   }
```

```
 7.     protected void finalize() {
 8.         System.out.println("Object no longer useful.");
 9.     }
10. }
```

Assume another class makes use of an instance of this class. No other classes contain the sentence in line 8. You run the program and see the output at line 8. What can you conclude?

A. The Counter object has been garbage-collected.

B. This object may not have been garbage-collected because the thread may still be running.

C. This object is eligible for garbage collection.

D. None of the above.

9. Given:

```
 1. class Test1 {
 2.     public static void main(String [] args) {
 3.         new Counter().start();
 4.         System.out.println("Welcome.");
 5.         // Possibly more code...
 6.     }
 7. }
 8.
 9. class Counter extends Thread {
10.     public void run() {
11.         for(int i=0;i<1000000;i++) {
12.             System.out.println(i);
13.             try {
14.                 this.sleep(100);
15.             } catch (InterruptedException ie) {}
16.         }
17.     }
18. }
```

A Counter object is created in line 3. As you can see, there is no reference variable for it. Is this Counter object ready for garbage collection at line 4?

A. Yes

B. No

C. Maybe

D. None of the above

10. Name the Runtime method that is used to invoke the finalize() methods on all objects that have no more reference variables: __________________________. (Fill in the blank.)

11. Given:

```
1.  class Test2 {
2.     public static void main(String [] args) {
3.        new Counting().run();
4.
5.        // Possibly more code...
6.     }
7.  }
8.
9.  class Counting {
10.    public void run() {
11.       for(int i=0;i<1000000;i++) {
12.          System.out.println(i);
13.       }
14.    }
15. }
```

A Counting object is created in line 3. As you can see, there is no reference variable for it. Is this Counting object eligible for garbage collection at line 4?

A. Yes

B. No

C. Maybe

D. None of the above

12. Given:

```
1.  class Test {
2.     String a = "hello";
3.     String b = "hello";
4.     public static void main(String [] args) {
5.        b = null;
6.        System.out.println(a);
7.        System.out.println(b);
8.     }
9.  }
```

An object is assigned to variable *b* in line 3. Is this object eligible for garbage collection at line 6?

A. Yes

B. No

C. Maybe

D. None of the above

13. Given:

```
1.  class Test {
2.      public static void main(String [] args) {
3.          String a = methodA();
4.          System.out.println(a);
5.          // Possibly more code...
6.      }
7.
8.      public static String methodA() {
9.          String s = "Study";
10.         String t = "studY";
11.         return s;
12.     }
13. }
```

Two objects are created in lines 9 and 10. Which of these statements are true concerning these objects? (Choose two.)

A. The object in line 9 is not eligible for collection at line 5.

B. The object in line 10 is not eligible for collection at line 5.

C. The object in line 9 is eligible for collection at line 5.

D. The object in line 10 is eligible for collection at line 5.

14. Given:

```
1.  class Test {
2.      public static void main(String [] args) {
3.          methodA();
4.          System.out.println("studY");
5.          // Possibly more code...
6.      }
7.
8.      public static String methodA() {
9.          String s = "Study";
10.         String t = "studY";
11.         return s;
12.     }
13. }
```

There are two objects created in lines 9 and 10. Which of these statements are true concerning these objects? (Choose two.)

A. The object in line 9 is not eligible for collection at line 5.

B. The object in line 10 is not eligible for collection at line 5.

C. The object in line 9 is eligible for collection at line 5.

D. The object in line 10 is eligible for collection at line 5.

15. When is the finalize() method called?

A. Immediately after the last reference variable for the object is removed

B. When the garbage collection determines that there are no more references to the object

C. After garbage collection takes place on an object

D. Only when a user calls the Runtime.runFinalization() method

16. Given:

```
1.  class Example {
2.     public static void main(String args[]) {
3.        new Example().useObject();
4.        System.out.println("Done!");
5.     }
6.     private void useObject() {
7.        String anObject =allocateObject();
8.        System.out.println(anObject);
9.     }
10.    private String allocateObject(){
11.       String myObject = new String("When will I be deleted?");
12.       return myObject;
13.    }
14. }
```

When will the object created as myObject become eligible for deletion?

A. When the allocateObject() method completes

B. When the call to System.out.println() completes in line 8

C. When the useObject() method completes

D. When the main program completes

17. Which method is overridden to perform cleanup when an object is no longer in use?

A. public void finalize(Object o)

B. public void finalize()

C. protected void finalize()

D. public boolean finalize()

18. Given:

```
1.  class Test extends Thread {
2.     MyClass mc = null;
3.
4.     public static void main(String [] args) {
5.        Test t = new Test();
6.        t.mc = new MyClass(t);
7.        t.start();
8.     }
9.
10.    public void run() {
11.       while(true) {
12.          String s = "Nothing really.";
13.          if (mc != null) {
14.             System.out.println("We have an object.");
15.             mc = null;
16.          }
17.       }
18.    }
19. }
20.
21. class MyClass {
22.    private Test t = null;
23.
24.    public MyClass(Test t) {
25.       this.t = t;
26.    }
27.
28.    protected void finalize() {
29.       t.mc = this;
30.    }
31. }
```

Assume the Test thread runs forever. Which of the following statements are correct? (Choose all that apply.)

A. This code will not compile.

B. This code will compile, but will cause errors when it is executed.

C. The finalize() method at line 28 will never run.

D. The MyClass object created in line 6 can never be garbage-collected.

E. The output at line 14 is guaranteed to be displayed only once.

19. Given:

```
1.  class Test {
2.      public static void main (String [] args) {
3.          String first = "Greetings ";
4.          {
5.              String second = "human.";
6.              System.out.println(first + second);
7.              System.out.println();
8.          }
9.          System.out.println("Now what?");
10.     }
11. }
```

Which of the following statements are correct?

A. This code will not compile because of line 7.

B. The "human" string is only eligible for collection after line 6.

C. The "human" string is only eligible for collection after line 8.

D. The "human" string is only eligible for collection when main() completes.

20. Given:

```
1.  class Test {
2.
3.      public static void main (String [] args) {
4.          String first = "Greetings ";
5.          String second = "human.";
6.          String third = "Grok.";
7.          first = second;
8.          second = first;
9.          third = second;
10.
11.         System.out.println("Now what?");
12.     }
13. }
```

Which of the following objects are eligible for collection at line 10? (Choose all that apply.)

A. "Greetings"

B. "human."

C. "Grok."

SELF TEST ANSWERS

The Behavior of the Garbage Collection System

1. ☑ **D**. In Java, the programmer does not have to perform any special actions to delete an object that is no longer in use. Rather, the system will automatically detect that the object is no longer used and will collect the object.
☒ **A** is incorrect, as there is no delete statement in Java. **B** is incorrect, as the finalize() method of an object is called automatically by the system and is never called by the programmer directly. **C** is incorrect; although calling System.gc() might cause the object to be collected, it is not required for the object to be collected.

2. ☑ **C**. Garbage collection is more reliable than most programmer-coded memory management. Garbage collection is designed to eliminate errors in memory management. It does not attempt to address memory efficiency or performance.
☒ **A** isn't a good answer because garbage collection will generally be slower overall than hand-written memory management. **B** is incorrect because garbage collection has been available in a variety of languages for a number of years. Garbage collection doesn't attempt to reduce the amount of memory that an object takes, so **D** isn't a good answer either.

3. ☑ **C**. Calling Runtime.gc() may have no effect, based on the virtual machine implementation. The Runtime.gc() (or the equivalent System.gc()) calls are requests to the virtual machine to run a garbage collection pass. The implementation of this call depends on the virtual machine under which you are running and may have no effect.
☒ **A** is incorrect, as there is never a guarantee that there will be enough memory for the next allocation request; this will always depend on the size of the request and the amount of memory available to the virtual machine. **B** is incorrect because the call may do nothing if it is not implemented in your virtual machine. **D** is incorrect because invoking Runtime.gc() before every memory allocation request would only add unnecessary overhead to your application without any benefits.

4. ☑ **B**. Requires some form of garbage collection, but not necessarily mark-sweep. The Java Virtual Machine specification requires that the virtual machine support garbage collection, but does not require that this garbage collection be implemented using the mark-sweep algorithm. It is true, however, that the mark-sweep algorithm is by far the most popular implementation, and is the implementation in Sun's JDK.
☒ **A** is incorrect because the virtual machine specification doesn't address how to implement memory management, only that memory management must be provided. The virtual machine

specification does not allow any form of manual memory management, however, so C is incorrect. D is incorrect because the specification clearly addresses the need for automatic memory management.

5. ☑ A. Can identify unused objects, even if they refer to each other. One advantage of the mark-sweep memory management algorithm is the ability to identify cycles of objects that only refer to each other internally. This allows these cyclically referenced objects to be collected and the memory recovered.
☒ B is incorrect, as mark-sweep is specifically designed to collect objects that refer to each other cyclically. C is incorrect, as mark-sweep may not be the fastest garbage collection system. The time it takes to evaluate objects to find out which objects are really alive imposes some overhead on the performance of the garbage collector. D is incorrect, although it could be for some implementation; mark-sweep will generally run when needed to free up memory, rather than regularly in another thread.

Writing Code That Explicitly Makes Objects Eligible for Collection

6. ☑ F. None of these are legal ways to call the garbage collector. System.gc() is one way to call it, and the other is by using an instance of Runtime. This can be accomplished by *Runtime.getRuntime().gc()*.
☒ A is incorrect because the Runtime.gc() method is specifically to call garbage collection. There is no guarantee that it will actually run, however. B is incorrect because *out* should not be included. C is incorrect because this is not the garbage collection method. D is incorrect because Runtime.gc() is not a static method; therefore, you need an instance of Runtime to call the method. E is incorrect because the only way to get a Runtime instance is with Runtime.getRuntime().

7. ☑ finalize(). The finalize() method is contained by all objects that can contain code to clean up an object before it is garbage collected.

8. ☑ C. When the finalize() method of an object runs, it means that the object no longer has any reference variables; therefore, it is eligible for collection.
☒ A is incorrect because the garbage collector does not necessarily run right after an object is finalized. B is incorrect because an object will not be finalized until the thread has finished. D is incorrect because we can conclude C.

9. ☑ B. Any threads that are still alive are not eligible for collection. This thread pauses for 1/10th of a second after each iteration, so it will still be executing when the next line of code executes.

☒ A and C are both incorrect because there is no possible way it would be eligible. **D** is incorrect because we can in fact conclude **B**.

10. ☑ runFinalization(). The Runtime method that is used to invoke the finalize() methods on all objects that have no more reference variables is runFinalization().

11. ☑ **A**. Counting is an unthreaded class. The run() method is a normal method and will execute in sequential order. The program will stop at line 3 until run() has finished executing, and then it will continue. At line 4, there are no variable references for it, so it is ready for garbage collection.
☒ **B** and **C** are both incorrect because it definitely is eligible for garbage collection. **D** is incorrect because we can in fact conclude **A**.

12. ☑ **B**. This is a difficult question that includes material introduced in Chapter 3. As you may recall, when Strings are assigned to variables, if the literal value of the string characters is the same, Java will assign the same object to all String variables that use that literal value at compile time. This means that both *a* and *b* refer to the same object. When we assign variable *b* to null in line 5, the object is still alive because *a* has a reference to it.
☒ **A** and **C** are both incorrect because *b* is definitely not eligible for garbage collection at line 6. **D** is incorrect because we can in fact conclude **B**.

13. ☑ **A** and **D**. **A** is correct because the object is passed out of methodA() and given a reference variable in line 3. It is available until the main() method ends, since the reference variable is never assigned to null or reassigned. **D** is correct because this is a local variable, even though it is a static method. Once methodA() is complete, there will be no other reference variables attached to the object created at line 10. In addition, the capitalization is different between *s* and *t*, so the compiler creates two separate String objects for each of these variables.
☒ **B** is incorrect because "Study" still has a reference variable at line 5. **C** is incorrect because "studY" has no reference variables at line 5.

14. ☑ **C** and **D**. **C** is correct because the object is never actually passed out of methodA(); therefore, there are no reference variables to it at line 5. **D** is correct because the String "studY" created in lines 4 and 10 both refer to the same object. The reference in line 10 ends once methodA() completes. There is no reference to it in line 4; therefore, it is eligible for collection in line 5.
☒ **A** is incorrect because there is no reference variable for "Study" at line 5. **B** is incorrect because "studY" has no reference variables at line 5; therefore, both objects in **A** and **B** are available for garbage collection.

15. ☑ **B.** The general contract of finalize() is that it is invoked if and when the JVM has determined that there is no longer any means by which this object can be accessed by any thread that has not yet died, except as a result of an action taken by the finalization of some other object or class that is ready to be finalized.
☒ **A** is incorrect because there is no guarantee that the finalize() methods for objects will run once there are no more references to it. **C** is incorrect because the finalize() code would be gone after the method is erased. **D** is incorrect because the runFinalization() method only suggests to the JVM to run the finalize() methods.

16. ☑ **C.** When the useObject() method completes. The object is eligible for deletion after the *last* reference that refers to it is dropped. For this code, the last reference is the anObject reference, which is dropped when the useObject() method completes.
☒ **A** is incorrect, as the object reference is returned from the method. This increases the number of references to the object, so the object isn't freed, even though the myObject references go out of scope. **B** is incorrect because the reference to the object is not dropped after the last usage of the reference, but rather when the scope that reference is in completes. **D** is incorrect, although the object may well not be collected until the program completes, as it is eligible for deletion as soon as the last reference is dropped.

17. ☑ **C.** The finalize() method is protected. This is one of the rare protected methods with which you should be familiar for the exam.
☒ **A, B,** and **D** are all incorrect because finalize() is not public, it doesn't accept an argument, and it doesn't return any value.

18. ☑ **D.** When the MyClass object loses its reference variable at line 15, it becomes eligible for object finalization. When the finalize() method is run at line 29, it gives the Test object a reference to itself again; hence, it is no longer eligible for garbage collection. The finalize() method is always run before garbage collection; therefore, this object cannot be garbage-collected. The only way it could die is if the Test thread also died, but we stated in the question that it runs forever. (In fact, it is still running on my PC to this day.)
☒ **A** and **B** are incorrect because this code is fully functioning. **C** is incorrect because the JVM may decide to run the finalize() method as soon as the *mc* variable is set to null in line 15. **E** is incorrect because once the finalize() method is run, *mc* will no longer be equal to null, so it will display the message again.

19. ☑ C. When a block of code has finished executing, any variables that are local to that block of code are eligible for collection.
☒ A is incorrect because println() has a no-arguments method. B is incorrect because, even though there are no more lines of code that reference this string, it is still not yet eligible. D is incorrect because it is eligible after the block ends after line 8.

20. ☑ A and C. Line 7 causes "Greetings " to lose its reference variable, so *first* will point to the "human." string. Line 8 doesn't change anything because *second* already points to the "human." string. Line 9 causes "Grok." to lose its reference variable.
☒ B is incorrect because all three variables point to the string "human."; therefore, it cannot be eligible for collection at line 10.

JAVA™

SUN CERTIFIED PROGRAMMER®

7

Overloading/ Overriding Runtime Type and Object Orientation

CERTIFICATION OBJECTIVES

- 7.01 Encapsulation in Object-Oriented Design
- 7.02 Designing and Implementing Tightly Encapsulated Classes
- 7.03 Describing is a and has a Class Relationships
- 7.04 Invoking Overridden or Overloaded Methods
- 7.05 Invoking Parental or Overloaded Constructors
- ✓ Two-Minute Drill
- Q&A Self Test

The questions on the Java Programmer Certification Exam will test your general understanding of object-oriented programming and your knowledge of Java's implementation of these concepts. Object-oriented programming in Java has many similarities to programming in other object-oriented languages, but it has a number of syntactic differences from other languages such as C++. In this chapter, you will learn how to recognize properly coded overridden and overloaded methods. You will also learn how to enumerate the valid—and invalid—techniques to invoke a superclass' constructor from the subclass using the super() method.

Before delving into the details specific to Java, we will first look at object-oriented programming in general. Encapsulation, the visibility of an implementation to outside classes, is at the core of object-oriented design. A programmer considers encapsulation issues when creating classes, and determines whether the members should be *public, private,* and so on. The other object-oriented concept that will be discussed is the often-confused difference between *is a* and *has a* relationships. An understanding of encapsulation, as well as *is a* and *has a* relationships, will be tested on the exam.

CERTIFICATION OBJECTIVE 7.01

Encapsulation in Object-Oriented Design

Two goals of encapsulation in object-oriented design are modularity and appropriate visibility. Modular classes are as independent (or loosely coupled) as is feasible. In other words, your code should be separated into different classes so that it only knows as much as is necessary about your other code. There are no right or wrong ways to write modular code, but there are several guidelines.

Visibility is the accessibility of methods and instance variables (members) to other classes and packages. When implementing a class, you determine the member visibility as *public, protected, package,* or *default,* based on this object-oriented concept. For example, Java has rules stating when a *protected* method may be accessed (as discussed in Chapter 2.) Deciding whether protected is appropriate is an encapsulation issue.

Writing Modular Code

As stated earlier, modular code keeps implementations isolated so that they depend on other code as little as possible. Although modular code doesn't affect how well your code executes, you will get many benefits by writing code this way. Consider the following code excerpt that is not modular:

```
public class Company {
    private Vector employeeNames;
    private Vector vendorNames;

    public Company() {
        employeeNames = new Vector();
        vendorNames = new Vector();
    }

    public void addEmployee(String empName) {
        employeeNames.add(empName);
    }

    public void addVendor(String vendName) {
        vendorNames.add(vendName);
    }
}
```

Company contains the implementation of adding *Employees* and *Vendors* in the same class. What would happen if the preceding code excerpt were representative of a large application with many programmers? If the application needed modifications to both the vendor and employee code, and the modifications were assigned to different programmers, then the programmers would have a very difficult task working together. They could easily erase or clobber each other's code because they would have to modify the same class. This is a simple example, but is a real concern in a real class containing much more code.

The representations of *Employees* and *Vendors* should be separated from each other. *Company* should still be able to access information about both, but there is no reason to keep the employee list and the vendor list implementations so closely coupled. To illustrate this point, we'll modify the design to expand the code into three classes.

Company.java

```
public class Company {
   private Employees employees;
   private Vendors vendors;

   public Company() {
      employees = new Employees();
      vendors = new Vendors();
   }

   public void addEmployeeName(String empName) {
      employees.addEmployeeName(empName);
   }

   public void addVendorName(vendName) {
      vendors.addVendorName(vendName);
   }
}
```

Employees.java

```
public class Employees {
   private Vector employeeNames;

   public Employees() {
      employeeNames = new Vector();
   }

   public void addEmployeeName(String empName) {
      employeeNames.add(empName);
   }
}
```

Vendors.java

```
public class Vendors {
   private Vector vendorNames;

   public Vendors() {
      vendorNames = new Vector();
   }

   public void addVendorName(String vendName) {
      vendorNames.add(vendName);
   }
}
```

The problem of two programmers working on the same class is now solved. One programmer can work on *Vendors*, while the other works on *Employees*. Another benefit of this change is that *Vendors* and *Employees* can undergo substantial revision without affecting any other class but themselves. For example, the programmer who is working on *Vendors* could change the representation of the *vendorNames* from a *Vector* to a *String* array without affecting the *Company* or *Employees* class.

This example illustrates a key distinction in encapsulation: the implementation versus the interface. In this context, interface does not necessarily mean a Java *interface*, although many interfaces to implementations are defined as such. This refers to a conceptual interface that outside classes use to access internal data. In the preceding example, the *Vendors* programmer can modify *vendorNames* (the implementation) without changing how other classes access *addVendorName* methods (its interface). As long as the interface's parameter list and return type don't change, you can change your implementation without affecting other classes in your application.

Knowing What Visibility Is Appropriate

As we have seen, making your code modular allows outside code to talk to your class' interface without having to know or depend on the implementation. Even though modularity helps enforce the use of an interface, programmers may still be able to circumvent how you intended them to use your code unless you give the appropriate visibility to the members. The following example defines a class *EmployeeInfo* and another class, *Accessor*, which uses *EmployeeInfo*.

EmployeeInfo.java

```
public class EmployeeInfo {
   public String firstName;
   public String lastName;
   public int salary;

   public EmployeeInfo() {}


   //Define the interface (accessor) methods for EmployeeInfo
   public void setFirstName(String fName) {
      firstName = fName.trim(); //remove leading or trailing spaces
   }

   public void setLastName(String lName) {
```

```
            lastName = lName.trim(); //remove leading or trailing spaces
        }

        public void setSalary(int sal) {
            if (sal > 0) //can't have a negative salary
                salary = sal;
        }
    }
```

The preceding class is used to store employee information. I created the application programming interface (API) to check the first name, last name, and salary before accepting them. Now, pretend someone else has written the following *Accessor* class.

Accessor.java

```
public class Accessor {
    public static populateData(EmployeeInfo eInfo) {
        eInfo.firstName = "  Sarah ";
        eInfo.lastName = "  Grande";
        eInfo.setSalary(-50000);
    }
}
```

Although I intended the accessor methods *setSalary(), setFirstName(),* and *setLastName()* to be the Interface to *EmployeeInfo*, another programmer evidently thought differently when writing *Accessor*. Because I gave others the ability to access my instance variables directly, I opened the door to letting them use my class in an unintended way. As a result, I gave my instance variables a visibility that is inappropriate to my goal of having others access my class only through the accessor methods.

One quick fix to EmployeeInfo is to change the visibility of the instance variables from *public* to *private*. This change is fine, but I would like to show you a different technique. Java allows you to divide the interface from the implementation more explicitly by defining an *interface* for the implementation class. The following code excerpt illustrates this facility.

EmployeeInfo.java

```
public interface EmployeeInfo {
   public void setFirstName(String fName);
   public void setLastName(String lName);
   public void setSalary(int sal);
}
```

EmployeeInfoImpl.java

```
public class EmployeeInfoImpl implements EmployeeInfo {
   private String firstName;
   private String lastName;
   private int salary;

   private EmployeeInfoImpl() {}

   public static EmployeeInfo create() {
      return (EmployeeInfo)(new EmployeeInfoImpl());
   }

   //Define the interface (accessor) methods for EmployeeInfo
   public void setFirstName( String fName) {
      firstName = fName.trim(); //remove leading or trailing spaces
   }

   public void setLastName( String lName) {
      lastName = lName.trim(); //remove leading or trailing spaces
   }

   public void setSalary( int sal) {
      if (sal > 0) //can't have a negative salary
         salary = sal;
   }
}
```

By providing the *EmployeeInfo* interface, we have explicitly defined which methods are intended for outside access. In fact, we have it set up so that an outside class cannot even create an *EmployeeInfoImpl* instance, because its constructor is declared *private.* Thus, we have enforced that others go through the *EmployeeInfo* interface and we have completely hidden the implementation outside *EmployeeInfoImpl.*

CERTIFICATION OBJECTIVE 7.02

Designing and Implementing Tightly Encapsulated Classes

Building on the distinctions of appropriate visibility and modularity, we will implement the framework of an object-oriented system. Here we will not have any code with which to work. Rather, we will only have a high-level description of the real-world model that we will make. The description of our application follows:

```
Create an object-oriented model for an inventory system. The
inventory has products and orders. Each product has a name and
a price. An order has one or more items in it. These order items
have to know what product is ordered and the quantity of items
ordered. Finally, an outside system needs some mechanism of
placing a new order and determining that order's total cost.
```

This high-level design only mentions a few of the components necessary for a fully functional inventory system, but it is sufficient for a simple object-oriented application.

Designing for Modularity

We will make this system modular by dividing the inventory system into separate concepts and determining their relationships with each other. We will not decide how these concepts will be implemented at this point, because that introduces a level of detail that is not yet necessary. The goal is to understand how the objects relate in the real world. Once we know that, we can express that relationship in Java.

When talking about the inventory system, we are describing something that appears, at least indirectly, to contain the concepts previously mentioned. In other words, the inventory *has a* list of available products rather than the available products having an inventory. In addition, the inventory system contains a list of orders, not vice versa. To take this idea of containment further, each order contains a list of the items in that order, and each order item contains exactly one product.

Stating the containment relationships of each concept gives us an insight into an approach for modularity. The concepts that we discussed earlier (inventory, orders, and products) are contained and are containers at some point, so it would be best to refer to them as independent entities. Other concepts that we did not mention, such as the product's price, are so integral to another concept (in this case, the product) that it would not be very useful to separate them into their own objects.

Designing for Appropriate Visibility

Now that we have determined how we want this system modularized, we will determine the information in each object that we want to be visible to other objects. The key here is to know what information each object will need in order to perform the tasks requested. For our design, we need the objects to be sufficiently visible for an outside system to create a new order and determine the order's cost.

To create a new order, an outside system will need to be able to tell the inventory system to do so. We also need the inventory system to place that order in the list of orders known by the inventory system. Furthermore, the order needs to be able to create a new item for each product in the order and add the order item to the list of items known by the order. The design didn't specifically state what information it would provide when creating new orders, but we have to know the products ordered and the number of items ordered. Therefore, we will assume that is the information provided.

Determining an order's cost doesn't really require anything out of the inventory system; the outside system just needs to query the order itself. To figure this calculation, the order needs to access the number of products in each item and the item's products. The order will then need to retrieve the price of the product.

Writing Encapsulated Classes

Given the visibility and modularity required for our object-oriented inventory system, we can now write the code. We can also use the description of our system from the previous two sections to comment our code so that other programmers will understand our justification for our design.

The code in this section is somewhat over-commented, but it should help you understand how a conceptual design is transformed into working code. I have also left out most of the class constructors and all of the method bodies. Other accessor methods that are not required for this limited example are omitted as well. Thus, this code is incomplete and will not compile.

InventorySystem.java

```
package com.acme.inventorysystem;
import java.util.Vector;

public class InventorySystem {
  /** The internal representation of the available products is private
   * because its implementation is irrelevant to outside classes.
   */
   private Vector availableProducts;

  /** The internal representation of the orders is also private.
   */
   private Vector currentOrders;

  /** createNewOrder() is public because outside systems need to be
   * able to create new orders. We assume that the outside system
   * will pass in the products and number of items ordered. This
   * constructor should also add the new instance to currentOrders.
   */
   public Order createNewOrder(Product [] products,
     int [] numItemsOrdered) {
     /* Body omitted */
     return null;
   }
}
```

Order.java

```
package com.acme.inventorysystem;
import java.util.Vector;

public class Order {
  /** The internal representation of the orderItems is private
   * because its implementation is irrelevant to outside classes.
   */
   private Vector orderItems;

  /** The constructor has default (package) visibility because
   * we do not want the outside system to create an order
   * without going through the InventorySystem's createNewOrder().
   * We do want other classes in this package to access it though.
   */
   Order(Product [] products, int [] numItemsOrdered) {
     /* Body omitted */ }
```

```
   /** computeCost() is public because the outside system needs to be
    * able to determine the cost of an order.
    */
    public double computeCost() {
     /* Body omitted */
     return 0.0;
    }
}
```

OrderItem.java

```
package com.acme.inventorysystem;
import java.util.Vector;

public class OrderItem {
   /** getProduct() has protected visibility because Order, another
    * class in this package needs access, but classes in
    * the outside system should not access this directly. We do
    * allow other classes in this package to access this, however.
    */
    protected Product getProduct() {
       /* Body omitted */
       return null;
   }

   /** numberOrdered() has protected visibility because Order,
    * another class in this package needs access, but classes in the
    * outside system should not access this directly. We do
    * allow other classes in this package to access this, however.
    */
    protected int numberOrdered() {
       /* Body omitted */
       return 0;
    }
}
```

Product.java

```
package com.acme.inventorysystem;
import java.util.Vector;

public class Product {
   /** getCost() is protected because Order, another class in this
    * package needs access, but classes in the outside system should
    * not access this directly.
    */
```

```
        protected double getCost() {
            /* Body omitted */
            return 0.0;
        }

       /** getName() is protected because though other classes in this
        * package may need access, but the outside system should not
        * access this directly.
        */
        protected String getName() {
            /* Body omitted */
            return null;
        }
    }
```

The preceding code has implemented the inventory system with the precise modularity and visibility required by the design. There is one more aspect of encapsulated design that should be mentioned. Although proper visibility is important to program design, so is maintenance. We may want an outside system to access the name and cost of *Product* in the future, so it may not be a bad idea to make those accessor methods public. Otherwise, we will have to change the code later. Appropriate visibility still applies here, although what is appropriate may be what you anticipate users will need to access for the life of your code.

on the Job

A knowledge of object-oriented techniques, including encapsulation, is essential to working on a software development team. Many productivity studies estimate a tenfold increase in productivity among programmers who know these techniques. There are many excellent books about object-oriented design on the market.

Benefits of Encapsulation

Because we wrote the inventory system with tightly encapsulated classes, we receive many benefits that will pay off later. We have hidden the implementation details of each class, and that will help if we need to *maintain* the code. For example, if we needed to change how we represented the *OrderItem* list in *Orders*, we would only have to change Orders. It is much easier to modify one class than to propagate changes throughout our inventory system.

Another benefit of encapsulation is *extensibility*, or the ease with which we can add to our existing code. If we had implemented the inventory system as one class, we would have to consider the ramifications to the entire system when adding functionality because we would have had interdependent code. Making a change in a large body of code also increases the chances that you will introduce a bug when adding a feature. For our code, suppose we needed to add billing statements to our inventory system. All we would have to do is to add a new *BillingStatement* class that has access to the `Orders` on the statement. We would not need to concern ourselves with the effect of this change on *OrderItem*, *Product*, or *InventorySystem*, because we have written modular code.

A final benefit from encapsulation is code *clarity*. Our code is very easy to understand for a new programmer because the code is divided along conceptual lines. Reading through large sections of code that serves many purposes is difficult because you cannot be sure what purpose eah piece of code serves. How our code is meant to be used is also clear because we make explicit visibilty rules that are enforced when instance variables and methods are accessible.

EXERCISE 7-1

Creating an Encapsulated Class

In this exercise, we are going to create a class with a tightly encapsulated API. This means the implementation details of the class will be hidden from programmers using the class, but methods that allow interaction will be public. We will create a class that averages a series of numbers. The programmer can add numbers to the object using the API and at any time request the average of all the numbers fed to it.

1. Create a class and call it Average. The API will contain a constructor, a method to add a number to the object, and a method to retrieve the average of all the numbers added to it.
2. The class will contain a double variable of the average. This will be kept private.
3. Create a method to allow the class to return the average of all numbers fed to it.
4. When a number is added to the class it will calculate a new average. The calculation for this is:

   ```
   avg = ((avg * total) + num)/(++total);
   ```

5. As you can see in the calculation, we will need to keep track of the total numbers added to the object. Make this variable private as well, since anyone

using this class never needs to know about this variable (we are hiding the implementation details).

The final code should look something like this:

```
class Average {
   private double avg;
   private int total;

   public Average() {
      total = 0;
      avg = 0.0;
   }

   public void store(double num) {
      avg = ((avg * total) + num)/(++total);
   }

   public double getAverage() {
      return avg;
   }

   public static void main(String [] args) {
      Average a = new Average();
      a.store(4);
      a.store(6);
      a.store(8);
      System.out.println("Average = " + a.getAverage());
   }
```

CERTIFICATION OBJECTIVE 7.03

Describing is a and has a Class Relationships

An often misunderstood distinction in object-oriented programming, and on the Java certification exam, is the difference between *is a* and *has a* class relationships. The confusion occurs when programmers have to determine whether one concept is a subclass of the other or is contained by the other. This section examines two implementations of the same set of classes to illustrate the distinction.

Building.java

```
public class Building {
    long length;
    long width;

    public Building(long len, long wid) {
        length = len;
        width = wid;
    }

    public long area() {
        return length * width;
    }
}
```

OfficeRoom.java

```
public class OfficeRoom extends Building {
    public OfficeRoom(long len, wid) {
        super(len, wid);
    }
}
```

This first implementation seems reasonable at first glance. We even use inheritance so that we do not have to rewrite the computation of area. This example, however, fails a fundamental rule of inheritance. One class may only be a subclass of another class, or an implementation of an *interface*, if the former *is a* type of the latter. In other words, *OfficeRoom* should not be a subclass of *Building*, because an office room is not a type of building; rather, a building *has an* office room.

The problem with this design becomes evident as you extend the functionality of Building. If we added an address and a janitorial service to *Building*, what would that say about an *OfficeRoom*? A room in an office does not usually have its own assigned janitor or address, but *OfficeRoom* would inherit those characteristics from *Building*. We could make the janitor and address attributes *private* so that they would not be visible to *OfficeRoom*, but we would block those characteristics to other potential subclasses of *Building*, like *House* or *Headquarters*, which may need those attributes.

The confusion here occurs because there are some overlapping characteristics between an office room and a building. The relationship is not an *is a* one, however. The key here is to recognize that the wrong relationship between these concepts makes adding a subclass a poor approach. The following code offers an alternative.

Building.java

```
public class Building {
    long length;
    long width;

    // The building has a number of office rooms:
    OfficeRoom [] officeRooms;

    public Building(long len, long wid, OfficeRoom [] ors) {
        length = len;
        width = wid;
        officeRooms = ors;
    }

    public long area() {
        return length * width;
    }
}
```

OfficeRoom.java

```
public class OfficeRoom {
    long length;
    long width;

    public OfficeRoom(long len, wid) {
        super(len, wid);
    }

    public long area() {
        return length * width;
    }
}
```

We see now how to code *has a* relationships between classes. A *Building* contains (in this case as an array) a number of *OfficeRoom* objects as shown in Figure 7-1. Now we can modify *Building* without having to consider the effects of *OfficeRoom*

FIGURE 7-1 Understanding *is a* and *has a* relationships

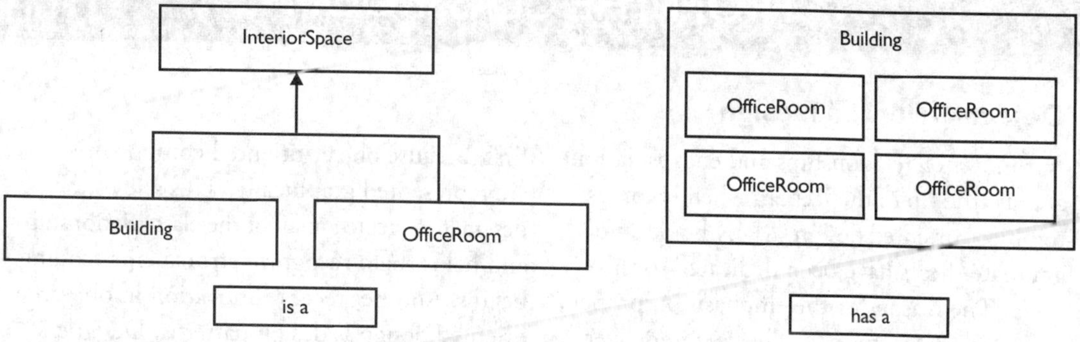

because of inheritance. We do have to write the *area* method a second time, but that is a small price to pay. If we wanted to, we could write a superclass, possibly called *InteriorSpace*, for both classes that implements area (Figure 7-1). Writing such a class is out of the scope of the exam, though.

exam Watch ***Ask yourself two questions when determining if the relationship between classes is "is a" or "has a." First ask: "Is the first class (for example, a circle) a type of the latter class (for example, a shape)?" If so, then the relationship is "is a." You also may ask: "Does the first class (for example, a building) contain one or more of the second class' type (for example, rooms)?" If so, then the relationship is "has a."***

Now that we have discussed some distinctions in object-oriented design, here are some possible scenario questions and their solutions.

SCENARIO & SOLUTION

What benefits do you gain from encapsulation?	Ease of code maintenance, extensibility, and code clarity.
What is the object-oriented relationship between a tree and an oak?	An *is a* relationship.
What is the object-oriented relationship between a city and a road?	A *has a* relationship.

FROM THE CLASSROOM

Object-Oriented Design

Is a and *has a* relationships and encapsulation are just the tip of the iceberg when it comes to object-oriented design. Many books and graduate theses have been dedicated to this topic. The reason for the emphasis on proper design is simple: money. The cost to deliver a software application has been estimated to be as much as 10 times more expensive for poorly designed programs. Having seen the ramifications of poor designs, I can assure you that this estimate is not far fetched.

Even the best object-oriented designers make mistakes. It is difficult to visualize the relationships between hundreds, or even thousands, of classes. When mistakes are discovered during the implantation (code writing) phase of a project, the amount of code that has to be rewritten can sometimes cause programming teams to start over from scratch.

The software industry has evolved to aid the designer. Visual object modeling languages, such as the Unified Modeling Language (UML), allow designers to design and easily modify classes without having to write code first, because object-oriented components are represented graphically. This allows the designer to create a map of the class relationships and helps them recognize errors before coding begins. Another recent innovation in object-oriented design is design patterns. Designers noticed that many object-oriented designs apply consistently from project to project, and that it was useful to apply the same designs because it reduced the potential to introduce new design errors. Object-oriented designers then started to share these designs with each other. Now, there are many catalogs of these design patterns both on the Internet and in book form.

Although passing the Java certification exam does not require you to understand object-oriented design this thoroughly, hopefully this background information will help you better appreciate why the test writers chose to include encapsulation and *is a* and *has a* relationships on the exam.

—Jonathan Meeks, Sun Certified Java Programmer

CERTIFICATION OBJECTIVE 7.04

Invoking Overridden or Overloaded Methods

Java and other object-oriented languages allow classes to have multiple methods with the same name. Knowing which of the identically named methods is called will frequently be asked on the exam. Specifically, the exam tests your knowledge about overloaded and overridden methods. Methods are *overloaded* when there are multiple methods in the same class with the same names, but with different parameter lists (arguments). Methods are *overridden* when the subclass has a method with the same name, parameter list, and return type as the superclass.

Let's start with an example to illustrate a simple case of overloaded methods.

```
public class MyTest {
   public void printNumbers(int a, int b) {
      System.out.println(a);
      System.out.println(b);
   }

   public void printNumbers(int a, int b, int c) {
      System.out.println(a);
      System.out.println(b);
      System.out.println(c);
   }
}
```

The compiler will know which *printNumbers* to call based on the parameter list. If there are two arguments, it will call the former, and if there are three arguments, it will call the latter method.

The following is an example to illustrate a simple case of overridden methods.

MyParent.java

```
public class MyParent {
   public void printClassName () {
```

```
        System.out.println("MyParent");
    }
}
```

MyChild.java

```
public class MyChild extends MyParent {
    public void printClassName() {
        System.out.println("MyChild");
    }
}
```

The compiler is able to determine which *printClassName* is called, depending on the object on which the method is called. If the object is a *MyChild*, then the output will be MyChild. If the object is a *MyParent*, then the output will be MyParent.

exam Watch

The rules that determine which overloaded and overridden methods are called are quite tricky. The exam will present methods that will violate the rules and result in compiler errors. Pay very close attention to the next two sections, and note which parameter lists are valid for overloaded and overridden methods.

Properly Overridden Methods

The most obvious overridden method is like the one in the previous section in which the keywords, the visibility, and the thrown exceptions are identical. (In the previous section there were no exceptions thrown or special keywords.) The return types and parameter lists must be identical, but other keywords in the method can differ between the parent and the subclass.

An overridden method may be made more *public* than the method in the parent class. It may not be made more *private*, or *restrictive*. In other words, a subclass may not change the interface of the parent class. Therefore, the following code will not compile because the *print()* is *private* in the subclass, whereas it is *public* in the superclass.

```
public class MySuperClass {
    public void print() {
    }
}

public class MySubClass extends MySuperClass {
    private void print() {
    }
}
```

The exceptions thrown by a subclass' method may be equal to or fewer than those thrown in the superclass' method. The overridden method must explicitly declare which methods it can throw, however. An overridden method does not *inherit* the exceptions thrown by the superclass.

Although it is fairly simple to realize that an overridden method can have fewer exceptions than in the superclass without adding any new exceptions, there is one subtle case that looks incorrect but actually is a valid overridden method.

```
public class MySuperClass {
   public void setID( int id) throws Exception {
   }
}

public class MySubClass extends MySuperClass {
   public void setID( int id) throws NullPointerException {
   }
}
```

The preceding example looks as if the overridden *setID()* method is adding an exception not listed in *MySuperClass*. This is not the case, though, because *NullPointerException* is a subclass of *Exception* (see Chapter 5. Therefore, *NullPointerException* is an *Exception*, so the preceding example illustrates a valid overridden method.

There is one final caveat that should be mentioned concerning overridden methods. The keyword *synchronized* may appear in overridden methods as a trick question on the exam. An overridden method and the method in the superclass may declare their methods *synchronized* independently of one another. In other words, if the superclass method is synchronized and the subclass is not, the classes will still compile (and vice versa).

Overridden Methods and Underlying Types

We now know which overridden methods are valid, but there can occasionally be some ambiguity as to which method is called in special situations. Examine the following code:

```
class A {
   public void print() {
      System.out.println('A');
   }
}
```

```
class B extends A {
    public void print() {
        System.out.println('B');
    }
}

class Test {
    public static void main(String [] args) {
        A a = new A();
        B b = new B();
        A a2 = new B();

        a.print();
        b.print();
        a2.print();
    }
}
```

In the preceding example, it is easy to determine that the first two print() calls will have *A* and *B* as output, respectively. However, what about the third *print()* call? The answer depends on the *underlying type* of the object, or the type of the object that is created. The fact that the object is cast to type A is irrelevant. Because the third object is created as type B, the *print()* call will call the method in B and have *B* as output.

Properly Overloaded Methods

There is only one criterion for determining whether overloaded methods can compile: all of the overloaded methods must have parameter lists that are unique enough for Java to know which method to call. Return types, visibility, thrown exceptions, and keywords play no part in determining valid overloaded methods.

For simple overloaded methods where there are different numbers of parameters, it is easy to determine which overloaded method is called. Examine the following example:

```
public class Test {
    //first print method
    private void print() {
    }

    //second print method
    private void print(int j) {
```

```
        }

        public static void main(String [] args) {
            Test t = new Test();
            t.print(3);
        }
    }
```

Because there is only one *print()* method with one parameter, it is obvious that the second `print` method will be called in *main()*. When there are overloaded methods that have the same number of parameters and very similar types in the parameter list, determining which methods will be called—or if the code will compile—is more difficult (and more likely to be tested for the exam).

```
public class Test {
    //first print method
    public void print(int a, long b, long c) {
        System.out.println("First");
    }

    //second print method
    public void print( long a, long b, long c) {
        System.out.println("Second");
    }
}
```

If we call *print(1, 2, 3)*, what will happen? The answer is that the code would call the first method because the parameters most closely match its parameter list. Java only has to cast two of the three parameters for the first method, but it would have to cast all three from *int* to `long` for the second method. If I called *print(1L, 2L, 3L)*, however, the code would call the second method. The first *print()* cannot accept the first parameter in *print(1L, 2L, 3L)* because `long` requires a greater degree of precision than `int`. Java always chooses the overloaded method with the closest matching parameter list that isn't more specific than the parameters allow. Let's examine another example:

```
public class SecondTest {
    //first print method
    public void print(int a, long b, long c) {
    }

    //second print method
```

```
        public void print(long a, int b, long c) {
        }

        public static void main(String [] args) {
            new SecondTest().print(1, 2, 3);
        }
    }
```

The final scenario that I will discuss is when neither overloaded method more closely matches the other. The preceding code example does not compile because the appropriate *print()* method call is ambiguous. Strangely enough, if we were to change the *print()* call to *print(1L, 2, 3),* the code would compile because only one of the methods (the second one) allows a long in the first parameter. Thus, it is the method calls themselves that determine overloaded method ambiguity. One exception to this is if the parameter lists are identical. Overloaded methods with identical parameter lists never compile, regardless of the method calls to them.

exam Watch

Methods can be overloaded by different arguments, not by different return type. It is the number of arguments, the type of arguments, and the order of the type of arguments that matters.

EXERCISE 7-2

Calling Overloading Methods

In order to become more familiar with calling overloaded methods, let's try to create some overloaded methods in actual code. We will create a class with three methods. Each method will have a different parameter list of arguments. The actual method itself will just output a word belonging to a sentence, and it will be up to you to call these methods in the proper order in order to output a sentence.

1. Create a class and create three methods with identical names.
2. The return types of the methods are irrelevant, but the arguments must all be unique. You can choose any arguments you like.

3. The output from each method will produce one word to the screen. You can choose any words you like. At this point, the program should compile, as long as the parameter list for each method is slightly different

4. Now try calling your methods from the main method. If there is any ambiguity as to which method you intend to call, the code will produce a compile error.

The final code should look something like the following code. Note that I added a small HasA class to make the output of this program more relevant—this is not required, however.

```
class HasA {}

class IsA extends HasA {
   public static void sayIt(int a, long b) {
      System.out.println(" HasA ");
   }

   public static void sayIt(int a, double b) {
      System.out.print(" is a ");
   }

   public static void sayIt(int a, int b) {
      System.out.print(" IsA ");
   }

   public static void main(String [] args) {
      sayIt(1,1);
      sayIt(1,1.0);
      sayIt(1,1L);
   }
}
```

When this code is executed, the result is as follows:

```
IsA  is a  HasA
```

CERTIFICATION OBJECTIVE 7.05

Invoking Parental or Overloaded Constructors

Class constructors are able to call overloaded constructors both in their class and in their superclass. To call another constructor in the same class, you can call *this()* in the first line of the body in the calling constructor. Placing *this()* in any other place will result in a compiler error.

```
public class MyClass {
   String title;

   //Calling constructor
   public MyClass() {
      this("Default Title");
      //rest of the body
   }

   //Called constructor
   public MyClass(String t) {
      title = t;
   }
}
```

In the preceding example, the calling constructor calls the second constructor with a default title. The second constructor executes its body before returning, and the calling constructor then executes the remainder of its body.

In addition to being able to call another constructor in the same class, you can also call a superclass constructor from the subclass constructor method. The rules for using super() are similar to this() (such a call must also be placed in the first line of the constructor), but there are a few effects that are different.

```
public class MySuper {
   //first constructor
   public MySuper() {
      System.out.println("Super1");
   }

   //second constructor
```

```
    public MySuper( String title) {
        System.out.println("Super2");
    }
}

public class MySub extends MySuper {
    //first constructor
    public MySub() {
        super("the title");
        System.out.println("Sub1");
    }

    //second constructor
    public MySub(String title) {
        System.out.println("Sub2");
    }
}
```

The first *MySub()* is fairly straightforward. *MySub()* first calls the second constructor in *MySuper,* prints out *Super2,* and then finishes calling the remainder of the *MySub()* and prints out `Sub1`.

The second *MySub()* is a little less obvious. Every class constructor, when that class extends another, always calls *super().* If there is not an explicit *super()* call in the constructor, Java will call one with no arguments. Therefore, the second `MySub` constructor first calls the no-args *MySuper(),* prints *Super1,* and then executes the rest of *MySub's* second constructor and prints *Sub2.*

exam Watch

Many people get confused about the differences between this() and super() on the exam because the functionality is similar. Remember that a constructor always calls super() (possibly implicitly) when that class extends another. The constructor this() is never called unless it is explicitly invoked. Calls to this() and super() cannot be used in the same constructor—it will not compile.

If the no-args constructor is not present in *MySuper,* then the code will not compile. This scenario is very easy to overlook on the exam. Even though super() is not explicitly called, Java will expect a no-args constructor in the superclass if a subclass constructor does not explicitly invoke another superclass constructor. Keep in mind that if no constructor is provided for a class, then Java will supply a default no-args constructor. When you have written your own constructors, Java will not automatically supply the no-args constructor.

The following example code demonstrates these concepts:

```
public class A {
   public A( String title) {
      System.out.println("A");
   }
}

public class B extends A {
   public B( String title) {
      System.out.println("B");
   }
}
```

Looking at the preceding code you might think all is well, but in fact, it will not compile because B() implicitly calls a no-args constructor for A, but a no-args version of A() is not defined. Because we wrote the constructor A(String title) for A, Java did not create a default no-args constructor.

Now that you have a better understanding of overriding and overloading methods and constructors, here are some possible scenario questions and their solutions.

SCENARIO & SOLUTION

What is the one valid criterion that determines if overloaded methods are valid?	The parameter lists for each must be different enough so that finding the matching method for every method call is unambiguous.
What elements of overridden methods must be identical?	The parameter list and the return type.
Which internal constructor keyword may be called implicitly?	super()

CERTIFICATION SUMMARY

This chapter covered general design considerations of object-oriented programming and the finer points of overloaded and overridden methods. An understanding of encapsulation, or the hiding of implementation details to other modules, will help you with the encapsulation-specific questions on the exam and give you the background knowledge needed to understand and answer other questions on the exam.

The distinction between *is a* and *has a* relationships will help you answer questions on the exam that ask you to choose the best object-oriented design. These questions can be especially tricky because the code for each answer may compile correctly. This distinction will also prove useful outside the exam, as it is the source of many poor designs.

Overloading and overriding methods may appear similar on the surface, because they both involve multiple methods with the same name, but the rules governing both differ. Overloaded methods must only have unique parameter lists to determine which calls are handled by which methods. Overridden methods, on the other hand, must have the same return type and parameter lists as the superclass method that is being overridden. Specific rules determine the allowable differences in method visibility and thrown exceptions of overridden methods.

Finally, you can use *this()* and *super()* in a class constructor to call constructors in the same class or in the parent class, respectively. It is important to note that *super()* is always called in a constructor when its class extends another, and that the default *super()* requires a no-args constructor in the parent class.

✓ TWO-MINUTE DRILL

Here are some of the key points from each certification objective in Chapter 7.

Encapsulation in Object-Oriented Design

- ❑ Encapsulated code uses modularity and appropriate visibility to separate the interface from the implementation.

Designing and Implementing Tightly Encapsulated Classes

- ❑ In encapsulation, an interface defines the methods and instance variables to which other classes and packages have access. The implementation contains the "under the hood" details that are not visible outside that class or package.

Describing is a and has a Class Relationships

- ❑ An is a relationship occurs when the subclass is a type of the superclass or interface.
- ❑ A has a relationship occurs when one class is contained by another class.

Invoking Overridden or Overloaded Methods

- ❑ Overloaded methods are methods with the same name in the same class type.
- ❑ Overloaded methods only have to have the same method name. The parameter list must vary. The return type, the visibility, and the exceptions thrown may optionally vary.

- Overridden methods are methods with the same name and parameter list that exist in different classes in a class hierarchy.
- Overridden methods must have the same method name and parameter list. The accessibility of an overriding method (the method in the child class) may not be more restrictive.
- The exception thrown by an overriding method must be equal to or a subclass down in the hierarchy of the exceptions thrown by the overridden method. It is also legal for the overriding method to not throw any exceptions at all.
- The overridden method that is called is determined by the underlying object's type, not the type to which the object is cast.

Invoking Parental or Overloaded Constructors

- Use *this()* to call another constructor from the body of a constructor in the same class. The parameters in *this()* must match the parameter list you intend to call.
- Use *super()* to call a parental constructor from the body of a constructor in the child class. The parameters in *super()* must match the parameter list you intend to call.
- The call to *this()* or *super()* must be made in the first line of the constructor. Calls to *this()* or *super()* cannot be used in the same constructor.
- When a constructor does not have an explicit *super()* call, Java will automatically call a no-args *super()*.
- You will get a compiler error when you have either an explicit or an implicit no-args *super()* call when you do not have a no-args constructor in the parent class. Keep in mind, though, that Java will automatically include a no-args constructor when that class doesn't have any other constructor written.

SELF TEST

The following questions will help you measure your understanding of the material presented in this chapter. Read all of the choices carefully, as there may be more than one correct answer. Choose all correct answers for each question.

Encapsulation in Object-Oriented Design

1. Methods and variables that do the background work of a class are known as implementation details. The implementation details of a tightly encapsulated class should be given which access?

A. Public

B. The default

C. Private

D. Protected

E. It does not matter

Designing and Implementing Tightly Encapsulated Classes

2. Which of the following is *not* a benefit of encapsulation?

A. Clarity of code

B. Code efficiency

C. The ability to add functionality later on

D. Modification requires less coding changes

Describing is a and has a Class Relationships

3. Given:

```
public class Rectangle {
}

public class Square extends Rectangle {
}
```

What is the relationship between *Rectangle* and *Square*?

A. has a

B. is a

C. It's both an *is a* and *has a* relationship.

D. The relationship is neither an *is a* or a *has a* relationship.

4. Given:

```
public class Vehicle {
   private Engine theEngine
}

public class Engine {
}
```

What is the relationship between *Vehicle* and *Engine*?

A. has a

B. is a

C. It's both an *is a* and *has a* relationship.

D. The relationship is neither an *is a* or a *has a* relationship.

5. Given:

```
public interface Moveable {
   public void moveObject();
}

public class Bitmap implements Moveable {
   public void moveObject() {
      //body omitted
   }
}
```

What is the relationship between *Movable* and *Bitmap*?

A. has a

B. is a

C. It's both an *is a* and *has a* relationship.

D. The relationship is neither an *is a* nor a *has a* relationship.

Invoking Overridden or Overloaded Methods

6. Given:

```
class SuperTest {
    public double getNumber() {
        return Math.random() * 100;
    }
}

class Test extends SuperTest {
    public int getNumber() {
        return (int)(Math.random() * 100);
    }
    public static void main(String [] args) {
        Test t = new Test();
        System.out.println(t.getNumber());
    }
}
```

Which of these results could occur from this code? (Choose all that apply.)

A. 59

B. 34.234

C. 134.234

D. 134

E. 100

F. This code will not compile.

7. Given:

```
class SuperTest {
    public double getNumber() {
        return Math.random() * 100;
    }
}

class Test extends SuperTest {
    public int getNumber(int max) {
        return (int)(Math.random() * max);
    }

    public Integer getNumber(int max) {
```

```
13.         int temp = (int)(Math.random() * max);
14.         return new Integer(temp);
15.     }
16.
17.     public static void main(String [] args) {
18.         Test t = new Test();
19.         System.out.println(t.getNumber());
20.     }
21. }
```

Which of these statements is true?

A. The code will not compile correctly because line 19 is trying to call a method that does not exist for the class Test.

B. The code does not compile because of line 12.

C. The code does not compile because of line 14.

D. There is no ambiguity as to the return type in line 12; therefore, this code will compile and output a double value greater than or equal to 0 and less than 100.

E. This code will not compile because the *getNumber()* methods in the Test class must all have return types of double.

8. Given:

```
1.  public class A {
2.     public static void main(String [] args) {
3.        new A().printResult(1, "abc", 4);
4.     }
5.     private void printResult(int a, long b, int c) {
6.        System.out.println(a + b + c);
7.     }
8.     private void printResult(long a, String b, int c) {
9.        System.out.println(a + b + c);
10.    }
11. }
```

Which of these statements is true?

A. The code will not compile correctly because a long and a String may not be added together in line 9.

B. The code will compile and run and will display *1abc4* in the standard output.

C. The code will compile and run and will display *11234* in the standard output.

D. The code will compile and will throw a NumberFormatException.

9. When a subclass method has the same name, parameter list, and return type as a method in the parent class, this method is said to be what?

A. Extended

B. Overloaded

C. Overextended

D. Overridden

10. Which of the following must match exactly for overloaded methods to compile correctly? (Choose all that apply.)

A. The parameter list

B. The return type

C. The exceptions thrown

D. None of the above

11. Given:

```
public class Test {
    public static void main(String [] args) {
        new Test().foo(1, 2);
    }
    private void foo(int a, int b) {
        System.out.println("int");
    }
    private void foo(long a, int b) {
        System.out.println("long");
    }
}
```

What will happen when you compile and run this program?

A. The code will compile and run, and display *int.*

B. The code will compile and run, and display *long.*

C. The code will not compile.

D. The code will compile, but throw a runtime exception when executed.

12. Given:

```
public class Parent {
    public void execute() throws Exception {
```

```
        //body omitted
    }
}
public class Child extends Parent {
    private void execute() throws ClassCastException {
        //body omitted
    }
}
```

What will happen when you compile this program?

A. The program will compile successfully.

B. The program will not compile because the *execute()* in the subclass throws a different exception than in the parent class.

C. The program will not compile because the *execute()* in the subclass has less accessibility than in the parent class.

D. The program will not compile because the *execute()* in the subclass has less accessibility *and* throws a different exception than in the parent class.

13. Given:

```
public class A {
    public void baz() {
        System.out.println("A");
    }
}
public class B extends A {
    public static void main(String [] args) {
        A a = new B();
        a.baz();
    }
    public void baz() {
        System.out.println("B");
    }
}
```

What will happen when you compile and run this program?

A. The program compiles, runs, and displays *A* in the standard output.

B. The program compiles, runs, and displays *B* in the standard output.

C. The program compiles, but throws a runtime exception.

D. The program does not compile.

14. Given:

```
public class A {
    public static void main( String [] args) {
        new A().baz(1, 2);
    }
    private void baz(int a, int b); {
        System.out.println("baz");
    }
    private void foo(int a, int b) {
        System.out.println("first");
    }
    private boolean foo(int a, int b) {
        System.out.println("second");
        return true;
    }
}
```

Which of the following statements is true?

A. The program compiles, runs, and displays *first* in the standard output.

B. The program compiles, runs, and displays *second* in the standard output.

C. The program compiles, runs, and displays *baz* in the standard output.

D. The program does not compile.

15. Given:

```
public class Test {
    protected void start() throws ClassCastException {
        //body omitted
    }
}

public class Child extends Test {
    public void start() throws Exception {
        //body omitted
    }
}
```

What will happen when you compile this program?

A. The program will compile successfully.

B. The program will not compile because the *start()* in the subclass throws a different exception than in the parent class.

C. The program will not compile because the *start()* in the subclass is public, whereas it is protected in the parent class.

D. The program will not compile because the *start()* in the subclass has different accessibility *and* throws a different exception than in the parent class.

16. When two or more methods in the same class have the same name, they are said to be what?

A. An implementation detail

B. Overridden

C. An interface

D. Overloaded

17. Given:

```
public class Example {
    public static void main( String [] args) {
        new Example ().locate( 1.0, 2);
    }
    private void locate ( double a, long b) {
        System.out.println( "double-long");
    }
    private void locate ( long a, int b) {
        System.out.println( "long-int");
    }
}
```

What will happen when you compile and run this program?

A. The code will compile, run, and display *double-long.*

B. The code will compile, run, and display *long-int.*

C. The code will not compile.

D. The code will compile, but throw a runtime exception when executed.

Invoking Parental or Overloaded Constructors

18. Given:

```
class SuperTest {
    public SuperTest() {
        System.out.print(" Super! ");
    }
}
```

```

class Test extends SuperTest {
    public static void main(String [] args) {
        new Test();
    }
    public Test() {
        super();
        this(" Great! ");
    }

    public Test(String name) {
        System.out.print(name);
    }
}
```

What is the result of this code?

A. Great! Super!

B. Super! Great!

C. Super! Super! Great!

D. Great!

E. Super!

F. This code will not compile.

19. Given:

```
1.  public class Test {
2.      public static void main(String [] args) {
3.          new Test(4);
4.      }
5.      public Test() {
6.          System.out.println("okay");
7.      }
8.      public Test(int i) {
9.
10.     }
11. }
```

Which of the following lines of code should be inserted at line 11 so that the output of the program is okay?

A. super();

B. this;

C. Test();

D. this();

E. super();

20. Given:

```
public class MySuper {
   public MySuper(int i) {
   }
}
public class MySub extends MySuper {
   public MySub() {
      super(2);
   }
}
```

Which of these statements is true?

A. The program does not compile because *MySuper* does not have a no-args constructor.

B. The program compiles, but throws a runtime exception when it cannot find the no-args *MySuper* constructor.

C. The program compiles and runs without error.

21. Given:

```
public class MySuper {
   public MySuper() {
      System.out.println( "MySuper");
   }
}

public class MySub extends MySuper {
   public static void main( String [] args) {
      new MySub();
   }
   public MySub() {
      System.out.println( "MySub");
   }
}
```

What will happen when you compile and run this program?

A. The program will compile, run, and will display *MySub* in the standard output.

B. The program will compile, run, and will display *MySuper* in the standard output.

C. The program will not compile.

D. The program will compile run, and will display *MySuper* and *MySub* in the standard output.

22. Given:

```
1.  public class Parent {
2.      public Parent() {
3.          System.out.println("good");
4.      }
5.      public Parent(int j) {
6.          System.out.println("bad");
7.      }
8.  }
9.  public class Example extends Parent {
10.     public static void main(String [] args) {
11.         new Example();
12.     }
13.     public Example() {
14.
15.     }
16. }
```

What code should be inserted in line 14 so that the output of the program is *good*?

A. this()

B. super

C. Parent()

D. Leave it blank.

SELF TEST ANSWERS

Encapsulation in Object-Oriented Design

1. ☑ C. *private* keeps other classes from viewing the implementation details, which is a primary goal of encapsulated classes.
   ☒ A is incorrect because it will allow any class to see the details. B and D are incorrect because these will allow other classes in the same package to see the details.

Designing and Implementing Tightly Encapsulated Classes

2. ☑ B. Encapsulation does not make code run any faster. It only keeps code more organized.
   ☒ A, C, and D are incorrect because all are direct benefits of code organization.

Describing *is a* and *has a* Class Relationships

3. ☑ B. Because *Square* extends *Rectangle*, and a square is a type of rectangle, the relationship is *is a*.
   ☒ A and C are both incorrect because *Square* does not contain *Rectangle*, or vice versa. D is incorrect because the relationship is one of *is a*.

4. ☑ A. *Vehicle* contains an instance variable pointing to an *Engine* reference, and a vehicle contains an engine.
   ☒ B and C are incorrect because this is not a case of one class containing another. D is incorrect because this is a case of *has a*.

5. ☑ B. Implementing an interface is another type of an *is a* relationship.
   ☒ A and C are incorrect because the type *Movable* does not contain a *Bitmap*. D is incorrect because the relationship is *is a*.

Invoking Overridden or Overloaded Methods

6. ☑ F. The problem lies in line 8. When a subclass overrides a superclass method, the return type must be the same. The only way to have this code compile successfully is to change the return type of Test.getNumber() to a double value (or by changing the return type of SuperTest.getNumber() to an int value).
☒ A, B, C, D, and E are all incorrect for the reasons stated above. If line 8 were fixed, then B would be the only possible answer.

7. ☑ B. Methods with the same name in the same class may not have the same method parameters as each other, even if the return type is different.
☒ A is incorrect because it inherits the no-arguments getNumber() method from SuperClass. C is incorrect because this is a valid way to create and return an Integer object. D is incorrect because return type is irrelevant when it comes to overloaded methods—it is the different argument parameters that matter. E is incorrect. Overloaded methods can have different return types.

8. ☑ B. The first argument is acceptably cast to a long.
☒ A is incorrect because adding a *String* to an *int* or a long is the same as string concatenation. C is incorrect because this output does not describe the effect of using + on a *String*. D is incorrect because this code runs without error.

9. ☑ D. Overridden methods have the same name, parameter list, and return type in the subclass as in the parent class.
☒ A is incorrect because it applies to a parent-child class relationship. B is incorrect because it refers to methods in the same class type with differing parameter lists. C is a nonsensical term.

10. ☑ D. Only the method name must match exactly for overloaded methods.
☒ A is incorrect because the parameter list should actually be different for overloaded methods. B is incorrect because the return type does not have to match exactly (although two methods with identical names and parameter lists are not allowed to have different return types). C is incorrect because exceptions only apply to overridden methods.

11. ☑ A. Although both methods seem like they could accept the method call, *foo(1, 2)* will print *int* because Java chooses the parameter list that is closest to the parameters in the call. *foo(1, 2)* would have to cast the first parameter from *int to long* in the second method, but no casting is needed for the first overloaded method.
☒ B is incorrect because it would only execute the second method with a call of *foo(1L, 2)*. C is incorrect because the code does in fact compile. D is incorrect because no runtime exceptions are thrown.

12. ☑ C. The only problem with this code is that the subclass version of *execute()* is private, whereas it is public in the parent class. Throwing a different exception is fine, as long as the exception in the subclass is a subset of that in the parent class.
☒ A is incorrect because this will not compile. B and D are incorrect because they all state that the *throws* clause is part of the problem, but in fact an overridden method can throw a subclass of the parent methods *throws* clause or no exceptions at all.

13. ☑ B. Although the object is cast as type A, the underlying type of the object upon which *baz()* is called is *type B.*
☒ A is incorrect because it claims that the method is called based on the type to which the object is cast, but in fact it is based on the object that it was initialized as. C is incorrect because no exception is thrown. D is incorrect because there are no compilation errors.

14. ☑ D. Even though *foo()* is never called, both parameter lists are identical. Therefore, we know that the parameter lists cannot ever be unique enough to distinguish one from the other. The *foo()* method at line 11 has a return value of boolean, but the code will still not compile because this does not distinguish overloaded methods.
☒ C is incorrect because the code doesn't compile. A and B are also incorrect because *foo()* is never called.

15. ☑ B. The problem here is that the exception in *Child* is more general than the one thrown in the parent class. Thus, the exception in *Child* is not a subclass of the one thrown in *Test.*
☒ A is incorrect because the program will not compile. C is incorrect because the subclass is more accessible, which is perfectly legal. D is incorrect for the same reason.

16. ☑ D. Methods in the same class with the same name are overloaded.
☒ A and C refer to terms used in encapsulation. B refers to methods with the same name in different classes.

17. ☑ A. 1.0 matches the double parameter in the first *locate()*, and 2 is cast up to a long.
☒ B is incorrect because 1.0 cannot automatically be cast to a double. C and D are incorrect because the code runs and compiles fine.

Invoking Parental or Overloaded Constructors

18. ☑ F. This code will not compile because *super()* and *this()* must be the first line of the constructor, and they cannot exist in the same constructor method.
☒ A, B, C, D, and E are all incorrect because the code will not compile. B would be correct if line 12 were removed.

19. ☑ D. *this()* is used within a constructor to call another constructor in the same class.
☒ A is incorrect because *super()* is used to invoke constructors in the parent class. B is incorrect because this is used to get a reference to an instance of your class. C will not compile. E is incorrect because *super* is used to refer to an instance of the superclass.

20. ☑ C. *MySuper* does not need a no-args constructor because *MySub()* explicitly calls the *MySuper* constructor with an argument. It is valid as long as any constructor for a superclass is run.
☒ A and B are incorrect because they assume that *MySuper* needs a no-args constructor.

21. ☑ D. *MySub()* implicitly calls super(), which is the same as a call to the *MySuper()* constructor.
☒ A is incorrect because it does not account for *MySuper()* being called. B is incorrect because it does not account for *MySub()* being called. C is incorrect because the program compiles successfully.

22. ☑ D. Leaving it blank would cause *super()* to be called automatically by the constructor.
☒ A is incorrect because this line results in a compile error, since the constructor is attempting to invoke itself. B is incorrect because it is not syntactically correct. C is incorrect because *Parent()* is an invalid call to the Parent constructor.

8

Inner Classes

CERTIFICATION OBJECTIVES

- 8.01 Static Inner Classes
- 8.02 Member Inner Classes
- 8.03 Local Inner Classes
- 8.04 Anonymous Inner Classes
- 8.05 Inner Class Access to an Enclosing Class
- ✓ Two-Minute Drill
- Q&A Self Test

Inner classes were an addition to the Java Development Kit 1.1 (JDK1.1). They can increase the clarity of your code by allowing you to create classes close to where they are being used; within another class. This is useful if you have behavior related to a class that shouldn't actually be implemented by that class or is not used by any other class. You can place that behavior in an inner class. Inner classes allow you to group related classes and thus reduce namespace clutter. In this section, we discuss the different types of inner classes and look at some examples.

Inner classes are classes defined at a scope smaller than a package. For example, you can define an inner class inside another class, inside a method, and even as part of an expression. Inner classes are classes nonetheless and behave just like any other class. They can extend other classes and they can implement interfaces. There are four types of inner classes:

- Static inner classes (also called nested classes)
- Member inner classes
- Local inner classes
- Anonymous inner classes

Each one of these will be discussed in further detail in the following sections.

CERTIFICATION OBJECTIVE 8.01

Static Inner Classes

Static inner classes are the simplest form of inner classes. They behave much like top-level classes except that they are defined within the scope of another class, namely the enclosing class. For example:

```
package mypackage;
public class EnclosingClass {
   private static int staticvar=0;
   public int instancevar=0;

   public static class StaticInnerClass {
   }
}
```

The fully qualified class name for the inner class in this example is mypackage.EnclosingClass.StaticInnerClass. The Java compiler creates two separate class files for this example: EnclosingClass.class and EnclosingClass$StaticInnerClass.class. Inner classes cannot have the same name as the enclosing class. The key point is that a static inner class is compiled into a completely separate *.class* file from the outer class.

Static inner classes have no implicit references to instances of the enclosing class and can access only static members and methods of the enclosing class. Because an inner class is defined within the enclosing class, it has access to private static members of the enclosing class. Because the inner class in the previous example is static, it can access only the *staticvar* variable, even though it is private. It cannot access the *instancevar* variable because it is not static, regardless of the fact that it is public.

Static inner classes are often used to implement small helper classes such as iterators. An *iterator* provides the necessary behavior to get to each element in a collection without exposing the collection itself. In classes containing and manipulating collections, it is good practice to return an iterator instead of the collection containing the elements you want to iterate over. This shields clients from internal changes to the data structures used in your classes.

Let's say you want to specify a week as a week number (for example, 1 to 52) within a year and find out what dates are in that given week. The following example treats a week as a collection of seven days. To find out what dates are in a given week, you create a Week as

```
Week week = new Week(weekNr,year);
```

and then ask the week for the days in that week by calling

```
week.getDays();
```

exam Watch ***You will not have to know anything about the Iterator interface for the exam.***

The return type of the getDays() method is *Iterator*. Iterator is an interface defined in the java.util package. Its interface is defined as follows:

```
package java.util;
public interface Iterator {
   public boolean hasNext();
   public Object next();
   public void remove();
}
```

In the following example, the Iterator interface is realized through the use of a static inner class called DayIterator. The DayIterator class definition starts at line 23 in the example code. The getDays() method of the Week class (line 11) creates a DayIterator by passing itself as a parameter to its constructor. The DayIterator uses the week's getWeeknr() and getYear() accessor methods to initialize an instance of GregorianCalendar (also from the java.util package) with the correct year and week. In this example, you can see that static inner classes can implement any arbitrary interface, just like any class can. Because the DayIterator claims to implement the Iterator interface, it must provide implementations for all the methods specified in the Iterator interface.

Even though removing a day from a week doesn't make sense, we must still provide an implementation for the Iterator's remove() method, as shown at line 44. The method's body is left empty. The DayIterator keeps track of the current day of the week in a private member called *index*, which is initialized to zero. As long as this index is less than seven, the DayIterator's hasNext() method will return *true*, indicating that there are more days to follow in this week. Each time you call the next() method (line 39), it uses the Calendar to calculate the Date based on the current value of *index*, after which it increments the index using index++.

```
1.  import java.util.*;
2.  public class Week {
3.     private int weeknr;
4.     private int year;
5.
6.     public Week(int weeknr, int year) {
7.        this.weeknr = weeknr;
8.        this.year = year;
9.     }
10.
11.    public Iterator getDays() {
12.       return new DayIterator(this);
13.    }
14.
15.    public int getWeeknr() {
16.       return weeknr;
17.    }
18.
19.    public int getYear() {
20.       return year;
21.    }
22.
23.    public static class DayIterator implements Iterator {
24.
```

```
      private int index = 0;
      private Calendar cal = null;

      DayIterator (Week aWeek) {
         cal = new GregorianCalendar();
         cal.clear();
         cal.set(Calendar.YEAR, aWeek.getYear());
         cal.set(Calendar.WEEK_OF_YEAR, aWeek.getWeeknr());
      }

      public boolean hasNext() {
         return index < 7;
      }

      public Object next() {
         cal.set(Calendar.DAY_OF_WEEK, index++);
         return cal.getTime();
      }

      public void remove() {
         // not implemented
      }
   }

   public static void main(String[] args) {
      // list the days of the week
      if (args.length < 2) {
         System.err.println("Usage: java Week <weeknr> year>");
         System.exit(1);
      } else {
         try {
            int weeknr = Integer.parseInt(args[0]);
            int year = Integer.parseInt(args[1]);
            Week wk = new Week(weeknr, year);
            for (Iterator i=wk.getDays();i.hasNext();) {
               System.err.println(i.next());
            }
         } catch (NumberFormatException x) {
            System.err.println("Illegal week or year");
         }
      }
   }
}
```

The main() method in this example demonstrates how to use the Week.getDays() method to print the days of the week. This method parses the week number and the year from the command-line arguments and then creates an instance of Week using these arguments. The for loop at line 59 creates an Iterator by calling the getDays() method and will keep looping until the Iterator's hasNext() method returns false. Each object returned by the Iterator is an instance of Date, so the output produced by the following command line:

```
java Week 10 1999
```

is as follows:

```
Sat Feb 27 00:00:00 EST 1999
Sun Feb 28 00:00:00 EST 1999
Mon Mar 01 00:00:00 EST 1999
Tue Mar 02 00:00:00 EST 1999
Wed Mar 03 00:00:00 EST 1999
Thu Mar 04 00:00:00 EST 1999
Fri Mar 05 00:00:00 EST 1999
```

Note that the try-catch block in the main() method is needed to cope with illegal command-line arguments that are not numbers that can be parsed to a valid int. Also note that this example does produce strange results for the first week of the year. This is a Calendar problem and is not related to the use of inner classes, so we made no attempts to fix this problem.

CERTIFICATION OBJECTIVE 8.02

Member Inner Classes

Inner classes defined in an enclosing class without using the static modifier are called *member inner classes.* They are members of the enclosing class just like instance variables (which are called members in C++ terminology). Unlike static inner classes, member inner classes (or simply member classes) can access all members of the enclosing class, regardless of their level of protection. In other words, all public, package, protected, and private members are visible to instances of the member class. To gain this access, you must provide an instance of the enclosing class when you create a new instance of a member class. A new syntax was invented for this purpose when they added inner classes to the JDK1.1. This new syntax treats the new operator as if it is a method of the enclosing class. The following is an example:

```
public class EnclosingClass {
   private int instVar = 1;

   public class MemberClass {
      public void innerMethod() {
         // it is okay to do something with instVar here
      }
   }

   public MemberClass createMember() {
      return this.new MemberClass();
   }
}
```

Note how the MemberClass instance is created in the createMember() method. The new operator has to be prefixed with an instance of the enclosing class, in this case *this.* Note that in this particular case, when the enclosing instance is *this*, you don't have to explicitly write it, you simply use new MemberClass(). In other words, the preceding code still would be legal if the following method was substituted:

```
public MemberClass createMember() {
   return new MemberClass();
}
```

This can be the cause of great confusion because if you need to create an instance of a member class outside of the scope of the enclosing class, you *do* need to use an instance of the enclosing class to create the member instance:

```
EnclosingClass ec = new EnclosingClass();
EnclosingClass.MemberClass mc = ec.new MemberClass();
```

or, if you're into one-liners:

```
EnclosingClass.MemberClass mc = new EnclosingClass().new MemberClass();
```

Another new syntax invented for the use of inner classes in the JDK1.1 has to do with the meaning of the keyword *this.* When in the scope of a member class, *this* refers to the instance of the member class. But how do you refer to the enclosing instance? The answer is to prefix the *this* keyword with the class name of the enclosing instance to which you want to refer. The same new syntax applies to the keyword *super*.

```
public class EnclosingClass {

  public class MemberClass {
     public void innerMethod() {
        // 'this' refers to an instance of
           EnclosingClass.MemberClass
        /* 'EnclosingClass.this' refers to an instance of
           EnclosingClass */
        // 'super' refers to the superclass of MemberClass (Object)
        /* 'EnclosingClass.super' refers to the superclass of
           EnclosingClass */
     }
  }
}
```

Member classes are compiled to separate class files just like static inner classes, so this example creates a file called EnclosingClass$MemberClass.class in addition to the EnclosingClass.class file. Like static inner classes, member classes cannot have the same name as the enclosing class. In addition, member inner classes cannot have static members. Only interfaces, top-level classes, and static inner classes can have static members.

The following example is a modification of the Week example from the preceding section. We modified it so that the DayIterator class (line 17) is now a member class that can access the Week's *weeknr* and *year* members directly (lines 24 and 25). The DayIterator no longer takes the Week as a constructor argument. We also modified the getDays() method to use the proper *this.new* syntax in line 14.

```
1.  import java.util.*;
2.  public class Week {
3.     private int weeknr;
4.     private int year;
5.
6.     public Week(int weeknr, int year) {
7.        this.weeknr = weeknr;
8.        this.year = year;
9.     }
10.
11.    public Iterator getDays() {
```

```
      // DayIterator is not static and therefore
      // needs an enclosing instance (this)
      return this.new DayIterator();
   }

   public class DayIterator implements Iterator {

      private int index = 0;
      private Calendar cal = null;

      DayIterator () {
         cal = new GregorianCalendar();
         cal.clear();
         cal.set(Calendar.YEAR, year);
         cal.set(Calendar.WEEK_OF_YEAR, weeknr);
      }

      public boolean hasNext() {
         return index < 7;
      }

      public Object next() {
         cal.set(Calendar.DAY_OF_WEEK, index++);
         return cal.getTime();
      }

      public void remove() {
         // not implemented
      }
   }
    public static void main(String[] args) {
        // identical to main of the Static inner class example
    }
}
```

An inner class is a member of its enclosing class, much the same as an instance variable or a method is a member of its enclosing class. As you may recall, member methods can contain local variables that use the same name as instance variables in the class. The same thing goes for inner classes. An inner class can contain a variable using the same name as a variable of the enclosing class. The following class demonstrates how these variables are accessed:

```
class Enclosing {
   private int year = 1;
```

```
    public static void main(String [] args) {
        Enclosing enc = new Enclosing();
        Enclosing.Inner inner = enc.new Inner();
        System.out.println("Enclosing = " + enc.year);
        System.out.println("Inner = " + inner.year);
        inner.checkVars();
    }

    class Inner {
        int year = 2;
        void checkVars() {
            System.out.println("Enclosing = " + Enclosing.this.year);
System.out.println("Inner = " + this.year);
        }
    }
}
```

EXERCISE 8-1

Instantiating a Member Class

In this exercise we will attempt to create a member class and instantiate it from the enclosing class. This will give you a better understanding of the syntax involved in handling member classes.

1. Create an enclosing class called *OuterHull* and a main() method, which will remain empty for now. The enclosing class also has a String variable called ship. You can give any value you want to this string.
2. Create an inner class called *InnerCore* and a method called communicate(). The inner class also has a String variable called ship, with the value "Shuttle Craft."
3. Use the main method to create an instance of *OuterHull* and *InnerCore.* Within the main method, output the instance variable *ship*, as well as the member class *ship* variable. Then call the method communicate().
4. Within the communicate() method, output the enclosing class variable *ship*, as well as the inner class variable *ship.*

The final code should look something like this:

```
class OuterHull {
    private String ship = "U.S.S. Enterprising";
    public static void main(String [] args) {
        OuterHull outer = new OuterHull();
        OuterHull.InnerCore inner = outer.new InnerCore();
        System.out.println("OuterHull = " + outer.ship);
        System.out.println("InnerCore = " + inner.ship);
        inner.communicate();
    }

    class InnerCore {
        String ship = "Shuttle Craft";
        void communicate() {
            System.out.println("OuterHull = " + OuterHull.this.ship);
            System.out.println("InnerCore = " + this.ship);
        }
    }
}
```

CERTIFICATION OBJECTIVE 8.03

Local Inner Classes

The preceding two forms of inner classes, static and member inner classes, were both defined at the class scope. You can also define inner classes within the scope of a method, or even smaller blocks within a method. We call this form of inner class a *local inner class.* This is by far the least used form of inner class. There are very few cases in which you would ever need a named local inner class because most problems can be solved with the other types of inner classes.

In the following example, we place the complete DayIterator inner class inside the getDays() method of the Week class (line 16). Local inner classes, like local variables, cannot be declared public, protected, private, or static. Like member inner classes, local inner classes cannot have static members, and they cannot have the same name as the enclosing class in which they are defined. Local inner classes can access certain kinds of local variables and method arguments of the enclosing method. Access to local variables and method arguments is restricted. These restrictions are an important certification objective, and we discuss them separately later in this chapter. At line 41 in this example, the DayIterator's toString() method accesses the local variable of the getDays() method called *text.*

```
1.  import java.util.*;
2.
3.  public class Week {
4.
5.     private int weeknr;
6.     private int year;
7.
8.     public Week(int weeknr, int year) {
9.        this.weeknr = weeknr;
10.       this.year = year;
11.    }
12.
13.    public Iterator getDays() {
14.       final String text = "DayIterator for week " + weeknr +
15.          " of " + year;
16.       class DayIterator implements Iterator {
17.
18.          private int index = 0;
19.          private Calendar cal = null;
20.
21.          DayIterator (Week aWeek) {
22.             cal = new GregorianCalendar();
23.             cal.clear();
24.             cal.set(Calendar.YEAR, aWeek.getYear());
25.             cal.set(Calendar.WEEK_OF_YEAR, aWeek.getWeeknr());
26.          }
27.
28.          public boolean hasNext() {
29.             return index < 7;
30.          }
31.
32.          public Object next() {
33.             cal.set(Calendar.DAY_OF_WEEK, index++);
34.             return cal.getTime();
35.          }
36.
37.          public void remove() {
```

```
        // not implemented
      }

      public String toString() {
        return text;
      }
    }
    return new DayIterator(this);
  }

  public int getWeeknr() {
    return weeknr;
  }

  public int getYear() {
    return year;
  }

  public static void main(String[] args) {
    // same as before
  }
}
```

CERTIFICATION OBJECTIVE 8.04

Anonymous Inner Classes

Anonymous inner classes are local inner classes that don't have a class name. You use an anonymous class when you want to create and use a class but don't want to bother with giving it a name or using it again. In the preceding example, you'll notice that we're using syntax that is different from that of a normal class definition. The keyword *class* is missing, and there are no modifiers (public, protected, and so on). The keywords *extends* and *implements* are missing too. These keywords aren't allowed because we create anonymous inner classes through another extension to the *new* operator syntax. That means the complete class definition is actually part of a Java expression. Right after the *new someClass()* syntax, you write a curly brace and start to write a class definition. It's that simple!

The lack of a class name has a number of implications for the definition and use of inner classes. You can't define constructors for an anonymous inner class because you can't name them. They must always (implicitly) extend a superclass or implement some interface, even though you never use the *extends* or *implements* keywords. Without a superclass or interface, you don't have a class name to refer to for the new operator.

When you compile the preceding source code, the Java compiler creates the files EnclosingClass$1.class, InnerSuperClass.class, and EnclosingClass.class. The Java compiler writes multiple anonymous inner classes in an enclosing class into sequentially numbered class files prefixed with the name of the enclosing class and a dollar sign. Note that when you create anonymous inner classes inside other inner classes, such as member classes or static inner classes, their numeric postfix is appended to the outermost enclosing class, not the inner class in which they are defined. So instead of Outer$Inner$1.class, you'll see Outer$1.class even if the anonymous inner class is defined in the Outer.Inner class.

on the Job

Anonymous classes are most commonly used in user interface adapters to perform event handling, such as for Abstract Window Toolkit (AWT) and Swing events. Inner classes have visibility to members of the enclosing class, which makes it easy to access AWT components defined by the enclosing class.

Here is an example of an event handler for AWT that uses an anonymous inner class to handle a button event.

```
import java.awt.Frame;
import java.awt.Button;
import java.awt.event.ActionEvent;
import java.awt.event.ActionListener;

public class DemoFrame extends Frame {
   public DemoFrame() {
      addButton("Hello world");
   }

   private void addButton(final String text) {
      Button b = new Button(text);
      b.addActionListener(new ActionListener() {
         public void actionPerformed(ActionEvent e) {
            // handle the button-pressed event
            System.err.println("Button " + text + " pressed");
         }
      });
      add(b);
   }
```

```
    public static void main(String[] args) {
        (new DemoFrame()).show();
    }
}
```

In this example, it looks like we create an instance of an ActionListener, but ActionListener is an interface, so how can it be instantiated? It can't. What is really instantiated by the *new ActionListener() {}* syntax is the anonymous inner class defined on the fly after the curly brace that implicitly implements the ActionListener interface. Note the absence of the *implements* keyword. Like local inner classes, anonymous inner classes cannot be public, protected, private, or static. The syntax for anonymous inner classes does not allow for any modifiers to be used.

Anonymous inner classes have access to local variables and method arguments governed by the same restrictions as local inner classes. These restrictions are detailed in a later section.

Using anonymous inner classes is most effective when they are small and implement only one method or very few small methods. Reading inline class definitions is difficult and gets very confusing when the definition of the inner class is long. Let's return to our Week example once more.

```
import java.util.*;

public class Week {

   private int weeknr;
   private int year;

   public Week(int weeknr, int year) {
      this.weeknr = weeknr;
      this.year = year;
   }

   public Iterator getDays() {
      return new Iterator() {
      private int index = 0;
      private Calendar cal = null;

         private Calendar getCalendar () {
            if (cal == null) {
               cal = new GregorianCalendar();
               cal.clear();
```

```
21.                     cal.set(Calendar.YEAR, year);
22.                     cal.set(Calendar.WEEK_OF_YEAR, weeknr);
23.                 }
24.                 return cal;
25.             }
26.
27.             public boolean hasNext() {
28.                 return index < 7;
29.             }
30.
31.             public Object next() {
32.                 getCalendar().set(Calendar.DAY_OF_WEEK, index++);
33.                 return getCalendar().getTime();
34.             }
35.
36.             public void remove() {
37.                 // not implemented
38.             }
39.         };
40.     }
41.
42.     public static void main(String[] args) {
43.         // identical to previous examples
44.     }
45. }
```

Note that at line 13 the day iterator is now created as an anonymous inner class implementing the Iterator interface. Because it is anonymous, it does not have a constructor. We had to find another way to initialize our GregorianCalendar object. We chose a technique called *lazy initialization*. By initializing the *cal* member to null at line 15, the getCalendar() method at line 17 initializes it the first time that it is called by the iterator's next() method.

An alternative to lazy initialization is using an *instance initializer*. An instance initializer is a block of code (not a method!) that automatically runs every time you create a new instance of an object. In effect, it is an anonymous constructor! Of course, instance initializers are rather limited; because they don't have arguments, you can't overload them, so you can have only one of these "constructors" per variable. The method definition in the following example replaces the getDays() method in the previous example. It initializes the anonymous day iterator using an instance initializer.

```
public Iterator getDays() {
   return new Iterator() {

      private int index = 0;
      private Calendar cal = new GregorianCalendar();
      { // instance initializer
         cal.clear();
         cal.set(Calendar.YEAR, year);
         cal.set(Calendar.WEEK_OF_YEAR, weeknr);
      } // end instance initializer

      public boolean hasNext() {
         return index < 7;
      }

      public Object next() {
         cal.set(Calendar.DAY_OF_WEEK, index++);
         return cal.getTime();
      }

      public void remove() {
         // not implemented
      }
   };
}
```

The size of the anonymous inner class in this example is borderline acceptable and slightly on the big side. For the day iterator, we prefer to use the first version of the example using static inner classes because this is the simplest form and makes the meaning of the inner class the most explicit.

EXERCISE 8-2

Creating an Anonymous Inner Class

In this exercise we will create an anonymous inner class. The syntax for the creation of an anonymous inner class is somewhat unique in the Java language. For this reason, many people are not familiar with how this is done. This exercise attempts to familiarize you with this.

1. Create an enclosing class and give it any name. Also, create a main() method. This is the method that will indirectly contain our anonymous class.
2. The enclosing class will also contain a static method called startThread(). This static method will take a Thread as an argument, and it will start the Thread object that it is given.
3. Back to the main() method, we are now going to call the static method startThread, but within the brackets of the argument we will define our anonymous Thread class. This thread class will print the words "Thread started" 10 times.
4. The final code should look something like this:

```
class Anonymous {
   public static void main(String [] args) {
      startThread(new Thread() {
         public void run() {
            for(int i=0;i<10;++i) {
               System.out.println("Thread running.");
            }
         }
      });
   }

   public static void startThread(Thread t) {
      t.start();
   }
}
```

CERTIFICATION OBJECTIVE 8.05

Inner Class Access to an Enclosing Class

In the preceding sections, you have learned that an inner class has full access rights to its enclosing class. The access rules get slightly more complicated when we look at local inner classes and anonymous inner classes. These can still access all the instance variables and methods of the enclosing class, but because they are defined within the context of a method, you might expect that they could also access local variables and method arguments. This is where the keyword *final* comes in. The rule is that a local or an anonymous inner class can access only those local variables and method arguments that are declared *final*. This means that you cannot change the value of local variables from within the code of the inner class. They are read-only.

```
public class MyClass {
    public void enclosingMethod(final String arg1, int arg2) {
        final String local = "A local final variable";
        String nonfinal = "A local non-final variable";
        Object obj = new Object() {
            public String toString() {
                return local + "," + arg1;
            }
        };
    }
}
```

exam watch

Local inner classes may only make reference to final variables. This may not seem to make any sense until you look at why this rule is in effect. Normally classes contain, among other things, methods. In the case of a local inner class, it is the method that contains the class. This can lead to some strange behavior because the class has no sequential relationship to the variables inside the method. That's where the final variable becomes useful. A final variable can't be changed; hence it won't lead to strange behavior when it is accessed.

Within the toString() method of the anonymous subclass of Object, we can access both the local variable called *local* and the method argument arg1. We cannot access arg2 or nonfinal. If you absolutely have to change the value of some variable in the enclosing scope (this should be extremely rare) you can use the following trick:

```
public class MyClass {
    public void enclosingMethod(final String arg1, int arg2) {
        final int[] trick = new int[1];

        Runnable runner = new Runnable() {
            public void run() {
                trick[0] = 5;
            }
        };
    }
}
```

SCENARIO & SOLUTION	
How would you define a local inner class that needs to access an argument of the enclosing method?	Declare the method parameter as final.
How would you define an anonymous inner class that needs constructor behavior?	Use an instance initializer or lazy initialization.
What is the best type of inner class to use that doesn't directly access any instance variables of the enclosing class?	A static inner class.
What is the type of inner class that has direct access to the instance variables of the enclosing class?	A member inner class.
What syntax can you use to get a reference to the enclosing class from within a member inner class?	Use the *EnclosingClass.this* syntax.

In this example, the array of integers called *trick* is declared final. That means you can never assign another array of integers to the variable trick, but it doesn't mean that its elements are final, so it is perfectly okay to assign a value to the only element in the trick array. Because the trick array is final, it is accessible from within the inner class as well.

CERTIFICATION SUMMARY

In this chapter you have learned everything about inner classes that you will need to know for the exam and more. Inner classes are classes defined within the scope of an enclosing class. There are four kinds of inner classes: static inner classes, member inner classes, local inner classes, and anonymous inner classes. Inner classes have full access rights to the members of the enclosing class, so they can access private members as well as public and protected ones.

Static inner classes can access only static members of the enclosing class. Member inner classes need an instance of the enclosing class when they are created, hence the *object.new* syntax. To refer to the instance of the enclosing class from within an inner class, use the *EnclosingClass.this* syntax.

Local and anonymous inner classes can access only those objects declared as *final* in their enclosing scope. Anonymous inner classes are not given a name by which you can refer to them; hence they can't have their own constructor. Instance initializers can be used in place of an actual constructor to initialize variables of the anonymous inner class.

TWO-MINUTE DRILL

Here are some of the key points from each certification objective in Chapter 8.

Static Inner Classes

- ❑ Only top-level classes, interfaces, and static inner classes can have static members.
- ❑ Static inner classes can access only static members of the enclosing class.

Member Inner Classes

- ❑ To create an instance of a member inner class, you need a reference to an instance of the enclosing class (new syntax for *new*).
- ❑ An inner class is a member of its enclosing class, much the same as an instance variable or a method is a member of its enclosing class.

Local Inner Classes

- ❑ Local and anonymous inner classes can access local variables from their enclosing scope only if it is declared final.
- ❑ Local and anonymous inner classes cannot be defined as private, protected, public, or static.

Anonymous Inner Classes

- ❑ An anonymous inner class cannot have a constructor.
- ❑ Anonymous inner classes are often used for event handling in AWT and Swing.

Inner Class Access to an Enclosing Class

- ❑ Inner classes are defined within the scope of an enclosing class.
- ❑ There are static, member, local, and anonymous inner classes.

- Inside the scope of an inner class, the keyword *this* refers to the instance of the inner class, not the enclosing class. To get a reference to the enclosing instance, prefix *this* with the name of the enclosing class (new syntax for *this* and *super*).
- Inner classes have full access rights to the members of the enclosing class. Most inner classes, especially local and anonymous inner classes, should be small to improve readability.

SELF TEST

The following questions will help you measure your understanding of the material presented in this chapter. Read all of the choices carefully, as there may be more than one correct answer. Choose all correct answers for each question.

Static Inner Classes

1. Given:

```
public class MyMap implements Map {
    private static class MapEntry {
    }
}
```

There are two filenames generated by the Java compiler for this code. (Choose all that apply.)

A. MyMap.class

B. MyMap.MapEntry.class

C. MyMap$MapEntry.class

D. MyMap$MapEntry

2. Briefly examine the following code:

```
import java.util.*;
class Week {
   private String[] days = {"M","T","W","Th","F"};

   public DayIterator getDays() {
      return new DayIterator();
   }

   private static class DayIterator {
      int index = 0;
      public void next() {
         System.out.println(days[index++]);
      }
   }
   public static void main(String[] args) {
      Week w = new Week();
      DayIterator di = w.getDays();
      di.next();
```

```
19.     }
20.  }
```

Which of the following statements are true?

A. This code compiles, and when it runs the output is M.

B. This code does not compile because the *days* array in line 3 is private.

C. This code does not compile because the *days* array in line 3 is not static.

D. This code does not compile because the DayIterator class in line 9 is private.

E. This code does not compile because line 6 attempts to create an instance of the static DayIterator class in line 9.

3. Given:

```
public class Foo {
   int var = 10;
   public class Test {
      public static void main(String[] args) {
         System.out.println("Foo$Test: var = " + var);
      }
   }
}
```

Which of the following statements about the code is correct? (Choose all that apply.)

A. The result of java Foo$Test is Foo$Test: var = 10.

B. This code does not compile because Foo$Test cannot access the instance variable *var*.

C. This code does not compile because Foo$Test can't have a static main() method.

D. This code does not compile because you can't access *var* from a static method.

4. Given:

```
class Foo {
   int total;
   static class Increment extends Thread {
      public void run() {
         ++total;
      }
   }
}
```

Which of the following changes to the code will make it valid?

A. Add a semicolon at the end of the inner class definition.

B. Get rid of the static keyword.

C. Declare the variable total as final.

D. Nothing. The code compiles and runs fine.

Member Inner Classes

5. Given:

```
class EnclosingClass {
    public class Inner {
        Inner(int a) {/* Constructor Code */}
    }
}

class SubClassOfInner extends EnclosingClass.Inner {
    // how to write a constructor?
}
```

What is the correct way to write a constructor for the SubClassOfInner class?

A. There is no correct way to provide a constructor in this scenario.

B. SubClassOfInner(int a) { super(a); }

C. SubClassOfInner(EnclosingClass outer, int a) { outer.super(a); }

D. SubClassOfInner(int a) {EnclosingClass.super(a);}

6. Given:

```
1.  public class MyClass {
2.      private class MyRunner implements Runnable {
3.          public void run() {
4.              // do something
5.          }
6.      }
7.      public static void main(String[] args) {
8.          (new Thread(new MyRunner())).start();
9.      }
10. }
```

This code does not compile. Which of the following statements is the reason why it does not compile?

A. Line 8 should create an instance of MyRunner with new MyClass.MyRunner().

B. MyRunner in line 2 is private.

C. The code is missing an import statement for Thread from java.lang.

D. The code should create an instance of MyRunner with an enclosing instance of MyClass.

7. Which of the following are correct ways to create an instance of an inner class called Outer.Inner from outside the scope of the Outer class? Assume Inner is a public static inner class that has no defined constructor.

A. Outer.new Inner()

B. (new Outer()).new Inner();

C. (new Outer()).new Outer.Inner();

D. new Outer.Inner();

8. Given:

```
public class Foo {
    protected int x = 3;
    private int y = 5;
    private class Bar {
        private int x = 8;
        public Bar() {
            Foo.this.x = y;
        }
        public int getValue() {
            return x*y;
        }
    }
    public int getValue() {
        return (new Bar()).getValue();
    }
    public static void main(String[] args) {
        System.err.println((new Foo()).getValue());
    }
}
```

What number is returned by getValue(), assuming the enclosing class creates an instance of Bar using *this.new*?

A. 15

B. 24

C. 25

D. 40

9. Which of the following classes or interfaces can have static members? (Choose all that apply.)

A. Top-level classes

B. Static inner classes

C. Interfaces

D. Member classes

Local Inner Classes

10. Given:

```
import java.util.Hashtable;
class Foo {
    String[] keys;
    String[] names;
    public Hashtable buildHash(String start) {
class MyHash extends Hashtable {
    public MyHash() {
        super();
    }
    public void initHash(String str) {
        for (int i=0; i < keys.length; i++)
            if (names[i].startsWith(str))
                put(keys[i], names[i]);
        }
    }
    MyHash h = new MyHash();
    h.initHash(start);
    return h;
    }
}
```

What is wrong with this code?

A. Nothing. This code is correct.

B. The keys and names arrays must be declared public.

C. The start parameter of buildHash must be declared final.

D. The str parameter of initHash must be declared final.

Anonymous Inner Classes

11. Given:

```
public class Foo {
    int a = 10;
    int c = 30;
    public Runnable getRunnable() {
       int a = 20;
       return new Thread() {
          public void run() {
                int b = a+c;
          }
       };
    }
}
```

What will be the value of *b* after the assignment in the run() method?

A. 30

B. 40

C. 50

D. This code doesn't compile.

12. Given:

```
import java.util.Iterator;
public class Foo {
    public Iterator getIterator() {
       return new public Iterator() {
          public void remove() {}
          public Object next() {return null;}
          public boolean hasNext() {return false;}
       };
    }
}
```

Which of these statements is true?

A. This code returns a new Foo.Iterator when you call getIterator().

B. This code returns a new Iterator when you call getIterator().

C. This code doesn't compile because an Iterator interface method is missing.

D. This code doesn't compile because the syntax of the inner class creation is wrong.

13. Given:

```
import java.util.Iterator;
public class Foo {
    public static class Week {
        public Iterator getIterator() {
            return new Iterator() {
                public void remove() {};
                public Object next() {return null;}
                public boolean hasNext() {return false;}
            };
        }
    }
}
```

Which class files are generated when you compile this code?

A. Foo.class, Foo$1.class, Foo$Week.class

B. Foo.class, Foo.Week$1.class, Foo$1$Week.class

C. Foo.class, Foo$Week.class, Foo$Week$1.class

D. Foo.class, Foo$Week.class, Foo$Week$Iterator.class

14. Given:

```
import java.util.HashMap;
public class Foo {
    public static class Week {
        public HashMap getMap() {
            return new HashMap() {
                public HashMap(int size) {}
                public Object put(Object key, Object value) {}
            };
        }
    }
}
```

Which class files are generated when you compile this code?

A. None, the code doesn't compile.

B. Foo.class, Foo$HashMap.class, Foo$Week.class

C. Foo.class, Foo$Week$1.class, Foo$Week.class

D. Foo.class, Foo$Week.class, Foo$Week$HashMap.class

15. Given:

```
1.  public class Foo {
2.     private int total;
3.     public Runnable getRunnable() {
4.        return new Thread() {
5.           public void run() {
6.              ++total;
7.           }
8.        };
9.     }
10. }
```

Which line change will make this code compile?

A. 2. public int total;

B. 3. public Thread getRunnable() {

C. 2. private final int total;

D. Nothing, the code is fine.

Inner Class Access to an Enclosing Class

16. Which of the following statements are correct? (Choose all that apply.)

A. Inner classes are defined within the scope of another class.

B. Inner classes can subclass other classes and they can implement interfaces.

C. Inner classes cannot be static.

D. There are four different kinds of inner classes: top-level, static, member, and anonymous.

17. Given:

```
public class Foo {
   public Runnable getRunnable(String name) {
      return new Thread() {
         public void run() {
            setName(name);
         }
      };
   }
}
```

Which line change will make this code compile?

A. 4. `protected void run() {`

B. 2. `public Thread getRunnable(String name) {`

C. 2. `public Runnable getRunnable(final String name) {`

D. Nothing, the code works fine.

18. Given:

```
class Foo {
    protected class Bar {
        protected Bar() {
            System.out.println("Foo.Bar");
        }
    }
    private Bar b;
    Foo() {
        System.out.println("Foo");
        b = this.new Bar();
    }
}
class FooToo extends Foo {
    protected class Bar {
        protected Bar() {
            System.out.println("FooToo.Bar");
        }
    }
    public static void main(String[] args) {
        new FooToo();
    }
}
```

What is printed to the output?

A. Nothing. This code fails to compile.

B. Foo
Foo.Bar

C. Foo
FooToo.Bar

D. FooToo
FooToo.Bar

19. Given:

```
1.  class A {
2.      int var = 0;
3.      class B {
4.          int var = 1;
5.          public void C() {
6.              int x = var;
7.
8.          }
9.      }
10. }
```

Which line of code, inserted at line 7, would allow you to access an instance of *var* from the A class?

A. int y = this.var;

B. int y = A.this.var;

C. int y = var;

D. int y = super.var;

E. int y = A.var;

20. You want to modify some local value defined in the enclosing scope of an anonymous inner class from within that anonymous inner class. What are your options to accomplish this? (Choose all that apply.)

A. Store the value in an array that is declared final and modify the array element.

B. Make sure the value is an object stored in a final local variable and use a method on that object to modify it.

C. This can't be done.

D. Don't define the value as final and simply modify it.

SELF TEST ANSWERS

Static Inner Classes

1. ☑ A and C. A is correct because this top-level class will be produced. C is correct because inner classes compile to separate files, and their filenames are prefixed with the name of the enclosing class followed by a dollar sign.
   ☒ B is incorrect because a dollar sign is missing. D is incorrect because the suffix *class* is missing.

2. ☑ C. Static inner classes can access only static members of the enclosing class. The day array is not static, so it can not be accessed from within a static inner class.
   ☒ A is incorrect because this code does not compile. B and D are both incorrect for the same reason. An inner class can view all instance variables of an enclosing class, even if it is given private access. E is incorrect because a static inner class may be instantiated. The static modifier means this inner class may be instantiated without an instance of the enclosing class.

3. ☑ C and D. This code has two problems. First, Test is a member class; therefore, it can't have static members, and thus no main method. Second, if you would make the Test class static so that it can have a main(), you wouldn't be able to access the *instance variable* var from the static main() method.
   ☒ A is incorrect because the code will not compile. B is incorrect because the inner class Test is able to access the variable *var* (if this code compiled).

4. ☑ B. A static class may not make reference to an instance variable. This will cause a compiler error.
   ☒ A is incorrect because a semicolon is not necessary. C is incorrect because this only applies when referencing a local variable. D is incorrect because the code will generate an error.

Member Inner Classes

5. C. Because the constructor of Inner needs a handle to an instance of the enclosing class, it must be initialized, but the problem is that you don't have one available in the derived class. The SubClassOfInner inherits only from the inner class, not the enclosing class. The only way to avoid this problem is to pass in the handle to the enclosing instance explicitly and use the object.super() syntax to attach to the handle. Instantiation would work like the following:

```
EnclosingClass ec = new EnclosingClass();
SubClassOfInner sci = new SubClassOfInner(ec, 10);
```

☒ A is incorrect because it is possible to create a constructor. **B** is incorrect because in order to use the constructor, it needs an instance of the enclosing class. **D** is incorrect because it needs to have an actual instance of the enclosing class to work properly.

6. **D.** MyRunner is a member class and needs an enclosing instance to be created. In this example, you can create one as in

```
(new Thread((new MyClass()).new MyRunner())).start();
```

☒ **A** is incorrect because it is okay to create an instance in this way. **B** is incorrect because there is still visibility to MyRunner within the enclosing class. **C** is incorrect because the classes from java.lang are automatically imported for all Java classes.

7. ☑ **D.** Because Inner is a static inner class, it does not need an instance of the Outer class to be created, which renders **C** invalid.
☒ **A**, **B**, and **C** are all incorrect because the syntax is not correct.

8. ☑ **D.** The line Foo.this.x = y in the Bar constructor changes the value of the member *x* of the *enclosing* class to 5. However, the expression x*y in getValue() uses the member *x* declared in the *inner* class, which has the value 8. 8*5 = 40.
☒ **A**, **B**, and **C** are all incorrect because the program flow, described for the correct answer, does not produce any of these results.

9. ☑ **A**, **B**, and **C**. **A** is correct because top-level classes can contain static members, as described earlier in this book. **B** is correct because static inner classes can of course contain static members. **C** is correct because interfaces can contain static elements, as described earlier in the book.
☒ **D** is incorrect because member classes are not allowed to contain static members.

Local Inner Classes

10. ☑ **A.** The local inner class MyHash has full access to the keys and names arrays, even if they were private.
☒ **B** is incorrect because the inner class can still access these variables, even though it is not declared public. **C** is incorrect because the inner class does not attempt to access the start parameter directly; therefore, it does not need to be final. The start value *is* passed into a

method of the inner class, but this is valid. **D** is incorrect because the method initHash() actually belongs to the inner class; therefore, it does not need to be final. Only parameters belonging to the enclosing method must be final if they are accessed. Be aware of strange indenting on the Sun exam. They will often do this to attempt to throw you off.

Anonymous Inner Classes

11. ☑ **D.** This code doesn't compile because at the scope level of the anonymous inner class definition; only the local variable *a* is visible, hiding the instance variable. This local variable has to be declared final to access it from within the run() method.
☒ **A, B,** and **C** are all incorrect because the code will not compile.

12. ☑ **D.** You cannot use modifiers in the creation of anonymous inner classes, and the parentheses on Iterator are missing. The correct syntax is 'new Iterator() {…}', without the keyword public. Note that this single error actually causes five(!) compilation errors.
☒ **A** and **B** are incorrect because the code will not compile, therefore it cannot be executed. **C** is incorrect because the syntax for the inner class creation is valid.

13. ☑ **A.** The inner class Week has one anonymous inner class in addition to Foo$Week.class and the top-level class Foo.class.
☒ **B** and **C** are both incorrect because you would expect Foo$Week$1.class to be the correct name of the generated class file, but the compiler ignores the inner classes in the numeric naming scheme of the anonymous inner classes. **D** is incorrect because an anonymous inner class is given a numeral, not the name of the class it extends or the interface it implements.

14. ☑ **A.** Anonymous inner classes cannot define constructors.
☒ **B, C,** and **D** are all incorrect because the class will not compile; therefore, it will not produce any output.

15. ☑ **D.** It is completely legal for a local or anonymous inner class to access variables from the enclosing class, even non-final variables.
☒ **A** is incorrect because the variable total is still visible to the inner class, even though it is private. **B** is incorrect because Thread implements Runnable, therefore Thread is a legal return type. **C** is incorrect because anonymous inner classes can access class variables, even if they are not final. Only local (method) variables need to be final if the anonymous inner class needs to access it.

Inner Class Access to an Enclosing Class

16. A and B. A is correct because inner classes are always within the scope of another class, even if it is within a method of that class. B is correct because it is perfectly legal for inner classes to extend other classes or implement interfaces.
☒ C is incorrect because an inner class can in fact be defined as static. D is incorrect because a top-level class is just a normal class, not an inner class. The four kinds of inner classes are *local*, static, member, and anonymous.

17. ☑ C. Local and anonymous inner classes can access only final local variables and parameters of the enclosing method.
☒ A is incorrect because changing the access modifier to protected will not work. B is incorrect because Thread extends Runnable; therefore, a return type of Runnable is valid. D is incorrect because the code does not work.

18. ☑ B. FooToo's default constructor invokes Foo's constructor, which in turn prints "Foo" and creates an instance of Bar. Recall that the class name of Bar in Foo is Foo$Bar and the class name of FooToo's Bar is FooToo$Bar! This means that Foo creates an instance of its own Bar and not the Bar in FooToo; hence the output "Foo.Bar" and not "FooToo.Bar." In effect, with respect to inheritance, the *protected* inner class Bar behaves as if it were *private*.
☒ A is incorrect because the code will compile and run fine. C and D are incorrect because the program flow will not produce this output.

19. ☑ B. In class B you can access var by using A.this.var to access A's var.
☒ A is incorrect because this.var refers to B's var. C is incorrect because it also refers to B's var. D is incorrect because the keyword super would refer to the superclass of B, which is Object. E is incorrect because it would be able to access var in this manner only if it were static.

20. ☑ A and B. A is correct because even though the array itself is final, its elements are not and can therefore be modified from within the anonymous inner class. B is correct because even though the variable referencing the object can't be changed, the object itself can be modified using its own methods, or, if it has public non-final members, by changing those members directly.
☒ C is incorrect because it is possible. D is incorrect because if the variable comes from the enclosing method, it must be declared final.

JAVA™

SUN CERTIFIED PROGRAMMER®

9

Threads

CERTIFICATION OBJECTIVES

- 9.01 Creating, Instantiating, and Starting New Threads
- 9.02 Transitioning Between Thread States
- 9.03 Putting Threads to Sleep
- 9.04 Concurrent Access Problems and Synchronized Threads
- 9.05 Communicating with Objects by Waiting and Notifying
- 9.06 Deadlocked Threads
- 9.07 Scheduling Threads Using Priority and Yielding
- ✓ Two-Minute Drill
- Q&A Self Test

In this chapter you'll learn all about threads and how they can be used to create complex behavior in programs. A *thread* is a single sequential flow of control within a program. A thread can be thought of as a software *engine* that can process a sequence of instructions. In older languages, such as Basic, there was only one such engine. In modern languages, however, there can be many threads; each running at the same time, independently of one another.

The various modern languages implement multithreading in different ways, and the resulting program is usually tied to the underlying operating system. Java was designed with this in mind from the beginning, and it provides all the necessary tools to easily create threads that function across multiple platforms.

A good knowledge of how to use threads is essential when creating complex applications, but there is a steep learning curve for some of these concepts. This will be one of the most difficult, if not *the* most difficult chapter in the entire book. Some thread topics in this chapter are easy to master, such as making a thread sleep. Other sections may require reading through the material three or four times before the topic sinks in, such as object locks and synchronizing threads using other objects. For the certification exam you will be expected to know how to run threads and how to make them cooperate with each other in an effective way.

CERTIFICATION OBJECTIVE 9.01

Creating, Instantiating, and Starting New Threads

Imagine a stockbroker application with a lot of complex behavior that the user can initiate. One of the operations could be "download last stock option prices," another could be "check prices for warnings," and a third, time-consuming operation could be "analyze historical data for company x."

In a one-thread environment these actions are executed one after the other. The next action can be executed only when the previous one has finished. If a historical analysis takes half an hour, and the user selects to perform a download and check afterward, a warning may come too late to buy or sell some stock.

This is the sort of application that benefits greatly from multithreading. Ideally, the download should occur in the background (that is, in another thread). This would allow other internal processes to occur at the same time, such as a warning message that needs to be communicated instantly. Meanwhile, the user can interact with other parts of the application. Another improvement would be to perform the historical analysis in yet another thread, so the user can work with the rest of the application while the results are being calculated.

Now how would we go about creating this sort of threaded behavior with Java? The first step to writing a multithreaded application is to identify the instruction set that will be executed by the thread. In Java you provide these instructions in a *public void run()* method; this method is executed when the thread is started. There are two ways of creating a thread: extending the Thread class and implementing the Runnable interface.

Creating a Thread by Extending the Thread Class

Extending the thread class is the easiest way to create a thread. Quite often, the behavior that you want to perform in a separate thread is tightly related to an object, and the main reason to create the object is to have it execute that parallel behavior only once. In this case you can keep things easy by defining the behavior in a new class that extends Thread.

Defining

The Thread class has a public run() method. You can override this method to include your functionality as part of an extended Thread class:

```
public class MyThread extends Thread {
   public void run() {
      // Your instructions here
   }
}
```

Note that the signature of the run() does not throw any checked exceptions. This means that your run() method cannot throw any exceptions either. The compiler will complain if there are any uncaught checked exceptions.

Instantiating

Once you have the class, you get an instance of it, typically by calling the no parameter constructor:

```
MyThread testThread = new MyThread();
```

You can use any constructor that you define in your extended class. As in any other classes, the default constructor for the superclass (that is, the Thread() constructor method) will be called automatically.

Creating a Thread by Implementing the Runnable Interface

A class that implements the Runnable interface can extend any other class, and its main purpose may be unrelated to any thread behavior. Additionally, an instance of this class can be the target of one or more threads throughout its life. It is a lot more flexible than extending Thread, but it requires an extra step.

Defining

The Runnable interface defines only one method:

```
public void run();
```

You can write a class that implements the method, as shown in the following example:

```
public class MyRunnable implements Runnable {
   public void run() {
      // Your instructions here
   }
}
```

This run() method is similar to the run() method of Thread, in that it should not throw any checked exceptions.

Instantiating

Once you have a class, you have to create an instance of it by calling any constructor that you have defined or the default:

```
MyRunnable firstRunnable = new MyRunnable();
```

This instance of your class will constitute the target of the thread. Now that you have the instance, you create a Thread object by passing the target as a parameter:

```
Thread testThread = new Thread(firstRunnable);
```

Starting an Instance of a Thread

Whether you created it from a subclass of Thread or from a Runnable target, the instance of Thread that you now have does nothing different from any other object. It has variables that you can access and methods that you can call, but it is not doing anything on its own. It is ready to run, but it is not running yet, and it won't do so until you tell it to start running. You do this by calling the start() method on the Thread instance:

```
testThread.start();
```

This starts a new flow of execution with your instructions and returns immediately. From that moment onward, the instructions that you specified in the run() method will be executing in parallel to whatever follows the start() method call.

In the case of using a Runnable target, its run method is not called directly, but it is called by the default run method of the Thread instance. So the effect is the same; there is now a separate thread executing instructions in the run method that you specified.

You can call start() only once on a thread. If you try to start a thread that has been started already, you will get an IllegalThreadStateException. This is an unchecked exception, so you don't have to worry about catching this.

exam Watch

The Thread methods suspend(), resume(), and stop() have all been deprecated in Java 2 because they were deadlock prone. These methods will not be mentioned on the Java 2 exam.

CERTIFICATION OBJECTIVE 9.02

Transitioning Between Thread States

It is in the running state that most things of interest happen to threads. They execute their run() methods concurrently with other threads, they cooperate, share resources, and they even compete with each other to get their own tasks done.

Because instructions can be performed only one at a time in a single CPU computer, threads have to take turns running. Usually the threads are switching so fast between one another that the user gets the impression of true parallelism (we will discuss this more in the scheduling section of this chapter). For the moment, remember that there is never a guarantee that a thread will execute a series of instructions in one go; it may be switched at any time and get its turn later. If there is more than one CPU available, threads may truly run in parallel.

Once a thread is started, it is not guaranteed to be running all the time. The Java virtual machine (JVM) could switch over to another thread and execute it for a while, giving it some CPU time. These various states are standard Java terms used to describe the state of a thread at any given time during execution. There are essentially five states a thread can be in:

- **New thread** This is the state the thread is in when it is first created but before the start() method is called. Calling the Thread constructor does not start a thread executing! Once the thread is started, the thread scheduler can begin allocating it CPU time.
- **Runnable** This is the state a thread is in when it is legal for it to be running, but the thread scheduler is not giving it any CPU time.
- **Running** This state occurs when the thread scheduler allocates CPU time for the thread. There are times when a running thread will transition into another state, such as waiting, runnable, or dead.
- **Waiting/blocking** A thread in the waiting state is literally waiting for some event to be satisfied. Once that event occurs it will leave the waiting state and go to the runnable state, as shown in Figure 9-1. A thread can be placed into the waiting state because of a sleep() or wait() method call. (This will be thoroughly discussed later in the chapter.) Sun refers to this as the *Not Runnable* state.
- **Dead** A thread will cease execution when the run() method completes. When this occurs, the thread is dead. A dead thread cannot be restarted.

FIGURE 9-1

Transitioning between thread states

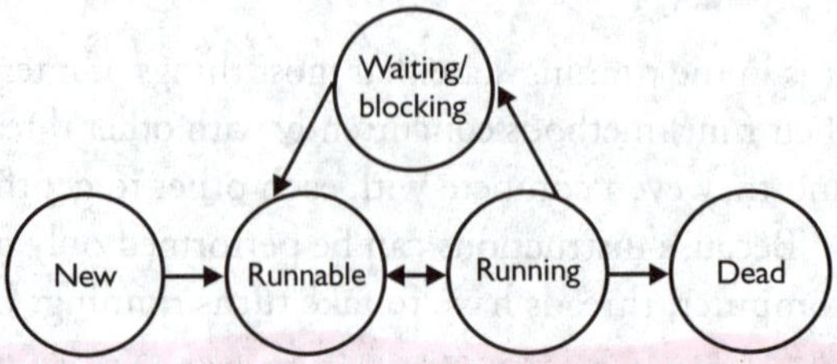

Let's review the life of a typical thread. The thread starts when the constructor is executed. Once the method start() is called, the thread enters the *runnable* state where it remains until the thread scheduler allocates time for it. The thread can transition into only one state from here; the *running* state (Figure 9-1). While in the running state, part or all of the run() method will get executed. If the scheduler allocates time to another thread, this thread will reenter the runnable state.

If a call to sleep() is made, the thread will enter the *waiting* state. Once the appropriate time has elapsed, the thread will reenter the runnable state and eventually the running state again. When the code in run() has completed, the thread becomes *dead.* There is no way for it to transition out of the dead state, much like people.

Notice that the waiting and blocking states depend on an event happening outside of the thread's control. If this event never happens, the thread can become permanently stuck. This is called *deadlocking*, which will be discussed later in the chapter.

on the job

You can get a reference to the currently running thread by calling the static method Thread.currentThread(). While developing and testing, it is usually easier to skip using a proper debugging tool and just include some instances of System.out.println in your code, including Thread.currentThread(). Even more useful is to dump the stack trace of the current thread by calling the static method Thread.dumpStack().

CERTIFICATION OBJECTIVE 9.03

Putting Threads to Sleep

Sometimes there is a need to delay any further execution of the current thread for a while. This section will discuss why this is needed and how to put threads to sleep.

Imagine a hypothetical thread that runs in a loop, downloading the latest stock prices and analyzing them. Downloading prices one after another would be a waste of time, as most of them would be quite similar, and even more, it would be incredibly wasteful because it would consume too much bandwidth.

The simplest way to solve this problem is to include a delay of five minutes after each download. You can do this in Java by calling the sleep() method of Thread.

This is a static method that will make the current thread go to sleep for the specified number of milliseconds, as follows:

```
Thread.sleep(5*60*1000);
```

The sleep() method accepts an argument of type long, which indicates the number of milliseconds for which it should sleep. The preceding example will make the current thread sleep for five minutes while other threads keep running. The sleep() method also throws an exception of type InterruptedException that must be dealt with.

While a thread is sleeping, a different thread may interrupt it by using the Thread instance method interrupt():

```
sleepingThread.interrupt();
```

If a thread has been interrupted, an internal *flag* (in the interrupted Thread instance) is set to indicate this, and the sleeping thread wakes up prematurely. The sleep() method will throw an InterruptedException immediately when this happens. The thread will never go to sleep if the flag was already set when sleep() was called, and will throw the exception instead.

Because of this exception, the sleep() call is typically surrounded inside a try-catch block, as follows:

```
try{
   Thread.sleep(sleepingTime);
}
catch(InterruptedException e){
   // do something about it
}
```

InterruptedException is a checked exception, so the compiler will complain if you don't catch it or specify that the current method throws it.

You should be aware of the context the thread will run in and be able to predict whether it is going to be interrupted. If you are quite sure that no other thread is going to interrupt the thread, or you don't care about exiting gracefully, it is common to not take any action in the catch section. In this example it is a good opportunity to break out of the loop. The run method for this thread would look like the following:

```
public void run(){
    while(true){
        //download stock prices
        // Analyze and report
        try{
           Thread.sleep(5*60*1000);
        } catch(InterruptedException e){
           break;
        }
    }
}
```

In this example, the thread will download stock prices, analyze and report, and then go to sleep for five minutes. After the sleep delay (if not interrupted) it will do the loop again.

During the sleeping state, the thread doesn't get a turn at the CPU. It becomes a candidate for running only after the sleep period has elapsed or the thread is interrupted. Note that there is no instance version of sleep(), so it is not possible to make other threads go to sleep directly.

exam Watch

All code in Java is run in threads, including the main() method which is often considered the main thread. For this reason, if Thread.sleep() is called from the main() method it will still cause the main() code to pause.

At any moment a thread can check its own interrupted status by using the static method:

```
Thread.interrupted(); // Returns boolean
```

This method will also automatically clear the flag, so if interrupted() is called twice in a row, the second call will return false.

Any thread can check another's interrupted status by using the instance method:

```
otherThread.isInterrupted(); // Returns boolean
```

This method, contrary to interrupted(), does not affect the flag in any way. The only way to change a thread's interrupted status from a different thread is to call interrupt() on the target thread.

EXERCISE 9-1

Creating a Thread and Putting It to Sleep

In this exercise we will create a simple counting thread. It will count to 100, pausing one second between each number. Also, in keeping with the counting theme, it will output a string every ten numbers.

1. Create a class and extend the Thread class. As an option, you can implement the Runnable interface.
2. Override the run() method of Thread. This is where the code will go that will output the numbers.
3. Create a for loop that will loop 100 times. Use the modulo operation to check whether there are any remainder numbers when divided by ten.
4. Use the static method Thread.sleep() to pause. The long number represents milliseconds.

The final code should look something like this:

```
class TheCount extends Thread {
  public void run() {
    for(int i = 1;i<=100;++i) {
      System.out.print(i + "  ");
      if(i % 10 == 0)
        System.out.println("Hahaha");
      try {
        Thread.sleep(1000);
      } catch(InterruptedException e) {}
    }
  }

  public static void main(String [] args) {
    new TheCount().start();
  }
}
```

CERTIFICATION OBJECTIVE 9.04

Concurrent Access Problems and Synchronized Threads

This section deals with the problems that can arise when different threads access the same information. It also explains how to use the *synchronized* keyword to avoid these problems.

Complexities can arise when using threads because the threads often share information to some degree. Keep in mind that there is no guarantee that two lines of code will be executed one after the other by the CPU. A different thread may take its turn, even with the following instruction:

```
i++;
```

Post-incrementing a variable is executed by the CPU not in one step, but in three:

1. Bring i to register.
2. Add 1 to register.
3. Store register onto i.

The CPU may swap over to a different thread at any time between these steps. Without proper protection, a supposedly co-operating thread may modify some variables at the wrong moment, thereby upsetting the results of an unprotected thread. The following section discusses the ways in which Java can deal with these problems.

Using Synchronized to Transmit Groups of Variables between Multiple Threads

There is a very flexible way of marking a group of variables that should have "exclusive use" for a thread. This involves using the *synchronized* keyword. Imagine two threads: Thread A and Thread B, both of which contain references to the same

StatusInfo object. Consider an application in which Thread A modifies a status object every few seconds, and Thread B analyzes this status object when needed, always expecting it to be the most recent status generated. The code for only the status object could look something like this:

```
public class StatusInfo {
    private float temperature, pressure, nitroConcentration;
    public void update(float temperature, float pressure, float
nitroConcentration){
        this.temperature = temperature;
        this.pressure = pressure;
        this.nitroConcentration = nitroConcentration;
    }
    public void analyze(){
        if(isDangerousCombination(temperature, pressure,
            nitroConcentration))
            stopChemicalManufacture();
    }
}
```

Without coordinating the access to the *StatusInfo* object, Thread A might see the status object in mid-modification, when some of the variables are new and some old, as shown in Figure 9-2. This is highly undesirable, even more so because there is no way to predict when these inconsistencies might happen. It depends on the odd chance that the CPU switches to Thread B at just the wrong moment. If the chance is very low, the software might seem to work fine while testing, only to fail later in production for no apparent reason.

The solution to guarantee safe behavior is to *lock* the object while it is being modified, so that the analyzer thread cannot read the information until the current modifications are finished. When an object is locked, no other threads can access the object until the lock is removed.

FIGURE 9-2

Threads accessing the same object concurrently

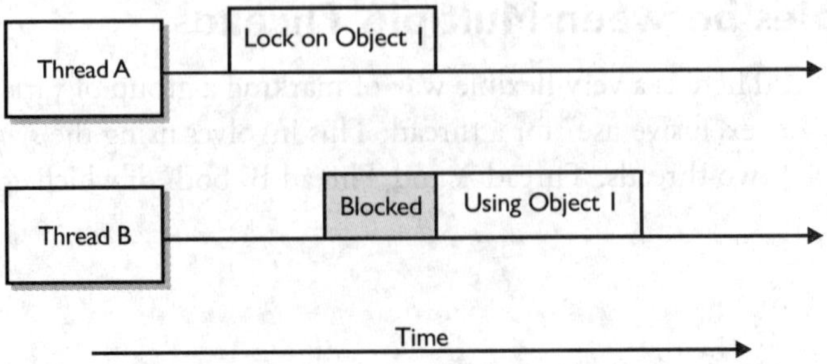

In Java this is achieved with synchronized blocks of code. A thread can enter a synchronized block only if it can lock the object. Otherwise, the thread temporarily becomes *blocked* at the entrance of the synchronized block, and it will get in only when the owner of the lock releases it, as shown in Figure 9-3. Many threads may be blocked in this way, but they will get the lock only one at a time, in an orderly fashion.

on the job

When many threads are trying to get a lock and it becomes available, only one of them will get it, but which one exactly varies between different systems. You should not make your code dependent on the particular order in which the threads will get the locks.

You could make the previous code safe by synchronizing the update() and analyze() methods. Simply add the *synchronized* keyword to the method declaration, as shown in lines 4 and 11 of the following code:

```
1.  public class StatusInfo {
2.     private float temperature, pressure, nitroConcentration;
3.
4.     public synchronized void update(float temperature, float pressure,
5.        float nitroConcentration){
6.        this.temperature=temperature;
7.        this.pressure=pressure;
8.        this.nitroConcentration=nitroConcentration;
9.     }
10.
11.    public synchronized void analyze() {
12.       if(isDangerousCombination(temperature, pressure,
13.          nitroConcentration)
14.          stopChemicalManufacture();
15.    }
16. }
```

In this way, when thread A (the status thread) enters the update() method, it acquires the lock of the StatusInfo object. In other words, thread A locks the object and thus prevents other threads that are sharing the same object from calling either of the synchronized methods. It releases the lock only when the method is finished. In the same way, thread B (the analyzer thread) acquires the lock upon entering the analyze() method, and it will release it upon finishing.

When either of the threads wants to get the lock but it is already taken, the thread goes from the running state to the *blocked* state. In this state the thread does nothing; it is simply stuck until the lock is released. Only after the lock is released does the thread go back to the running state, continuing in the normal way.

FIGURE 9-3

A thread locking an object

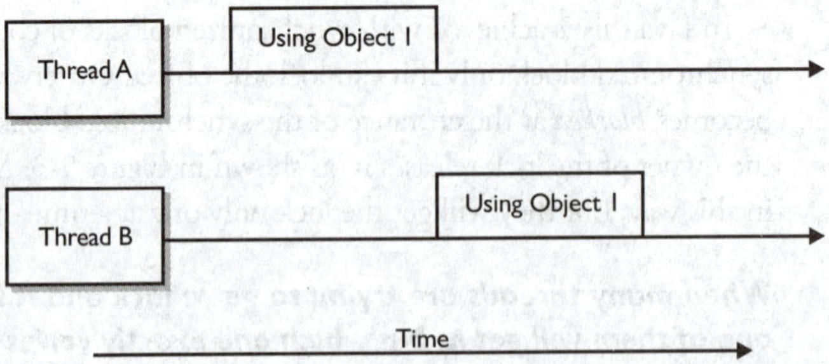

In Java, any object can be locked by a synchronized block of code. Synchronized methods always get the lock on the instance of the class from which the method is executed. So, when a synchronized method runs in an object, it is guaranteed the entire method will execute without other threads calling other synchronized methods in the object. In other words, all other threads are locked out of the object until the method finishes executing.

It is also possible to lock just a portion of a method (a block of code). A block of code can obtain a lock on an object by specifying that a block of code is synchronized on that particular object in the following way:

```
void notFullySynchronizedMethod(Object otherObject) {
    // Unsynchronized instructions here
    synchronized(otherObject){
        //Safe instructions here
    }
    // More unsynchronized instructions here
}
```

Note that a synchronized method is just a shortcut for obtaining a lock on the *this* object. Examine the following synchronized method:

```
public synchronized void analyze() {
    if(isDangerousCombination(temperature, pressure,
        nitroConcentration)
        stopChemicalManufacture();
}
```

The preceding method is actually the same as the following:

```
public void analyze() {
    synchronized(this){
        if(isDangerousCombination(temperature, pressure,
```

```
                 nitroConcentration)
                 stopChemicalManufacture();
         }
     }
```

Let's try locking an unsynchronized object in some real code. Remember the StatusInfo data object presented at the top of this section? It was not originally thread safe. Imagine a scenario where several threads read and manipulate the data of a single StatusInfo object. We will attempt to make a thread class that will read data from the StatusInfo object. We want to make sure the data in the StatusInfo object is not altered while our class is reading it. How would we accomplish this? Examine the following code:

```
1.  class Reactor extends Thread {
2.     StatusInfo si;
3.     public Reactor(StatusInfo si) {
4.        this.si = si;
5.     }
6.
7.     public void run() {
8.        while(true) {
9.           synchronized(si){
10.             if(isDangerousCombination(si.temperature, si.pressure,
11.                si.nitroConcentration)
12.                stopChemicalManufacture();
13.          }
14.       }
15.    }
16. }
```

As you can see in the constructor at line 3, the StatusInfo object could potentially be shared by many objects in different threads. We take care of the problem of unsynchronized data in line 9 by locking access to the StatusInfo object while we read the data. This will block out all other threads from manipulating the StatusInfo object while we read the data from it.

EXERCISE 9-2

Synchronizing a Block of Code

In this exercise we will attempt to synchronize a block of code. Within that block of code we will get the lock on an object so that other threads cannot modify it while the block of code is executing. We will be creating three threads that will all attempt to manipulate the same object. Each thread will output a single letter 100 times, and then increment that letter by one. The object we will be using is StringBuffer. We could synchronize on a String object, but strings cannot be modified once they are created so we would not be able to increment the letter without generating a new String object. The final output should have 100 As, 100 Bs, and 100 Cs all in unbroken lines.

1. Create a class and extend the Thread class.
2. Override the run() method of Thread. This is where the synchronized block of code will go.
3. For our three threaded objects to share the same object, we will need to create a constructor that accepts a StringBuffer object in the argument.
4. The synchronized block of code will obtain a lock on the StringBuffer object from step 3.
5. Within the block, output the StringBuffer 100 times and then increment the letter in the StringBuffer. You can check Chapter 11 for StringBuffer methods that will help with this.
6. Finally, in the main() method, create a single StringBuffer object using the letter *A*, create three instances of our class, and start all three of them.

Don't despair if it takes many tries to figure out this exercise. It's a pretty challenging topic. Your code might look something like this when completed:

```
class InSync extends Thread {
   StringBuffer letter;

   public InSync(StringBuffer letter) {
      this.letter = letter;
   }

   public void run() {
      synchronized(letter) {
         for(int i = 1;i<=100;++i) {
            System.out.print(letter);
         }
         System.out.println();
         // Increment the letter in StringBuffer:
```

```
15.             char temp = letter.charAt(0);
16.             ++temp;
17.             letter.setCharAt(0, temp);
18.          }
19.       }
20.
21.       public static void main(String [] args) {
22.          StringBuffer sb = new StringBuffer("A");
23.          new InSync(sb).start();
24.          new InSync(sb).start();
25.          new InSync(sb).start();
26.       }
27.    }
```

Just for fun, try removing lines 9 and 18 then run the program again. It will be unsynchronized, and the sequence will not print the letters in three continuous lines.

CERTIFICATION OBJECTIVE 9.05

Communicating with Objects by Waiting and Notifying

This section discusses the signaling system available to Java threads to ensure the proper order of execution between them. As discussed previously, a thread can interrupt another sleeping thread by calling the interrupt() method. This can be used to coordinate when a thread executes some action. Unfortunately this is focused on the thread, and usually we want to make a signal according to the object that we are dealing with (that is, the object that is ready for further processing).

For example, imagine two interdependent threads: thread A and thread B. Thread A needs to get a value from thread B, but it takes a while for thread B to calculate that value. In this case, thread A must wait until thread B signals that the calculation is completed.

The solution is to use the methods wait(), notify(), and notifyAll(). This enables signaling in a more object-oriented approach than interrupting threads, because it is based on the objects that the threads are dealing with.

Using wait() and notify() by Two Interdependent Threads

Here I'll present an example of two threads that depend on each other to proceed with their execution, and I'll show how to use wait() and notify() to make them interact safely and at the proper moment.

Think of a computer-controlled machine that cuts pieces of fabric into different shapes and an application that allows users to specify the shape to cut. The current version of the application has only one thread, which first asks the user for instructions and then directs the hardware to cut that shape, repeating the cycle afterward.

```
public void run(){
    while(true){
        // Get shape from user
        // Calculate machine steps from shape
        // Send steps to hardware
    }
}
```

This design is not optimal because the user can't do anything while the machine is busy and while there are other shapes to define. Some improvement is required.

A simple solution is to separate the processes into two different threads, one of them interacting with the user and another managing the hardware. The user thread sends the instructions to the hardware thread and then goes back to interacting with the user immediately. The hardware thread receives the instructions from the user thread and starts directing the machine immediately. Both threads use a common object to communicate, which holds the current design being processed.

The following pseudocode shows this design:

```
public void userLoop(){
    while(true){
        // Get shape from user
        // Calculate machine steps from shape
        // Modify common object with new machine steps
    }
}

public void hardwareLoop(){
    while(true){
        // Get steps from common object
        // Send steps to hardware
    }
}
```

The problem now is to get the hardware thread to process the machine steps as soon as they are available. Also, the user thread should not modify them until they have all been sent to the hardware. The solution is to use wait() and notify(), and also to synchronize some of the code.

The methods wait() and notify() are instance methods of Object. In the same way that every object has a lock, every object can have a list of threads that are waiting for a signal from the object. A thread gets on this list by executing the wait() method of the target object. From that moment, it doesn't execute any further instructions until the notify() method of the target object is called. If many threads are waiting on the same object, only one will be chosen to proceed with its execution. If there are no threads waiting, then no particular action is taken. Let's take a look at some real code that shows one object waiting for another object to notify it (take note, it is somewhat complex):

```
class ThreadA {
   public static void main(String [] args) {
      ThreadB b = new ThreadB();
      b.start();

      synchronized(b) {
         try {
            System.out.println("Waiting for b to complete...");
            b.wait();
         } catch (InterruptedException e) {}
      }
      System.out.println("Total is: " + b.total);
   }
}

class ThreadB extends Thread {
   int total;

   public void run() {
      synchronized(this) {
         for(int i=0;i<100;i++) {
            total += i;
         }
         notify();
      }
   }
}
```

This program contains two objects with threads; ThreadA contains the main thread and ThreadB has a thread that calculates the sum of all numbers from 0 to 99. As soon as line 4 calls the start() method, ThreadA will continue with the next line of code in its own class, which means it could get to line 12 before ThreadB has finished the calculation. To prevent this, we use the wait() method in line 9.

Notice in line 6 the code synchronizes itself with the object *b*—this is because in order to call wait() on the object, ThreadA must own a lock on *b*. For a thread to call wait() or notify(), the thread has to be the owner of the lock for that object. When the thread waits, it temporarily releases the lock for other threads to use, but it will need it again to continue execution. It is common to find code such as the following:

```
synchronized(anotherObject) { // this has the lock on anotherObject
    try {
        anotherObject.wait(); // the thread releases the lock and waits
        // To continue, the thread needs the lock, so it may be blocked
        // until it gets it.
    } catch(InteruptedException e){}
}
```

The preceding code waits until notify() is called on *anotherObject.*

```
synchronized(this) {
    notify();
}
```

This code notifies any thread currently waiting on the *this* object.

The lock can be acquired much earlier in the code, such as in the calling method. Note that if the thread calling wait() does not own the lock, it will throw an IllegalMonitorStateExeption. This exception is not a checked exception, so you don't have to catch it explicitly. You should always be clear whether a thread has the lock of an object in any given block of code.

Notice in lines 7–10 there is a try-catch block around the wait() method. A waiting thread can be interrupted in the same way as a sleeping thread, so you have to take care of the exception:

```
try{
    wait();
} catch(InterruptedException e) {
    // Do something about it
}
```

In the fabric example, the way to use these methods is to have the hardware thread wait on the shape to be available and the user thread to notify after it has written the steps.

The machine steps may comprise global steps, such as moving the required fabric to the cutting area, and a number of substeps, such as the direction and length of a cut. As an example they could be:

```
int fabricRoll;
int cuttingSpeed;
Point startingPoint;
float[] directions;
float[] lengths;
etc..
```

It is important that the user thread does not modify the machine steps while the hardware thread is using them, so this reading and writing should be synchronized. The resulting code would look like this:

```
class Operator extends Thread {
   public void run(){
      while(true){
         // Get shape from user
         synchronized(this){
            // Calculate new machine steps from shape
            notify();
         }
      }
   }
}
class Machine extends Thread {
   Operator operator; // assume this gets initialized
   public void run(){
      while(true){
         synchronized(operator){
            try {
               operator.wait();
            } catch(InterruptedException ie) {}
            // Send machine steps to hardware
         }
      }
   }
}
```

The machine thread, once started, will immediately go into the waiting state and will wait patiently until the operator sends the first notification. At that point it is the operator thread that owns the lock for the object, so the hardware thread gets stuck for a while. It is only after the operator thread abandons the synchronized block that the hardware thread can really start processing the machine steps.

While one shape is being processed by the hardware, the user may interact with the system and specify another shape to be cut. When the user is finished with the shape and it is time to cut it, the operator thread attempts to enter the synchronized block, maybe blocking until the machine thread has finished with the previous machine steps. When the machine thread has finished, it repeats the loop, going again to the waiting state (and therefore releasing the lock). Only then can the operator thread enter the synchronized block and overwrite the machine steps with the new ones.

Having two threads is definitely an improvement over having one, although in this implementation there is still a possibility of making the user wait. A further improvement would be to have many shapes in a queue; therefore reducing the possibility of requiring the user to wait for the hardware.

There is also a second form of wait() that accepts a number of milliseconds as a maximum time to wait. If the thread is not interrupted, it will continue normally whenever it is notified or the specified timeout has elapsed. This normal continuation consists of getting out of the waiting state, but to continue execution it will have to get the lock for the object:

```
synchronized(a){ // The thread gets the lock on a
   a.wait(2000); // The thread releases the lock and waits for notify
   // But only for a maximum of two seconds
   // The thread reacquires the lock
   // More instructions here
}
```

Using notifyAll When Many Threads May Be Waiting

In some applications, it is preferable to notify all of the threads that are waiting on a particular object. If so, you only have to call the method notifyAll() on the object

```
targetObject.notifyAll(); // Will notify all waiting threads
```

or, more likely, the object can choose to notify on its own:

```
notifyAll(); // Will notify all waiting threads
```

All of the threads will be notified and start competing to get the lock. As the lock is used and released by each thread, all of them will get into action without a need for further notification.

As I said earlier, an object can have many threads waiting on it, and using notify() will affect only one of them. Which one exactly is not specified and depends on the JVM implementation, so you should never rely on a particular thread being notified in preference to another.

In cases in which there might be a lot more waiting, the best way to do this is by using notifyAll(). Let's take a look at this in some code. In this example there is one class that performs a calculation and many readers that are waiting to receive the completed calculation. At any given moment many readers may be waiting.

```
class Reader extends Thread {
   Calculator c;

   public Reader(Calculator calc) {
      c = calc;
   }

   public void run() {
      synchronized(c) {
         try {
            System.out.println("Waiting for calculation...");
            c.wait();
         } catch (InterruptedException e) {}
      }
      System.out.println("Total is: " + c.total);
   }

   public static void main(String [] args) {
      Calculator calculator = new Calculator();
      calculator.start();
      new Reader(calculator).start();
      new Reader(calculator).start();
      new Reader(calculator).start();
   }
}

class Calculator extends Thread {
   int total;

   public void run() {
```

```
31.         synchronized(this) {
32.            for(int i=0;i<100;i++) {
33.               total += i;
34.            }
35.            notifyAll();
36.         }
37.      }
38.   }
```

This program starts the calculator with its calculation, and then starts three threads that are all waiting to receive the finished calculation (lines 18–24). Note that if the run() method at line 30 used notify() instead of notifyAll(), there would be a chance that only one reader would be notified, instead of all the readers.

CERTIFICATION OBJECTIVE 9.06

Deadlocked Threads

Threads sometimes get stuck for awhile trying to get a lock on an object. Imagine two threaded objects: Object A and Object B. Sometimes situations can occur in which Object A has a lock on itself and is also waiting for the lock to be freed on Object B. Object B also has a lock on itself and is waiting for the lock to be freed on Object A. This situation is called *deadlock* (also known as thread starvation or deadly embrace). In its simplest form, there are only two threads participating, as in the following example:

```
public class DeadlockRisk {
   private static class Resource {
      public int value;
```

```
4.      }
5.      private Resource resourceA = new Resource();
6.      private Resource resourceB = new Resource();
7.      public int read() {
8.          synchronized(resourceA) { // May deadlock here
9.              synchronized(resourceB) {
10.                 return resourceB.value + resourceA.value;
11.             }
12.         }
13.     }
14.
15.     public void write(int a, int b) {
16.         synchronized(resourceB) { // May deadlock here
17.             synchronized(resourceA) {
18.                 resourceA.value = a;
19.                 resourceB.value = b;
20.             }
21.         }
22.     }
23. }
```

Assume that read() is started by one thread and write() is started by another. If there are two different threads that may read and write independently, there is a risk of deadlock at line 8 or 16. The reader thread will have resourceA, the writer thread will have resourceB, and both will get stuck forever waiting for the other to back down.

Code like this almost never results in deadlock because the CPU has to switch from the reader thread to the writer thread at a particular point in the code, and the chances of deadlock occurring are very small. The application may work fine 99.9 percent of the time.

The preceding simple example is easy to fix; just swap the order of locking for either the reader or the writer at lines 16 and 17 (or lines 8 and 9). More complex deadlock situations can take a long time to figure out.

FROM THE CLASSROOM

Deadlocking

Deadlock is one of those problems that can be difficult to debug, especially because things just stop happening and there are no friendly exception stack traces to study. The situation might be difficult, or even impossible to replicate, because it depends on when the JVM thread scheduler switches from one thread to another.

The best way to avoid deadlocked applications is to plan in advance. A well-designed application will never have the possibility of deadlock occurring. You have to consider all the different paths that a thread will follow and the different combinations of locks that it will acquire in each path. This tree of paths can be combined with the trees for other threads, making it easy to detect possible deadlocks. If conflicting locks appear, change the design before it is too late.

For simple applications it is generally a good idea to use blocks that are mostly synchronized on the appropriate object. This way all the synchronized code can be found on the same file. Try to keep locks on objects for the minimum amount of time possible. Also, it is generally a good idea to avoid circular *paths of execution* where threads may go from object to object only to call the same objects again. In six words: To avoid deadlocks, keep it simple.

—Diego Moriarty, Sun Certified Java Programmer and Developer

CERTIFICATION OBJECTIVE 9.07

Scheduling Threads Using Priority and Yielding

As mentioned earlier in the chapter, it is not possible to predict when the currently executing thread will become dormant and a different one will become active. Nor is it possible to predict which thread will be chosen next. It all depends on the JVM and the underlying operating system. Even so, there are some sure ways of getting your threaded application to perform reliably on any platform.

The first thing to consider is when does the current thread lose its turn at the CPU? The current thread will always lose its turn when the yield() method is called, which is a static method of Thread:

```
Thread.yield(); // Current thread will give up the turn on the CPU
```

Using yield() is always a conscious decision by the programmer; it is used to give up the turn voluntarily.

exam Watch

Note that yield() is a static method of Thread. If you have a reference to a thread (otherThread) and you call yield on it (otherThread.yield()), what actually happens is the current thread will yield, not the other one. No thread can make another thread yield.

Besides yielding, the turn is always given up when the current thread sleeps, waits, or does a blocking input/output (I/O) operation. Blocking I/O operations are, for example, the ones that read information from a stream, and after some information arrives from the stream, the thread will attempt to get turns off the CPU again.

In most systems, the turn is also lost when a higher priority thread becomes a candidate to run (either after starting, waking up, being notified, or returning from a blocking I/O), but this behavior is not guaranteed for all systems.

There are some systems that will forcefully switch to another thread if the turn is not given up after some amount of time. This is called *time-slicing*. You should be careful about making any assumptions. Many programs work fine in one system because, by luck, they rely on the absence of time-slicing (or the opposite; they work by relying on time-slicing). It is only when these programs are tested on different systems that problems arise.

The second thing to consider is which thread will be the next to execute. Java allows the programmer to specify the priorities of threads. The intention of the priorities is to suggest that no low priority thread executes while a higher priority one needs executing, although this is not guaranteed either.

The Thread member method setPrority() accepts an integer between 1 and 10. For clarity, Thread has the constants MIN_PRIORITY, NORM_PRIORITY, and MAX_PRIORITY, which are 1, 5, and 10 respectively. It is used as follows:

```
realTimeThread.setPriority(Thread.MAX_PRIORITY);
```

on the job

When running functions triggered by the user, it is easy to end up having the DispatchThread running for a few seconds in graphical user interface (GUI) applications. During this time, the GUI seems unstable (native components get refreshed, but paint() methods don't get called), and the GUI doesn't respond to any more actions. On these occasions, the users will get a better experience if the action is performed in a separate, lower priority thread, even if it only lasts for some seconds. This is at the cost of explicitly taking care of concurrent access problems.

Now that you have a better understanding of Java Threads, here are some possible scenario questions and their answers.

SCENARIO & SOLUTION

Which method would you call to delay the current thread for one second?	Thread.sleep(1000)
What is the name of the method that is used to signal to all threads waiting on the object that they can continue?	notifyAll()
Which method would you call to begin a thread executing?	start()
Which method would you call to move the thread from the running state to the runnable state?	yield()
What is the name of the Thread method that causes a thread to stop until it receives a signal from an object?	None! There is no method like this defined in the Thread class. The wait() method is defined in the Object class.

CERTIFICATION SUMMARY

This chapter contains all the required information regarding the use of threads that you will need to apply on the Certification Exam. Threads can be created by either extending the Thread class or implementing the Runnable interface. The only method that must be overwritten in the Runnable interface is the run() method; however, the start() method is used to begin the thread.

There are issues to take into consideration concerning interaction between the program code and other threads. To ensure that the JVM executes a block of code in a thread without other threads interrupting, use the *synchronized* keyword. To coordinate activity between different threads, use the wait(), notify(), and notifyAll() methods. We discussed how threads can go through the different states of runnable, running, and dead and when threads go in and out of the sleeping, waiting, blocking on I/O, and acquiring a lock state.

✓ TWO-MINUTE DRILL

Here are some of the key points from each certification objective in Chapter 9.

Creating, Instantiating, and Starting New Threads

- ❑ Threads are created by extending Thread and overriding the public void run() method.
- ❑ Thread objects can also be created using the constructor with a Runnable argument.
- ❑ You can call start() on a Thread object only once. If start() is called more than once on a Thread object it will throw a RuntimeException.
- ❑ It is legal to create many Thread objects using the same Runnable object in the constructor.

Transitioning Between Thread States

- ❑ Once a new thread is started, it will always enter the runnable state, the running state, and finally the dead state.
- ❑ The thread scheduler can move a thread back and forth between the runnable state and the running state.
- ❑ A running thread may enter the waiting state by a call from wait() or sleep().
- ❑ When the sleep or wait is over, the thread can only reenter the runnable state.
- ❑ A dead thread cannot be started again.

Putting Threads to Sleep

- ❑ Sleeping is used to delay execution for a period of time, and no locks are released.
- ❑ The intended use of interrupt() is to signal a thread that it should stop sleeping or waiting.
- ❑ Threads that are in the waiting or sleeping state can be interrupted, but threads that are blocking I/O or getting a lock cannot.

Concurrent Access Problems and Synchronized Threads

- ❑ Synchronized blocks of code can get *exclusive use* of an object.

Communicating with Objects by Waiting and Notifying

- ❑ The synchronized wait() method is used to wait for a signal from a particular object.
- ❑ The synchronized notify() method is used to send a signal to one and only one of the threads that are waiting for it.
- ❑ The synchronized method notifyAll() works in the same way as notify, only it sends the signal to all of the threads waiting on the object.

Deadlocked Threads

- ❑ Deadlocking is when thread execution grinds to a halt because the code is waiting for locks to be removed from objects.
- ❑ Deadlocking can occur when a locked object attempts to access another locked object that is trying to access the first locked object.

Scheduling Using Priority and Yielding

- ❑ The yield() method is used to give up control and allow other threads to run.
- ❑ The setPriority() method is used on Thread objects to give threads a priority of between 1 (low) and 10 (high).

SELF TEST

The following questions will help you measure your understanding of the material presented in this chapter. Read all of the choices carefully, as there may be more than one correct answer. Choose all correct answers for each question.

Creating, Instantiating, and Starting New Threads

1. Given:

```
1.  class MyThread extends Thread {
2.
3.     public static void main(String [] args) {
4.        MyThread t = new MyThread();
5.        t.run();
6.     }
7.
8.     public void run() {
9.        for(int i=1;i<3;++i) {
10.          System.out.print(i + "..");
11.       }
12.    }
13. }
```

What is the result of this code?

A. This code will not compile due to line 4.

B. This code will not compile due to line 5.

C. 1..2..

D. 1..2..3..

2. Which of the following methods are defined by the Runnable interface?

A. start()

B. stop()

C. resume()

D. run()

E. suspend()

3. The following block of code creates a Thread using a Runnable target:

```
Runnable target = new MyRunnable();
Thread myThread = new Thread(target);
```

Which of the following classes can be used to create the target, so that the preceding code compiles correctly?

A. public class MyRunnable extends Runnable{public void run(){}}

B. public class MyRunnable extends Object{public void run(){}}

C. public class MyRunnable implements Runnable{public void run(){}}

D. public class MyRunnable extends Runnable{void run(){}}

E. public class MyRunnable implements Runnable{void run(){}}

4. Given:

```
 1. class MyThread extends Thread {
 2.
 3.    public static void main(String [] args) {
 4.       MyThread t = new MyThread();
 5.       t.start();
 6.       System.out.print("one. ");
 7.       t.start();
 8.       System.out.print("two. ");
 9.    }
10.
11.    public void run() {
12.       System.out.print("Thread ");
13.    }
14. }
```

What is the result of this code?

A. Compilation fails due to line 7.

B. Compilation succeeds but an exception is thrown at line 7 when run.

C. *Thread one. Thread two.*

D. None of the above.

5. Given:

```
public class MyRunnable implements Runnable {
   public void run() {
      // some code here
```

```
    }
}
```

What is the proper way to create and start this thread?

A. new Runnable(MyRunnable).start();

B. new Thread(MyRunnable).run();

C. new Thread(new MyRunnable()).start();

D. new MyRunnable().start();

6. Given:

```
1.  class MyThread extends Thread {
2.
3.     public static void main(String [] args) {
4.        MyThread t = new MyThread();
5.        Thread x = new Thread(t);
6.        x.start();
7.     }
8.
9.     public void run() {
10.       for(int i=0;i<3;++i) {
11.          System.out.print(i + "..");
12.       }
13.    }
14. }
```

What is the result of this code?

A. The code fails to compile due to line 5.

B. 1..2..3..

C. 0..1..2..3..

D. 0..1..2..

Putting Threads to Sleep

7. Given:

```
class Test {

   public static void main(String [] args) {
      printAll(args);
   }
```

```
    public static void printAll(String[] lines) {
        for(int i=0;i<lines.length;i++){
            System.out.println(lines[i]);
            Thread.currentThread().sleep(1000);
        }
    }
}
```

The static method Thread.currentThread() returns a reference to the currently executing Thread object. What is the result of this code?

A. Each String in the array *lines* will output, with a one-second pause.

B. Each String in the array *lines* will output, with no pause in between because this method is not executed in a Thread.

C. Each String in the array *lines* will output, and there is no guarantee there will be a pause because currentThread() may not retrieve this thread.

D. This code will not compile.

8. Given:

```
public class MyThread extends Thread {
    public void run() {
        try {
            for(int i=1;i<5;i++) {
                System.out.print(i + " ");
                if(i > 2)
                    interrupt();
                sleep(1000);
                if(interrupted())
                    break;
            }
        }
        catch(InterruptedException e) {
            System.out.print("caught");
        }
    }
}
```

Assume another object creates an instance of this Thread and starts it. What is the output of this thread?

A. 1

B. 1 2

C. 1 2 3

D. 1 caught

E. 1 2 caught

F. 1 2 3 caught

G. None of the above

Concurrent Access Problems and Synchronized Threads

9. Assume you have an object that is used to contain two values: *a* and *b*. Which of the following methods in its class can prevent concurrent access problems? (Choose all that apply.)

A. public int read(int a, int b){return a+b;}
public void set(int a, int b){this.a=a;this.b=b;}

B. public synchronized int read(int a, int b){return a+b;}
public synchronized void set(int a, int b){this.a=a;this.b=b;}

C. public int read(int a, int b){synchronized(a){return a+b;}}
public void set(int a, int b){synchronized(a){this.a=a;this.b=b;}}

D. public int read(int a, int b){synchronized(a){return a+b;}}
public void set(int a, int b){synchronized(b){this.a=a;this.b=b;}}

E. public synchronized(this) int read(int a, int b){return a+b;}
public synchronized(this) void set(int a, int b){this.a=a;this.b=b;}

F. public int read(int a, int b){synchronized(this){return a+b;}}
public void set(int a, int b){synchronized(this){this.a=a;this.b=b;}}

Communicating with Objects by Waiting and Notifying

10. Which method is used to signal all threads waiting on an object that they may continue? (Fill in the blank.)

______________________ is used to signal all threads waiting on an object that they may continue.

11. Which class or interface defines the wait(), notify(), and notifyAll() methods?

A. Object

B. Thread

C. Runnable

D. Class

E. None of the above

12. Of the following objects, which can have locks? (Choose all that apply.)

A. Thread objects

B. Runnable objects

C. Primitive types

D. Object objects

13. What is the purpose of notifying a thread that is in the waiting state?

A. To signal that the lock that it was waiting for is now available

B. To prevent it getting turns at the CPU

C. To make it throw an InterruptedException

D. To set the notified flag

E. To signal that it should proceed in executing instructions

F. To signal that there are no more instructions to execute

14. Which of the following are methods of the Object class? (Choose all that apply.)

A. notify();

B. notifyAll();

C. isInterrupted();

D. synchronized();

E. interrupt();

F. wait(long msecs);

G. sleep(long msecs);

H. yield();

I. synchronized(Object lock);

15. Given:

```
public class WaitTest {
   public static void main(String [] args) {
      System.out.print("1 ");
      synchronized(args){
         System.out.print("2 ");
```

```
6.            try {
7.                args.wait();
8.            }
9.            catch(InterruptedException e){}
10.        }
11.        System.out.print("3 ");
12.    }
13. }
```

What is the result of trying to compile and run this program?

A. It fails to compile because the IllegalMonitorStateException of wait() is not dealt with in line 7.

B. 1 2 3

C. 1 3

D. 1 2

E. At runtime it throws an IllegalMonitorStateException when trying to wait.

F. It will fail to compile because it has to be synchronized on the *this* object.

16. Assume the following method is properly synchronized and the exception is caught:

```
wait(2000);
```

After calling this method, when will the thread become a candidate to get another turn at the CPU?

A. After the thread is interrupted, the thread is notified, or two seconds have elapsed

B. After the thread is interrupted or two seconds after the thread is notified

C. Two seconds after the thread is notified or interrupted

D. After the thread is interrupted or two seconds have elapsed

17. When should notifyAll() be used instead of the notify() method?

A. When there is one thread waiting for notification on the specific object

B. When all the objects that the thread has locked should be notified

C. When many threads are waiting on a waitAll method for the specified object

D. When there might be more than one thread waiting for notification on the specified object

E. When all waiting threads on the system should be notified

F. When there might be one thread waiting for notification on the specific object

Scheduling Using Priority and Yielding

18. Given:

```
public class ThreadTest extends Thread {
    public static void main(String [] args) {
        new ThreadTest(1);
        new ThreadTest(2);
        System.out.println("main ");
    }
    private int val;
    private ThreadTest(int val) {
        this.val = val;
        start();
    }
    public void run() {
        System.out.print(val + " ");
    }
}
```

What will be the output from this program?

A. 1 2 main

B. 2 1 main

C. main 1 2

D. main 2 1

E. 1 main 2

F. 2 main 1

G. Any of the above

H. None of the above

19. Assume you create a program and one of your threads (called backgroundThread) does some lengthy numerical processing. What would be the proper way of setting its priority to ensure that the rest of the system is very responsive while the thread is running? (Choose all that apply.)

A. backgroundThread.setPriority(Thread.LOW_PRIORITY);

B. backgroundThread.setPriority(Thread.MAX_PRIORITY);

C. backgroundThread.setPriority(1);

D. backgroundThread.setPriority(Thread.NO_PRIORITY);

E. backgroundThread.setPriority(Thread.MIN_PRIORITY);

F. backgroundThread.setPriority(Thread.NORM_PRIORITY);

G. backgroundThread.setPriority(10);

H. backgroundThread.setPriority(0);

20. Which method can be called on a Thread instance to make sure it never again receives a turn at the CPU?

A. yield(0);

B. exit(0);

C. yield();

D. setDaemon();

E. setDaemon(0);

F. interrupt();

G. None of the above

SELF TEST ANSWERS

Creating, Instantiating, and Starting New Threads

1. ☑ C. Line 5 calls the run() method, so the run() method executes as a normal method should.
☒ A is incorrect because this is the proper way to create an object. **B** is incorrect because it is legal to call the run() method, even though this will not start a true thread. The code after line 5 will not execute until the run() method is complete. **D** is incorrect because the for loop only does two iterations.

2. ☑ **D.** Only run() is defined by the Runnable interface.
☒ A, B, C, and E are all incorrect because they are methods of the Thread class. Also, the methods resume(), suspend(), and stop() have all been deprecated in Java 2.

3. ☑ **C.** The class correctly implements the Runnable interface with a legal public void run() method.
☒ A is incorrect because interfaces are not extended, they are implemented. **B** is incorrect because even though the class would compile and it has a valid public void run method, it does not implement the Runnable interface, so the compiler would complain when creating a Thread with an instance of it. **D** is incorrect because it tries to extend, not to implement, the Runnable interface. In addition, the run method should be public. **E** is incorrect because the run method should be public.

4. ☑ **B.** When the start() method is attempted on a single Thread object, the method will throw an IllegalThreadStateException (you will not need to know this exception name for the exam). Even if the thread has finished running it is still illegal to call start() again.
☒ A is incorrect because compilation will succeed. For the most part, the Java compiler only checks for illegal syntax, but if methods are legally called compilation will succeed. **C** is incorrect because of the preceding reason, but it is also incorrect because there is no guarantee of the execution order of threads. **D** is incorrect because there is a correct answer.

5. ☑ **C.** Because the class implements Runnable, an instance of it has to be passed to the Thread constructor, and then the instance of the Thread has to be started.
☒ A is incorrect. There is no constructor like this for Runnable because Runnable is an interface, and it is illegal to pass a class name to any constructor. **B** is incorrect for the same reason; you can't pass a class name to any constructor. **D** is incorrect because MyRunnable doesn't have a start() method.

6. ☑ **D.** The thread MyThread will start and loop three times (from 0 to 2).
☒ A is incorrect because the Thread class implements the Runnable interface; therefore, in line 5,

Thread can take an object of type Thread as an argument in the constructor. B and C are incorrect because the variable *i* in the for-loop starts with a value of 0 and ends with a value of 2.

Putting Threads to Sleep

7. ☑ The sleep() method must be enclosed in a try-catch block, or the method printAll() must declare it throws the InterruptedException.
☒ A is incorrect, but it would be correct if the InterruptedException was dealt with. B is incorrect, but it would still be incorrect if the InterruptedException was dealt with because all Java code, including the main() method, runs in threads. C is incorrect. The sleep() method is static, so even if it is called on an instance it still always affects the currently executing thread.

8. ☑ F. The thread prints the numbers and in the last loop, when *i* is 3, it will set the interrupted flag. This will force the last of the sleep method calls to throw an InterruptedException immediately and print *caught* after the already printed numbers.
☒ A, B, and C are incorrect because they count on the InterruptedException never being thrown. D and E are incorrect because they count on the interrupt flag being set before *i* is 3.

Concurrent Access Problems and Synchronized Threads

9. ☑ B and F. By marking the methods as synchronized, the threads will get the lock of the *this* object before proceeding. Only one thread will be either setting or reading at any given moment, thereby assuring that read() always returns the addition of a valid pair.
☒ A is incorrect because it is not synchronized; therefore there is no guarantee that the values added by the read() method belong to the same pair. C and D are incorrect; only objects can be used to synchronize on. E is incorrect because it is not possible to select other objects to synchronize on when declaring a method as synchronized. Even using *this* is incorrect syntax.

Communicating with Objects by Waiting and Notifying

10. ☑ notifyAll().The notifyAll() method is used to signal all threads waiting on an object that they may continue.

11. ☑ A. The Object class defines these thread-specific methods.
☒ B, C, and D are incorrect because they do not define these methods. And yes, the Java API does define a class called Class, though you do not need to know it for the exam.

12. ☑ A, B, and D. All objects in Java can be locked by another thread.
☒ C is incorrect because primitive types cannot be locked.

13. ☑ E. A waiting thread is waiting for a different thread to signal that it is time to proceed, typically because some data has been updated or made available.
☒ A is incorrect because waiting threads do not wait on a lock; they wait on an object. **B** is incorrect; a waiting thread is not taking turns on the CPU. The notify() method takes the thread out of this state and into a similar state when it tries to get a lock to proceed in executing. **C** is incorrect because interrupt() is used to make it throw an InteruptedException. **D** is incorrect; there is no such flag. **F** is incorrect because notify is used precisely when there are more instructions to execute.

14. ☑ A, B, and F. They are all related to the list of threads waiting on the specified object.
☒ C, E, G, and H are incorrect answers. The methods isInterrupted() and interrupt() are instance methods of Thread. The methods sleep() and yield() are static methods of Thread. **D** and **I** are incorrect; such methods don't exist because synchronized is a keyword and the synchronized() construct is part of the Java language.

15. ☑ D. 1 and 2 will be printed, but there will be no return from the wait call because no other thread will notify the main thread, so 3 will never be printed. The program is essentially frozen at line 7.
☒ A is incorrect; IllegalMonitorStateException is an unchecked exception so it doesn't have to be deal with explicitly. **B** and **C** are incorrect; 3 will never be printed, since this program will never terminate because it will wait forever. **E** is incorrect because IllegalMonitorStateException will never be thrown because the wait() is done on *args* within a block of code synchronized on args. **F** is incorrect because any object can be used to synchronize on, and furthermore, there is no *this* when running a static method.

16. ☑ A. Either of the three will make the thread become a candidate for running again.
☒ B and C are incorrect because the thread will become a candidate immediately after notification, not two seconds afterwards. **D** is also incorrect because the thread may become a candidate after interruption.

17. ☑ D. No matter how many threads are waiting on notification from the specified object, notifyAll() should be used if there is a possibility that there are more threads waiting on the specified object than the one we intended to notify. Just using notify may notify another thread, and the intended thread might never be notified, and so the application may freeze.
☒ A and F are incorrect because notify() should only be used if only one thread is waiting. **B** is incorrect; objects are not notified, threads are. **C** is incorrect because there is no such waitAll() method. **E** is incorrect because there is no way of notifying all waiting threads on the system simultaneously.

Scheduling Using Priority and Yielding

18. ☑ **G.** It is not possible to tell what the output will be. There is no way of knowing exactly when threads will get a turn at the CPU, in which order, and if they preempt the currently running one. These considerations are JVM/platform dependent.
☒ **A, B, C, D, E,** and **F** are incorrect answers because none of them can be guaranteed for all platforms, although for some particular JVM/platforms it is possible to predict their particular outputs. The best possible answer, therefore, is **G. H** is incorrect because it will always be one of the above, regardless of the platform.

19. ☑ **C** and **E.** In **E**, the constant Thread.MIN_PRIORITY is the lowest priority that a Thread can have, and the background thread should have a very low priority or the lowest. Answer **C** is correct because the value of Thread.MIN_PRIORITY is 1, although for code clarity it is recommended to use the Thread.MIN_PRIORITY.
☒ **A** and **D** are incorrect because there are no such variables in the Thread class. **B** is incorrect; using MAX_PRIORITY would make other threads have less chances of getting a turn of the CPU, even to the point of freezing until the numerical processing is finished. **F** is incorrect because the thread would still compete for the CPU time and even delay other threads. **G** is incorrect because 10 is the value of MAX_PRIORITY, so *i* would be equivalent to answer **B. H** is incorrect because the allowed range for thread priorities is 1 through 10.

20. ☑ **G.** There is no method call to force a thread to never get a turn at the CPU again.
☒ **A** is incorrectly called because yield takes no parameter, and it is a static method, not an instance method. **B** is incorrect; Thread doesn't have an exit() method. **C** is incorrect because yield() can be used by the current thread to give up control of the CPU, but it will get another turn later. **D** and **E** are incorrect because setting the Deamon state does not stop the thread in any way, and further, setting the Daemon state requires one boolean parameter. **F** is incorrect. The interrupted flag of the thread will be set, and if sleeping or waiting, it will throw an InterruptedException, but it will still get turns at the CPU.

10

The java.lang.Math Class

CERTIFICATION OBJECTIVES

10.01	Using the java.lang.Math Class
✓	Two-Minute Drill
Q&A	Self Test

This chapter covers one of the more straightforward testing objectives of the Java Certified Programmer exam, the java.lang.Math class. This class contains methods that can calculate standard mathematical functions, including trigonometry functions. The methods you will need to know for the exam are abs(), ceil(), floor(), max(), min(), random(), round(), sin(), cos(), tan(), and sqrt(). The exam will test your knowledge of what each of these methods will do when given a number. It may also test you on the Math class method signatures. You may have to know, for instance, that Math.round() could take a float or a double as an input parameter and returns an int or a long.

CERTIFICATION OBJECTIVE 10.01

Using the java.lang.Math Class

The java.lang package defines classes that are fundamental to the Java language. For this reason, all classes in the java.lang package are imported automatically, so there is no reason to include an import statement for this. The package defines class wrappers for all primitive types such as Boolean, Byte, Character, Double, Float, Integer, Long, Short, and Void as well as Object, the class from which all Java classes inherit. The package also contains the Math class, which is used to perform basic mathematical operations.

The Math class defines two approximations of the mathematical constants *pi* and *e*. Math.PI is a double value that is close to the ratio of a circle's circumference to its diameter. Math.E is a double value that is close to the base of the natural logarithms. The signatures of them are as follows:

- public final static double Math.PI
- public final static double Math.E

Because all methods of the Math class are defined as static, it's unnecessary to create an instance to access the functionality. In fact it's not possible to create an instance of the Math class because the constructor method is private. It is also not possible to extend the class, because it is final. The main reason these classes are final is because final classes are more efficient and execute faster (many Java application programming interface (API) classes are final for this reason).

Methods of the java.lang.Math Class

The methods of the Math class are static and are accessed like any static method, through the class name. The following sections describe the Math methods and include examples of how to use them.

abs

The abs() method returns the absolute value of the argument. Invoking Math.abs(99) returns 99, and invoking Math.abs(-99) also returns 99. The method is overloaded to handle an int, a long, a float, or a double argument. In all but two cases, the returned value is non-negative. If the argument is equal to Integer.MIN_VALUE or Long.MIN_VALUE, then the returned result is the same as the argument, which is less than zero. Examine the following code:

```
public class MathTest {
   public static void main(String [] argh) {
      System.out.println("Min Int = " + Math.abs(Integer.MIN_VALUE));
      System.out.println("Min Long = " + Math.abs(Long.MIN_VALUE));
   }
}
```

In this example, we are actually calling two separate methods. The first method is the overloaded abs() method for an int value, and the second method is the overloaded abs() method for a long value. In both methods, we are using the constant MIN_VALUE for an integer and a long. The results are as follows:

```
Min Int = -2147483648
Min Long = -9223372036854775808
```

It is not possible to do the same with the float overloaded abs() methods because Float.MIN_VALUE and Double.MIN_VALUE equals the smallest positive numbers; hence, the value will not be negative. The signatures of the abs() method are as follows:

- public static int abs(int a)
- public static long abs(long a)
- public static float abs(float a)
- public static double abs(double a)

ceil

The ceil() method returns the smallest double that is greater than or equal to the argument and equal to the nearest integer value. In other words, the argument is rounded up to the nearest integer equivalent.

Let's look at some examples of this in action, just to make sure you are familiar with the concept. All the following calls to Math.ceil() return the double value 9.0:

- Math.ceil(9.0)
- Math.ceil(8.4)
- Math.ceil(8.8)

Negative numbers are similar, but just remember that -9 is larger than -10! All the following calls to Math.ceil() return the double value -9.0:

- Math.ceil(-9.0)
- Math.ceil(-9.4)
- Math.ceil(-9.8)

There is only one ceil() method with the following signature:

- public static double ceil(double a)

floor

The floor() method returns the largest double that is less than or equal to the argument and equal to the nearest integer value. This method is the antithesis of the ceil() method.

All the following calls to Math.floor() return the double value 9.0:

- Math.floor(9.0)
- Math.floor(9.4)
- Math.floor(9.8)

As before, keep in mind that with negative numbers, -9 is less than -8! All the following calls to Math.floor() return the double value –9.0:

- Math.floor(-9.0)

- Math.floor(-8.4)
- Math.floor(-8.8)

The signature of the floor() method is as follows:

- public static double floor(double a)

exam Watch

The floor() and ceil() methods only use double values. There are no overloaded methods for integral numbers, because the function would only end up returning the integral number It was given.

max

The max method compares the two arguments and returns the greater value. For example, invoking Math.max(1024, -5000) returns 1024. This method is overloaded to handle int, long, float, or double arguments. If the input parameters are the same, max returns a value equal to the two arguments. The signatures of the max() method are as follows:

- public static int max(int a, int b)
- public static long max(long a, long b)
- public static float max(float a, float b)
- public static double max(double a, double b)

min

The min() method is the antithesis of the max() method; it compares the two arguments and returns the lesser value. For example, invoking Math.min(0.5, 0.0) returns 0.0. This method is overloaded to handle int, long, float, or double arguments. If the input parameters are the same, min returns a value equal to the two arguments. The signatures of the min() method are as follows:

- public static int min(int a, int b)
- public static long min(long a, long b)
- public static float min(float a, float b)
- public static double min(double a, double b)

FROM THE CLASSROOM

Overloaded Methods in the Math Class

The knowledge required for the Math class is pretty straight forward, but sometimes there can be confusion with overloaded methods. Of the 11 methods that are required for the exam, only abs(), max(), min(), and round() are overloaded. The first three are overloaded to handle int, long, float, and double values. The round() method is overloaded to accept float and double arguments, and it returns int or long, respectively.

Sometimes it is possible to use two different parameter types in the arguments, as is the case with min() and max(). For example, when calling max() we could give arguments of one int and one long value, as in:

```
max(2, 3L)
```

Because there are methods long max(long, long) and int max(int int) there seems to be some ambiguity as to what will be returned. To resolve this ambiguity, we will use information from Chapter 6 on overloaded methods. In this case, the method will use max(long, long) because an integer can be implicitly cast into a long value, but a long cannot be implicitly cast into an integer. So, the return value will be a long as well.

—Brian Bagnall, Sun Certified Java Programmer and Developer

EXERCISE 10-1

Using the Math Class

In this exercise we will interrogate some numbers using the abs(), ceil(), and floor() methods of the Math class. Find the absolute, ceiling, and floor values of the following numbers: 10.5, -10.5, Math.PI, and 0. Try to do this with as little code as possible.

1. Create a class and a main() method to perform the calculations.
2. Store these numbers in an array of double values.
3. Use a for-loop to go through the array and perform the tests on each of these numbers.

4. The final code should look something like this:

```
class NumberInterrogation {
    public static void main(String [] argh) {
        double [] num = {10.5, -10.5, Math.PI, 0};
        for(int i=0;i<num.length;++i) {

System.out.println("abs("+num[i]+")="+Math.abs(num[i]));

System.out.println("ceil("+num[i]+")="+Math.ceil(num[i]));

System.out.println("floor("+num[i]+")="+Math.floor(num[i]));
            System.out.println();
        }
    }
}
```

Try to figure out what the results of these calculations will be before running the program.

---

random

The random() method returns a random double that is greater than or equal to 0.0 and less than 1.0. The random() method does not take any parameters. The signature of the random() method is as follows:

- public static double random( )

exam Watch

You will not have to know anything about java.util.Random for the exam.

round

The round() method returns the closest integer to the argument. The algorithm is to add 0.5 to the argument and truncate to the nearest integer equivalent. This method is overloaded to handle a float or a double argument.

The methods ceil(), floor(), and round() all take floating-point arguments and return integer equivalents. If the number after the decimal point is less than 0.5, Math.round() is equal to Math.floor(). If the number after the decimal point is greater than or equal to 0.5, Math.round() is equal to Math.ceil(). Table 10-1 shows some examples of the round() method with the results.

TABLE 10-1

Determining the Return Values for the Round Method

Method Arguments	Return Value
Math.round(10.5)	11.0
Math.round(10.1)	10.0
Math.round(10.0)	10.0
Math.round(-10.0)	-10.0
Math.round(-10.4)	-10.0
Math.round(-10.5)	-10.0
Math.round(-10.6)	-11.0

Most people are familiar with rounding, but keep in mind that with negative numbers a number at the .5 mark will round up to the *larger* number. For example, the number -10.5 will round up to -10. The signatures of the round() method are as follows:

- public static int round(float a)
- public static long round(double a)

sin

The sin() method returns the sine of an angle. The argument is a double representing an angle in radians. Degrees can be converted to radians by using Math.toRadians() (which is not covered on the exam). For example, invoking Math.sin(Math.toRadians(90.0)) returns 1.0. The signature of the sin() method is as follows:

- public static double sin(double a)

cos

The cos() method returns the cosine of an angle. The argument is a double representing an angle in radians. For example, invoking Math.cos(Math.toRadians(0.0)) returns 1.0. The signature of the cos() method is as follows:

- public static double cos(double a)

tan

The tan() method returns the tangent of an angle. The argument is a double representing an angle in radians. For example, invoking Math.tan(Math.toRadians(45.0)) returns 1.0. The signature of the tan() method is as follows:

- public static double tan(double a)

exam Watch

Sun does not expect you to be a human calculator. The certification exam will not contain questions that require you to verify the result of calling methods such as Math.cos(0.623).

sqrt

The sqrt() method returns the square root of a double. For example, invoking Math.sqrt(9.0) returns 3.0. What if you try to do the square root of a negative number? After all, the actual mathematical square root function returns a complex number (comprised of real and imaginary parts) when the operand is negative. The Java Math.sqrt() method returns NaN instead of an object representing a complex number. NaN is a bit pattern that denotes "not a number." The signature of the sqrt() method is as follows:

- public static double sqrt(double a)

EXERCISE 10-2

Rounding Random Numbers

In this exercise we will round a series of random numbers. The program will generate ten random numbers between 0 and 100. Round each one of them, then print the results to the screen. Try to do this with as little code as possible.

1. Create a class and a main() method to perform the calculations.
2. Use a for-loop to go through ten iterations.

3. Each iteration should generate a random number using Math.random(). To get a number between 0 and 100 simply multiply the random number by 100. Print this number to the screen.
4. Round the number using the Math.round() method. Print the rounded number to the screen.
5. The code should look something like this:

```
class RandomRound {
    public static void main(String [] argh) {
        for(int i=0;i<10;++i) {
            double num = Math.random() * 100;
            System.out.print("The number " + num);
            System.out.println(" rounds to " + Math.round(num));
        }
    }
}
```

As a bonus, it is interesting to note whether the numbers look random. Is there an equal number of even and odd numbers? Are they grouped more towards the top half of 100 or the bottom half? I've found the algorithm to be quite good in all respects.

That's all you will need to know for the exam on the Math class! Table 10-2 summarizes the method signatures of the math class. The exam will likely test your knowledge of these methods, and will make sure you know the correct return types from these methods. The next section continues with the remaining methods of the Math class.

TABLE 10-2

Required Method Signatures for the Exam

static int abs(int a)	static long abs(long a)
static float abs(float a)	static double abs(double a)
static double ceil(double a)	static double floor(double a)
static int max(int a, int b)	static long max(long a, long b)
static float max(float a, float b)	static double max(double a, double b)
static int min(int a, int b)	static long min(long a, long b)
static float min(float a, float b)	static double min(double a, double b)
static double random()	static int round(float a)
static long round(double a)	static double sin(double a)
static double cos(double a)	static double tan(double a)
static double sqrt(double a)	

Methods Not Covered on the Exam

The following methods will not be tested on the exam, even though they are part of the java.lang.Math class. Feel free to skip this section if you are only interested in learning material for the exam. The sample questions at the end of the chapter will not test you on this material.

acos

The acos() method returns the arc cosine of the angle. The argument is a double representing an angle in radians. The method is defined only for an input angle in the range of 0.0 through PI. The signature of the acos() method is as follows:

- public static double acos(double a)

asin

The asin() method returns the arc sine of the angle. The argument is a double representing an angle in radians. The method is defined only for an input angle in the range of –PI/2 through PI/2. The signature of the asin() method is as follows:

- public static double asin(double a)

atan

The atan() method returns the arc tangent of the angle. The argument is a double representing an angle in radians. The method is defined only for an input angle in the range of –PI/2 through PI/2. The signature of the atan() method is as follows:

- public static double atan(double a)

atan2

The atan2() method returns the Polar coordinate equivalent of the input Cartesian coordinate. The arguments represent a location in a rectangular plane. The signature of the atan2() method is as follows:

- public static double atan2(double a, double b)

exp

The exp() method returns the value of the constant *e* raised to the power of the input parameter. The mathematical constant *e* is represented by the constant approximation Math.E. The signature of the exp() method is as follows:

- public static double exp(double a)

log

The log() method returns the logarithm of the input parameter. The calculated logarithm uses the constant *e* as the base. The method is defined for an argument greater than 0.0. The signature of the log() method is as follows:

- public static double log(double a)

pow

The pow() method returns the first argument raised to the power of the second argument. For example, 2^3 can be called as Math.pow(2, 3), and it will return a double of 8.0. This method will throw an ArithmeticException if the first argument is 0.0 and the second argument is not greater than 0.0, or if the first argument is less than 0.0 and the second argument is not equal to a whole number. The signature of the pow() method is as follows:

- public static double pow(double a, double b)

rint

The rint() method returns the closest integer equivalent to the argument. When there are two integer equivalent values of equal distance from the argument, the even integer equivalent is returned. For example, invoking Math.rint(12.9) returns 13.0.

Both the following calls to Math.rint() return the double value 8.0:

- Math.rint(7.5)
- Math.rint(8.5)

The signature of the rint() method is as follows:

- public static double rint(double a)

toDegrees

The toDegrees() method takes an argument representing an angle in radians and returns the equivalent angle in degrees. For example, invoking Math.toDegrees(Math.PI * 2.0) returns 360.0. The signature of the toDegrees() method is as follows:

- public static double toDegrees(double a)

toRadians

The toRadians() method takes an argument representing an angle in degrees and returns the equivalent angle in radians. For example, invoking Math.toRadians(360.0) returns 6.283185, which is 2 * PI. This method is useful for converting an angle in degrees to an argument suitable for use with the trigonometric methods (cos, sin, tan, acos, asin, and atan). The signature of the toRadians() method is as follows:

- public static double toRadians(double a)

Now that you have a better understanding of the methods of the Math class, here are some possible scenario questions and their answers.

SCENARIO & SOLUTION

What method creates a random number?	Math.random()
The result obtained from calling Math.random() is never equal to 1.0. True or false?	True
Which method is used to round a number?	Math.round()
Math.min() is overloaded only for float and double. True or false?	False
What is the correct signature for the random method?	static double random()

CERTIFICATION SUMMARY

As the Math class relates to the certification exam, you will not be expected to reproduce complicated mathematical algorithms in your head or know the cosine of an angle. However, you will need to know how to calculate the result of calling abs(), ceil(), floor(), max(), min(), and round() with any given values. Know the method signatures in Table 10-2. The exam will test your ability to remember method signatures or to follow simple algorithms. Most questions on the Math class are quite simple, as long as you've spent the time to commit to memory the Math class methods and their calling signatures.

There is ample time to take the test and you are allowed to use scratch paper to work out results. I would suggest using scratch paper to draw a number line for all questions involving ceil(), floor(), max(), min(), or round(). You can graph the number or numbers from the question in the following manner.

```
 | - - - - - - - - - - | - - - - - - - - - - | - - - | - - - - - | - - - - - - - - - - |
-4.0                  -3.0                  -2.0  -1.7       -1.0                    0.0
```

Let's look at some examples. If the number from the question is –1.7, then the following answers should be automatic.

- What is Math.ceil(-1.7)? Move to the right, to the first integer equivalent.
- What is Math.floor(-1.7)? Move to the left, to the first integer equivalent.
- What is Math.round(-1.7)? Select the closest integer equivalent. If the decimal is .5, then always move to the *larger* number.

If the question involves two numbers and Math.min or Math.max, the number furthest to the left on the number line is the min and the number furthest to the right on the number line is the max. This may appear like overkill, but the goal is to not miss any questions that should be givens.

✓ TWO-MINUTE DRILL

Here are some of the key points from the certification objective in Chapter 10.

Using the java.lang.Math Class

- ❑ The abs() method is overloaded to take an int, a long, a float, or a double.
- ❑ The abs() method can return a negative if the argument is the minimum int or long value equal to the value of Integer.MIN_VALUE or Long.MIN_VALUE, respectively.
- ❑ The max() method is overloaded to take int, long, float, or double arguments.
- ❑ The min() method is overloaded to take int, long, float, or double arguments.
- ❑ The random() method returns a double greater than or equal to 0.0 and less than 1.0.
- ❑ Random does not take any arguments.
- ❑ The methods ceil(), floor(), and round() all return integer equivalent doubles.
- ❑ The round() method is overloaded to take a float (the other method takes a double).
- ❑ The methods sin(), cos(), and tan() take a double angle in radians
- ❑ The method sqrt() can return NaN if the argument is NaN or less than zero.

SELF TEST

The following questions will help you measure your understanding of the material presented in this chapter. Read all of the choices carefully, as there may be more than one correct answer. Choose all correct answers for each question.

Using the java.lang.Math Class

1. Calling Math.abs(10.4) returns which value?

A. 10.0

B. 10.4

C. 11.0

D. –10.4

2. Given:

```
1.  public class AbsExample {
2.      public static void main(String args[]) {
3.          float x = -5.6f;
4.          float absX = Math.abs(x);
5.          System.out.println("The abs of " +  x + " is " + absX);
6.      }
7.  }
```

Which answer best describes the result of running this program?

A. A compiler error occurs at line 4.

B. The abs of –5.6 is 5.6.

C. The abs of –5.6 is –5.6.

D. The abs of –5.6 is –5.

3. Calling Math.ceil(-5.5) results in which value?

A. –5.5

B. –5.0

C. –6.0

D. –4.0

4. To better understand how the ceil method works, the following program is written to output the index of the values array when the ceil method return is the same as the input parameter.

```
1.   public class CeilExample {
2.      public static void main(String args[]) {
3.         float values[] = {1.0f, 1.2f, 1.4f, 1.6f, 1.8f, 2.0f};
4.         float ceilValues[] = new double[values.length];
5.         for (int i = 0; i < values.length; i++) {
6.            ceilValues[i] = Math.ceil(values[i]);
7.         }
8.         for (int i = 0; i < values.length; i++) {
9.            if (values[i] == ceilValues[i]) {
10.              System.out.println(i);
11.           }
12.        }
13.     }
14.  }
```

Which answer best describes the result of running the program?

A. 0, 5

B. 0, 1, 2, 3, 4, 5

C. The program runs, but no output is written.

D. Compilation fails because of an error at line 6.

5. Calling Math.ceil(25.9) results in which value?

A. 25.9

B. 30.0

C. 25.0

D. 26.0

6. The result of calling Math.floor(-0.5) is what value?

A. 0.0

B. –1.0

C. 1.0

D. 0.5

7. Given:

```
public class FloorExample {
   public static void main(String args[]) {
```

```
3.          double values[] = {-2.3, -1.0, 0.25, 4};
4.          int cnt = 0;
5.          for (int i = 0; i < values.length; i++) {
6.              if (Math.floor(values[i]) == Math.ceil(values[i])) {
7.                  ++cnt;
8.              }
9.          }
10.         System.out.println("The results are the same " + cnt +
11.             " time(s)");
12.     }
13. }
```

What is the result?

A. The results are the same 0 time(s)

B. The results are the same 2 time(s)

C. The results are the same 4 time(s)

D. A compiler error at line 6.

8. Calling Math.floor(96.4) yields which result?

A. 96.4

B. 95.0

C. 96.0

D. 97.0

9. Which of the following are valid calls to Math.max? (Choose all that apply.)

A. Math.max(1, 4)

B. Math.max(2.3, 5)

C. Math.max(1, 3, 5, 7)

D. Math.max(-1.5, -2.8f)

10. Calling Math.max(8.2, 6.9) returns which value?

A. 8.2

B. 8.0

C. 6.9

D. 7.0

11. Calling Math.min(8.2, 6.9) returns which value?

A. 8.2

B. 8.0

C. 6.9

D. 7.0

12. Given:

```
1.  public class MinDouble1 {
2.      public static void main(String args[]) {
3.          double setA[] = {1.1, 1.5, -3.6};
4.          double setB[] = {1.1, 1.4, 3.6};
5.          for (int i = 0; i < setA.length; i++) {
6.              if (Math.min(setA[i], setB[i]) ==
7.                  Math.max(setA[i], setB[i])) {
8.                  System.out.println("Min and Max are the same at " +
9.                      i);
10.             }
11.         }
12.     }
13. }
```

What output is produced running this program?

A. Min and Max are the same at 0

B. Min and Max are the same at 1

C. Min and Max are the same at 2

D. A compiler error at line 6.

13. Calling Math.min(1, 8.25) returns which type and value?

A. int 1

B. long 1L

C. float 1.0f

D. double 1.0

14. Given:

```
public class RandomExample {
    public static void main(String args[]) {
        int num = Math.random() * 5;
        if(num >= 5.0) {
```

```
5.          System.out.println("The number is >= to 5.0");
6.       }
7.       else {
8.          System.out.println("The number is less than 5.0");
9.       }
10.    }
11. }
```

Running this program yields which of the following?

A. The number is >= to 5.0

B. The number is less than 5.0

C. Either A or B

D. A compiler error at line 3.

15. Given:

```
1.  public class RandomExample {
2.     public static void main(String args[]) {
3.        double seed = Math.PI;
4.        Math.random(seed);
5.        for (int i = 0; i < 10; i++) {
6.           System.out.println(Math.random());
7.        }
8.     }
9.  }
```

The preceding program is run three times on the same platform. What statements are true?

A. Each run produces the same ten random numbers.

B. Each run produces a different set of ten random numbers.

C. The seed value is added to each random number.

D. A compiler error occurs at line 4.

16. What statements are true about the result obtained from calling Math.random()? (Choose all that apply.)

A. The result is less than 0.0.

B. The result is greater than or equal to 0.0.

C. The result is less than 10.0.

D. The result is greater than 1.0.

17. Which method in the Math class is used to round a number? (Fill in the blank.)

The method to round a number is ________________.

18. For which arguments are the results from round and floor the same? (Choose all that apply.)

A. –1.3

B. 0.4

C. 6.2

D. –2.7

E. 100

19. Calling Math.round(9.5) returns which result?

A. 9

B. 9.5

C. 10

20. Assume we are calling the Math.max() method as follows:

```
Math.max(2L, 300);
```

What type of number will be returned?

A. double

B. int

C. long

D. float

E. This example would never compile.

21. Choose all the valid sin method signatures. (Choose all that apply.)

A. static double sin(double a)

B. static float sin(float a)

C. static double sin(double a, double b)

D. static float sin(float a, float b)

22. For which ranges of values is the sin method defined? (Choose all that apply.)

A. greater than or equal to 0.0

B. –PI / 2 through PI / 2

C. 0.0 through 360.0

23. What are the valid signatures for the sqrt method? (Choose all that apply.)

A. static int sqrt(int a)

B. static long sqrt(long a)

C. static float sqrt(float a)

D. static double sqrt(double a)

24. What value is returned from calling Math.sqrt(0.0)?

A. 0.0

B. NaN

C. ArithmeticException is thrown.

D. A compiler error is generated by calling Math.sqrt(0.0).

25. Given:

```
1.  public class SqrtExample {
2.      public static void main(String args[]) {
3.          double value = -9.0;
4.          System.out.println("The sqrt of "
5.              + value + " is " + Math.sqrt(value));
6.      }
7.  }
```

What is the result?

A. The sqrt of –9.0 is 3.0

B. The sqrt of –9.0 is –3.0

C. The sqrt of –9.0 is NaN

D. A compiler error at line 5.

SELF TEST ANSWERS

Using the java.lang.Math Class

1. ☑ B. 10.4. The abs() method returns the absolute value of the expression, which means in effect the negative sign is removed. The absolute value of 10.4 is 10.4.
   ☒ A and C are incorrect because these results might occur from some other rounding method. D is incorrect because the only time abs() will return a negative value is if the input parameter is Integer.MIN_VALUE or Long.MIN_VALUE.

2. ☑ B. The abs of –5.6 is 5.6. The abs method will return the value of the input parameter when the parameter is greater than zero and the negative of the input parameter when the parameter is less than zero.
   ☒ A is incorrect because the abs() method is overloaded to take a float and return a float. No compiler errors result from line 4. C and D are incorrect because the abs() method does not return negative numbers.

3. ☑ B. The smallest integer equivalent that is greater than or equal to –5.5 is –5.0.
   ☒ A is incorrect because the result of calling ceil() will only return integer equivalent values. C is incorrect because –6.0 is less than –5.5. D is incorrect because –4.0 is not the smallest number greater than –5.5.

4. ☑ D. The compiler reports that an explicit cast is needed to convert a double into a float. The method signature for the ceil method is public static double ceil(double a).
   ☒ A, B, and C are incorrect because the program does not compile. If the float on line 4 were changed to a double, then *A* would be correct. Calling ceil() with an integer equivalent returns the input parameter. Calling Math.ceil(8.0) returns 8.0, whereas calling Math.ceil(8.2) returns 9.0.

5. ☑ D. 26 is the closest integer value that is greater than 25.9.
   ☒ A is incorrect because the ceil() method always returns an integer equivalent. B is incorrect because it doesn't round to the nearest 0 digit number. C is incorrect because ceil() never returns a value less than the argument.

6. ☑ B. –1.0. Floor returns the largest integer equivalent that is less than or equal to the argument. –1.0 is the largest integer equivalent that is less than –0.5.
   ☒ A, C, and D are all incorrect because the result of calling floor is never greater than the argument.

7. ☑ **B.** The results are the same 2 time(s). When the value is –2.3, Math.floor() is –3.0 and Math.ceil() is –2.0. When the value is –1.0, Math.floor() is –1.0 and Math.ceil() is –1.0. When the value is 0.25, Math.floor() is 0.0 and Math.ceil() is 1.0. When the value is 4, Math.floor() is 4.0 and Math.ceil() is 4.0.
☒ **A** and **C** are incorrect because the only time floor() and ceil() are equal is when the argument is an integer equivalent. **D** is incorrect because the program compiles and runs without error. There is nothing wrong with line 6; the values are all compatible with a double.

8. ☑ **C.** 96.0. Remember the number line; 96.0 is the first number found by moving to the left on the number line from the argument 96.4.
☒ **A** is incorrect because floor always returns an integer equivalent. **B** is incorrect because 95.0 is not the first number found to the left of 96.4 on the number line. **D** is incorrect because the floor method never returns a value greater than the argument.

9. ☑ **A, B,** and **D.** The max method is overloaded to take two arguments of type int, long, float, and double.
☒ **C** is incorrect because Math.max() does not take three parameters.

10. ☑ **A.** 8.2. The value of 8.2 is the maximum value given 8.2 and 6.9.
☒ **B** and **D** are incorrect because the max() method will always return a value equal to one of the two arguments. **C** is incorrect because 8.2 is greater than 6.9.

11. ☑ **C.** 6.9. Regardless of the order in which the arguments appear in the call to min, the lesser value is the min result. 6.9 is less than 8.2.
☒ **A** is incorrect because 8.2 is greater than 6.9 and the min() method always returns the lesser of the two arguments. **B** and **D** are incorrect because the min() method will always return a value equal to one of the two arguments.

12. ☑ **A.** Min and Max are the same at 0. At the first array location for setA() and setB(), the values are the same. Because the values are the same, the min() and the max() of two equal values are the same.
☒ **B** and **C** are incorrect because at the second and third array locations for setA() and setB(), the values are different. Two numbers that are not equal will result in different min() and max() values. **D** is incorrect because the program compiles and runs without errors.

13. ☑ **D.** double 1.0. The 8.25 argument is a double and causes the static double min(double a, double b) method to be called.
☒ **A, B,** and **C** are incorrect because the return value is a double and not an int, a long, or a float.

14. ☑ D. The random() method returns a double value, so it is illegal to assign this to the *int* variable.
☒ A, B, and C are all incorrect because the program does not compile. A is incorrect, and even if line 3 was fixed *num* would still never be greater than or equal to 5 because the random number is always less than 1.0. B is incorrect, but could be correct if line 3 was fixed. The random method always returns a value greater than or equal to 0.0 and less than 1.0. The test at line three would always fail and line 8 would be printed out each time the program is executed.

15. ☑ D. A compiler error occurs at line 4.
☒ A is incorrect because the program does not compile and run. If line 4 is removed, running the program subsequent times produces a different result each time. B is incorrect because the program does not compile or run. C is incorrect because a seed is not used in the Java random method.

16. ☑ B and C. The result is greater than or equal to 0.0 and the result is less than 10.0. The range of values returned from random is a value that is greater than or equal to 0.0 and less than 1.0.
☒ A is incorrect because random() does not return negative values. D is incorrect because numbers greater than or equal to 1.0 are outside the range of returned values.

17. ☑ round(). The round() method is used to round a number in the Math class.

18. ☑ B, C, D, and E. 100. Math.round(0.4) is 0 and Math.floor(0.4) is 0.0. Math.round(6.2) is 6 and Math.floor(6.2) is 6.0. Math.round(-2.7) is –3 and Math.floor(-2.7) is –3.0. Math.round(100) is 100 and Math.floor(100) is 100.0.
☒ A is incorrect. Math.round(-1.3) is –1 and Math.floor(-1.3) is –2.0.

19. ☑ C. 10. By using the algorithm in which you add 0.5 to the argument and truncating, you get 10.
☒ A is incorrect because round() always returns a value greater than or equal to the argument. 9 is definitely less than 9.5. B is incorrect because round() returns an int or a long.

20. ☑ C. This question uses material from Chapter 7 on calling overloaded methods. The method will cast the int to a long and use the Math.max(long, long) method, which returns a long.
☒ A, B, and D are incorrect because these values are not returned by this method call. E is incorrect because there is no ambiguity in the method call.

21. ☑ A. static double sin(double a). There is only one valid signature for each trigonometric function. The valid signature takes a double argument for an angle in radians and returns a double result.
☒ B, C, and D are incorrect because there are no valid sin() method signatures that take a float argument or more than one argument.

22. ☑ **A, B,** and **C.** The signature for sin takes a double argument in radians and the function is defined for all real values.
☒ There are no incorrect answer choices.

23. ☑ **D.** static double sqrt(double a). The sqrt() method takes a double argument and returns the square root as a double value.
☒ **A, B,** and **C** are incorrect because the sqrt() method is not defined to take an int, a long, or a float.

24. ☑ **A.** 0.0. The sqrt function is defined for all values greater than or equal to 0.0.
☒ **B** is incorrect because NaN is returned when the argument is less than 0.0 or NaN. **C** is incorrect because Math.sqrt() does not throw exceptions. **D** is incorrect because it is syntactically correct to call the sqrt() method with any value.

25. ☑ **C.** The sqrt of –9.0 is NaN. The sqrt method returns NaN whenever the argument is less than 0.0.
☒ **A** is incorrect because –9.0 is less than 0.0 and sqrt() always returns NaN given a negative argument. **B** is incorrect because sqrt() never returns a negative number. **D** is incorrect because the program compiles and runs without errors.

11

Strings

CERTIFICATION OBJECTIVES

- 11.01 Creating and Working with Strings in Java
- 11.02 Storage of Strings and String Immutability
- 11.03 Using the StringBuffer Class
- 11.04 Constructors and Methods for the String Class
- 11.05 Constructors and Methods for the StringBuffer Class
- ✓ Two-Minute Drill
- Q&A Self Test

Text display is central to most applications. It is one of the easiest and most common ways to get a message across to a user. For this reason, the Java language has provided a fleshed-out application programming interface (API) for interacting with strings of text characters, or simply *strings*, as they are known throughout the industry. Like many other computer languages, Java has facilities to create and modify strings, to display them on the screen, or to write them to files. Many of the commands are similar to other programming languages such as C++, Basic, or Pascal.

In this chapter, we will explore how to work with the String class and the StringBuffer class. We will also learn about the string operations that are occurring behind the scenes that must be understood in order to pass the certification exam. This includes learning the concept of String immutability and how this affects the results of program execution. Let's begin the chapter by learning how strings are created.

CERTIFICATION OBJECTIVE 11.01

Creating and Working with Strings in Java

A String object is used to reference a string literal. All string literals in Java, such as "abc," are implemented as instances of the String class. A string literal is basically a string of zero or more characters enclosed in double quotation marks. Strings can store uppercase and lowercase letters, numbers, punctuation, and white space. All characters in String objects are stored in *Unicode*. Unicode is a two-byte character encoding system that includes thousands of international language symbols. Because of this, a string can hold text from writing systems used all over the world. However, programmers who are used to C or C++ will find that strings use twice as much memory. For example, the contents of the string "Hello, world." will be 26 bytes long because it holds 13 two-byte characters. There is no limitation in Java on the potential length of a string, other than memory limitations.

Creating a string can be deceptively simple. For example:

```
String myName = "Pill Bug";
```

This constructor is reminiscent of a primitive constructor. Keep in mind that Strings are not primitives. They are objects, defined in the Java API in the java.lang package. They can also be constructed just like any other object. For example, the preceding code example is simply shorthand for the following:

```
String myName = new String("Pill Bug");
```

Java programmers use methods within the String class to work with string variables. For example, there is a method in the String class named concat() that can be used to combine strings. The following code is an example of string concatenation.

```
String a = "hello ";
String b = "Pill Bug";
String c = a.concat(b); // c = "hello Pill Bug"
```

Java provides shorthand for string concatenation by overloading the + (plus) operator. The following instructions have the same effect:

```
String a = "hello ";
String b = "Pill Bug";
String c = a + b;
```

It is important to be aware, however, that the + operator is merely a shortcut to other method calls, just as the double quotation marks can be used as a shortcut to calling a string constructor directly.

exam Watch

If a string appears on either side of the + operator, the result is a String, and the Object.toString() method is called on any arguments that are not Strings. The certification test often has a code sample in which a number is concatenated to a String, so it is important to understand that this is allowed.

Note that string concatenation is actually done using StringBuffer objects, not the concat() method of the String class.

Despite a few shortcuts provided by the Java language, strings are objects, and the String class is just another class. Strings can be the arguments of methods or they can be returned by methods. They can be used in arrays or in other classes. All Java objects use the method toString() to return a String representation, including String objects. In other words, the String method toString() returns itself!

CERTIFICATION OBJECTIVE 11.02

Storage of Strings and String Immutability

Many programmers with backgrounds in other languages are confused when they look at the methods of the String class. None of the methods defined actually change the referenced string object, they just return another string object. For instance, in the string concatenation example discussed earlier, the statement c = a.concat(b) doesn't change either of the string variables *a* or *b*. It creates a new string, and assigns that string to *c*.

It's important to understand that in the Java programming language, once a string is created, it is *immutable*. Its contents can never be changed. There is no method that changes the contents of a string; there are only methods that take the source string as input and return another string. Strings in Java are not data structures that can be operated on; they can only be referenced.

The reason for this is that a String object is not the string itself, it is just a reference to an in-memory location that contains a string of characters. The following source code provides an example of storage allocation for strings.

```
String a = "hello";
String b = "hello";
String c = "hello";
```

FIGURE 11-1

Variables sharing string objects at compile time

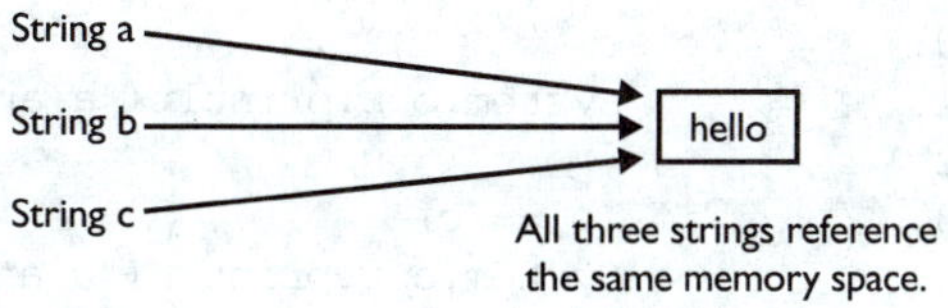

To save space and reduce complexity, even though three strings are initialized, the Java compiler creates only a single memory space for storing the text *hello*, as shown in Figure 11-1. That memory space is shared by all three String objects, and the variables *a*, *b*, and *c* are simply pointers to that space.

Any changes to a single string would clearly affect all three. Therefore, by disallowing the direct manipulation of strings, the Java environment prevents changes in one string from impacting others.

String references can, however, be reassigned. Consider the following example:

```
String a = "hello";
String b = "hi";
String c = a;
c = b;
```

Two areas in memory are allocated for string storage. The first holds *hello* and the second holds *hi*, and the string variable *c* points to first one then the other, as shown in Figure 11-2.

Understanding string storage also explains some idiosyncrasies in string comparison in Java. Consider the following:

```
public class Test {
    public static void main(String args[]) {
        String a = "java";
        String b = "java";
        String x = "ja";
        String y = "va";
        String c = x + y;
        if (a == b)
```

```
            System.out.println("a and b are the same object");
        else
            System.out.println("a and b are not the same object");

        if (b == c)
            System.out.println("a and c are the same object");
        else
            System.out.println("a and c are not the same object");
    }
}
```

When this Java source code is executed, the contents of the String variables a, b, and c will be the same: the string "java." However, they will not all point to the same memory location, and thus the second comparison will fail. The output will look like this:

```
a and b are the same object
a and c are not the same object
```

Even though the contents of *a* and *c* are the same, the word *java*, the string objects *a* and *c* do not point to the same memory location, so the comparison will fail. When the if statements are reached, the internal memory structures associated with these variables will look like Figure 11-3.

The == operator is not the appropriate operator to use to determine the equality of string contents. Instead, the equals() method should be used. It is highly likely, however, that the certification exam will have questions regarding code samples similar to the preceding example to ensure you have an understanding of how strings are allocated.

FIGURE 11-2

Variables point to immutable string objects

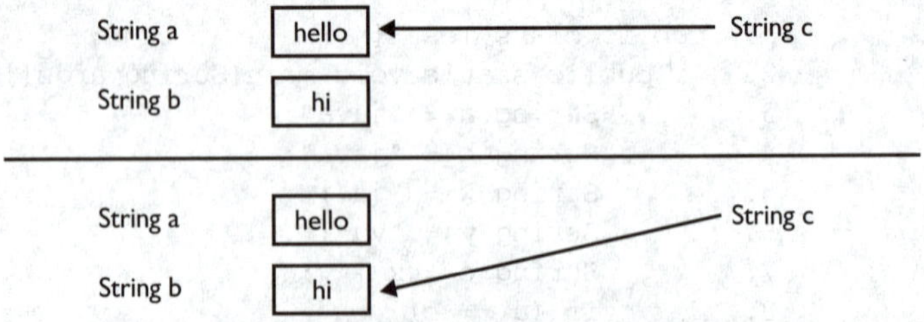

At first c references the same memory space as String a. When c is reassigned, it then points to the same space as String b.

FIGURE 11-3

Compile time strings versus runtime generated strings

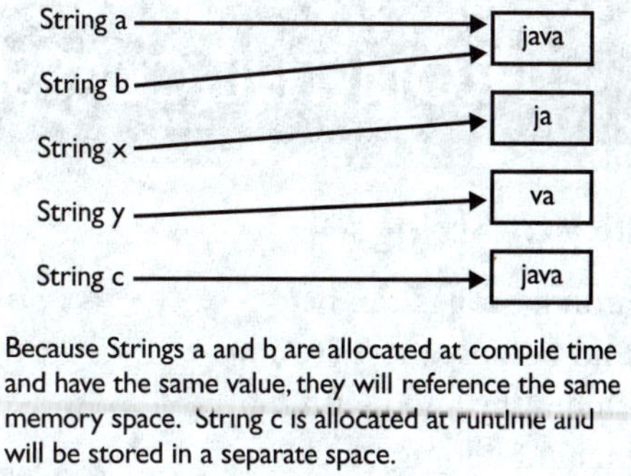

Programmers with a background in C may be concerned about needlessly creating strings. In a case where a string variable is reused over and over, the contents of many of the steps along the way may be lost. For example:

```
String y = "yes";
String n = "no";
String m = "maybe";
String s = "I vote " + y;
String s = "I vote " + n;
String s = "I vote " + m;
```

In the preceding example, the strings "I vote yes", "I vote no", and "I vote maybe" are created at runtime. The memory contents then look like Figure 11-4.

This looks like it wastes a lot of memory, but as we learned in Chapter 6, Java has automatic garbage collection to clean up unused objects.

FIGURE 11-4

String objects with no reference variables

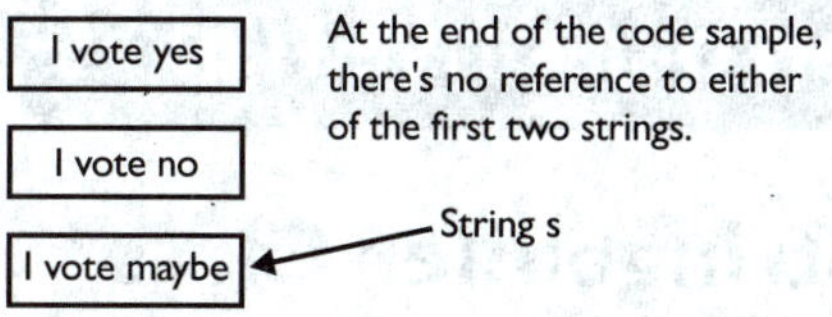

FROM THE CLASSROOM

The Immutability of Strings

Some concepts regarding Strings can be difficult to understand because there are a lot of things going on under the hood with the Java compiler. The main building block concepts you should be aware of are:

- All string "modifications" actually return new String objects.
- String variables with the same string literal value at compile time will be assigned to the same string object.
- Shorthand string operations are actually calling real underlying methods.

Consider the following code:

```
String a = "string";
a = a + "A";
```

This code looks simple enough, but when we analyze what is really going on it gets a little more complicated. When the compiler reads this syntax, it computes the following:

```
String a = new String("string");
a = new StringBuffer(a).append("A").toString();
```

The shorthand code just makes it easier and more intuitive for us to make these method calls. When we look at it this way, it's obvious why a simple concatenation operation is creating a whole new String object.

—Brian Bagnall, Sun Certified Java Programmer and Developer

CERTIFICATION OBJECTIVE 11.03

Using the Stringbuffer Class

The main problem with the String class is that it is based upon immutable string contents. Certain types of problems can be solved much more easily and efficiently if a string can be directly modified. Java provides an alternate class, StringBuffer, for these types of situations. A StringBuffer is a string that can be modified. StringBuffers are used internally to implement many of the methods in the String class.

A StringBuffer can hold only a certain amount of characters upon creation. This is known as its capacity. A StringBuffer has a default capacity of 16 characters, but the programmer typically defines the capacity upon creation. For example, the following line creates an empty StringBuffer with a capacity of 100 characters.

```
StringBuffer b = new StringBuffer(100);
```

A StringBuffer can also be created from an existing string.

```
StringBuffer b = new StringBuffer("hello");
```

This creates a StringBuffer with a capacity of 21 (16 plus the length of the string argument) that contains the string *hello*. Unlike a string, however, the text *hello* can be changed.

StringBuffer capacity is not particularly important, however, as StringBuffers automatically grow when characters are added beyond their initial capacity. Setting sufficient capacity is simply a matter of efficiency; changing the capacity of a StringBuffer requires allocating and deallocating additional memory, which can be an expensive operation.

Here is a common example from Sun that highlights the differences between Strings and StringBuffers:

```
public String reverseIt(String source) {
    int c, len = source.length();
    StringBuffer dest = new StringBuffer(len);
    for (c = (len - 1); c >= 0; c--) {
        dest.append(source.charAt(c));
    }
    return dest.toString();
}
```

The preceding method reverses the characters in a string. A StringBuffer, dest, is created to hold the intermediate results. The for loop takes characters from the end of the string to the beginning, using the charAt() method of the String class, and appends them to the end of the StringBuffer using the append() method of that class. The StringBuffer is then converted to a string using the toString() method, and returned. Because StringBuffers can be modified, it's the best class to use to store intermediate string operations.

If the code had been written using the String object internally instead of StringBuffers, it would have required allocating a single character string for every character in the source string. This would have run much slower. StringBuffers make the code much more efficient.

It should be noted that the StringBuffer class is thread-safe and its methods are synchronized. If methods are called on the same string by multiple threads, then one method call must finish before another is begun. This prevents the two threads from getting unexpected results.

exam Watch

String and StringBuffer are not the same class, and the exam will definitely ask questions that test whether this is understood. Look out for code samples that try to use StringBuffer methods on String variables and vice versa. These code samples are invalid and will not even compile. The toString() method must be used to convert a StringBuffer to a String before String methods can be used on it.

CERTIFICATION OBJECTIVE 11.04

Constructors and Methods for the String Class

A string can be constructed and initialized using either a String value, a String variable, or a StringBuffer object. Table 11-1 contains constructors that are frequently used to create String objects.

TABLE 11-1 Constructors Used to Create String Objects

Syntax	Description	Example
String()	Initializes and constructs a String object containing no characters. It is the same as String("");	String();
String(String value)	Initializes and constructs a String object. The contents are a copy of the passed String.	String("Hello world.");
String(StringBuffer buffer)	Initializes and constructs a String object. The contents are identical to the sequence of characters stored in the StringBuffer object.	String(new StringBuffer());

Some of the methods that are typically used for working with strings are described in the following sections.

equals(String str)

The *equals()* method of the String class is the preferred way to check for string equality because the == operator does not accurately test the character contents. The equals() method returns true if the contents of the target string are identical to the source string; otherwise, it returns false. The match is case-sensitive, so differences in case will return false. A null argument will also return false.

```
String x = "hello";
String y = "HellO";
if (x.equals(y) == false) {
   System.out.println("The two strings are not equal.");

  System.out.println("equals() is case sensitive".);
}
```

equalsIgnoreCase(String str)

The *equalsIgnoreCase()* method allows programmers to determine the equality of strings without taking case into account. The method returns true if the two strings are identical, even if the case is different. Otherwise, the method returns false. A null argument will also return false.

```
String x = "hello";
String y = "HellO";
if (x.equalsIgnoreCase(y)) {
   System.out.println("The two strings are equal.");
   System.out.println("equals() is case insensitive".);
}
```

compareTo(String str)

The *compareTo()* method of the String class is used to put strings in alphabetical order. If the target string is higher in the alphabet than the referenced string, this method returns a negative number. If the string is lower in the alphabet, it returns a positive number. If the string is identical, then a zero is returned. This method is commonly used in sorting operations. Comparisons are based upon Unicode representations of the characters.

```
String s1 = "one";
String s2 = "two";
String s3 = "three";
if (s1.compareTo(s2) < 0) {
   // Returns true, because the string "one" appears before "two"
   // in the alphabet.
   System.out.println("one appears before two");
}
if (s2.compareTo(s3) > 0) {
   // Returns true, because the string "two" appears after "three"
   // in the alphabet.
   System.out.println("three appears before two");
}
```

toUpperCase()

The *toUpperCase()* method returns a string identical to the original string, except that any lowercase characters are changed to uppercase. The original string is unchanged, of course, only the string returned is different. Note: If the string is already uppercase, a reference to the original string is returned.

```
String s1 = "HELLO WORLD";
String s2 = "hello world";
if (s1.equals(s2.toUpperCase())) {
   System.out.println("String s1 is equal to uppercase s2");
}
```

toLowerCase()

The *toLowerCase()* method returns a string identical to the original string, except that any uppercase characters are changed to lowercase. Note: If the string is already lowercase, a reference to the original string is returned.

```
String s1 = "HELLO WORLD";
String s2 = "hello world";
if (s2.equals(s1.toLowerCase())) {
   System.out.println("Lowercase string s1 is equal to string s2");
}
```

charAt(int index)

The *charAt()* method returns the character at the specified position in the string. The position is zero-based, so that s.charAt(0) returns the first character in the string, s.charAt(1) is the second character, and so on until s.charAt(s.length()-1), which returns the last character.

```
String s = "hello world";
char c1, c2, c3;
c1 = s.charAt(0);  // returns 'h'
c2 = s.charAt(6);  // returns 'w'
c3 = s.charAt(10); // returns 'd'
```

substring(int start)

The *substring()* method returns a portion of a string from within another string. The substring() method is overloaded and has two forms. The first method call accepts one argument and returns the remainder of the string from the indicated character.

```
"nonfiction".substring(3); // returns "fiction"
```

Notice in the preceding example that we use the string literal to call the substring() method. As mentioned before, string literals are implemented as instances of the String class; therefore, it is valid to call all of the String class methods from a string literal.

substring(int start, int end)

The second overloaded *substring()* method call requires two arguments and returns the portion of the string from the first indicated position to the character before second indicated position. The resulting length of the string is (*end–start*).

The arguments are zero-based, so that the first character is referenced as position 0, and the last character is referenced as length()-1. Figure 11-5 is a graphical representation of this.

```
s1 = "wired".substring(2);   //  s1 is set to "red"
s2 = "substring".substring(3,6);  // s2 is set to "str"
```

FIGURE 11-5

Using the substring() method

wired
01234 "wired".substring(2,5) returns "red"

substring
012345678 "substring".substring(3,6) returns "str"

indexOf(char ch), indexOf(char ch, int index), indexOf(*String s*), *indexOf(String s, int index)*

The *indexOf()* method searches a string for a character or string and, if found, returns the first position at which the target is found. Like other methods, the location is zero-based, so that a returned position of zero would indicate that the target was found at the beginning of the original string. If the target character or string is not found, the method returns a value of -1. Note: The match is case-sensitive.

```
String s = "Welcome to Java 2";
int x1, x2, x3, x4, x5;
x1 = s.indexOf("W");  // returns 0, first position
x2 = s.indexOf("e");  // returns 1, second position
// (e appears twice in the string, but IndexOf
// only returns the first occurrence)
x3 = s.indexOf("J");  // returns 11
x4 = s.indexOf("2"); // returns 16
x5 = s.indexOf("java"); // returns -1 because it's case-sensitive
```

The indexOf() method is also overloaded to accept a second parameter indicating the position with which to begin the search. This can be used to find all of the occurrences of a certain character or string.

lastIndexOf(char ch)

The *lastIndexOf()* method, like indexOf(), searches a string for a character and, if found, returns the first position at which the target character is found. However, unlike indexOf(), the search starts at the end of the string. As with indexOf(), the method can also be called with a second parameter to begin the search at another location, though the search still continues from right to left.

```
String s = "hello world";
int x1, x2;
```

```
x1 = s.lastIndexOf("l");  //  Returns 9, the position of last l
x2 = s.lastIndexOf("o",5);  // Returns 4, the o in hello
```

startsWith(String str)

The *startsWith()* method of the String class tests whether the string begins with a specific sequence of characters. An alternate method call begins the test using a specific offset, and is similar to substring(). The following example shows two calls to startsWith() that both return true:

```
public class Test {
   public static void main(String args[]) {
      String s = "knowledge";
      if (s.startWith("know")) {  // returns true
         System.out.println("knowledge begins with know");
      }
      if (s.startsWith("led",4)) {  // returns true
         System.out.println("starting at position 4 it begins led");
      }
   }
}
```

trim()

The *trim()* method is used to remove white space from the beginning and the end of a string. White space includes not only spaces but any control characters as well (ASCII characters such as tabs or form feeds). The returned string will still contain white space within the string; only leading and trailing white space will be removed.

```
String s1 = "   remove leading and trailing white space    ";
String s2 = s1.trim();
System.out.println(s2);
//  this line will print "remove leading and trailing white space"
```

exam Watch

Passing the Java certification exam requires the ability to read short segments of Java code and quickly identify the principles of the language that are being tested. This is much more important than knowing syntax. For example, there probably won't be a question that asks, "What is the syntax of the charAt() method?" But there may be a question that shows a code sample that uses both charAt() and indexOf() on a string variable and then asks what results are returned. Understanding syntax alone is not enough to answer this type of question.

EXERCISE 11-1

Using the String Class

In this exercise we will attempt to become familiar with some of the methods contained in the String class. The program will start with the string "A man of many talents" and attempt to call some methods on it.

1. Convert all the characters to uppercase.
2. Find the position in the text of "AL" (which is capitalized now).
3. Using the position of "AL," create a new string that contains all the characters before "AL" and all the characters after.
4. Output the final string.

The final code should look something like this:

```
class Manipulate{
   public static void main(String [] args) {
      String x = "A man of many talents";
      x = x.toUpperCase();
      int pos = x.indexOf("AL");
      x = x.substring(0,pos) + x.substring(pos + 2, x.length());
      System.out.println(x);
   }
}
```

CERTIFICATION OBJECTIVE 11.05

Constructors and Methods for the Stringbuffer Class

StringBuffers, like strings, can hold a series of String characters, but individual characters within the string can be changed. StringBuffers also have an attribute named *capacity*, which is the maximum number of characters that the StringBuffer can hold. This capacity will grow automatically if characters are appended and the length of the string grows beyond the current capacity.

Table 11-2 contains constructors that are frequently used to create StringBuffer objects.

Some of the methods that are typically used for working with StringBuffers are described in the following sections. Methods that act upon StringBuffers are often destructive, meaning the contents may be changed.

capacity()

The *capacity()* method of the StringBuffer class returns the current capacity of the StringBuffer object.

```
String s = "hello world";
int c;
StringBuffer buf = new StringBuffer(s);
c = buf.capacity();  // will be set to 27
```

reverse()

The *reverse()* method reverses the contents of the referenced StringBuffer object.

```
StringBuffer buf = new StringBuffer("hello");
buf.reverse();
System.out.println(buf.toString());  // prints out the text 'olleh'
```

Like all objects, the StringBuffer class has a toString() method that can be used to return a String value.

TABLE 11-2 Constructors Used to Create StringBuffer Objects

Syntax	Description	Example
StringBuffer()	Initializes and constructs an empty StringBuffer object with a default capacity of 16 characters. It is the same as StringBuffer(16);	StringBuffer();
StringBuffer (int capacity)	Initializes and constructs an empty StringBuffer object with the specified capacity.	StringBuffer (100);
StringBuffer (String value)	Initializes and constructs a StringBuffer object. The contents are identical to the passed string, and its capacity is equivalent to 16 plus the length of the String argument.	StringBuffer ("Hello world.");

setCharAt(int index, char ch)

The *setCharAt()* method of the StringBuffer class changes a character at a specific position to another character. The positional argument, like most other String and StringBuffer positions, is zero-based, so that 0 is the first character of the StringBuffer.

```
StringBuffer buf = new StringBuffer("java");
buf.setCharAt(0,'J');
buf.setCharAt(2,'V');
System.out.println(buf.toString());  // prints "JaVa"
```

append(Object obj)

The *append()* method appends, in order, the character sequence from the string representation of a target object to the end of the referenced StringBuffer. This method is usually called with a string as the argument, but the method is overloaded to support objects, ints, floats, and character arrays. The capacity of the StringBuffer object will grow to accommodate the added characters.

```
StringBuffer buf = new StringBuffer("Test");
buf.append("ing");
System.out.println(buf.toString());  // prints "Testing"
buf.append(123);
System.out.println(buf.toString());  // prints "Testing123"
```

insert(int index, Object obj)

The *insert()* method of the StringBuffer class inserts characters into the object at a specific position. It takes two arguments: a position and an object, typically a string, though the method is overloaded to support many other arguments such as objects, ints, floats, characters, and character arrays. The second object is converted to a sequence of characters, and those characters are inserted *at* the position specified by the first argument. Like all positional arguments, it is zero-based. See Figure 11-6 for an example.

```
StringBuffer buf = new StringBuffer("mod");
buf.insert(1,"eth");
System.out.println(buf.toString());  // prints "method"
```

FIGURE 11-6

Using the insert() method

```
mod <--- eth        "eth" is inserted into "mod" with
012                 the syntax buf.insert("eth",1)

                    The result is "method"
method
012345              And now eth is at position 1
```

delete(int start, int end)

The *delete()* method deletes characters from within a StringBuffer. It takes two arguments, a starting position and an ending position. The ending position is actually the character after the last character to be deleted. If the ending position is beyond the end of the string, all characters after the starting position are removed. If the starting position and the ending position are the same, no characters are deleted. The positional arguments, like all others in the String and StringBuffer objects, are zero-based. Thus, zero references the first character in the String, and one less than the length of the StringBuffer represents the last character in the string. Figure 11-7 shows this example.

```
public class Test {
    public static void main(String args[]) {
        StringBuffer buf = new
            StringBuffer("We'll delete characters from this sentence");
        buf.delete(0,13);
        buf.delete(10,99);
        System.out.println(buf.toString());  // displays "characters"
    }
}
```

FIGURE 11-7

Using the delete() method

buf.delete(0,13) deletes the first thirteen characters.

```
[We'll delete ]characters from this sentence
[0123456789012]345678901234567890123456789 01
[0000000000111]11111112222222222333333333344
```

buf.delete(10,99) deletes from position 10 to the end of the String.

```
characters[ from this sentence]
0123456789[0123456789012345678]
0000000000[1111111111222222222]
```

length()

The *length()* method returns the length of the StringBuffer's character content. If the StringBuffer is empty, the method will return a zero.

```
StringBuffer buf = new StringBuffer("");
System.out.println("The length is " + buf.length());
// prints "The length is 0"
```

EXERCISE 11-2

Using the Stringbuffer Class

In this exercise we will attempt to become familiar with some of the methods contained in the StringBuffer class. Follow these instructions and see if the final program produces a viable sentence.

1. Construct a StringBuffer object with the string literal "It takes a big man to cry".
2. Create another StringBuffer called *spell*, and make it contain these words: "nam taht ta hgual".
3. Reverse the character order in *spell*, and append it to the first string buffer.
4. Insert the following string literal in between these two sentences (at position 25):
   " but it takes a bigger man to "

The final code should look something like this:

```
class Sayings {
   public static void main(String [] args) {
      StringBuffer x = new StringBuffer("It takes a big man to cry");

      StringBuffer spell = new StringBuffer("nam taht ta hgual");
      spell.reverse();
```

```
        x.append(spell);

        x.insert(25, " but it takes a bigger man to ");

        System.out.println(x);
    }
}
```

Notice that we are directly manipulating the characters in the StringBuffer objects. This contrasts with Exercise 11-1 in which we created a new String object using each method.

You now know more than you've ever dreamed about strings and string buffers. Let's take a look at some possible Scenario & Solution questions about strings and string buffers.

SCENARIO & SOLUTION	
How would you obtain a string representation of a Date object?	Use the toString() method. Every class in Java inherits this method from the Object class.
How can you find out the size of a string?	Call the length() method of the string.
What is the method call to get the first character from the string "Spider"? (Include any arguments.)	Use charAt(0). This will return a character primitive.
How can you modify the string object containing "Monkeys" into "Monkey"?	You can't. String objects are immutable and can't be modified.
Name the primary difference between the String class and the StringBuffer class.	The String class stores an array of characters that can't be modified. The StringBuffer class stores an array of characters that can be modified.

CERTIFICATION SUMMARY

Almost all programming languages have facilities for working with strings of characters. However, strings in Java have some unique properties that should be understood before taking the Java certification test. Strings in Java are implemented using the String class of the java.lang package.

After a string is constructed, its contents can never be changed. The String object itself may be reassigned to another set of contents, but its individual contents may not be changed. This is known as string immutability. String contents are also shared at compile time; String objects that are defined with the same contents will reference the same location. This is another reason that strings are immutable. Strings have a few simple constructors, and several methods that can be used to return uppercase or lowercase strings, trimmed strings, lengths, the positions of characters, or other information. There is also an equals() method that is used to determine whether strings are equal.

A second class, the StringBuffer class, provides the ability to work with text on a character-by-character basis. In this class, the text is not immutable and can be changed. StringBuffers have a specific capacity that is defined at creation time, but this can be extended automatically. StringBuffers are typically constructed from Strings, and are converted back to Strings using the toString() method. Much like the String class, this class has methods for appending, inserting, and deleting characters.

✓ TWO-MINUTE DRILL

Here are some of the key points from each certification objective in Chapter 11.

Creating and Working with Strings in Java

- ❑ String operations are carried out by the String class, which can be found in the java.lang package.
- ❑ Strings can be constructed with the following syntax:

```
String s = new String(<string literal>);
```

- ❑ Strings can be concatenated with the overloaded + operator. If a string is involved in an expression using the + operator, the result is considered a string, and the toString() method is called for all nonstring objects involved.

Storage of Strings and String Immutability

- ❑ In Java, strings are immutable. Their contents can never be changed.
- ❑ Text for strings defined at compile time and strings with identical contents may share the same memory space.

Constructors and Methods for the String Class

- ❑ None of the methods for the String class change the actual contents of the string; they only return new values.
- ❑ The equals() method is used to compare two strings and determine whether they are identical. The == operator should not be used, as it will only determine whether the two string variables reference the same object.
- ❑ The indexOf() and lastIndexOf() methods of the String class can be used to search a string's contents for a specific character or sequence of characters.

Using the StringBuffer Class

- ❑ A second class, StringBuffer, is used for operations that require working with strings on a character-by-character basis. StringBuffers are not immutable; their contents can be changed.
- ❑ StringBuffers are initialized with a certain character capacity. If this capacity is exceeded, the StringBuffer object automatically grows.

Constructors and Methods for the StringBuffer Class

- ❑ The setCharAt(), insert(), delete(), and append() methods are used to work with individual characters and strings of characters in StringBuffers.
- ❑ All positional arguments for methods in the String or StringBuffer classes are zero-based. The first character is referenced as zero.

SELF TEST

The following questions will help you measure your understanding of the material presented in this chapter. Read all of the choices carefully, as there may be more than one correct answer. Choose all correct answers for each question.

Storage of Strings and String Immutability

1. Which of the following methods is used to change the contents of the string *World* to also include the characters *Hello*?

A. trim()

B. insert()

C. append()

D. None of these

2. Given:

```
public class Test {
   public static void main(String args[]) {
      String a  = "foo";
      String b = "bar";
      a = a + b;
   }
}
```

Will the preceding code compile?

A. Yes

B. No

3. Given:

```
public class Test {
   public static void main(String args[]) {
      String a  = "New";
      String b = a;
      a += "t";
      if (a == b)
         System.out.println("a and b are the same");
      else
```

```
9.             System.out.println("a and b are not the same");
10.        }
11.    }
```

When this code is executed, what will be the output?

A. a and b are the same

B. a and b are not the same

C. Nothing. This code will not compile due to line 5.

4. Which of the following statements is *not* true?

A. Strings can be initialized using the = operator with a string literal value.

B. The toString() method can be used to return a String value from a StringBuffer object.

C. All strings are terminated with a null (ASCII 0) character.

D. It is impossible to change the contents of a String variable.

5. Given:

```
public class foo {
    public static void main(String[] args) {
        String a = "    java    ";
        String b = "         java";
        if (a.trim() == b.trim())
            System.out.println("a == b");
        if (a.trim().equals(b.trim()))
            System.out.println("a equals b");
    }
}
```

What is the output of this Java program?

A. Nothing. The program will not compile.

B. a == b

C. a equals b

D. Both B and C.

6. Given:

```
public class Test {
    public static void main(String args[]) {
        String s1 = new String ("one");
        StringBuffer s2 = new StringBuffer("three");
        s1.append("1");
```

```
6.         s2.append("2");
7.         if (s1.equals(s2))
8.             System.out.println("The two strings are equal");
9.     }
10. }
```

What is the result of this code?

A. It will print "The two strings are equal."

B. There will not be any output.

C. An exception will be thrown at line 5.

D. The code will not compile.

Using the StringBuffer Class

7. Which of the following is true about the StringBuffer class in Java?

A. StringBuffer objects have a specific character capacity.

B. StringBuffer objects inherit all of the methods of the String class.

C. The contents of StringBuffer variables can be initialized using the = operator.

D. The contents of StringBuffer objects can compared using the == operator.

Constructors and Methods for the String Class

8. Given:

```
public class Test {
    public static void main(String args[]) {
        String a = "ALL YOUR BASE";
        String b = a.toUpperCase();
        if (a == b)
            System.out.println("a and b are the same");
        else
            System.out.println("a and b are not the same");
    }
}
```

When this class is executed, what will be the output?

A. a and b are the same.

B. a and b are not the same.

9. Given:

```
public class Test {
    public static void main(String args[]) {
        String a = "Java";
        System.out.println(a.length);
    }
}
```

What is the result of this code?

A. 3

B. 4

C. 5

D. This code will not compile.

10. Given:

```
String a = "Java";
System.out.println(a.length());
```

When this fragment of code is executed, what will be the output?

A. 3

B. 4

C. 5

D. This code will not compile.

11. Given:

```
String a = "Java is great.";
System.out.println(a.charAt(a.length()));
```

When this fragment of code is executed, what will be the output?

A. "."

B. "t"

C. "J"

D. The code will generate an exception.

12. Given:

```
String a = "Java is great.";
System.out.println(a.indexOf("i"));
```

When this fragment of code is executed, what will be the output?

A. 5

B. 6

C. 7

D. The code will generate an exception.

13. Given:

```
String a = "xxxJava is great.xxx";
System.out.println(a.substring(0, a.lastIndexOf('x') - 2));
```

What is the output of this code fragment?

A. "xxxJava is great."

B. "xxxJava is great.xx"

C. "xxxJava is grea"

D. "x"

14. Which of the following lines are legal to construct and initialize a string? (Choose all that apply.)

A. String s = "test";

B. String s = new String "test";

C. String s = new String();

D. String s = new String("test");

Creating and Working with Strings in Java

15. Given:

```
public class Test {
    public static void main(String args[]) {
        String a = "ABCabc";
        String b = a.toString();
        if (a == b)
            System.out.println("A is the same as B");
        else
            System.out.println("A is not the same as B");

        if (a.equals(b))
            System.out.println("A equals B");
        else
```

```
            System.out.println("A does not equal B");
        }
    }
```

A. A is the same as B
   A equals B

B. A is not the same as B
   A equals B

C. A is the same as B
   A does not equal B

D. A is not the same as B
   A does not equal B

16. Given:

```
String a = "There are " + 90 + 9 + " bottles of beer on the wall.";
```

What is the result of this code?

A. There are 99 bottles of beer on the wall.

B. There are 909 bottles of beer on the wall.

C. Nothing. This code is ambiguous and will not compile.

17. Given:

```
class MyObject {
    public static void main(String[] arg) {
        MyObject mo = new MyObject();
        String a = "My object is " + mo;
    }
}
```

Will this code compile?

A. Yes

B. No

18. How many bytes of storage are required to store each character in a string?

A. 1

B. 2

C. 3

D. 4

E. The number of bytes depends upon the character.

Constructors and Methods for the StringBuffer Class

19. Given:

```
StringBuffer b = new StringBuffer("abcdefg");
b.delete(3,6);
b.append("hij");
System.out.println(b.toString());
```

What is the output of this code fragment?

A. abcghij

B. abcdefghij

C. abfghij

D. abchij

E. The code will not compile.

20. Given:

```
StringBuffer buf = new StringBuffer("Test");
```

If a StringBuffer is constructed with this syntax, what would the original capacity be?

A. 4

B. 16

C. 32

D. 20

E. Unlimited

F. It is impossible to tell.

SELF TEST ANSWERS

Storage of Strings and String Immutability

1. ☑ **D.** Strings are immutable. There are no methods that change the contents of an existing String object.
☒ **A** is incorrect because the trim() method removes white space. **B** and **C** are incorrect because these methods apply to StringBuffers and not Strings.

2. ☑ **A.** The code will compile. This code causes a new String object to be created and the object reference of the String object *a* is changed to reference the new string.
☒ **B** is incorrect because the code will compile.

3. ☑ **B.** Because operators like += change the object reference, and not the object itself, changes that occur to *a* using these operators do not affect other objects with the same initial reference.
☒ **A** is incorrect because the statement *a+="t";* changes the variable's reference, so that it no longer points to the initial string. This makes the comparison fail. **C** is incorrect because the assignment operator += is also overloaded to handle strings.

4. ☑ **C.** Strings in Java are not terminated with a null character, as in the C language.
☒ **A** is true because strings can be initialized using the = operator as a shorthand method of string construction. **B** is true because a String value can be returned from any object by using the toString() method. The statement in **D** is true because strings are immutable. Their contents can never be changed.

5. ☑ **C.** The Java virtual machine (JVM) will create two separate strings to hold the result of the a.trim() and b.trim() operations, so the == operator will receive different object references and return false. The result of trimming any string is to return the string with no leading or trailing white space, so because both strings are otherwise identical, both will be returned as *java* and the equals() method will return true.
☒ **A** is incorrect because the program will compile. **B** and **D** are incorrect because the two string references will not point to the same location, so the a == b comparison will fail.

6. ☑ **D.** There is no append() method for the String class, so the line s1.append("1") will generate an error at compile time. Strings are immutable, so an append() method doesn't make any sense conceptually.
☒ **A, B,** and **C** are all incorrect because the code won't compile.

Using the StringBuffer Class

7. ☑ All StringBuffer objects have a set character capacity that is specified when the variable is constructed.
☒ B is incorrect because StringBuffer is a completely different class from the String class, and does not inherit its methods. C is incorrect because the = operator can be used only to initialize Strings, not StringBuffers. D is incorrect because the == operator only determines whether object references are equal, and does not test the actual contents.

Constructors and Methods for the String Class

8. ☑ A. The toUpperCase() method returns a reference to the original string if it is already in uppercase.
☒ B is incorrect because the a == b comparison succeeds due to *a* and *b* pointing to the same underlying object.

9. ☑ D. The length() method is being referenced as an instance variable and not as a method. The correct code to print the length of the string *a* would be: System.out.println(a.length());
☒ A, B, and C are incorrect because the code will not compile.

10. ☑ B. The length() method returns the exact number of characters in the string. (Java does not include *null* characters to terminate strings like C does.)
☒ A and C are incorrect because the length() method returns a value of 4, not 5 or 3. There are four characters in the string *Java.* D is incorrect because the code will compile.

11. ☑ D. The code will generate an exception. The first character in a Java string is at position 0. The last character is at position length() - 1, so this code will generate a StringIndexOutOfBounds exception.
☒ A, B, and C are incorrect because if an exception is generated when executing the first line, the second will never be reached.

12. ☑ A. The first character in a Java string is at position 0, so the indexOf() method will parse through the String *a* and find the first *i* at location 5.
☒ B is incorrect because string indexes in Java are based on zero, not one. C is incorrect, as the indexof() method will return 5, not 7. D is incorrect because the code will compile.

13. ☑ A. The lastIndexOf() method returns the index of the last *x*, which is also the last character in the string. The substring() method returns the portion of the string from the character at index 0 (the first character in the string) to this index - 2, yielding the string in answer *A*.

☒ B, C, and D are incorrect because the position returned by the lastIndexOf() method, 19, doesn't match any of the answers.

14. ☑ A, C, and D. *C* and *D* are correct because they are valid constructors for the String class. The Java language also provides programmers with a shortcut to string construction, as shown in *A*.
☒ B. This is not valid syntax in any way.

Creating and Working with Strings in Java

15. ☑ A. Calling the toString() on a String object always returns the object reference of the string itself. After the initialization, *a* and *b* will reference the same String object, therefore the == operator will return true. Because the equals() method evaluates whether the contents of the String object are the same, and both *a* and *b* refer to the same String object, their contents must be the same, so the equals() method will also return true.
☒ B is incorrect because the a == b comparison will succeed, not fail, due to the String references being the same. C is incorrect because the a.equals(b) comparison will succeed due to the contents of the string variables being equal. D is incorrect because both comparisons will succeed.

16. ☑ B. Java automatically converts all primitive types to a string when the + operator is used with strings.
☒ A is incorrect because the math equation is not calculated first. C is incorrect because this compiles fine.

17. ☑ A. All classes inherit from the Object class, and the Object class defines a default toString() method. This means all objects have a toString() method which can be called, and all objects can be referenced as strings.
☒ B is incorrect because the code will compile due to the string concatenation succeeding.

18. ☑ B. All Java characters are two bytes long.
☒ E would be correct for many other programming languages, but not for Java. A, C, and D are simply false.

Constructors and Methods for the StringBuffer Class

19. ☑ A. The second line, b.delete(3,6) deletes the characters *def* from the source string, leaving the characters abcg. The next line, b.append("hij") appends those three characters to the string, which gives the final result, abcghij.
☒ E is incorrect because there is nothing stopping the code from compiling. **B** and **C** are incorrect because the delete method deleted the characters *def* from the string. **D** is incorrect because the character *g* was never deleted.

20. ☑ D. When a StringBuffer is constructed using a string as an argument, the capacity is set to 16 plus the length of the target string. *Test* is four characters in length, so the capacity is initially four.
☒ A is incorrect because it only accounts for the length of the constructor string. **B** would be correct if no string argument was given, as the default capacity for a StringBuffer is 16. **C** is incorrect; there is no reason why the capacity would be equal to 32. **E** and **F** are incorrect because even though the capacities of StringBuffers can grow as the variable grows, all StringBuffer variables have a specific capacity when constructed.

12

The java.util Package

CERTIFICATION OBJECTIVES

- 12.01 The Collections Framework
- 12.02 Collection Interfaces and Classes
- ✓ Two-Minute Drill
- Q&A Self Test

There are many useful classes in the java.util package, but for the exam you will only need to know about collections. Collections are new for Java 2.0, and they are extremely useful when dealing with sets of data. There are several different types of collections, each slightly different in behavior. For the exam, you will need to know the interfaces and classes and the behavior they deliver.

CERTIFICATION OBJECTIVE 12.01

The Collections Framework

In a general sense, a collection is an element used to store data. For Java, a *collection* is an object used to store other objects, similar to an array. Two common examples of collections are Hashtables and Vectors. Don't worry if you haven't heard of these or used them before; they will be covered in this chapter.

An array can store primitives or objects, but Java collections can store only objects. Primitive types cannot be added to a collection, so it is necessary to use the wrapper classes (found in the java.lang package) such as Integer and Double in lieu of primitives. The following is a simple example of a Hashtable using a wrapper class:

```
import java.util.*;
class CollectionTest {
    public static void main (String [] args) {
        Hashtable ht = new Hashtable();
        ht.put("Key1",new Integer(12));
    }
}
```

The preceding code is easy to analyze. It first creates a Hashtable object, and then adds an Integer object with the key *Key1*. Keys are used to store and retrieve objects.

There are three elements in Java that make up collections:

- **Interfaces** Define the methods that each type of collection must implement.
- **Implementations** Actual classes such as Hashtable and Vector.
- **Algorithms** Methods that store, retrieve, and manipulate elements in a collection.

Collectively, these elements create what is known as the *collections framework.* The collections framework did not exist in the Java Development Kit 1.1 (JDK 1.1), though it did have some of the same classes such as Vector and Hashtable.

The new collections framework is very powerful and gives the following benefits, as outlined by Sun Microsystems:

- Reduces programming effort—methods such as sorting algorithms are already written.
- Increases program speed and quality.
- Allows interoperability among unrelated application programming interfaces (APIs)—programmers can use their classes with other classes that use the collections framework.
- Reduces the effort to learn and use new APIs.
- Reduces the effort to design new APIs—the architecture is already designed and method names are already chosen for you.
- Fosters software reuse—classes that use the collections framework can be used in any class that uses collections in its methods.

There are four properties that collections may or may not possess, as shown in Table 12-1. These are the properties you must know to differentiate between collection types.

TABLE 12-1 The Four Properties of Collections

Property	Description
Sorted	Ascending order, sorted naturally using the equals() object method. An example is a membership list for a club.
Ordered/Unordered	A collection can keep a specific order determined by where the object is placed in the collection. For example, a deck of cards is ordered because each card is pulled from the top.
Allows duplicates	Duplicate objects are sometimes allowed in a collection. An example is a collection of hockey cards, some of which might be duplicates.
Uses keys	Collections sometimes use a key object to reference the underlying stored object. For example, governments often store information about citizens using a social security number.

Now that we have learned the four basic properties that describe a collection's behavior, let's examine the objects used to define the Java collections framework.

CERTIFICATION OBJECTIVE 12.02

Collection Interfaces and Classes

The interfaces in the collections framework are the foundation of collections. By using these interfaces, collections can be passed into other methods, regardless of the details of a particular collection.

There are six interfaces that make up the core collections framework. Some of these interfaces extend other interfaces to form a hierarchy, as shown in Figure 12-1. Notice *Map* and *SortedMap* do not extend the Collection interface. *Map* and *SortedMap* are still known as collections, however, even though in strict Java terms they are not Collection types.

Each of these interfaces (except for *SortedSet* and *SortedMap*) also has an abstract class that has some of the methods already implemented. For example, the Collection interface has a class called AbstractCollection, and the Set interface has a class called AbstractSet. We will now examine the interfaces individually.

Collection Interface

The Collection interface is very general in its handling of groups of objects. In theory it accepts any group of objects, whether duplicates are present or not, and stores them in no particular order. This is "in theory" because the Collection interface is not directly implemented by functional classes. Let's examine some of the major methods defined by the Collection interface.

FIGURE 12-1

Hierarchy of the collections framework interfaces

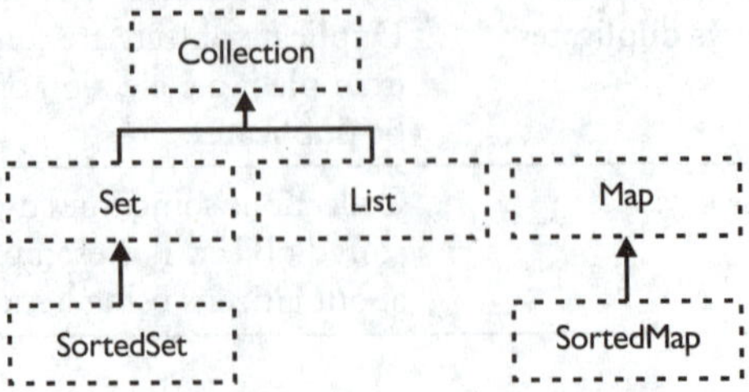

exam
Watch

The exam will not question you on methods within each type of collection or on how to implement the collections framework. However, it is recommended that you run through the method descriptions to get an idea of how the collection classes work. There is nothing worse than taking an exam on a topic you partially comprehend. On the other hand, do not try to memorize these methods. Instead, learn the types of collections and their general behavior. You will need to know which classes and interfaces are sorted, which are ordered, which allow duplicates, and which use keys.

boolean add(Object element)

The *add()* method adds the specified element to the collection. If the set has successfully changed, the method will return true.

boolean remove(Object element)

The *remove()* method removes the specified element from the collection. If the set has successfully changed, the method will return true.

int size()

The *size()* method returns the number of elements in the set (its cardinality).

boolean isEmpty()

The *isEmpty()* method returns true if the set contains no elements.

boolean contains(Object element)

The *contains()* method returns true if the set contains the specified element.

boolean containsAll(Collection collection)

The *containsAll()* method returns true if the collection contains all of the elements in the specified collection.

boolean addAll(Collection collection)

The *addAll()* method appends all of the elements in the specified collection to the specified collection.

void clear()

The *clear()* method removes all elements from the collection.

void removeAll(Collection collection)

The *removeAll()* method removes all elements that are contained in the collection passed as an argument.

void retainAll(Collection collection)

The *retainAll()* method is the mirror image of the removeAll() method. The retainAll() method deletes all elements *except* the elements that are contained in the collection passed as an argument.

There are no functional classes that directly implement the Collection interface. AbstractCollection is the only class that directly implements the interface, but it is abstract and therefore not functional. There are many subinterfaces of Collection that are used to define functional classes, as shown in Figure 12-2.

on the job

Some programmers have wondered why the methods do not follow the standard JavaBean methodology of using the is, has, set, and get prefixes. The reason this was not followed is because previous versions of Java had collection objects such as Hashtable and Vector that used similar method calls. Sun decided to follow this common naming convention. In addition, a collection is not a Bean and therefore does not need to stick to this methodology.

FIGURE 12-2

Collections framework hierarchy including classes

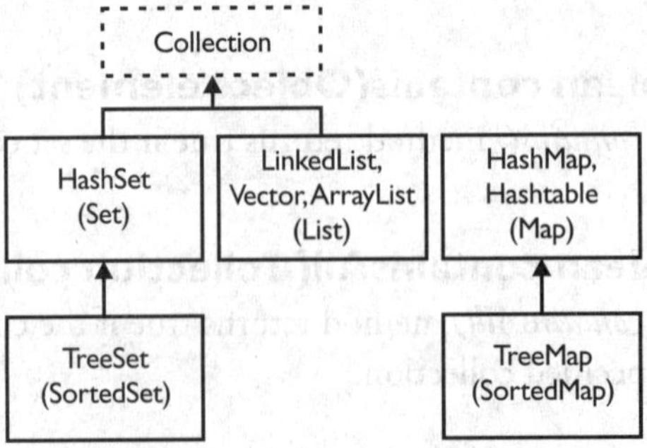

Set

A Set is unique because it does not allow duplicate objects to enter the collection of elements. The Set interface is a subinterface of Collection; therefore, it contains all of the methods of the Collection interface. The Set interface does not define any new methods, however. The difference is that the add() and addAll() methods check for duplication of objects using the equals() method on each object.

The only functional class in the Java 2 API that directly implements the Set interface is HashSet (see Figure 12-2). Let's examine the HashSet class with some sample code:

```
import java.util.*;
class SetTest {
   public static void main (String [] args) {
      HashSet hs = new HashSet();
      hs.add("Chess");
      hs.add("Poker");
      hs.add("Solitaire");
      hs.add("Chess");
      hs.add(null);
      System.out.println(hs);
   }
}
```

The preceding code attempts to add the String object *Chess* twice to the Set. It also adds the *null* value to the collection. The code compiles fine, but let's take a look at the output.

```
C:\Java projects\SetTest>java SetTest
[Poker, Solitaire, Chess, null]
```

As you can see, the program runs fine but it does not add the String object Chess more than once, because sets may not contain duplicates. The add() method actually returns a boolean value of *false* if the object already exists in the set, so it is possible to see if an object failed to be added. The null value is added, but only one null can exist in a set. And, as is characteristic of Sets, the collection is unsorted and unordered.

on the job

You may want to make your own type of collection using the collections framework. To do this, you will need to implement the collections interfaces. If your new class will not use one of the predefined methods in the interface, you have the option of throwing an UnsupportedOperationException. For example, if your collection is read-only, you could throw this exception if the method add() is used. This will signal to any methods using your collection class that this operation is not available. The UnsupportedOperationException is an extension of RuntimeException, so there is no need to call the operation within a try-catch block.

Sorted Set

The SortedSet interface is similar to the Set interface, except that the elements in the set are stored in ascending order. Once again, the elements are nonduplicating. The SortedSet interface includes all of the methods of Set because it extends Set, but also adds a few more to take advantage of the fact that it is sorted.

All elements inserted into a SortedSet must implement the Comparable interface (or be accepted by the specified Comparator Interface). You can get away with adding only one normal object to a SortedSet, but as soon as there is more than one it will try to compare them to sort them. When this happens the class will throw an exception.

Additionally, each element must be mutually comparable, which means that they have to be of the same type so they can be compared against one another. You just can't put any type of object in a SortedSet.

Object first()

The *first()* method returns the first (lowest index) element currently in this sorted set.

Object last()

The *last()* method returns the last (highest index) element currently in this sorted set.

SortedSet subSet(Object fromElement, Object toElement)

The *subSet()* method returns a view of the portion of this sorted set whose elements range from *fromElement*, inclusive, to *toElement*, exclusive.

SortedSet headSet(Object toElement)

The *headSet()* method returns a view of the portion of this sorted set whose elements are strictly less than *toElement*.

SortedSet tailSet(Object fromElement)

The *tailSet()* method returns a view of the portion of this sorted set whose elements are greater than or equal to *fromElement*.

The TreeSet class is the only class to implement the SortedSet interface directly. Let's examine the TreeSet class in some sample code:

```
import java.util.*;
class SortedSetTest {
    public static void main (String [] args) {
        SortedSet set = new TreeSet();
        set.add("Chess");
        set.add("Whist");
        set.add("Checkers");
        set.add("Blackjack");
        set.add("Chess");
        System.out.println(set);
        SortedSet end = set.tailSet("Checkers");
        System.out.println(end);
    }
}
```

This code adds several String objects to TreeSet and outputs it to the screen. It then uses the tailSet() method to print the last part of this collection. The results of executing this class are as follows:

```
C:\Java projects\SetTest>java SortedSetTest
[Blackjack, Checkers, Chess, Whist]
[Checkers, Chess, Whist]
```

The tailSet() method pulled out the elements that were equal to or greater than the "Checkers" string object. Notice that the set is in ascending order even though the elements were added randomly. This is one of the properties of a SortedSet, along with not allowing duplicates.

List

A List is *ordered*. This allows a List to maintain an order as objects are added and removed from the collection. This is not the same as sorted! Sorted objects form a hierarchy based on how the objects compare to each other, such as alphabetical sorting. An ordered collection keeps the order in which objects were added to it.

A List can also contain duplicate entries of objects. The List interface adds several methods, all of which deal with the List collection being ordered. The added methods contain an index or index numbers that are used to specify a certain ordered object in the List.

void add(int index, Object element)

The *void()* method inserts the specified element at the specified position in the List.

boolean addAll(int index, Collection collection)

The *addAll()* method appends all of the elements in the specified collection to the end of the List in the order that they are returned by the specified collection's iterator.

Object get(int index)

The *get()* method returns the element at the specified position in the List.

int indexOf(Object element)

The *indexOf()* method searches for the first occurrence of the given argument and tests for equality using the equals method.

int lastIndexOf(Object element)

The *lastIndexOf()* method returns the index of the last occurrence of the specified object in the List.

Object remove(int index)

The *remove()* method removes the element from the specified position in the List and returns that element.

Object set(int index, Object element)

The *set()* method replaces the element at the specified position in the List with the element passed as an argument. There are three functional classes that implement the List interface (see Figure 12-2):

- **LinkedList** Elements in a LinkedList are queued at the beginning of the list and removed from the end. This is often used for buffering operations.
- **Vector** A growable array of objects.
- **ArrayList** This class is roughly equivalent to Vector, except that it is unsynchronized. This means that if multiple threads are accessing an ArrayList object, this object must be externally synchronized.

Let's look at an example of a class that implements the List interface. Everyone loves the Vector class, so let's take a look at it in a simple example:

```
import java.util.*;
class VectorTest {
   public static void main (String [] args) {
      Vector v = new Vector();
      v.add("Zak");
      v.add("Gordon");
      v.add(0, "Duke");
      v.add("Lara");
      v.add("Zak");
      System.out.println(v);
      String name = (String)v.get(2);
      System.out.println(name);
   }
}
```

The preceding code creates a Vector and adds several names to it. Notice the third name, Duke, is added with an index variable. This inserts it in the 0 slot in the List, which is the first slot. The class also uses the get() method to retrieve a name, using the index 2. To retrieve the object from the list, it is necessary to cast the object to a string, as you can see in the code. This is necessary when retrieving objects from all collections. The output from this program is as follows:

```
C:\Java\Booktest>java VectorTest
[Duke, Zak, Gordon, Lara, Zak]
Gordon
```

The preceding code shows that the elements retain the order in which they are placed into the list. The List is guaranteed to keep this order, but a Set has no guarantee of keeping this order over time. We added the string *Zak* to the collection more than once, and the List stored the duplicate entry. This demonstrates that a List is ordered and allows duplicate elements.

Map

A *Map* stores objects that are identified by unique keys. Each key can map to one element at most. A Map may not store duplicate keys. It can, however, store duplicate objects. Objects are stored in Map collections in no particular order.

The Map interface does not extend the Collection interface (see Figure 12-1), so in strict terms it is not a Collection type. In general terms, however, it is part of the Java collections architecture. There are two common collections that directly implement the Map interface, as we saw in Figure 12-2: Hashtable and HashMap.

The HashMap class is roughly equivalent to Hashtable, except that HashMap is not synchronized for threads, and it permits null values to be stored. The Hashtable was present in the JDK 1.1; however, it did not use the collections framework as Java 2, and so it did not implement the Map interface. The overall functionality of the new Java 2 Hashtable is the same as it was in the JDK 1.1, and it has been reworked so that it now implements the Map interface.

We saw a small demonstration of Hashtable earlier in this chapter, so let's instead examine the HashMap class. The following code stores several objects in a HashMap and then retrieves them using keys:

```
import java.util.*;
class HashMapTest {
   public static void main (String [] args) {
      HashMap hm = new HashMap();
      hm.put("Game1","Hearts");
      hm.put(null, "Chess");
```

```
        hm.put("Game3", "Checkers");
        hm.put("Game3", "Whist");
        hm.put("Game4", "Chess");
        System.out.println(hm);
    }
}
```

The preceding code adds several String objects to the HashMap using keys, which also happen to be Strings. Although the keys are String objects in this example, it is possible to use any object as a key; however, it is not legal to use a primitive as a key. Notice that the code attempts to place two titles under the same key, *Game3*. This code will compile successfully, but the output might be unexpected. Looking at the preceding code, which title will it display, *Checkers* or *Whist*?

```
C:\Java\Maptest>java HashMapTest
{Game4=Chess, Game3=Whist, Game1=Hearts, null=Chess}
Hockey Game
```

As we can see, it stored Whist, so the last object to be added under a key will be stored. The code shows that *null* can be used for objects or keys. Also, notice the objects are stored in no particular order. Objects may be duplicated in this set, as shown by the Chess element.

The Map interface defines several methods that manipulate objects using keys. A lot of these methods are also defined in the Collection interface, but because Map does not extend Collection it must redefine them.

void clear()

The *clear()* method removes all mappings from this map.

boolean containsKey(Object key)

The *containsKey()* method returns true if this map contains a mapping (element) for the specified key.

boolean containsValue(Object value)

The *containsValue()* method returns true if this map maps one or more keys to the specified value.

Set entrySet()

The *entrySet()* method returns a Set view of the mappings contained in this map.

boolean equals(Object o)

The *equals()* method compares the specified object with this map for equality.

Object get(Object key)

The *get()* method returns the element that maps to the specified key.

int hashCode()

The *int hashCode()* method returns the hash code value for this map. This is an integer representation of the key used to store the element.

boolean isEmpty()

The *isEmpty()* method returns true if this map contains no key-value mappings.

Set keySet()

The *keySet()* method returns a set view of the keys contained in this map.

Object put(Object key, Object value)

The *put()* method associates the specified value with the specified key in this map.

void putAll(Map t)

The *putAll()* method copies all of the mappings from the specified map to this map.

Object remove(Object key)

The *remove()* method removes the mapping for this key from the map, if present.

int size()

The *size()* method returns the number of key-value mappings in this map.

Collection values()

The *values()* method returns a collection view of the values contained in this map.

The preceding methods define the behavior of a Map. This guarantees it can store duplicate objects with nonduplicate keys in an unordered, unsorted collection. Now let's examine a special type of Map called a SortedMap.

SortedMap

SortedMap is similar to Map, except the objects are stored in ascending order according to their keys. Like Map, there can be no duplicate keys, and the objects themselves may be duplicated. One very important difference with SortedMap objects is that the key may not be a null value.

As with SortedSet, each key must implement the *Comparable* interface (or be accepted by the specified comparator). Additionally, each key must be mutually comparable so they can be compared to each other.

TreeMap is the only core API class to implement the SortedMap interface directly, so let's examine this in some code:

```
import java.util.*;
class TreeMapTest {
   public static void main (String [] args) {
      Map titles = new TreeMap();
      titles.put(new Integer(3), "Checkers");
      titles.put(new Integer(1), "Euchre");
      titles.put(new Integer(4), "Chess");
      titles.put(new Integer(2), "Tic Tac Toe");
      System.out.println(titles);
   }
}
```

Notice the order of the keys before the program is executed. Now let's examine the output.

```
C:\Java\Booktest>java TreeMapTest
{1=Euchre, 2=Tic Tac Toe, 3=Checkers, 4=Chess}
```

This output demonstrates that SortedMap collections are automatically sorted in ascending order by key. In this case we used Integer objects as keys.

FROM THE CLASSROOM

Sorting Objects

You might wonder how the SortedMap and SortedSet types manage to sort objects. After all, what is there about an object that determines whether one object should appear before another? According to the Java API, these elements are sorted by the natural ordering of the elements. In most cases, this natural ordering comes from the use of the Comparable interface.

The Comparable interface is contained in the java.lang package. Objects that implement this interface can be compared to one another, and it can be determined whether one object is less than, equal to, or greater than another object in the natural ordering. Some common Java objects that implement this interface include Character, File, Long, Short, String, Float, Integer, Byte, Double, BigInteger, BigDecimal, Date, and CollationKey.

The only method defined in the Comparable interface is compareTo(). This accepts a single Object as an argument and returns an integer value. If the value is a negative integer, the object is less than the object in the argument. If the value is a positive integer, the object is greater than the object in the argument. If the value is zero, the object is equal to the object in the argument. By using the Comparable interface, it would be possible for you to create an object that would allow itself to be sorted by the SortedSet and SortedMap collection classes.

—Brian Bagnall, Sun Certified Java Programmer and Developer

The SortedMap interface implements all the methods in the Map interface, as well as the following:

Comparator comparator()

The *comparator()* method returns the comparator associated with this sorted map, or null if it uses its keys' natural ordering.

Object firstKey()

The *firstKey()* method returns the first (lowest index) key currently in this sorted map.

Object lastKey()

The *lastKey()* method returns the last (highest index) key currently in this sorted map.

SortedMap headMap(Object toKey)

The *headMap()* method returns a view of the portion of this sorted map whose keys are strictly less than *toKey*.

SortedMap subMap(Object fromKey, Object toKey)

The *subMap()* method returns a view of the portion of this sorted map whose keys range from *fromKey*, inclusive, to *toKey*, exclusive.

SortedMap tailMap(Object fromKey)

The *tailMap()* method returns a view of the portion of this sorted map whose keys are greater than or equal to *fromKey*.

Together, these methods enable a SortedMap to behave like a SortedSet that uses keys. This concludes the discussion on the core collections architecture of the Java 2 platform. The five subinterfaces of the Collection interface are shown in Table 12-2, along with their corresponding behaviors. In the final section of this chapter we will examine the Collections class that allows for additional operations to be performed on collections objects.

TABLE 12-2 Summary of Collection Interfaces

	Sorted	Ordered	Uses Keys	No Duplicates
Set				X
SortedSet	X			X
List		X		
Map			X	
SortedMap	X		X	

EXERCISE 12-1

Choosing the Correct Collection Type

In this exercise we will create a mock Domain Name System (DNS). A DNS is used to look up IP addresses when given a Web site name, such as *www.javasoft.com.* We will create a class that uses a collection to store three Internet Protocol (IP) addresses and their respective domain names. It will, in effect, be a Domain Name System. The class should look up the domain name as a string and return the IP address, also a string.

1. Decide the properties of the DNS that you will be creating. In this case, it is a nonsorted, nonduplicating, unordered collection using keys.
2. Choose the appropriate collection type to store our data. The one you choose is completely up to you, but in this case Hashtable seems to be the best choice.
3. We will call the class DNS. Enclose the Hashtable object in this class.
4. Provide methods to retrieve and store domain names and IP addresses.

We included a main() method to test the class. Your final program should look something like this:

```
import java.util.*;
class DNS {
   Map addresses;

   public DNS() {
      addresses = new Hashtable();
      addAddress("java.sun.com","192.18.97.137");
      addAddress("www.syngress.com", "204.146.80.99");
      addAddress("www.mysterysite.com", "216.65.63.102");
   }

   public void addAddress(String domainName, String ip) {
      addresses.put(domainName, ip);
   }

   public String getIP(String domainName) {
```

```
        return (String)addresses.get(domainName);
    }

    public static void main (String [] args) {
        DNS server = new DNS();
        String sunIP = server.getIP("java.sun.com");
        System.out.println(sunIP);
    }
}
```

on the Job

The Collections class (not to be confused with the Collection interface) contains static methods that perform operations on various collections. Most of the operations perform some type of sorting routine on the collection. The good thing about this is that if you decide to make your own type of collection and use one of the interfaces in the collection architecture, your collection should work flawlessly with the static methods in the Collections class!

exam Watch

It is good to know about the methods in the Collections class for the real world because they can save you valuable programming time and the methods are very efficient. For the exam, however, you will not need to know any method names from this class.

Now that you have a better understanding of collections, refer to the following Scenario & Solution for some possible attributes for a collection, followed by the correct collection interface.

SCENARIO & SOLUTION

What type of collection is nonduplicating, unsorted, and unordered?	Set
What type of collection allows duplicating, but is ordered?	List
What type of collection allows duplicating elements, but is unsorted and uses unique keys?	Map
What type of collection is nonduplicating and sorted?	SortedSet
What type of collection allows duplicating and is sorted by unique keys?	SortedMap

CERTIFICATION SUMMARY

Hopefully you have been able to get through this chapter in less time than it took for previous chapters. The main information that you should concentrate on from this chapter is the four properties that collections may possess: sorting, ordering, allowing duplicates, and using keys. You should also know the interfaces and classes that make up the collections framework.

The Collection interface is at the top of the collections hierarchy (except for Map). Two subinterfaces extend this interface directly: List and Set. SortedSet directly extends Set. Map is at the top of its own hierarchy, and it has one subinterface called SortedMap.

The behavior of each of these types is actually quite easy to pin down. A Set allows no duplicates, a List is the only type that is ordered, and a Map is the only type that uses keys. There are two subtypes that have the extra feature of being sorted: SortedSet and SortedMap. A SortedSet is a Set that is sorted, and likewise a SortedMap is a Map whose keys are sorted. That is about all you need to know about the java.util package for the exam!

✓ TWO-MINUTE DRILL

Here are some of the key points from each certification objective in Chapter 12.

The Collections Framework

- ❑ The four properties that differentiate collections are *sorted, ordered, allows duplicates*, and *uses keys.*
- ❑ In strict terminology, a set cannot be both ordered and sorted.
- ❑ An ordered set keeps track of the sequence in which objects are added to it. It is unsorted, however.
- ❑ A sorted set uses the natural ordering of its objects, such as alphabetical.

Collection Interfaces and Classes

- ❑ A Set can store only unique objects, not duplicates.
- ❑ A List keeps the objects indexed in a definite order.
- ❑ A Map stores objects according to keys.
- ❑ SortedSet stores objects in ascending order without duplicates.
- ❑ SortedMap stores objects in ascending order using keys.
- ❑ The null object can't be used to sort objects, so a SortedSet can't contain objects that are null. Likewise, a SortedMap can't contain keys that are null.
- ❑ HashSet implements the Set interface.
- ❑ TreeSet implements the SortedSet interface.
- ❑ LinkedList, Vector, and ArrayList implement List.
- ❑ HashMap and Hashtable implement the Map interface.
- ❑ TreeMap implements the SortedMap interface.

SELF TEST

The following questions will help you measure your understanding of the material presented in this chapter. Read all of the choices carefully, as there may be more than one correct answer. Choose all correct answers for each question.

The Collections Framework

1. Which of the following properties apply to a deck of cards?

   A. Ordered

   B. Sorted

   C. Duplicating

   D. Uses keys

2. Which of the following properties apply to an address book containing names and phone numbers? (Choose all that apply.)

   A. Ordered

   B. Sorted

   C. Duplicating

   D. Uses keys

Collection Interfaces and Classes

3. Which of the following interfaces form the framework for a nonduplicating, unsorted, unordered collection?

   A. List

   B. Map

   C. Set

   D. Collection

4. Which of the following classes directly implement the Set interface?

   A. Vector

   B. LinkedList

C. HashSet

D. Hashtable

5. Which of the following classes would be appropriate to use for a list of one-of-a-kind baseball cards? (Assume you throw away all duplicates.) Keep in mind that you are not interested in sorting these or in their order.

A. Vector

B. TreeMap

C. Hashtable

D. TreeSet

E. HashSet

6. Which of the following interfaces form the framework for a nonduplicating, sorted collection?

A. SortedList

B. SortedMap

C. SortedSet

D. List

7. Which of the following classes directly implement the SortedSet interface?

A. Vector

B. LinkedList

C. HashSet

D. TreeSet

E. Hashtable

8. You are creating a program that stores a list of the members in your Monday night bowling league. It would be nice to have them stored alphabetically. Which of the following classes would you use?

A. Vector

B. TreeMap

C. Hashtable

D. TreeSet

E. HashSet

9. Which of the following interfaces form the framework for a duplicating, ordered, unsorted collection?

   A. List
   B. Map
   C. Set
   D. Collection

10. Which of the following classes directly implement the List interface? (Choose all that apply.)

   A. Vector
   B. LinkedList
   C. HashSet
   D. TreeSet
   E. Hashtable

11. Which of the following classes would be appropriate to use for a deck of cards?

   A. Vector
   B. TreeMap
   C. Hashtable
   D. TreeSet
   E. HashSet

12. Which of the following interfaces form the framework for an unsorted, unordered collection that uses keys to access elements?

   A. List
   B. Map
   C. Set
   D. Collection

13. Which of the following classes directly implement the Map interface? (Choose all that apply.)

   A. Vector
   B. LinkedList
   C. HashSet
   D. Hashtable
   E. HashMap

14. Which of the following methods are defined by the Map interface? (Choose all that apply.)

A. get()

B. add()

C. set()

D. put()

E. remove()

15. Which of the following classes would be appropriate to use for a telephone directory listing?

A. TreeMap

B. Vector

C. Hashtable

D. TreeSet

E. HashSet

16. Which of the following interfaces form the framework for a sorted collection that uses keys?

A. SortedList

B. SortedMap

C. SortedSet

D. List

E. Map

17. Which of the following classes directly implement the SortedMap interface?

A. Vector

B. ArrayMap

C. HashMap

D. Hashtable

E. TreeMap

18. Given:

```
import java.util.*;
class Inventors {
   public static void main (String [] args) {
      Set dir = new TreeSet();
      dir.put("Jon G.", "555-5553");
      dir.put("Al E.", "555-1978");
```

```
 7.        dir.put("Tom E.", "555-1330");
 8.        dir.put("Alex B.", "555-7165");
 9.        System.out.println(dir);
10.     }
11.  }
```

What is the output of this program when it is compiled and run?

A. {Al E.=555-1978, Alex B.=555-7165, Jon G.=555-5553, Tom E.=555-1330}

B. { Jon G.=555-5553, Al E.=555-1978, Tom E.=555-1330, Alex B.=555-7165}

C. The program won't compile because of line 4.

D. The program won't compile because of lines 5 through 8.

E. Something else will prevent the program from compiling.

19. Given:

```
 1.  import java.util.*;
 2.  class MadameCthulhu {
 3.     public static void main (String [] args) {
 4.         Map tarot = new HashMap();
 5.         tarot.put("Lovers", "you will have romance");
 6.         tarot.put("Justice", "justice will be yours at last");
 7.         tarot.put("The Fool", "beware what friends tell you");
 8.         tarot.put("Death", "you better make a will");
 9.         Collections.shuffle(tarot);
10.         String card = (String)tarot.firstKey();
11.         String prediction = (String)tarot.get(card);
12.         System.out.println("Madam Cthulhu has picked " + card);
13.         System.out.println("She says " + prediction + "!");
14.     }
15.  }
```

Which lines will prevent this code from compiling successfully? (Choose all that apply.)

A. Line 4

B. Line 9

C. Line 10

D. Line 11

E. Lines 5-8

20. Given:

```
1.  import java.util.*;
2.  class ComicBooks {
3.     public static void main (String [] args) {
4.        Map comics = new TreeMap();
5.        comics.put(new Integer(404),"Spiderman");
6.        comics.put(new Integer(437),"X-Men");
7.        comics.put(new Integer(461),"The Hulk");
8.        comics.put(new Integer(459),null);
9.        String comic = comics.get(new Integer(461));
10.       System.out.println(comic);
11.    }
12. }
```

What will occur when this class is compiled and run?

A. It will not compile because an Integer object can't be used as a key in lines 5–8.

B. It will not compile because of line 8.

C. It will not compile because of line 9.

D. It will compile and run fine.

SELF TEST ANSWERS

The Collections Framework

1. ☑ A. A deck contains individual cards which, when pulled off the top of the deck one after another, form a definite order.
☒ B is incorrect because a deck of cards is shuffled with no sorting (unless someone is cheating). C is incorrect because each card in a deck is unique; therefore, there are no duplicates. D is incorrect because there is no mapping of keys to refer to the cards in a deck.

2. ☑ B and D. B is correct because the names are stored in alphabetical order (probably by last name). D is correct because the name acts as the key to retrieve, store, and sort the phone numbers.
☒ A is incorrect because, although they are sorted, they are not ordered in the sense of keeping a sequence and index of objects in the collection. C is incorrect because the key may not be duplicated. In this case, a single person may not be duplicated in the phone book.

Collection Interfaces and Classes

3. ☑ C. A Set does not allow duplicate objects to be stored. It also is unsorted and unordered.
☒ A is incorrect because a List allows duplicates. B is incorrect because a Map allows duplicates and uses a key, which is not required. D is incorrect because a Collection is a very general Interface that theoretically allows anything, including duplicates.

4. ☑ C. HashSet is the only class in the Java API to directly implement the Set interface.
☒ A, B, and D are incorrect because they do not use the Set interface.

5. ☑ E. A HashSet stores objects in an unordered, unsorted manner without allowing duplicates.
☒ A is incorrect because a Vector keeps objects ordered, which is unnecessary for this example. B is incorrect because a TreeMap is sorted. C is incorrect because Hashtable uses a key to manipulate items, which is unnecessary for this example. D is incorrect because TreeSet uses the SortedSet interface; hence the objects are sorted.

6. ☑ C. A SortedSet does not allow duplicate objects to be stored, but it has the additional property of being sorted.
☒ A is incorrect because a SortedList does not actually exist. B is incorrect because a SortedMap uses keys, which are not required. D is incorrect because a List allows duplicates.

7. ☑ D. TreeSet is the only class in the Java API to directly implement the SortedSet interface.
☒ A, B, C, and E are incorrect because they do not use the SortedSet interface.

8. ☑ D. A TreeSet is a SortedSet, which sorts items in ascending order without allowing duplicates.
☒ A is incorrect because a Vector is not sorted (technically you can sort this using the Collections class method sort(), but it does not do it automatically on the fly). B and C are incorrect because TreeMap and Hashtable use a key to manipulate items, which is unnecessary for a list of names. E is incorrect because objects placed in a HashSet are not sorted.

9. ☑ A. List allows duplicate objects to be stored, but it has the additional property of being ordered.
☒ B is incorrect because a Map uses keys, which are not required. C is incorrect because a Set is not ordered. D is incorrect because a Collection is a very general interface for collections without any specific behavior.

10. ☑ A and B. Both Vector and LinkedList implement the List interface directly.
☒ C, D, and E are incorrect because they do not use the List interface.

11. ☑ A. Vector keeps items ordered. It does allow duplicates, but it is still the best choice for cards, especially if several decks of cards are combined into one.
☒ B is incorrect because a TreeMap is sorted, and cards must be able to be shuffled. C is incorrect because Hashtable uses a key to manipulate items, which is unnecessary in a deck of cards. D is incorrect because TreeSet uses the SortedSet interface, so the objects are sorted. E is incorrect because objects placed in a Set such as HashSet are unordered, so it would be difficult and inaccurate to attempt to use this class for a deck of cards. A real deck of cards is shuffled randomly, yet it does have an order.

12. ☑ B. Map is the only type that uses keys to access the elements. It also is unsorted and unordered.
☒ A is incorrect because a List is ordered and does not use a key. C is incorrect because a Set does not use a key. D is incorrect because a Collection is a very general interface that allows anything, including duplicates.

13. ☑ D and E. Hashtable and HashMap both directly implement the Map interface.
☒ A, B, and C are incorrect because they do not use the Map interface.

14. ☑ A, D, and E. All of these methods are part of the Map interface.
☒ B is incorrect because add() is used only for classes implementing the Collection interface. C is incorrect because the set() method is completely made up.

15. ☑ **A.** TreeMap uses a key (the name) to store other objects (the phone number). The keys will be sorted in ascending order.
☒ **B** is incorrect because a Vector is unsorted. **C** is incorrect because Hashtable is also unsorted. **D** and **E** are incorrect because TreeSet and HashSet do not use keys; hence the phone numbers will not be sorted by name.

16. ☑ **B.** SortedMap stores objects in a sorted collection using keys.
☒ **A, C,** and **D** are incorrect because none of these collections use keys. **E** is incorrect because a Map is not sorted.

17. ☑ **E.** TreeMap is the only class in the Java API to directly implement the SortedMap interface.
☒ **A, B, C,** and **D** are incorrect because they do not use the SortedMap interface.

18. ☑ **D. D** is correct because TreeSet does not use the method put(), it uses add(). Also, TreeSet does not use keys.
☒ **A** is incorrect because only TreeMap would cause this output. **B** is incorrect because HashMap or Hashtable would give this output. **C** is incorrect because this line will compile fine—it is when we try to use the method put() that the compiler complains. **E** is incorrect because of the preceding reasons.

19. ☑ **B** and **C. B** will not work because the shuffle() method requires a List object. HashMap is a Map object and does not implement the List interface. On a conceptual level, for things to be shuffled they must be ordered and unsorted. Any type that does not keep order will not work for shuffling. **C** causes compilation to fail because the method firstKey() is part of the SortedMap interface, not the Map interface. On a conceptual level, Map is not sorted or ordered, therefore there would be no way to get the first key.
☒ **A** is incorrect because line 4 declares a Map object properly. **D** is incorrect because this is the proper way to retrieve an object from a Map collection. The compiler will not complain about line 11. **E** is incorrect because these lines properly add objects to the HashMap using keys.

20. ☑ **C.** When an object is retrieved from any collection, it must be cast into the appropriate Object type. In this case, it must be cast into a String, as follows:
String comic = (String)comics.get(new Integer(461));
☒ **A** is incorrect because any object can be used as a key. It is primitive types that can't be used as keys. **B** is incorrect because Map objects can store null values both as keys and as objects (SortedMap may not, however). **D** is incorrect because this class does not compile.

13

The java.awt Package: The Basics

CERTIFICATION OBJECTIVES

- 13.01 Components
- 13.02 Containers
- 13.03 Layout Managers
- 13.04 Menus
- 13.05 Painting
- ✓ Two-Minute Drill
- Q&A Self Test

The java.awt package defines an easy to use application programming interface library (API) to create and manipulate graphical components. The API includes a variety of familiar components, such as buttons and labels. These components are typically added to containers such as panels or frames. There is a species of Abstract Window Toolkit (AWT) component that is used to create menus. These MenuComponents are not subclasses of Component, and will be discussed separately in this chapter.

One component in particular, the Canvas class, is used for painting to. We will go over the paint() method, the Graphics class, and the Graphics methods that allow us to draw images, shapes, and text to any graphical component.

Java also includes a large number of layout managers that help a programmer position the components on the screen, relative to one another. This chapter will discuss how containers, components, and layout managers are related. It will specifically focus on the various types of layout managers and the behavior you can expect from them.

CERTIFICATION OBJECTIVE 13.01

The java.awt Package

The java.awt package of the Java Development Kit (JDK) provides developers with an arsenal of objects to construct graphical user interfaces (GUIs). These classes and interfaces form what is known as the *Abstract Window Toolkit* (AWT). There are three main types of classes within the java.awt package:

- **Component** The base class for the visual AWT classes, including Container. It provides functionality for defining the appearance of the AWT component, the response (if any) to various events, and the instructions on how to render itself. Swing components also descend from java.awt.Component. JComponent is a subclass of java.awt.Component, so it follows that Swing components contain the inherited functionality of their AWT predecessors.
- **Container** A specialized component that holds other components. Because containers themselves are components, you can nest containers within containers to achieve a desired layout.

- **LayoutManager** An interface responsible for sizing and positioning components within a container. A layout manager is associated with a container and a reference to that layout manager is held as a member of the container class. There are over a dozen layout managers available in the standard Java software development kit (SDK) 1.3. If the LayoutManager attribute of a container is set to null then that container uses absolute positioning of the components it contains. Absolute positioning means that each component is placed and sized at the coordinates as defined by the getBounds() method.

exam Watch ***There are new components for the Java 2 platform called Swing components. These components offer more functionality than standard java.awt components, and they look the same across all platforms. Swing will not be tested on the exam, however.***

CERTIFICATION OBJECTIVE 13.02

Components

Components are those objects in the Java SDK that render graphical widgets. Every type of component inherits from java.awt.Component, as shown in Figure 13-1, and thus inherits all of the methods necessary to render itself. They also inherit the methods for capturing and processing events such as mouse movement and keyboard activity (event handling will be thoroughly discussed in Chapter 14).

exam Watch ***Remember that the Component class of the java.awt package is the ultimate superclass for all nonmenu graphical components.***

FIGURE 13-1

The Component hierarchy with some sample components

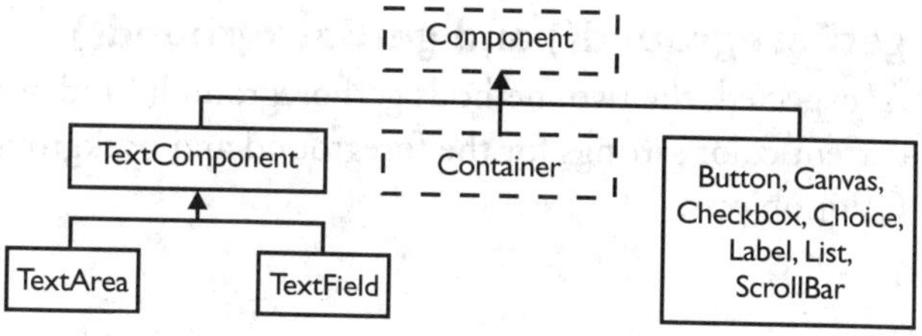

Component Methods

Component classes have many methods to perform those tasks that components must do. The abstract Component class itself has almost 200 methods, but you will not need to know all of these methods for the programmer exam. There are, however, certain methods that deserve closer attention as they perform some of the key functionality of components. Each component can customize its visual representation in a variety of ways. The most common properties of a component that are modified are its colors, fonts, and dimensions.

The dimensions of a component refer to its physical geometry on the screen, including the location and size. Components also contain methods for rendering (or painting) that component.

setForeground() and setBackground()

There are two methods for setting the color of a component, setForeground() and setBackground(). The setForeground() method defines the color that will be used to draw those items in the foreground of the component; the text color for example. The setBackground() method defines the color that will be used to draw the background of the component.

Both methods accept a Color object for an argument. For example, to set the color of the foreground of a component to red and the background to black, you would use the following:

```
myButton.setForeground(Color.red);
myButton.setBackground(Color.black);
```

If either the foreground color or the background color is not set using these methods, then the appropriate color setting of the parent container is used! So if the foreground color of a Frame is set to red and we add a Button object to the Frame, the button text will be red.

getForeground() and getBackground()

As expected, the two methods getForeground() and getBackground() return the current color settings for the foreground and background. These methods return Color objects.

setEnabled() and isEnabled()

A component can be enabled or disabled. When it is enabled, it is active to user interaction and can generate events. When it is disabled, typically, a user cannot affect the component. A disabled component is usually set to a grayish color to indicate it is not operational.

The setEnabled() method accepts a boolean value to indicate whether it should be enabled or disabled. Conversely, the isEnabled() method returns a boolean value indicating whether the component is enabled or disabled.

setVisible() and isVisible()

A component can be visible or invisible. When it is visible, it is displayed on the user GUI (assuming the parent container of this component is also visible). When it is invisible, the component is hidden from the user. Components are initially set to visible, except for top-level components such as Window objects.

These methods are similar to setEnabled() and isEnabled(). The setVisible() method accepts a boolean value to indicate whether the component should be visible. The isVisible() method returns a boolean value indicating whether the component is currently visible.

setFont() and getFont()

The java.awt.Component class provides a method for changing the font. This method is called setFont() and must be passed a java.awt.Font object in the method call. To retrieve the current font, the getFont() method may be called.

For example, the following code sets the font of a component:

```
myButton.setFont(new Font("SanSerif", Font.PLAIN, 14));
```

As with the colors of the component, if a font is not explicitly specified then the font of the parent component is inherited. So if we use setFont() to change the font of a Panel, then any component in Panel that has no font set will inherit the enclosing panel's font. (Remember, Component defines the setFont() method and Panel inherits from Container, which in turn inherits from Component.)

setSize() and getSize()

The methods setSize() and getSize() are used for setting or retrieving the dimensions of a component, respectively. For setting the dimensions, you can pass either two integers representing the width and height or a java.awt.Dimension object. The getSize() method exclusively returns a java.awt.Dimension object.

getPreferredSize()

The *preferred* size of a component is the minimum required dimensions a component needs to display properly. The method getPreferredSize() is used for retrieving the minimum dimensions of a component. The getPreferredSize() method returns a java.awt.Dimension object.

setLocation() and getLocation()

The methods setLocation() and getLocation() are used to set or retrieve the current location of the component within the container, respectively. The location of a component is defined as the upper-left corner of the component. For setting the location, you may pass in either two integer parameters representing the *x* and *y* coordinates of the upper-left corner or a java.awt.Point object. The getLocation() method exclusively returns a java.awt.Point object.

For example, the following code creates a Label within an application that will sit at location x = 100, y = 100, have a width of 300, and a height of 50:

```
Label label = new Label("A Label");
label.setLocation(100,100);
label.setSize(300,50);
```

setBounds() and getBounds()

There are also methods that perform the size and location tasks in one call. These methods are setBounds() and getBounds(). These methods pass and return the entire physical geometry of the component all at once. For the setBounds() method, you can pass either four integers representing the *x* and *y* coordinates and the width and height or pass one java.awt.Rectangle object. The getBounds() method exclusively returns a java.awt.Rectangle object.

It is only fair to warn you that the layout manager may ignore the size and location settings. It is at the layout manager's discretion to pay attention to all or some of these geometry settings or to ignore them completely.

paint()

The paint() method of a component is called by the system, not from within the application. If your class extends a component, you can override the paint(Graphics g) method of java.awt.Component so that you can define your own rendering characteristics. The paint() method is where all rendering takes place. When implementing your own paint() method, you use the graphics context provided to set the colors, the fonts, and to draw the various parts of the component.

repaint()

The repaint() method can be called directly from within an application. It makes a system call to repaint this component the first chance it gets.

update()

The update(Graphics g) method is called automatically when you (or the system) invokes the repaint() method. The most common experience with the update() method is to override it to call the paint() method. By using this technique, one can reduce or eliminate flickering when a component is redrawn. This flicker is caused by the default implementation of the update() method. Normally, the update() method calls the clearRect() method to erase the drawing space prior to drawing. This default process may cause the appearance of flickering. By overriding the update() method to call the paint() method, the flickering can be eliminated.

When a component is to be rendered, the methods are invoked in the following order:

1. repaint()
2. update()
3. paint()

on the job

The update() method of java.awt.Component clears the drawing rectangle prior to rendering the component. This causes flickering under certain circumstances. To alleviate this, it is customary to override the update() method in your custom component so it calls paint() directly and does not clear the screen.

AWT Components

For the exam, you should have some knowledge and experience with the most common AWT components. These components essentially act the same when they are placed into a container and subject to a layout manager (discussed later in the chapter). They also have most of the same methods (inherited from Component), with some extra methods added to take advantage of the GUI behavior in which the component specializes.

We will examine each of the AWT components in detail. For now, let's examine some basic code that displays the components. The following example creates a frame and places each AWT component in the frame:

```
import java.awt.*;
class AWTTest extends Frame {

   public AWTTest() {
      super("Components Test");
      this.setSize(300,300);
      this.setLayout(new FlowLayout());
      this.add(new Button("Button"));
      this.add(new Checkbox("CheckBox", true));

      Choice ch = new Choice();
      ch.add("Choice1");
      ch.add("Choice2");
      this.add(ch);

      this.add(new Label("Label"));

      class MyCanvas extends Canvas {
         public void paint(Graphics g) {
            g.drawString("Canvas",10,10);
         }
      }
      Canvas c = new MyCanvas();
      c.setBackground(Color.black);
      c.setForeground(Color.white);
      c.setSize(60, 50);
      this.add(c);

      List l = new List(4, false);
      l.add("List item 1");
      l.add("List item 2");
```

```
32.          this.add(l);
33.
34.          this.add(new Scrollbar(Scrollbar.VERTICAL, 0, 1, 0, 255));
35.          this.add(new TextArea("TextArea", 5, 40));
36.          this.add(new TextField("TextField"));
37.      }
38.
39.      public static void main (String [] args) {
40.          new AWTTest().setVisible(true);
41.      }
42.  }
```

For those that are familiar with the Java AWT, this code is very basic. The main class is called *AWTTest*, and it extends the container Frame to give us something to which we can add our components. The constructor performs some basic formatting to the frame, such as resizing the frame to 300 by 300 pixels in line 6, and giving the frame a layout manager in line 7. The rest of the code in the constructor creates all of the AWT component types and adds them to the frame. (Coding these components will be discussed in detail later.)

About the only surprise in the preceding code is the inner class used to create a canvas. A canvas is almost always created by extending the Canvas class, then overriding the paint() method to achieve the desired appearance, as shown in lines 19 to 21. We also changed the colors of the canvas in lines 24 and 25 to make it stand out from the frame.

When this code is compiled and executed, you should see something similar to Figure 13-2. The actual appearance of these AWT components will vary, depending on the operating system you are using. This is in contrast to Swing components, which appear the same no matter what operating system the application is executed on.

There are nine classes in the java.awt package that directly extend the Component class. You are probably familiar with the behavior of most of these classes from just using an operating system. Let's examine each of these components individually.

Button

Most users of popular operating systems such as Windows, Macintosh, or Linux (with the KDE or GNOME user interfaces) are very familiar with the behavior of a button. It is simply a component that initiates an action when the user clicks it.

The java.awt.Button class has two constructors: Button() and Button(String label). The second constructor returns a button labeled with the supplied string.

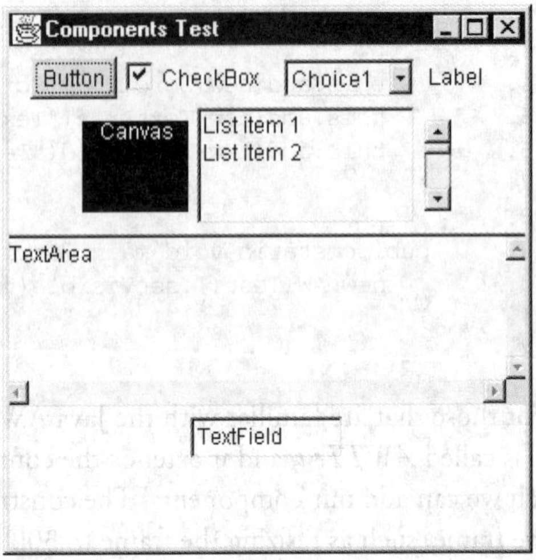

FIGURE 13-2

All of the basic Java AWT components

Alternately, the label can be set using the method setLabel(), and the label can be retrieved using getLabel().

Canvas

A canvas object is used for displaying graphics. A programmer can paint the canvas object with shapes, pixels, and text in many colors. Generally, highly graphical applications, such as video games, use a canvas to draw on. We will be discussing the Canvas class in more detail in the painting section of this chapter.

Checkbox

The checkbox can appear differently, depending on how it is used. When used individually, it displays a checkbox that is either on or off. As part of a checkbox group, it displays as radio buttons. Exactly one check box button in a CheckboxGroup can be on at any given time. Pushing any button sets it to on and forces any other button in the group to off. Examine the following code, which displays normal checkboxes, and a checkbox group:

```
import java.awt.*;
class CheckboxTest extends Frame {

    public CheckboxTest() {
```

```
5.          super("Checkboxes and Radio buttons");
6.          this.setSize(300,200);
7.          this.setLayout(new FlowLayout());
8.
9.          this.add(new Checkbox("Watermelons", true));
10.         this.add(new Checkbox("Kiwis", true));
11.         this.add(new Checkbox("Apples", true));
12.
13.         CheckboxGroup group = new CheckboxGroup();
14.         this.add(new Checkbox("Windows", group, true));
15.         this.add(new Checkbox("Linux", group, false));
16.         this.add(new Checkbox("Macintosh", group, false));
17.     }
18.
19.     public static void main (String [] args) {
20.         new CheckboxTest().setVisible(true);
21.     }
22. }
```

This code creates some regular checkboxes in lines 9 to 11 using a string and a boolean value that indicates whether it should be checked or not. The rest of the code creates a group of radio buttons. As you can see, it is extremely easy to make a group of checkboxes belong to the same group. Line 13 creates a CheckboxGroup, which conceptually ties the checkboxes together. In lines 14 to 16, the Checkbox constructor includes the CheckboxGroup object in the argument.

When this code is executed, you should see something similar to Figure 13-3.

Choice

The Choice class is essentially a drop-down menu of choices. The currently-selected choice is displayed on the screen, and the other choices are hidden until the user

FIGURE 13-3

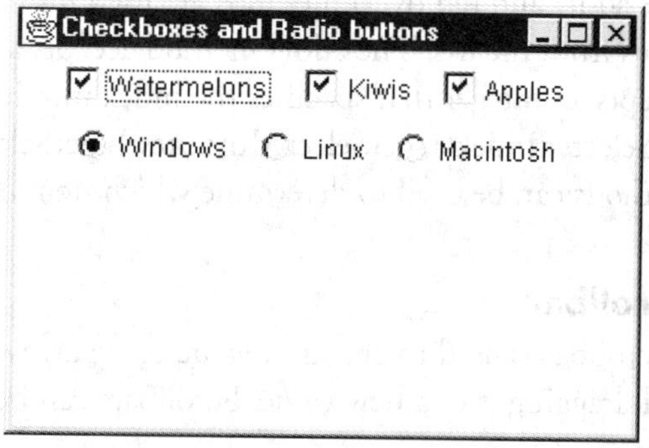

Checkboxes versus a CheckboxGroup (radio buttons)

clicks the component. The Choice class has one constructor that takes no arguments. Items can be added to the menu by invoking the add() method, using a string object in the argument.

Container

A container is a component (such as Frame or Applet) that can contain other components. This class type will be described thoroughly later in the chapter.

Label

The label is a simple component used for displaying text on the screen. Typically, there is no user interaction directly with a label. The Label class has a no-arguments constructor and a constructor that takes a string as the argument. It also has a third constructor that specifies the alignment of the text within the label using an integer value:

```
Label l = new Label("Dollars: ", Label.LEFT);
```

The Label class also uses the setText() and getText() methods for changing and retrieving the label text.

List

The List class displays a list of strings on the screen, and allows the user to select one or many of the items in the list. There are three constructors for the List class. The first is a no-arguments constructor, the second accepts an integer that specifies the number of rows for the list, and the third constructor accepts the number of rows and a boolean value that determines whether multiple selections are allowed.

The List class contains many extra methods that allow manipulation of the list. The add() and remove() methods are used for (you guessed it) adding and removing items from the list. The add() method accepts a string, and the remove() method accepts an integer that specifies the index number of the item to remove. The getSelectedIndex(), getSelectedIndexes(), getSelectedItem(), and getSelectedItems() methods can be used to determine which item or items are currently selected.

Scrollbar

A scrollbar is used to change a value using arrows or by grabbing the scrollbar and dragging it to a new value. Scrollbars can be either vertically or horizontally oriented, depending on the constructor used. By default, the scrollbar is vertical if orientation is not specified. The following constructor allows all values to be set:

```
Scrollbar(int orientation, int value, int visible, int minimum,
    int  maximum)
```

Text Components

The TextComponent has methods that allow basic text editing. It is not an abstract class, but it cannot be instantiated because the constructor is private. There are two subclasses of this component:

- **TextField** This provides a single line of text for editing.
- **TextArea** This provides multiple lines of text for editing. Scrollbars can also be invoked using one of the overloaded constructors.

FROM THE CLASSROOM

Creating Lightweight Components

It is possible for a programmer to create new components from scratch. This allows you, the developer, maximum flexibility over the functionality of your component, but it is a little more work than simply extending an existing component.

The most common way to create a new component is to create a class that extends the java.awt.Component itself. The benefit of this is that your component will already have much of the event handling and layout functionality built in already. This also has the advantage of being lightweight and not needing a native peer to render itself. Basically, this means that your new component will look the same across all platforms that support the Java Virtual Machine. (This is how the javax.swing components are created.)

There are two requirements for creating a new component in this manner. The first requirement is that you must provide a constructor in your component. You can either implement a constructor or allow the virtual machine to create a default constructor with no arguments. The other requirement is providing a means for the component to render itself. This entails overriding the paint() method of the java.awt.Component superclass and implementing the code that will draw the component on the screen.

—Jay Foster, BSEE

CERTIFICATION OBJECTIVE 13.03

Containers

Containers are special components that can contain other components. Components are added to a container by way of the add() method. The Container class defines five overloaded add() methods in total. Each container utilizes a layout manager (discussed later) to size and position those components within it.

As we saw earlier in this chapter, the Container class is a subclass of Component (see Figure 13-1). Looking even further down the object hierarchy there are many containers that are derived from the abstract Container class, as shown in Figure 13-4. All of the classes shown reside in the java.awt package except for Applet, which is in the java.applet package.

exam watch

The add() method is used to add component instances to the container. This includes the overloaded variants of add().

Container Methods

There are several methods defined by the Container class that are common to all containers. Of these, the most important are those that deal with adding components as well as performing the layout and sizing of components.

FIGURE 13-4

Hierarchy of the major Container classes

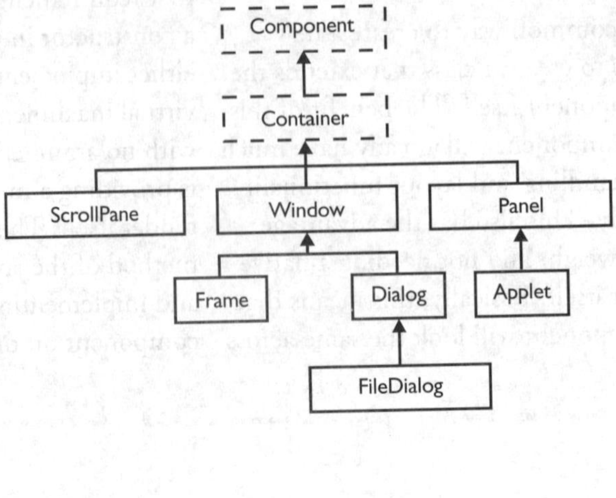

add()

The add() method of the java.awt.Container class is overloaded with several different methods. These give the container a great deal of flexibility when adding components to its collection. The overloaded add() methods are as follows:

- **add(Component component)** This method adds the specified component as the last object in the container.
- **add(Component component, int index)** This adds the specified component and inserts it into the specified position. Although the results of an invalid index vary from layout manager to layout manager, the general result is an exception of some sort. By using an index of -1 the component will be added to the last position.
- **add(Component component, Object constraints)** This add() method is special in that it provides the constraints object for those layout managers that require it. In fact, this method calls the addLayoutComponent() method of the container's layout manager.
- **add(String name, Component component)** This add() method is more or less the same as the add(Component, Object) method, except it specifically uses a String object. The Java API documents recommend using the add (Component, Object) method instead of this one.
- **add(Component component, Object constraints, int index)** This add() method provides the necessary information for those layout managers that require both a constraints object and an index to properly layout the component.

setLayout() and getLayout()

The setLayout(LayoutManager) method allows you to set the layout manager that will be responsible for the sizing and positioning of components within the container. Conversely, getLayout() allows you to retrieve the LayoutManager object being used for the container.

getComponent()

The getComponent() method retrieves a specified component from the container. The Container method getComponent(int n) is passed an argument of an integer value that specifies the index of the component to retrieve. There are three other similar methods of Container that allow retrieval of components.

getInsets()

The getInsets() method returns an Insets object of this container, which indicates the size of the container's border.

remove() and removeAll()

The remove() and removeAll() methods remove a specified component or all components from the container. The remove() method accepts either an index of the component to remove, or the actual Component object that should be removed.

validate()

When a container is *validated* it means the component layout is recalculated. The validate() method is generally called after components have been added or modified.

Types of Containers

There are several subclasses of Container that provide different functionality in the java.awt package. Many of these containers are *top-level containers,* meaning they can be displayed alone without needing to be placed within another object. The Window class and all of its subclasses are examples of top-level containers. We will now examine each of the major Container subclasses in more detail.

Panel

Panel is by far the simplest and most common of the Container classes. A panel is typically added to another container and is used to group components within a container. This behavior will be thoroughly examined in the Layout Manager section of this chapter.

The Applet class is a subclass of Panel. It is part of the java.applet package, however, and not the java.awt package. You should still be familiar with it.

If no LayoutManager is specified for a panel, then the FlowLayout manager is used by default.

on the Job

When creating your own layouts using panels, you will probably notice you end up nesting a lot of panels within panels. Don't get discouraged and feel you are not being efficient because you needed so many panels! It is typical for Java GUIs using AWT to require many panels and lots of code to achieve a desired effect.

ScrollPane

ScrollPane is a container that provides optional scroll bars to gain access to the part of the container that is presently off the viewable area. There is an option to have the scroll bars present all the time, or visible only when the content doesn't fit in the viewable portion of the container. Figure 13-5 shows a ScrollPane that contains the license agreement bundled with the latest Java 2 Development Kit.

Window

The Window class is a container with no decorations such as borders or menu bars. The Window container is a top-level container, so all classes that inherit from

FIGURE 13-5

ScrollPane is a subclass of the class Container

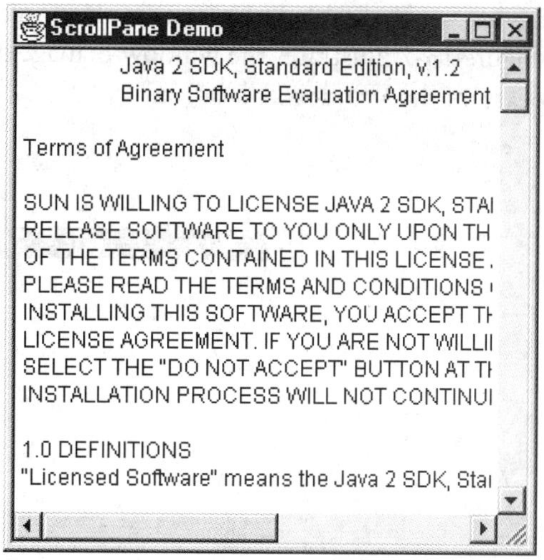

Window are also top-level containers. A typical use of the Window class is to present a splash for an application. Such screens usually do not need the decorations and controls associated with an application frame. A Window must have either a Frame, a Dialog, or another Window defined as its owner when it's constructed.

If no LayoutManager is specified for the Window container then a BorderLayout manager is used by default.

Frame

The Frame class is derived from the Window class (see Figure 13-4). The Frame class has decorations such as borders, titles, and menu bars. Like all subclasses of Window, the Frame container is a top-level container.

If no LayoutManager is specified then a BorderLayout manager is used by default, much like the Window class that it inherits from.

Figure 13-6 shows a blank frame. This illustrates the basic components of the graphical representation of the Frame class. Notice the standard window management controls at the top of the frame as well as the border. The border surrounding the frame can be used to resize the frame during execution. Of course, this resizing behavior can be disabled from within the program.

Figure 13-7 illustrates the window management menu of the Frame class as it appears on the Windows platform.

FIGURE 13-6

A blank frame

FIGURE 13-7

A frame with the window management menu

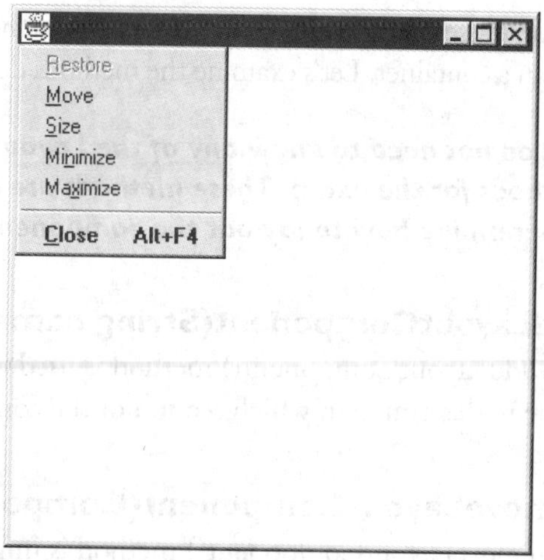

CERTIFICATION OBJECTIVE 13.04

Layout Managers

Layout managers are responsible for positioning and sizing components within a container. The type of layout manager that the parent container uses will determine where the components are positioned within that container.

Layout managers free the developer from having to calculate positions and sizes of each component. Given the fact that different platforms render each component differently, the task of manually calculating the appropriate size and position of a component such that the appearance of the application remains more or less the same across platforms would be quite daunting without the AWT package.

Fortunately, the layout managers are able to handle these tasks for the developer. Each layout manager knows how to position each of the components within the container and reposition them (if necessary) when the size of the parent container changes during runtime.

Layout Manager Interfaces

A class that wants to perform the role of a layout manager must either implement java.awt.LayoutManager or java.awt.LayoutManager2. Both of these interfaces define those methods necessary to determine how to position and size components within a container. Let's examine the methods defined by the LayoutManager interface.

exam Watch

You do not need to know any of the LayoutManager or LayoutManager2 methods for the exam. These methods are used only by the container object to determine how to lay out the components.

addLayoutComponent(String name, Component comp)

The addLayoutComponent() method is used by those layout managers that use a name to determine in which section of the container the component will be placed.

removeLayoutComponent(Component comp)

Th removeLayoutComponent() method is implemented by those layout managers that need to be able to remove a component from a container.

preferredLayoutSize(Container cont)

The preferredLayoutSize() method is called to provide the dimensions necessary to render the given container. It is up to the implementing layout manager to determine how those dimensions are calculated. Some layout managers step through each component and calculate the dimensions and position of each one, and other layout managers simply return the current size of the container.

minimumLayoutSize(Container cont)

The minimumLayoutSize() method should be implemented by layout managers to return the minimum size necessary to render the container.

layoutContainer(Container cont)

The layoutContainer() method is where most of the action takes place. It is here that the implementing layout manager class will size and position each component with the specified container.

The LayoutManager2 interface is a subinterface of the LayoutManager interface. The main difference is that LayoutManager2 provides for the sizing and positioning of components based upon a constraints object. Let's take a look at the methods defined by the LayoutManager2 interface.

addLayoutComponent(Component component, Object constraints)

The addLayoutComponent() method will add the specified component to the container. The constraints object will dictate to the layout manager how to render the component.

maximumLayoutSize(Container container)

The maximumLayoutSize() method introduces the concept of a maximum size to a container. If implemented by the layout manager, the container will not exceed the size returned.

getLayoutAlignmentX(Container container)

The getLayoutAlignmentX() method returns a float value representing the alignment of the container specified along the horizontal axis. The range of values for the return type is 0.0 to 1.0. Those values nearer to 0.0 mean an alignment more towards the left edge of the container. Those values nearer to 1.0 mean an alignment more towards the right edge of the container. A value of 0.5 means it is centered.

getLayoutAlignmentY(Container container)

The getLayoutAlignmentY() method returns a float value representing the alignment of the container specified along the vertical axis. The range of values for the return type is 0.0 to 1.0. Those values nearer to 0.0 mean an alignment more towards the top edge of the container. Those values nearer to 1.0 mean an alignment more towards the bottom edge of the container. A value of 0.5 means it is centered.

invalidateLayout(Container container)

The invalidateLayout() method will tell the layout manager that the current information about the layout of the specified container is no longer valid and should be purged from any cached information.

Types of Layout Managers

There are a variety of predefined layout managers in the Java Development Kit. Each one performs its role of sizing and positioning components in different ways. The following sections outline the predefined layout managers of the JDK.

GridLayout

The GridLayout arranges components in a grid within a container. Each cell in the grid is of equal dimensions. The GridLayout manager ignores the preferred size of each component and resizes them to exactly fit each cell's dimensions. As each component is added to the container, the GridLayout manager inserts them across each column until that row is filled and then starts at the first column of the next row.

It should be noted that explicitly setting the number of columns and rows either in the constructor or by calling the setRows() and setColumns() methods does not guarantee that you will get the expected number of columns. Due to the nature of the GridLayout class, the number of columns is calculated by the number of rows and the number of components added. The number of columns specified is respected only if the number of rows is not specified.

The following is an example of the GridLayout manager. Figure 13-8 is a visual representation.

```
import java.awt.*;
public class GridLayoutExample {
    public static void main(String args[]) {
        Frame f = new Frame("GridLayout Example");
        f.setBounds(0, 0, 300, 300);
        f.setLayout(new GridLayout(3, 3)); // 3 rows x 3 columns
        for(int i = 1; i <= 9; ++i) {
            Button b = new Button("Button " + i);
            f.add(b);
```

FIGURE 13-8

A GridLayout example

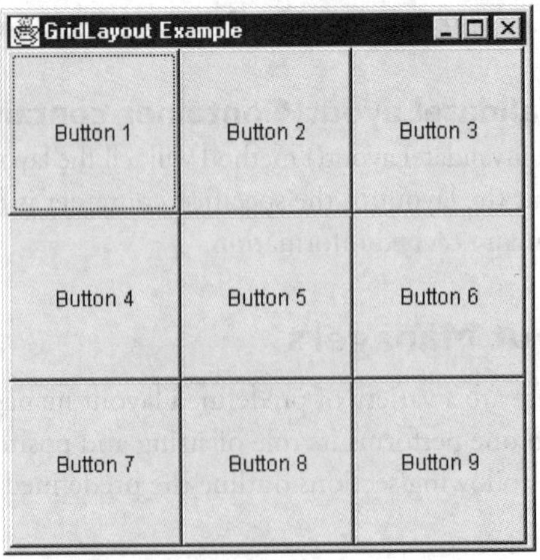

```
            }
            f.setVisible(true);
        }
    }
```

This class will generate a frame divided into a grid with nine cells, and with three cells per row. Each cell in the grid is of equal dimensions. When the frame is resized, all of the cells resize proportionally to remain the same size as each other.

FlowLayout

The FlowLayout class arranges components within the container from left to right. When the container runs out of room on the current row, FlowLayout resumes positioning components on the next row down. The FlowLayout manager respects the preferred size of each component.

The following code demonstrates FlowLayout, as shown in Figure 13-9.

```
import java.awt.*;
public class FlowLayoutExample {
   public static void main(String args[]) {
      Frame f = new Frame("FlowLayout Example");
      f.setBounds(0, 0, 300, 300);
      f.setLayout(new FlowLayout());
      for(int i = 1; i < 10; ++i) {
         Button b = new Button("Button " + i);
         f.setSize(100, 25);
```

FIGURE 13-9

A FlowLayout example

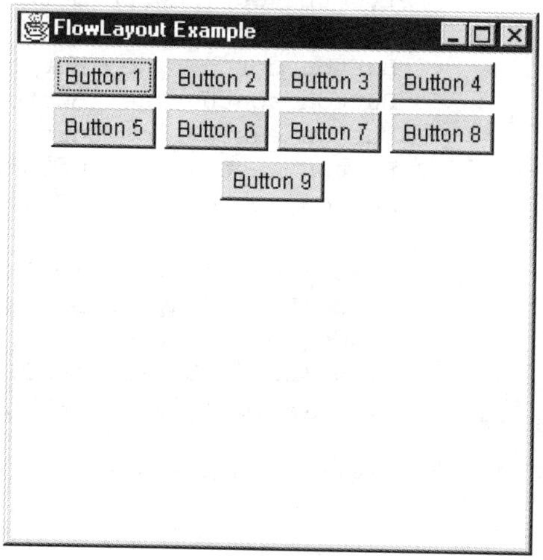

```
            f.add(b);
        }
        f.setVisible(true);
    }
}
```

This class will generate a frame containing nine buttons. Each row of buttons is centered on the vertical axis of the frame. As you resize the frame, notice that the buttons are rearranged into new rows or placed into existing rows as dictated by the size of each button and the size of the frame itself. In addition, notice that the buttons are sized according to their preferred size. This is in contrast to the GridLayout, where components take up as much space as possible.

BorderLayout

The BorderLayout layout manager divides the container into five areas. These areas are NORTH, SOUTH, EAST, WEST, and CENTER. The name of the area indicates where the component will be placed. All directional references are relative to the top of the container, which is considered NORTH.

The following class uses BorderLayout, as shown in Figure 13-10.

```
import java.awt.*;
public class BorderLayoutExample {
   public static void main(String args[]) {
      Frame f = new Frame("BorderLayout Example");
      f.setBounds(0, 0, 300, 300);
      f.setLayout(new BorderLayout());

      Button north = new Button("North");
      Button south = new Button("South");
      Button east = new Button("East");
      Button west = new Button("West");
      Button center = new Button("Center");

      f.add(BorderLayout.NORTH, north);
      f.add(BorderLayout.SOUTH, south);
      f.add(BorderLayout.EAST, east);
      f.add(BorderLayout.WEST, west);
      f.add(BorderLayout.CENTER, center);

      f.setVisible(true);
   }
}
```

FIGURE 13-10

A BorderLayout example

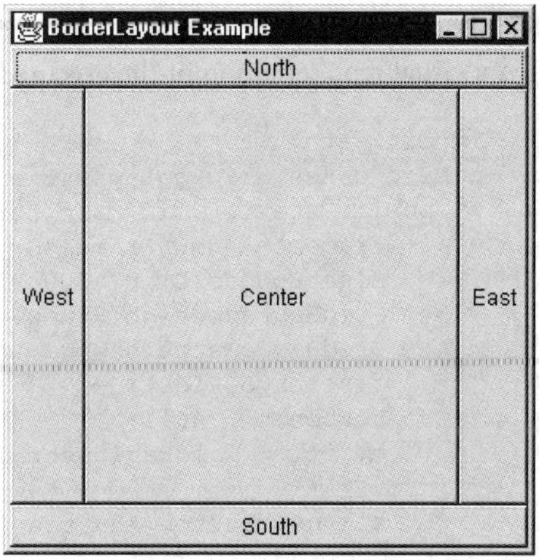

In this example, we create five buttons, label them in a descriptive manner (lines 8 to 12), and insert them into the five different sections of the container (lines 14 to 18). This example demonstrates the distinctive behavior of the BorderLayout class.

Any component placed within the NORTH or SOUTH areas of the container are resized to fill the entire *width* of the container, while the preferred *height* of the component is maintained. Any component placed within the EAST or WEST areas of the container are resized to fill the entire *height* of the container, while the preferred *width* of the component is maintained. Any component placed within the CENTER section of the container is resized to fill whatever space is left over after the other four sections have positioned components. The preferred size of any component in this CENTER section is ignored completely.

GridBagLayout

The GridBagLayout is similar to the GridLayout in that it places components on a grid. The difference is that components may span one or more rows or columns on the grid. In other words, it allows the placement of components that are aligned either vertically or horizontally without constraining those components to be the same height or width.

The GridBagLayout accomplishes this by defining a dynamic grid of cells. The constraints object that is passed when the component is added to the container determines how many cells the component will encompass. This constraint object is called a GridBagConstraints object.

The following code is an example of the GridBagLayout layout manager. Figure 13-11 is a visual representation of the executed code.

```
import java.awt.*;
public class GridBagLayoutExample {
    public static void main(String args[]) {
        Frame f = new Frame("GridBagLayout Example");
        f.setBounds(0, 0, 300, 300);
        GridBagLayout gb = new GridBagLayout();
        GridBagConstraints c = new GridBagConstraints();
        f.setLayout(gb);
        Button b = null;
        c.fill = GridBagConstraints.BOTH;

        b = new Button("Button 1");
        c.gridwidth = 1;
        c.gridheight = 1;
        gb.setConstraints(b, c);
        f.add(b, c);

        b = new Button("Button 2");
        c.gridwidth = 1;
        c.gridheight = 1;
        gb.setConstraints(b, c);
        f.add(b, c);

        b = new Button("Button 3");
        c.gridwidth = GridBagConstraints.REMAINDER;
        gb.setConstraints(b, c);
        f.add(b, c);

        b = new Button("Button 4");
        c.gridwidth = GridBagConstraints.RELATIVE;
        gb.setConstraints(b, c);
        f.add(b, c);

        b = new Button("Button 5");
        c.gridwidth = GridBagConstraints.REMAINDER;
        gb.setConstraints(b, c);
        f.add(b, c);

        b = new Button("Button 6");
        c.gridwidth = 1;
        gb.setConstraints(b, c);
```

```
        f.add(b, c);

        b = new Button("Button 7");
        c.gridwidth = GridBagConstraints.REMAINDER;
        gb.setConstraints(b, c);
        f.add(b, c);

        f.setVisible(true);
    }
}
```

In this example, we place seven buttons in three rows. Two of the buttons span multiple cells in the grid. There is no limit to the amount of complexity with which the grid can be defined and the components added. By virtue of this complexity, the GridBagLayout is the most flexible of the layout managers but is also the hardest to master.

CardLayout

The CardLayout layout manager treats each component as a card, with only one card being visible at any given time. Typically, a panel is used for the card and components are placed within the panel. That way, when a panel becomes hidden, all the components contained in the panel also become hidden. Whichever component was added first will be visible first when the container is displayed.

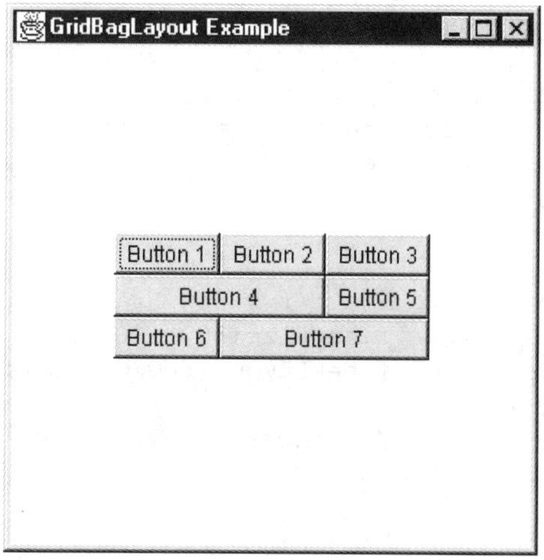

FIGURE 13-11

A GridBagLayout example

FIGURE 13-12

A CardLayout example

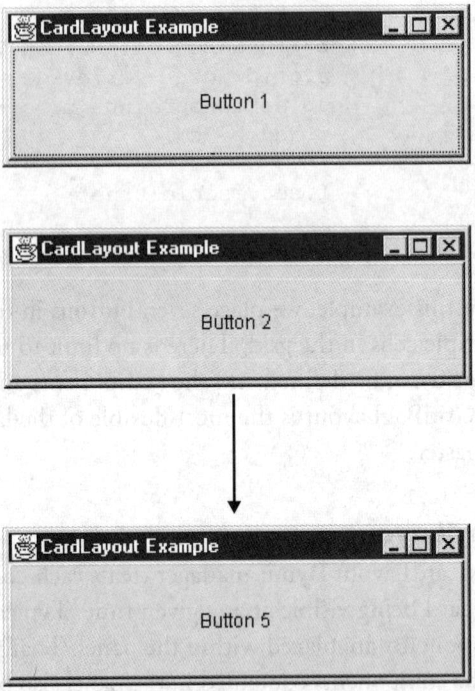

The following code is an example of the CardLayout layout manager. Figure 13-12 is a visual representation.

```
import java.awt.*;
import java.awt.event.*;
public class CardLayoutExample {
   public static void main(String args[]) {


      Frame f = new Frame("CardLayout Example");
      f.setSize(300, 100);
      f.setLayout(new CardLayout());

      /* Make a final copy of the reference to the Frame for
```

```
10.          the anonymous inner class below. */
11.       final Frame f1 = f;
12.       for(int i = 1; i <= 5; ++i) {
13.          Button b = new Button("Button " + i);
14.          b.setSize(100, 25);
15.          b.addActionListener(new ActionListener() {
16.             public void actionPerformed(ActionEvent ae) {
17.                CardLayout cl = (CardLayout)f1.getLayout();
18.                cl.next(f1);
19.             }
20.          } );
21.          f.add(b, "button" + i);
22.       }
23.       f.setVisible(true);
24.    }
25. }
```

In this example, we create a frame with a layout manager of CardLayout (line 7). We then add five buttons to this frame. Each button is assigned an anonymous action listener class that will receive the action event when the button is clicked and initiate the viewing of the next button in the card layout (lines 15 to 20). This process cycles over when the last button is reached.

No LayoutManager (null)

If the LayoutManager is set to null for a container, then absolute positioning is used to lay out the components. Each component will be sized and positioned according to its own parameters. The preferred size and position of the component will be respected.

The following is an example of a frame with its layout manager attribute set to null. Figure 13-13 is a visual representation.

```
import java.awt.*;
public class NullLayoutExample {
   public static void main(String[] args) {
      Frame f = new Frame("No LayoutManager Example");
      f.setSize(300, 300);
      f.setLayout(null);

      Button b1 = new Button("Button1");
```

```
        b1.setBounds(50, 50, 100, 100);
        Button b2 = new Button("Button2");
        b2.setBounds(100, 100, 100, 100);
        Button b3 = new Button("Button3");
        b3.setBounds(150, 150, 100, 100);

        f.add(b1);
        f.add(b2);
        f.add(b3);

        f.setVisible(true);
    }
}
```

In the preceding example, you can see how the preferred size and position of each component is respected. In this case, it results in an overlap of components. Resizing the container has no effect on the components it contains.

FIGURE 13-13

An example of a LayoutManager set to null

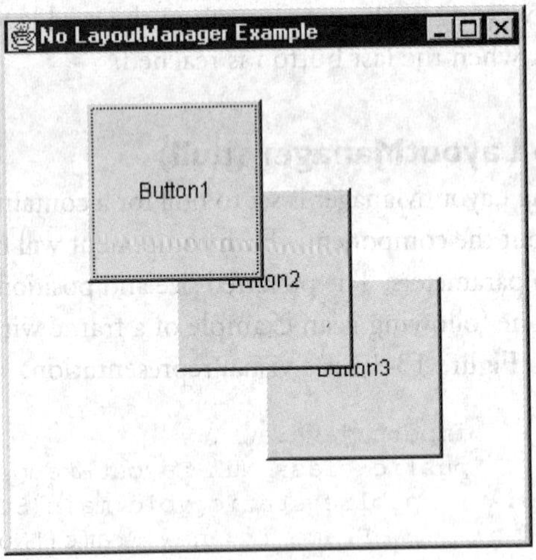

EXERCISE 13-1

Using Layout Managers

In this exercise, we will attempt to lay out some components in a frame according to a specific design specification. The top of the frame should contain one button, sized to its preferred size, situated on the leftmost side of the frame. The rest of the frame will consist of multicolored Canvas objects. This portion will use a GridBagLayout to position the Canvas objects. The first row will contain three panels of red, black, and blue colors. The second row will contain two panels of yellow and green. The yellow panel will take up two times the width of one red panel. The final product should look something like Figure 13-14.

Create an enclosing class called *TestPattern* and make it extend the Frame class. Also, create a no-arguments constructor where most of our GUI will be built, and a main() method which will create a new instance of the TestPattern class.

FIGURE 13-14

Layout Exercise

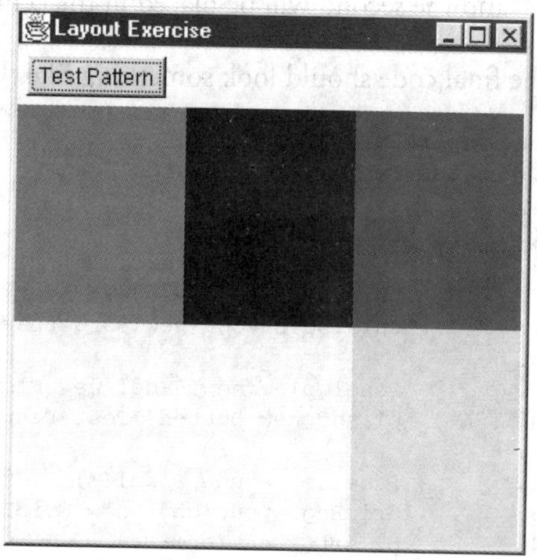

1. In the constructor, set the layout of our frame to BorderLayout. Also, create two panels. The first will use a FlowLayout, and the second a GridBagLayout. Make sure you initialize the FlowLayout using the argument FlowLayout.LEFT.
2. We will need to create a GridBagConstraints object. For the first row in the second panel, we will give the x and y dimensions a relative weight of 1.0. Add the red and black panels. For the last one, we want it to use up the remainder of the row, so we set the GridBagConstraints.gridwidth value to GridBagConstraints.REMAINDER, then add the final panel for this row.
3. For the second row, we want the yellow panel to take up two times the width of the previous panels. To do this, set the weightx value to 2.0 and then add the yellow panel.
4. Now we want the green panel to take up only the normal width, so set weightx back to 1.0 and change gridwidth to GridBagConstraints. REMAINDER and add the final panel.
5. Last, add the two panels to the Frame. The first goes in the North section, and the second will be placed in the center.

The final code should look something like this:

```
import java.awt.*;
class TestPattern extends Frame {

    public TestPattern() {
        super("Layout Exercise");
        this.setSize(300,300);
        this.setLayout(new BorderLayout());

        Panel p1 = new Panel(new FlowLayout(FlowLayout.LEFT));
        p1.add(new Button("Test Pattern"));

        Panel p2 = new Panel();
        GridBagLayout gb = new GridBagLayout();
        p2.setLayout(gb);

        GridBagConstraints gbc = new GridBagConstraints();
        gbc.fill = GridBagConstraints.BOTH;
        gbc.weightx = 1.0;
        gbc.weighty = 1.0;

        Panel panelA = new Panel();
        panelA.setBackground(Color.red);
        gb.setConstraints(panelA, gbc);
        p2.add(panelA);

```

```
26.        Panel panelB = new Panel();
27.        panelB.setBackground(Color.black);
28.        gb.setConstraints(panelB, gbc);
29.        p2.add(panelB);
30.
31.        Panel panelC = new Panel();
32.        panelC.setBackground(Color.blue);
33.        gbc.gridwidth = GridBagConstraints.REMAINDER; // End of row
34.        gb.setConstraints(panelC, gbc);
35.        p2.add(panelC);
36.
37.        gbc.weightx = 2.0; // Component takes up 2x width
38.        Panel panelD = new Panel();
39.        panelD.setBackground(Color.yellow);
40.        gbc.gridwidth = GridBagConstraints.RELATIVE;
41.        gb.setConstraints(panelD, gbc);
42.        p2.add(panelD);
43.
44.        gbc.weightx = 1.0; // Reset to 1x width
45.        Panel panelE = new Panel();
46.        panelE.setBackground(Color.green);
47.        gbc.gridwidth = GridBagConstraints.REMAINDER; // End of row
48.        gb.setConstraints(panelE, gbc);
49.        p2.add(panelE);
50.
51.        this.add(p1, "North");
52.        this.add(p2, "Center");
53.     }
54.
55.     public static void main (String [] args) {
56.        new TestPattern().setVisible(true);
57.     }
58. }
```

In the preceding code, we use the same GridBagConstraints object repeatedly instead of creating a new one for each panel, but a new one could be created each time. Sometimes programmers create a reusable method to handle some of the repetitious nature of using the GridBagLayout. There are some problems that can occur when trying to fulfill the design specification. If the panels are tiny squares (their preferred size) make sure you have the fill value set to GridBagConstraints.BOTH, as shown in line 17. If the panels appear scrunched-up vertically, then you are probably not setting the weighty value to 1.0, as shown in line 19.

Now that you have a better understanding of components, containers, and layout managers, refer to the Scenario & Solution for some possible scenario questions and their answers.

SCENARIO & SOLUTION	
Describe the relationship between components and containers.	A container is a special kind of component that can contain other components.
Describe the relationship between containers and layout managers.	The container holds a collection of components. The layout manager of the container is responsible for sizing and positioning those components.
How does a child component get its color settings if it does not explicitly set them itself?	The child component inherits the color settings from the parent component.
You want to create a top-level container that the user can resize. Which container do you use?	Frame. It is a top-level container that provides handles for resizing the Frame object
You want to create a splash screen that contains no decorations or menu bars. Which container do you use?	Window.
Which of the layout managers provided in the JDK always respects the preferred size of the components within the container?	FlowLayout.
Which of the layout managers provided in the JDK always ignores the preferred size of the components within the container?	GridLayout and CardLayout.
Which of the layout managers allows only one component to be visible at any given time?	CardLayout.

CERTIFICATION OBJECTIVE 13.05

Menus

Most people are familiar with menu systems in GUIs. They have been around since Xerox PARC pioneered them in the 1970s. Menus typically reside at the top of a Frame and drop down a list of menu items when the user clicks it. There are usually at least three different menu types that go into making a standard system: MenuBar, Menu, and MenuItem. All of these classes inherit from the abstract class MenuComponent, as shown in Figure 13-15.

FIGURE 13-15

Java AWT menu hierarchy

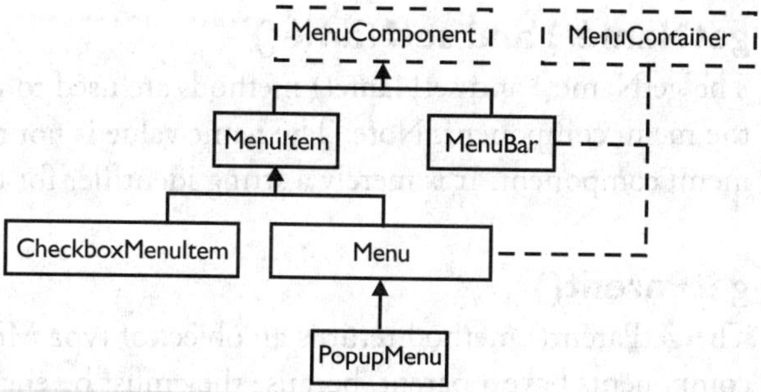

A *menu bar* is the strip along the top of the window that displays one or more words, typically from left to right. The menu bar can contain one or more *menus*. When a user clicks the menu, it will expand to display a list of *menu items*. A menu and a menu bar can both contain other menu components, so they both implement the MenuContainer interface. In fact, other objects that can contain menu items also implement this interface, such as Frame and even the abstract Component class.

Menu Methods

The MenuComponent class defines very few methods, because most menu components do not have a lot in common concerning their functionality. For instance, a menu bar is really quite different from a menu item. Let's examine some of the major methods of the MenuComponent class.

getFont() and setFont()

The getFont() and setFont() methods allow a programmer to set the type of font that a menu component will display as, or retrieve the type of font. Both methods use a Font object.

getName() and setName()

The getName() and setName() methods are used to retrieve or change the name of the menu component. Note: The name value is not the label that will appear on the menu component. It is merely a string identifier for this component.

getParent()

The getParent() method returns an object of type MenuContainer. *All* menu components have a parent, because they must be enclosed within some other object in order to exist. A menu cannot exist by itself.

Menu Components

There are five menu components in the java.awt package. Each of these components has specific behavior to perform one part of a menu system. The following sections examine those components and how they are used.

MenuBar

The MenuBar class has methods that will create a bar along the top of a Frame that can contain menus. Before the menu bar becomes visible to the GUI, however, it must be added to a Frame. This is done using the Frame.setMenuBar() method.

If the menu bar contains no menus then it will not appear in the GUI, not even as a blank bar. The most important MenuBar method to be familiar with is the add() method, which adds a Menu to itself, in order, from left to right. The add() method accepts only a Menu object as an argument.

Menu

When a menu is not selected, it is visible by its label on a menu bar. If a user selects the menu by clicking its label, the entire contents of the menu become visible. The main function of a Menu is to contain MenuItems. Because Menu itself is derived from the MenuItem class, a Menu can contain another Menu (known as a submenu).

The most important method of a Menu is the add() method. This takes a MenuItem (or a String) and adds it to the bottom of the menu. Another method called insert() accepts a MenuItem (or String) and an index that represents the location in the menu to which the item should be added. There is also an addSeparator() method that adds a small divider line to the menu list. Let's examine these methods in some code:

```
 1.  import java.awt.*;
 2.  class MenuTest extends Frame {
 3.
 4.     public MenuTest() {
 5.        super("Golf Caddy");
 6.        this.setSize(300,300);
 7.        this.setLayout(new FlowLayout());
 8.        this.add(new Label("Choose club."));
 9.
10.        Menu woods = new Menu("Woods");
11.        woods.add("1 W");
12.        woods.add("3 W");
13.        woods.add("5 W");
14.
15.        Menu irons = new Menu("Irons");
16.        irons.add("3 iron");
17.        irons.add("4 iron");
18.        irons.add("5 iron");
19.        irons.add("7 iron");
20.        irons.add("8 iron");
21.        irons.add("9 iron");
22.        irons.addSeparator();
23.        irons.add("PW");
24.        irons.insert("6 iron", 3);
25.
26.        MenuBar mb = new MenuBar();
27.        mb.add(woods);
28.        mb.add(irons);
29.        this.setMenuBar(mb);
30.     }
31.
32.     public static void main (String [] args) {
33.        new MenuTest().setVisible(true);
34.     }
35.  }
```

The preceding code creates two Menu objects. The *woods* Menu contains three strings. The constructor at line 10 gives the menu a label of *Woods.* The *irons* Menu is a little more fancy. It adds a separator just before the pitching wedge. Notice we accidentally forgot to add the 6 iron in the proper order. To remedy

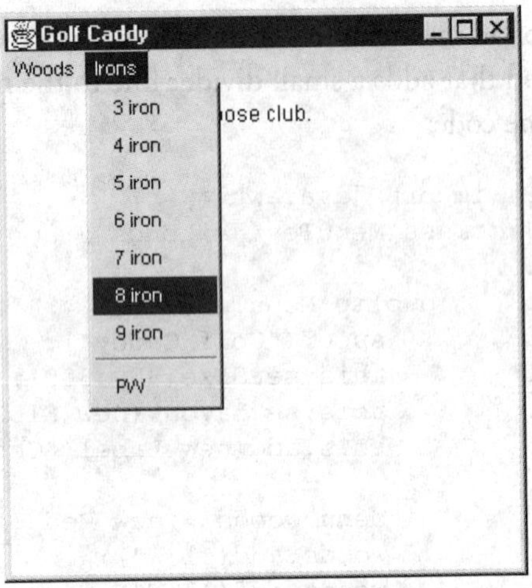

FIGURE 13-16

A simple menu system

this, the code uses the insert() method to place the 6 iron fourth down from the top. When this code is compiled and executed you should see something similar to Figure 13-16.

on the job

You may wonder why Strings can be added to a Menu because a String cannot react to user events. After all, a MenuItem is able to react to user events so it would seem to be more useful than adding a string. Actually, a Menu itself can react to user events, so it can determine which string was selected on its own.

MenuItem

A MenuItem is a label in a menu that can be selected by the user. All items in a Menu must belong to MenuItem or one of its subclasses. Notice in Figure 13-15 that Menu is a subclass of MenuItem. This design allows us to add Menus to other Menus (called a submenu). A third type of MenuItem is the CheckboxMenuItem. Let's examine all three of these with some Java code. We will alter our previous example for this demonstration:

```
1.  import java.awt.*;
2.  class MenuTest extends Frame {
3.
4.     public MenuTest() {
5.        super("Golf Caddy");
6.        this.setSize(300,300);
7.        this.setLayout(new FlowLayout());
8.        this.add(new Label("Choose club."));
9.
10.       Menu woods = new Menu("Woods");
11.       woods.add(new MenuItem("1 W"));
12.       woods.add(new MenuItem("3 W"));
13.       woods.add(new MenuItem("5 W"));
14.
15.       Menu irons = new Menu("Irons");
16.       irons.add("3 iron");
17.       irons.add("5 iron");
18.       irons.add("7 iron");
19.       irons.add("9 iron");
20.       irons.addSeparator();
21.       irons.add(woods);
22.       irons.addSeparator();
23.       irons.add(new CheckboxMenuItem("Putter", true));
24.
25.       MenuBar mb = new MenuBar();
26.       mb.add(irons);
27.       this.setMenuBar(mb);
28.    }
29.
30.    public static void main (String [] args) {
31.       new MenuTest().setVisible(true);
32.    }
33. }
```

The preceding example is similar to the previous example with some minor changes. Now we have used MenuItems instead of strings in lines 11 to 13. In line 21 we have added the menu *Woods* to the *Irons* menu. And finally, we have added a CheckboxMenuIitem in line 23. When this code is executed you will see something similar to Figure 13-17.

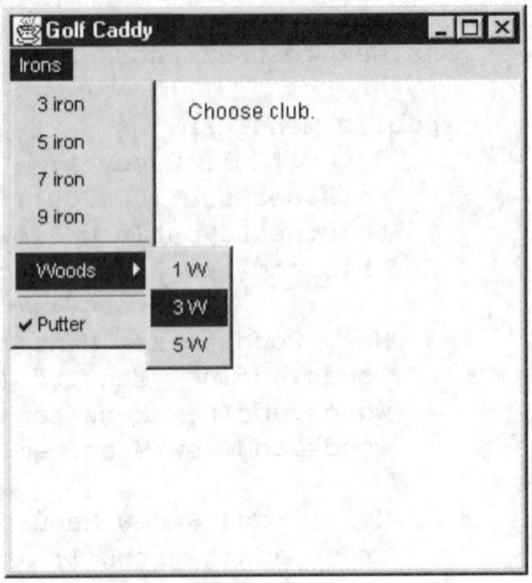

FIGURE 13-17

A menu containing another menu and a Checkbox MenuItem

CERTIFICATION OBJECTIVE 13.06

Painting

In our last topic for this chapter, we will teach you to paint with oils and canvas just like Bob Ross. Actually, we are not going to talk about oils, but we will be discussing the Canvas class in more detail. Java allows several objects to be *painted*, meaning we can draw shapes and text to them. Any object with a paint(Graphics g) method that we can override can be painted to. These classes include any class that has Component as a superclass. In most cases, however, the Canvas class is used because it is made specifically to paint to.

In the Components section, we briefly demonstrated how to paint to a Canvas. In this section, we will delve deeper into how this is accomplished and examine the Graphics class and some of its methods.

Overriding the paint() Method

All AWT Component subclasses contain a paint() method, including Canvas. In fact, the Canvas class exists primarily for painting. When a Canvas object is rendered to the screen, the paint() method is invoked. This method is invoked by the system, and not by you as the programmer. You can, however, indirectly invoke this method by calling the repaint() method.

To implement your own drawing and painting functionality, you can override the paint() method to execute your own code. The paint() method takes a Graphics object as its argument, enabling you to have access to the *graphics context* for the object. A graphics context is the area drawn to the screen for a GUI component. In fact, the Graphics object is analogous to the graphics context in that it gives us direct access to draw to the screen.

The following code demonstrates how to override the paint() method and how to use the Graphics object to render a few simple shapes to the screen.

```
import java.awt.*;
class SailBoat extends Canvas {

   public void paint(Graphics g) {
      setBackground(Color.red);
      g.setColor(Color.orange);
      g.fillOval(50, 50, 200, 200); // sun
      g.setColor(Color.blue);
      g.fillRect(0, 200, 300, 300); // water

      // sail:
      int sailX = 170;
      int sailY = 180;
      int [] x = {0 + sailX,10+ sailX,30+ sailX};
      int [] y = {30 + sailY,0 + sailY,30 + sailY};
      g.setColor(Color.white);
      g.fillPolygon(x, y, 3);
   }
}

class DisplayFrame extends Frame {
   public DisplayFrame() {
      super("Boat");
      this.setSize(300, 300);
      this.add(new SailBoat());
      this.setVisible(true);
   }

   public static void main (String [] args) {
      new DisplayFrame();
   }
}
```

The preceding program uses two classes: one to create a subclass of Canvas and one to override Frame and display our GUI. The paint() method is where the action occurs. It uses a few basic Graphics methods to draw some shapes to the screen (these will be covered later).

This use of an API is a little different compared to the way we use other Java API methods. Normally, we call a method from the Java API, but in this case we are creating a method and we just have to trust that the JVM will call our method on its own whenever it needs to draw the object to the screen. It can take a while to wrap your mind around this concept, but after using it a few times it becomes easy to understand. We will now examine the Graphics class in more detail.

The Graphics Class

The Graphics class is an abstract class that provides implementation for all of the low-level drawing methods. Because drawing may be performed differently on different platforms, there should not be one class that provides implementation for the system's drawing capabilities. So when it is implemented on each platform, a derived Graphics class is created that will provide the implementation for all of the drawing capabilities. All of this implementation is hidden by the Graphics class, which supplies the programmer with an interface to write code that uses graphics in a platform-independent way.

A Graphics object (commonly referred to as the graphics context) encapsulates the information, such as the current font, the current color, and coordinates information needed for basic rendering. The Graphics methods allow you to draw and fill an assortment of shapes, including lines, ovals, arcs, rectangles, and polygons, as well as methods for font and color manipulation. There are also methods to provide the capability to draw bitmapped images on a canvas.

Drawing Shapes

Java provides many methods that are capable of drawing almost any shape to the screen. Sun feels you should be familiar with some of these methods to become a certified programmer.

When any of the shape (or text) methods are called, they will draw the shape to the screen in the current color selected for the graphics context. It is up to you to change the color of the graphics to the color you want to render in using the Graphics.setColor() method.

The following section describes some of the more important shape drawing methods available in the Graphics class.

drawRect() and fillRect()

The drawRect() and fillRect() methods draw or fill a rectangle, using the supplied arguments. Both of these methods accept integer x and y coordinate arguments for the upper-left starting point, as well as integer values for the width and the height.

drawRoundRect() and fillRoundRect()

The drawRoundRect() and fillRoundRect() methods draw or fill a rectangle with rounded corners using this graphics context's current color. There are six integer arguments needed to define this object. The x, y, width, and height arguments give you the edges and size. There is also the horizontal diameter and vertical diameter of the arc for the four corners that determine the roundness of the corners.

draw3DRect() and fill3DRect()

The draw3Drect() and fill3Drect() methods draw or fill a 3-D highlighted rectangle using the current color. The edges will be highlighted so that it appears as if they are beveled and light is coming from the upper-left corner. Both of these methods take the same four arguments as the non-3D rectangle, plus an additional boolean argument that determines whether the rectangle appears to be raised above or sunken below the surface.

drawArc() and fillArc()

The drawArc() and fillArc() methods draw or fill the outline of a circular or elliptical arc covering the rectangle specified by the integer x, y, width, and height arguments supplied. There are also two integer arguments, one being the starting angle (0 degrees is at the 3 o'clock position), and another angle representing how far around the arc extends. A positive value indicates the rotation is clockwise, and a negative value is counterclockwise.

drawOval() and fillOval()

The drawOval() and fillOval() methods draw or fill an oval. The circle (or ellipse) fits within the rectangle specified by the four integer arguments: x, y, width, and height.

drawPolygon() and fillPolygon()

The drawPolygon() and fillPolygon() methods draw or fill a closed polygon that is defined by two arrays of integer x and y coordinates. Each pair of (x, y) coordinates defines a point. The third argument is an integer that defines the total number of line segments. The polygon is closed automatically by drawing a line that connects the final point to the first point (if those points are different).

There is an alternate overloaded method that accepts a Polygon object as well.

drawPolyline()

The drawPolyline() method draws a sequence of connected lines that are defined by two integer array arguments of x and y coordinates. Each pair of (x, y) coordinates defines a point. If the first point differs from the last point, then the figure is not closed.

drawLine()

The drawLine() method draws a line, using the current color, between the given integer starting points (x1, y1) and the end points (x2, y2).

drawString()

The drawString() method draws the text supplied in the first argument (a String) using the current font and color. The baseline of the leftmost character is at the x, y position using the next two integer arguments supplied.

getColor() and setColor()

The getColor() and setColor() methods get or set the drawing color. The setColor() method takes a Color object as its argument. This is the color that will be used until this method is invoked again with a new color.

Working with Text

The Font class provides a wide range of methods to work with fonts. There are two constructors for the Font class. The most commonly used one takes three arguments—the name, the style, and the point size. The style may be PLAIN, BOLD, ITALIC, or BOLD + ITALIC. The other constructor takes a Map argument with specified attributes. A platform-independent approach is taken when naming the fonts in

Java, and they are then mapped to local system fonts depending on the operating system. This means that the Font class is a representation of a font face that is present on the machine. Using the GraphicsEnvironment class' method, getAllFont() and retrieve an array of all available font faces on the system. They are returned as Font objects with a size of 1. From there, you can "derive" new Font objects with different sizes and styles by using one of the many varieties of the deriveFont() method. This is what you use to modify a Font.

The details of the implementation of the Font object are encapsulated in a FontMetrics object, which is created by invoking the getFontMetrics() method. There are methods that give you access to a number of important font-related properties. They are: getLeading(), getAscent(), getDescent(), and getHeight(). Text characters are displayed relative to a *baseline*, which is the line drawn along the bottom of all nondescending characters (descending characters are ones like g and y). These descending characters give you the *descent*—the number of pixels that descend below the baseline. The *ascent* is the number of pixels that the character ascends above the baseline. There is also the font's *leading*, which is the number of pixels between a font's *descent* and the *ascent* of the line of text that is directly below it. The *height* of the font is the sum of its ascent, descent, and leading.

EXERCISE 13-2

Painting to a Canvas

In this exercise, we will attempt to draw some shapes and text to a Canvas object. This will use most of the material from the preceding section. In our example, we will attempt to draw a self-portrait on the canvas with your name underneath.

1. Create an enclosing class called *SelfPortrait* and make it extend the Canvas class.
2. In previous AWT examples, we used the *is a* relationship with a Frame. In this example, we will use the *has a* relationship. Create a no-arguments constructor that creates an instance of the Frame class when the class is instantiated. Resize the frame appropriately and make it visible. Also, the class should add itself to the Frame object.
3. Override the public void paint(Graphics g) method of the Canvas class. This is the method that will draw the picture.

4. Now go nuts drawing an image of yourself. Don't forget to change the color using the Graphics.setColor() method.

   The final code should look similar to this:

```
import java.awt.*;
class SelfPortrait extends Canvas {

   public SelfPortrait() {
      this.setBackground(Color.yellow);

      Frame f = new Frame("Me"); // 'has a' Frame
      f.setSize(300, 400);
      f.add(this);
      f.setVisible(true);
   }

   public void paint(Graphics g) {
      setForeground(Color.pink);
      g.fillOval(50, 50, 200, 200); // face
      g.setColor(Color.black);
      g.fillOval(125, 150, 10, 10); // left eye
      g.fillOval(175, 150, 10, 10); // right eye
      g.fillRect(125, 115, 15, 5); // left brow
      g.fillRect(175, 115, 15, 5); // right brow
      g.drawArc(55, 150, 190, 40, 180, 180); // mouth

      g.setColor(Color.blue);
      g.setFont(new Font("Ariel", Font.BOLD, 22));
      g.drawString("Ike!", 130, 275);
   }

   public static void main (String [] args) {
      new SelfPortrait();
   }
}
```

This code will produce Figure 13-18, which seems like a suitable image on which to end the chapter.

FIGURE 13-18

A self-portrait of the author

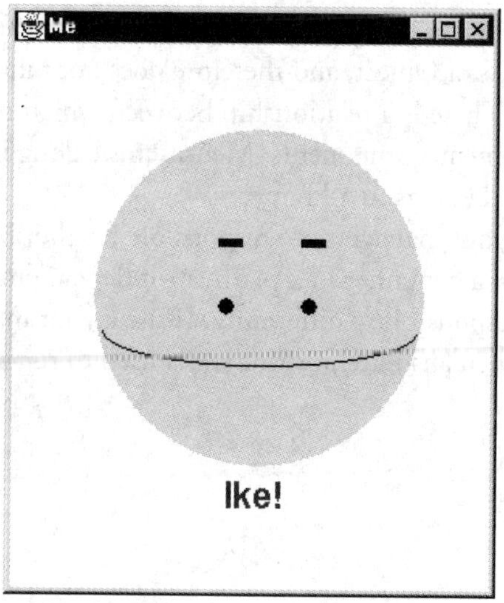

CERTIFICATION SUMMARY

This chapter covered one of the larger topics on the programmer exam: designing and coding with the Java AWT. The exam will focus on the behavior of the various classes in the java.awt package. Sun wants to make sure that, as a certified programmer, you know the tools of the trade and what they can do. The exam will test you on some of the major methods in these classes, but Sun does not expect you to be a walking API document.

All nonmenu graphical components of the Java Development Kit extend from java.awt.Component. As a result, they all exhibit similar behavior because they inherit the methods of that class. Containers are a special type of component that can contain other components. Because containers are components themselves, you can create nested containers. This is most frequently done using many Panel containers.

Canvas is a special-purpose Component used for painting graphics to. This is done by overriding the public void paint(Graphics g) method of Canvas. The methods to make painting to the screen are contained in the Graphics class.

All menu components are derived from the MenuComponent class, which is a subclass of Object, and therefore does not inherit any methods from the Component class. There is a relationship between which menu components can be contained in other menu components: MenuItems belong in Menus, which belong in a MenuBar, which belongs in a Frame.

Layout managers are responsible for the sizing and positioning of components within a container in a platform-independent manner. Each layout manager handles this responsibility differently. If the layout manager attribute of a container is set to null then absolute positioning is used to render components within a container.

✓ TWO-MINUTE DRILL

Here are some of the key points from each certification objective in Chapter 13.

Components

- ❑ The java.awt.Component class is the abstract superclass for all nonmenu graphical components in the java.awt package.
- ❑ A custom component can be created by extending an existing component subclass or by extending the java.awt.Component class directly.

Containers

- ❑ A container is a type of component that contains other components.
- ❑ A container is itself a subclass of component, so it is possible to nest containers within one another.

Layout Managers

- ❑ A container uses a layout manager to position the components that it contains. The layout manager is specified using the Container.setLayout() method.
- ❑ The layout manager for a container determines the size and position of each component within a container.
- ❑ If no layout manager is specified for a container then absolute positioning is used to determine each component's position.

Menus

- ❑ MenuComponent is at the top of the hierarchy for all menu subclasses. MenuComponent does not inherit from Component.
- ❑ A MenuBar must be associated with a Frame in order to be visible. This is accomplished using the Frame.setMenuBar() method.
- ❑ A MenuBar can have Menu objects added to it using the add() method.
- ❑ Menus can have MenuItems and all subclasses of MenuItem added to it using the add() method. Menu is a subclass of MenuItem, so a Menu can be added to another Menu.

Painting

- ❑ The Canvas class is used by creating a subclass of Canvas, then overriding the paint() method.
- ❑ All Components have a paint() method.
- ❑ To ask the GUI to refresh a component, the repaint() method can be called. There is no guarantee it will be refreshed right away.
- ❑ Images, text, and shapes can be rendered to a Canvas or any Component using the Graphics object associated with the paint() method.

SELF TEST

The following questions will help you measure your understanding of the material presented in this chapter. Read all of the choices carefully, as there may be more than one correct answer. Choose all correct answers for each question.

Components

1. Which of the following statements are true of the java.awt.Component class? (Choose all that apply.)

A. It is the ultimate superclass for all nonmenu graphical components.

B. It contains methods for handling events.

C. It contains methods for rendering.

2. Which method is used to set the background color of a component?

A. setColor(Color c)

B. setBackGround(Color c)

C. setBackGroundColor(Color c)

D. setForeGroundColor(Color c)

E. setBackground(Color c)

3. Given:

```
import java.awt.*;
class Test extends Frame {
   public Test() {
      super("Exam Question");
      this.setSize(300,300);
      this.setLayout(new BorderLayout());
      this.setForeground(Color.red);

      Panel p1 = new Panel();
      p1.setBackground(Color.black);
      p1.setForeground(Color.white);

      Panel p2 = new Panel();
      p1.setForeground(Color.red);

      p2.add(new Label("Label Test"));
```

```
17.             p1.add(p2);
18.             this.add(p1);
19.         }
20.
21.     public static void main (String [] args) {
22.             new Test().setVisible(true);
23.         }
24.     }
```

Which of the following sentences are accurate? (Choose all that apply.)

A. The label text in line 16 is white in color.

B. The label text in line 16 is red in color.

C. The layout manager of panel p2 overrides the layout manager of panel p1.

D. The panel p2 has a background color of black.

E. The label in panel p2 fills the entire area of panel p2.

4. Suppose you extend the class java.awt.Button with a new class called NewButton. NewButton defines the following constructors:

```
public NewButton(String label) { … }
public NewButton(String label, Color color) { … }
```

Now, by definition, the Button class has the following constructors:

```
public Button() { … }
public Button(String label) { … }
```

Based upon this information, which statements that attempt to instantiate NewButton will compile? (Choose all that apply.)

A. NewButton nb = new NewButton("Start");

B. NewButton nb = new NewButton("Start", 4);

C. NewButton nb = new NewButton();

D. NewButton nb = new NewButton("Start", new Color(255, 255, 255));

5. Which of the following method signatures are correct for the setSize() method of Component? (Choose all that apply.)

A. setSize(int width, int height)

B. setSize(int x, int y, int width, int height)

C. setSize(Dimension dim)

D. None of the above.

6. The getSize() method of Component returns what data?

   A. A single int

   B. A Dimension object

   C. A Rectangle object

7. Which of the following method signatures are correct for the setLocation() method of Component? (Choose all that apply.)

   A. setLocation(int width, int height)

   B. setLocation(int x, int y, int width, int height)

   C. setLocation(Point p)

   D. setLocation(Dimension dim)

   E. None of the above.

8. The getLocation() method of Component returns what data?

   A. A single int

   B. A Dimension object

   C. A Point object

   D. A Rectangle object

9. Which of the following method signatures are correct for the setBounds() method of Component? (Choose all that apply.)

   A. setBounds(int width, int height)

   B. setBounds(int x, int y, int width, int height)

   C. setBounds(Point p)

   D. setBounds(Rectangle rect)

   E. None of the above.

10. The getBounds() method of Component returns what data?

   A. A Dimension object

   B. A Rectangle object

   C. A Point object

Containers

11. Which methods are defined by java.awt.Container? (Choose all that apply.)

A. add(Component c, index index)

B. add(int index, Component c)

C. add(Component c)

D. add(Component c, Object constraints, Container parent)

E. add(Component c, Object constraints)

12. Which of the following containers are top-level containers? (Choose all that apply.)

A. Panel

B. ScrollPane

C. Window

D. Frame

13. What is the default layout manager for a Panel container?

A. BorderLayout

B. CardLayout

C. GridLayout

D. GridBagLayout

E. FlowLayout

F. null

14. What is the default layout manager for a Frame container?

A. BorderLayout

B. CardLayout

C. GridLayout

D. GridBagLayout

E. FlowLayout

F. null

15. What is the default layout manager for a Window container?

A. BorderLayout

B. CardLayout

C. GridLayout

D. GridBagLayout

E. FlowLayout

F. null

Layout Managers

16. Which of the following are valid area designations for the java.awt.BorderLayout layout manager? (Choose all that apply.)

A. NORTH

B. SOUTH

C. TOP

D. EAST

E. MIDDLE

F. CENTER

17. As part of your GUI design, you want to have a dialog that contains five buttons arranged vertically. These buttons must take up all of the space provided by the container of the dialog. These buttons are allowed to vary in size but must be the same size as each other no matter how the dialog is resized. Which strategy would you use?

A. Create a FlowLayout instance and pass that instance to the setLayout() method of the dialog's container. Then add each of the five buttons in turn to that container by calling the add(Component c) method for that container.

B. Create a BorderLayout instance and pass that instance to the setLayout() method of the dialog's container. Then add each of the five buttons in turn to that container by calling the add(Component c) method for that container.

C. Create a GridLayout instance using the constructor GridLayout(5, 1) and pass that instance to the setLayout() method of the dialog's container. Then add each of the five buttons in turn to that container by calling the add(Component c) method for that container.

D. null (no LayoutManager)

18. Assume that you have a Frame with a layout manager of FlowLayout. The alignment of the layout manager is LEFT. Which one sentence accurately describes the rendering of a Button added to this Frame?

A. The Button is at the top of the Frame. Its width is that of the entire Frame and its height is the preferred height of that Button.

B. The Button fills the entire Frame.

C. The Button is at the top left of the Frame and both its height and width are of the preferred size.

D. The Button is at the top right of the Frame and both its height and width are of the preferred size.

19. Assume that you have a panel that has a GridLayout as its layout manager. Which of the following statements is true regarding the placement of components within that container?

A. The components are placed top to bottom, then left to right.

B. The components are placed right to left, then top to bottom.

C. The components are placed left to right, then top to bottom.

20. The number of columns and rows in a GridLayout is dictated by either setting them in the constructor or by calling the setRows() and setColumns() methods.

A. True

B. False

21. Which of the following LayoutManagers will respect all dimensions of a component's preferred size?

A. FlowLayout

B. GridLayout

C. BorderLayout

D. None of the above

Menus

22. Which of the following classes can be added to a Menu using the add() method? (Choose all that apply.)

A. MenuComponent

B. Component

C. Menu

D. MenuBar

E. MenuItem

F. Frame

23. How can a programmer add a separator to a Menu? Assume there is a menu object called *myMenu.*

A. myMenu.add(MenuItem.SEPARATOR);

B. myMenu.add(new MenuItem("-"));

C. myMenu.addSeparator();

D. None of the above.

24. Which method call does a programmer use to ensure a MenuBar will appear at the top of a Frame?

A. MenuBar.setVisible(boolean b)

B. MenuBar.associate(Frame f)

C. MenuBar.setFrame(Frame f)

D. Frame.setMenuBar(MenuBar mb)

E. Frame.add(MenuBar mb)

F. Frame.addMenuBar(MenuBar mb)

G. The Frame constructor: Frame(MenuBar mb)

Painting

25. Which of the following methods are part of the Graphics class? (Choose all that apply.)

A. drawLine()

B. drawRectangle()

C. fillTriangle()

D. fillRoundRect()

E. drawArc()

F. drawCircle()

26. Study Figure 13-19.

Which of the following method calls will draw this image?

A. fillArc(50, 50, 200, 200, 160, 200)

B. fillArc(50, 50, 200, 200, 20, 340)

C. fillArc(50, 50, 200, 200, 20, 320)

D. fillArc(50, 50, 200, 200, 70, -340)

E. fillArc(50, 50, 200, 200, 70, 340)

27. How many arguments are there in the fillRoundRect() method?

A. 3

B. 4

C. 5

D. 6

E. 7

F. 8

28. Which method is used to refresh the graphics for a component? Make sure you use the correct capitalization. (Fill in the blank.)
Graphics are refreshed using: ____________________

FIGURE 13-19

Question 26 Exhibit

SELF TEST ANSWERS

Components

1. ☑ **A, B, and C.** The Component class is the superclass for all nonmenu graphical components. The Component class contains methods for both handling events and rendering itself.
☒ There are no incorrect answer choices.

2. ☑ **E.** The setBackground(Color c) method is used to set the background color of a component.
☒ **A, B, and C** are incorrect because there are no such methods in components that come with the JDK. **B** is incorrect because the G in Background should not be capitalized because Java is a case-sensitive language. **D** is incorrect because there is no method like this. Also, the setForeground() method is used to set the color for those items rendered in the foreground, such as text.

3. ☑ **B and D. B** is correct because the label does not explicitly set a foreground color; it inherits the foreground color of its enclosing container, in this case the red foreground color of its parent panel named p2. **D** is correct because in line 17 p2 is placed into container p1. The panel p2 does not explicitly set a background color so it inherits the background color of its parent container p1, which has a background color of black.
☒ **A** is incorrect because the label inherits its foreground color from its parent container, panel p2. **C** is incorrect because layout managers do not override each other in that manner. **E** is incorrect because although panel p1 has a layout manager of BorderLayout and having been inserted into area CENTER makes panel p2 the full size of panel p1, the default layout manager of panel p2 is FlowLayout, which means that the label retains its preferred size.

4. ☑ **A and D.** Both of these constructors are defined in the NewButton class.
☒ **B** is incorrect because it will not compile as there is no constructor in the NewButton class with a signature of (String, int). **C** is incorrect because it will not compile since constructors are not inherited.

5. ☑ **A and C.** Both methods describe valid method signatures for the setSize() method.
☒ **B** is incorrect because Component does not have a setSize() method that takes four integer arguments. **D** is incorrect because there is a correct answer choice.

6. ☑ **B.** The getSize() method of Component returns a Dimension object.
☒ **A** is incorrect because a single int would not provide sufficient information to describe the size of an object. **C** is incorrect because a Rectangle also includes information on the position of a component, which is not desired.

7. ☑ A and C. Both methods describe valid method signatures for the setLocation() method.
☒ B is incorrect because Component does not have a setLocation () method that takes four integer arguments. D is incorrect because Component does not have a setLocation() method that takes a Dimension argument.

8. ☑ C. The getLocation() method of Component returns a Point object with int members representing the x and y coordinates of the upper-left corner of the component.
☒ A is incorrect because a single int would be insufficient to describe the current position of the component. B is incorrect because the members of Dimension represent width and height, not absolute coordinates. D is incorrect because a Rectangle object stores four points of data.

9. ☑ B and D. Both methods describe valid method signatures for the setBounds () method.
☒ A is incorrect because Component does not have a setBounds () method that takes two integer arguments. C is incorrect because Component does not have a setBounds () method that takes a Point argument.

10. ☑ B. The getBounds() method of Component returns a Rectangle object, which is the best object to return four points of data.
☒ A is incorrect because a Dimension object contains only data on the width and height of the component. C is incorrect because a Point object contains only coordinates on the position of an object.

Containers

11. ☑ A, C, and E. These are all valid methods as defined by the java.awt.Container class.
☒ B and D are incorrect because they define methods that are not in java.awt.Container.

12. ☑ C and D. These are both top-level containers that can be displayed without needing to be enclosed within another container.
☒ A and B are incorrect because they are not top-level containers and need to be placed within a parent container.

13. ☑ E. The FlowLayout is the default layout manager of the Panel container.
☒ A, B, C, D, and F are all incorrect choices.

14. ☑ A. The BorderLayout is the default layout manager of the Frame container.
☒ B, C, D, E, and F are all incorrect choices.

15. ☑ A. The BorderLayout is the default layout manager of the Window container.
☒ B, C, D, E, and F are all incorrect choices.

Layout Managers

16. ☑ **A, B, D,** and **F.** These are all valid area designations for the BorderLayout layout manager.
☒ **C** and **E** are incorrect because they are not valid area designations for the BorderLayout layout manager.

17. ☑ **C.** A GridLayout divides the container into equally spaced cells. Each component that is added is resized to fill that cell. The preferred size for each component is ignored. When a container, the dialog in this case, is resized then all components within the container are resized to fit the new cell dimensions.
☒ **A** is incorrect because a FlowLayout respects the preferred size of each component and would not resize them when the dialog is resized. **B** is incorrect because each component is being added to the center part of the container. If a component is already in the center part of the container then it is replaced with the new component. In the end, only the fifth button will be visible. **D** is incorrect because the lack of a LayoutManager (null) will result in absolute positioning and preferred sizing regardless of the size of the dialog.

18. ☑ **C.** FlowLayout respects the preferred size of each of the components it manages. Because the alignment was set to LEFT, each row of components with the container will start at the left margin of that container.
☒ **A** is incorrect because the behavior it describes is indicative of a BorderLayout manager with the component being added to the NORTH section. **B** is incorrect because the behavior it describes is indicative of a BorderLayout manager with the component being added to the CENTER section. **D** is incorrect because although the respecting of the preferred size suggests a FlowLayout manager, the alignment is wrong.

19. ☑ **C.** When adding components to a container with a layout manager of GridLayout, the components are added from left to right then to the next row.
☒ **A** and **B** are incorrect as components are always inserted left to right in a row then down at column one of the next row.

20. ☑ **B.** The number of columns and rows in a GridLayout is dictated by either setting them in the constructor or by calling the setRows() and setColumns() methods.
☒ **A** is incorrect because the value passed in the setColumns() is ignored unless the number of rows has not been specified.

21. ☑ **A.** The FlowLayout manager class always respects the preferred size of each Component.
☒ **B** is incorrect because GridLayout ignores the preferred size of each component. **C** is incorrect because BorderLayout will ignore at least one dimension of the preferred size of a Component. BorderLayout ignores the preferred height of a component in the EAST and

WEST areas of the container, it ignores the preferred width of a component in the NORTH and SOUTH areas of the container, and it ignores all dimensions of the preferred size in the CENTER area of the container. **D** is incorrect because there is a correct answer choice.

Menus

22. ☑ **C** and **E**. Any object that inherits from MenuItem may be added to a Menu. Because Menu is a subclass of MenuItem, it too can be added to a Menu.
☒ **A**, **B**, **D**, and **F** are all incorrect because none of these classes inherits from MenuItem.

23. ☑ **C**. The Menu.addSeparator() method is used to add a separator line to a menu.
☒ **A** is incorrect because there is no constant called SEPARATOR. **B** is incorrect and only succeeds in adding a menu item that is a dash. **D** is incorrect because there is a correct answer choice.

24. ☑ **D**. This is the only method listed that will set the MenuBar with a Frame.
☒ **A** is incorrect because setVisible() is a Component method, not a MenuComponent method. **B**, **C**, and **F** are incorrect because they are completely made up method names. **E** is incorrect because it is how a Component is added to a Container, such as Frame. MenuBar is not a subclass of Component. **G** is incorrect because there is no constructor like this.

Painting

25. ☑ **A**, **D**, and **E**. These are all methods of the Graphics class.
☒ **B** is incorrect because the method to draw a rectangle is called drawRect(). **C** is incorrect because there is no drawTriangle() method. The closest thing to draw a triangle is drawPolygon(). **F** is incorrect because there is no drawCircle() method; there is a drawOval() method, however.

26. ☑ **C**. The fourth argument is the starting angle. The 3 o'clock position is 0 degrees, and the angle increases counterclockwise, so 20 degrees is a good start angle. The fifth argument is the angle the arc covers. 320 degrees brings the arc back to the 340 degree angle.
☒ **A**, **B**, **D**, and **E** are all incorrect angles to draw the desired picture. **B** is the closest, but the mouth will be pointing slightly upwards using these arguments.

27. ☑ **D**. The arguments are for x position, y position, width, height, arc width, and arc height.
☒ **A**, **B**, **C**, **E**, and **F** are all incorrect argument numbers.

28. ☑ repaint(). The repaint() method is used to refresh the graphics for a component. Make sure you use the correct capitalization.

14

The java.awt Package: Event Handling

CERTIFICATION OBJECTIVES

14.01 Java Events and Event Listeners

14.02 The java.awt.event Package

✓ Two-Minute Drill

Q&A Self Test

The Java 2 event model is literally where all the action occurs with the Java programming language. Interaction between the user and the PC is a fundamental part of computing, so it is important to know this topic to make a graphical user interface (GUI) easy to use. Although normally associated with graphical components, any object can be implemented to generate or receive events. The event model allows components to publish information about their state to other objects by generating *event objects* and delivering them to *event listeners*. This chapter will explore the event concepts you need to know to become a certified programmer.

CERTIFICATION OBJECTIVE 14.01

Java Events and Event Listeners

There is nothing magical about Abstract Window Toolkit (AWT) events. The mechanism for producing events consists of objects delivering objects to other objects using methods. The Java event mechanism consists of three objects:

- An event source
- An event object
- One or more event listeners

In a nutshell, *event sources* create *event objects* and deliver them to *event listeners*, as shown in Figure 14-1. The event object is the medium used by the event source to deliver pertinent information about a change in state to the event listeners.

Event Objects

An event object embodies information related to a particular type of event. Think of an event object as a messenger that relays news about the event that just occurred. In a computer program using a GUI, an event can be as simple as a mouse-click or a user pressing the ENTER key. At a minimum, an event object contains a reference to the object that caused the event (the event source). Usually, the event object also contains other data such as mouse position or a timestamp.

FIGURE 14-1 A single event source with multiple event listeners

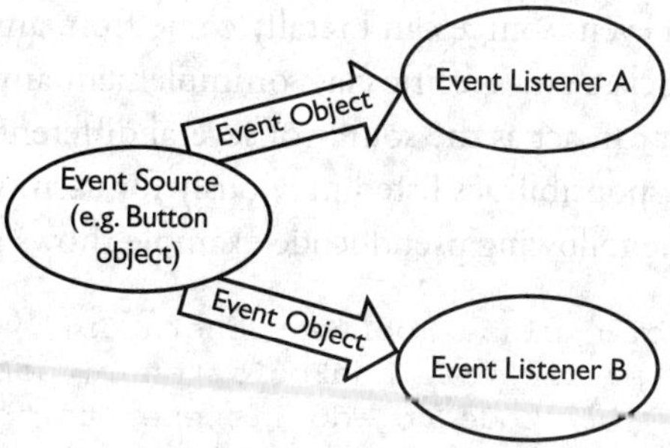

All event objects are defined in event classes that subclass java.util.EventObject. EventObject defines the following method used to get a reference to the source of the event:

```
public Object getSource();
```

The class of the event defines the event type. For instance, the class FooEvent defines events of type Foo.

The following example shows how easy it is to create an event. This code is an implementation of the hypothetical FooEvent:

```
public class FooEvent extends java.util.EventObject{
   public FooEvent(Object source){
      super(source);
   }
}
```

Event Sources

An event source is a component or object that generates events. A common example of an event source is a GUI button, although not all event sources need to be GUI components. For example, an internal timer object could be an event source that creates an event object once every second.

Event sources have three main responsibilities:

- Provide methods that allow other methods to add and remove event listeners.
- Maintain a list of interested event listeners.
- Contain logic to create and deliver event objects of the appropriate type (class) to all interested event listeners.

An event source can literally come from any object of any type. It does not have to subclass any specific class or implement any specific interface. Additionally, an object can act as the source of several different event types, provided that it fulfills the responsibilities listed previously for each type.

The following pseudocode example shows a class that generates Foo events:

```
public class FooEventGenerator{
   public void addFooListener(FooListener l){
      //Code to add listener to the list of listeners.
   }
   public void removeFooListener(FooListener l){
      // Code to remove listener from the list of listeners.
   }
   private void notifyFooListeners(){
      // Create a FooEvent with this as the source.
      FooEvent fooEvent = new FooEvent(this);
      // Deliver the event.
   }
}
```

Event Listeners

For an object to be notified of an event, the object must subscribe to the event source. To do this, it must implement the appropriate *listener interface*. All listener interfaces are subclasses of java.util.EventListener. EventListener does not define any methods and is used strictly as a marker interface. Each specialized listener interface defines at least one method that is used to deliver an event object to the listener. The method or methods defined in the listener interface normally take one parameter that is a subclass of EventObject. The following is an example definition of a FooEvent listener interface:

```
public interface FooListener extends java.util.EventListener{
   public void handleFooEvent(FooEvent evt);
}
```

Now that we have created a wonderful listener interface, let's create a class that becomes a listener of Foo events. To do this it must first implement the FooListener interface:

```
public class FooTest implements FooListener{
   // Implement the FooListener interface.
```

```
    public void handleFooEvent(FooEvent evt){
        System.out.println("Received FooEvent!");
    }
}
```

To receive events, event listeners must first register with an event source. Event listeners register for events using a well-known method provided by the event source. For example, instances of FooTest could register to receive FooEvents using code that looks something like this:

```
FooEventGenerator eventSource = new FooEventGenerator();
FooTest listener = new FooTest();
eventSource.addFooListener(listener);
```

Instances of FooTest can also unsubscribe from receiving FooEvents:

```
eventSource.removeFooListener(listener);
```

From the perspective of the event listener, events occur asynchronously. All events are delivered in the event source's thread of execution. Another way to think of this is that the event source *pushes* events to the event listeners.

CERTIFICATION OBJECTIVE 14.02

The java.awt.event Package

The java.awt.event package contains all of the events and corresponding event listener interfaces associated with AWT components. The following section will discuss the major classes and interfaces in this package. *Adapter classes* are also provided so the programmer doesn't have to manually implement each and every method in an event listener interface.

exam Watch

A lot of what is actually covered by the exam deals with the classes found in the java.awt.event package. You will need to be familiar with these classes and their methods to excel on the test. In this chapter, good old-fashioned memorization will likely be your best ally.

The AWTEvent Class

All event classes defined in the java.awt.event package are subclasses of java.awt.AWTEvent, which is itself a subclass of java.util.EventObject. Note that AWTEvent is in the java.awt package, not the java.awt.event package. AWTEvent defines the following methods.

`public int getID()`	Returns the event's integer event type.
`protected void consume()`	Consumes the event.
`protected boolean isConsumed()`	Tests to see whether this event has been consumed.
`public String paramString()`	Provides useful debug information.

Each AWTEvent has an integer *event type*. The event type is used to distinguish between events that share the same class but have a different purpose. For instance, a Mouse event is generated when a mouse button is pressed and released. The specific type of event can be determined by comparing the getID() value with MouseEvent.MOUSE_PRESSED and MouseEvent.MOUSE_RELEASED.

Sometimes AWT events are processed by the event source after event listeners are notified. If you don't want the event to be further processed by the event source you can *consume* the event using the consume() method

Events in the java.awt.event Package

Events in the java.awt.event package can be classified as either *semantic* or *low-level.* Semantic events occur as the result of a combination of low-level events. Generally, semantic events signify the primary purpose of a component. Take the semantic event ActionEvent for example. Button components fire Action events when the button is activated (pressed). TextField components fire Action events when the user enters text and then presses the ENTER key.

Low-level events, on the other hand, are finer grained than semantic events and tend to occur at a higher frequency. For example, a TextField fires the low-level KeyEvent whenever the user presses any key, not just after the user presses the ENTER key. Generally, a low-level event represents a low-level input or window-system occurrence on a visual component on the screen.

Semantic Events

ActionEvent, ItemEvent, TextEvent, and AdjustmentEvent are the only semantic events defined in the java.awt.event package. They provide a high-level view into the component that sources them. For example, a Button component generates an ActionEvent when it is selected and is also enabled. This keeps the programmer from having to deal with combinations of low-level events, such as MouseEvents, directly. Figure 14-2 displays the class hierarchy of semantic events defined in the java.awt.event package.

ActionEvent ActionEvent is the most important semantic event to be familiar with for the exam. ActionEvents occur as a result of the following actions:

- An item is double-clicked in a List component.
- A Button is selected.
- A MenuItem is selected.
- The ENTER key is pressed in a TextField component.

Each action event object contains a *command string* that can be accessed using the following method:

`Public String getActionCommand()`	Returns the command string for this ActionEvent object.

The command string contains the relevant data about the source or cause of the event. An Action event that is the result of a Button being activated contains the Button's text. An Action event that is the result of the ENTER key being pressed in

FIGURE 14-2

Semantic events class hierarchy

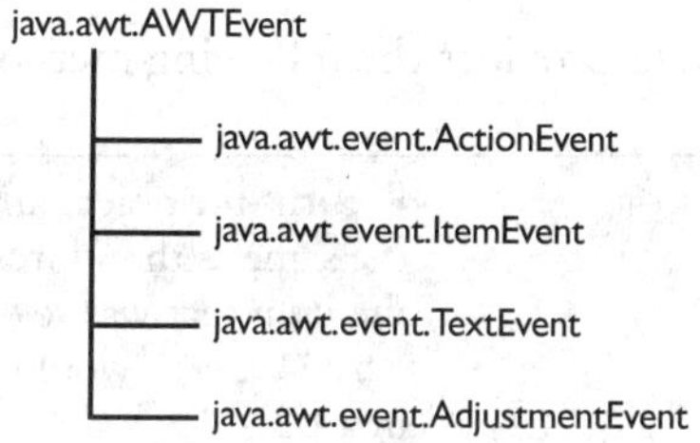

a TextField component returns the entered text. Similarly, the text that represents a MenuItem or item in a List component is returned when a MenuItem or List is the source of the Action event.

It is also possible for Java to detect whether a user was holding down a special key when the event occurred. The getModifiers() method provides information about modifier keys, such as SHIFT or ALT, that were held down at the time of the event. One interesting thing about this is that special hidden functionality can be provided if a user holds down a modifier key while clicking a button!

`Public int getModifiers()`	Returns the integer modifier field for this ActionEvent object.

The integer modifier field can be tested against public static values defined in ActionEvents that represent the various keys, such as ActionCommand.ALT_MASK.

TextEvent TextEvents occur as a result of the following actions:

- Text has changed in a TextField component.
- Text has changed in a TextArea component.

ItemEvent ItemEvents occur on any object that has items that are selectable. An ItemEvent can occur as a result of any of the following actions:

- A check box is selected or cleared.
- A CheckboxMenuItem is selected or cleared.
- An item is selected in a Choice component.
- One or more items are selected in a List.

ItemEvent provides the following methods:

`Public Object getItem()`	Returns the object affected by the selection. Note that this is not the same as the source component, but an object that represents the item that was selected in the source component. For example, `getItem()` would return a `String` that represents an item in a `List`.

`Public ItemSelectable getItemSelectable()`	Returns an `ItemSelectable` interface on the source component.
`Public int getStateChange()`	Returns an `int` value that is either `ItemEvent.SELECTED` or `ItemEvent.DESELECTED`.

AdjustmentEvent ScrollBar and ScrollPane objects generate Adjustment events when their scroll position changes. Scrolling is handled internally by these components, so we won't discuss Adjustment events in detail.

Low-Level Events

As we discussed earlier, low-level events are finer grained than semantic events and tend to occur at a higher frequency, such as key presses on a keyboard. The majority of these events are component events; that is, they subclass java.awt.event. ComponetEvent. The remaining events are AdjustmentEvent, InputMethodEvent, and InvocationEvent. The last two methods, InputMethodEvent and InvocationEvent, are rarely used and will not be discussed in detail. Figure 14-3 displays the hierarchy of low-level events defined in the java.awt.event package.

FIGURE 14-3

Low-level events in the java.awt.event package

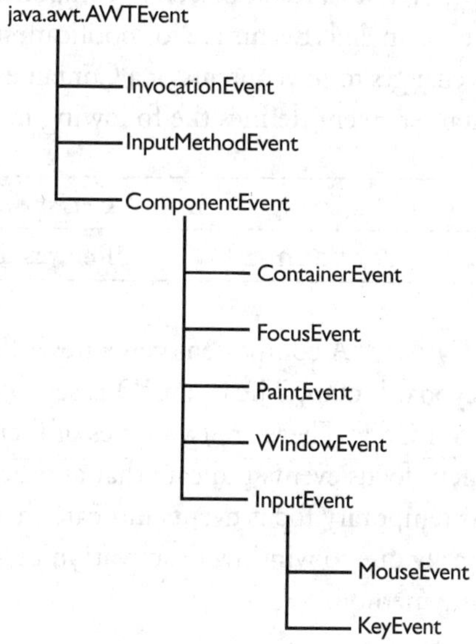

ComponentEvent A component generates a ComponentEvent when the component's size, position, or visibility has changed. ComponentEvents are for notification purposes only because the AWT automatically adjusts the size, position, and visibility of components internally.

ComponentEvent defines the following method to get the source component of the event.

`Public Component getComponent()`	Returns the event source as a Component.

The component returned by the getComponent() method is the same object that is returned by the getSource() method defined in EventObject. This is simply a convenience method that returns the source as a component so that you do not have to cast the object returned by the getSource() method. ItemEvent, WindowEvent, and ContainerEvent provide similar methods (getItemSelectable(), getWindow(), and getContainer()) for the same purposes. Note that ComponentEvent is a base class for many other low-level event classes.

ContainerEvent A *container* component, such as Panel, generates a ContainerEvent as a result of a child component being added or removed from the container. ContainerEvents are for notification purposes only. The AWT automatically handles changes to the contents of a Container component internally.

Container Event defines the following methods.

`Public Component getChild()`	Gets the affected child component.
`Public Container getContainer()`	Returns the event source as a Container.

FocusEvent A component generates a FocusEvent when it gains or loses keyboard focus. The event ID is set to either FOCUS_GAINED or FOCUS_LOST. There are two types of focus events, permanent and temporary. Permanent focus events indicate that another component has gained the focus, whereas temporary focus events indicate that the component has lost focus temporarily due to window deactivation or scrolling. FocusEvent defines the following method.

`Public boolean isTemporary()`	Returns *true* if the focus was lost temporarily.

InputEvent InputEvent is an abstract class that serves as the base class for MouseEvent and KeyEvent. InputEvent defines the following useful method to determine the time of the event.

`Public long getWhen()`	Returns a timestamp.

The InputEvent abstract class also provides the following methods to determine whether modifier keys were pressed when the event was generated.

`Public int getModifiers()`	Returns the integer modifier's flag.
`Public boolean isAltDown()`	Tests for the ALT key.
`Public boolean isAltGraphDown()`	Tests for the ALT-GRAPH key.
`Public boolean isControlDown()`	Tests for the CTRL key.
`Public boolean isMetaDown()`	Tests for the META key.
`Public boolean isShiftDown()`	Tests for the SHIFT key.

Input events are delivered to listeners *before* they are handled by their source component. This allows listeners and component subclasses to *consume* the event to keep the event from being processed in the default manner by the source. For example, consuming a mouse press event from a Button component will prevent the Button from being activated. If there are other listeners registered, however, they will still receive the event even if a listener down the chain consumed it.

The InputEvent class cleverly overrides the consume() method defined in AWTEvent and changes its visibility from *protected* to *public*. This allows listeners from other packages to effectively swallow the event before it gets back to the source component, thus stopping the event dead in its tracks.

KeyEvent A component generates Key events when it has the current input focus and the user presses a key. There are two basic types of Key events: *key pressed* events and *key typed* events. *Key typed* events are higher-level than key pressed events, and only occur when a logical sequence or combination that represents a character has been completed. For example, pressing SHIFT-A results in a key typed event with the character *A* (uppercase *a* because shift was held down). The event type of a key typed event is KEY_TYPED.

KeyEvent provides the following method to get the character represented by a key typed event.

`Public char getKeyChar()`	Returns the character represented by a key typed event.

Key pressed events occur for keys that don't have an associated character, or that must be used in combination with other keys to form a logical character. These are keys such as function keys, up and down arrow keys, and the SHIFT key. The event types for key pressed events are KEY_PRESSED and KEY_RELEASED.

KeyEvent provides the following method, which returns a *virtual key code* constant that represents the key.

`Public int getKeyCode()`	Returns a virtual key code constant that represents the key.

There are over 150 virtual key code constants defined in KeyEvent such as VK_F1, which represents the function key F1. (Note: Don't even think about trying to memorize these!)

MouseEvent Mouse events are very low-level in their nature. A component generates Mouse events in the following situations:

- A mouse button is pressed while the cursor is over the component.
- A mouse button is released while the cursor is over the component.
- A mouse button is clicked (pressed and released) while the cursor is over the component.
- When the cursor enters or exits the component's boundaries (great for displaying data about a component before the user commits to clicking).

Additionally, the component generates special *mouse motion events* in the following situations:

- The mouse is moved while it is over the component.
- The mouse is dragged (moved while a button is pressed) while it is over the component.

Mouse Motion events are special because they are delivered using a listener interface that is different from normal Mouse events. There are two separate listener interfaces for MouseEvents: MouseListener and MouseMotionListener. The second is used because mouse motion events occur at a high volume and frequency, but are superfluous to a listener that is only interested in mouse-clicks. Therefore, it would be inefficient to deliver events for every movement of the mouse pointer.

Mouse events contain information about click activity and cursor location. The methods pertaining to click activity are as follows.

`Public int getClickCount()`	Returns the number of mouse-clicks.
`Public boolean isPopupTrigger()`	True if the button pressed is the pop-up menu trigger for this platform.

The getClickCount() method is useful for testing for double-clicks. The isPopupTrigger() method is a necessary evil due to platform differences.

The getModifiers() method and *modifier flags*, defined in InputEvent, can be used to determine which mouse button was clicked. If more than one modifier is held down, the values are added together. All values are exactly one bit apart from one another, so a bitwise-AND operation can pick out individual modifiers. For example, the following code tests for a right mouse-click:

```
public void mouseClicked(MouseEvent e){
   if((e.getModifiers() & InputEvent.BUTTON3_MASK) != 0){
      System.out.println("Right Mouse Button Clicked!");
   }
}
```

MouseEvent defines the following useful methods to determine cursor location.

`Public int getX()`	Gets the *x* coordinate.
`Public int getY()`	Gets the *x* coordinate.
`Public Point getPoint()`	Gets the *x* and *y* coordinates as a Point object.
`Public void translatePoint (int x, int y)`	Translates the *x* and *y* coordinates by the given amount.

All coordinates are relative to the source component's coordinate system. The translatePoint() method is used to convert the coordinates to another coordinate system, such as that of the source component's container.

exam Watch ***Note that there is no separate MouseMotionEvent class. MouseEvent objects are used for all Mouse Motion events, but as mentioned earlier, are delivered using two separate listener interfaces: MouseListener and MouseMotionListener.***

WindowEvent A window generates Window events in the following situations:

- A window is about to close.
- A window is opened or closed.
- A window is activated or deactivated.
- A window is iconified or deiconified.

Window Event provides the following method to determine the window that caused the event.

`Public Window getWindow()`	Gets the source window.

PaintEvent Paint events are used internally to ensure serialization of paint operations in the AWT event thread. They are not intended to be used like other events and will not be discussed here. Note that there is no corresponding listener interface for PaintEvent.

EXERCISE 14-1

Action Events

In this exercise we will implement the ActionListener interface. This will require a Frame that contains a single button. It is the button that will be the event source. We will register our listener class with the Button object to handle events generated by it.

1. Create a class that extends Frame and give it any name you like. Make sure you import the java.awt and java.awt.event packages.

2. Create an inner class to handle events from the button. This class must implement the ActionListener interface, and it must define the method actionPerformed().
3. Inside the actionPerformed() method we will place some code to exit the program.
4. Inside the constructor for your frame, place code to set the size of the frame, create a button, and add an action listener to the button.

The completed code should look like this:

```
import java.awt.*;
import java.awt.event.*;
class ClosingWindow extends Frame {

   public ClosingWindow() {
      this.setLayout(new FlowLayout());
      this.setSize(300, 300);

      Button b = new Button("Close Window");
      b.addActionListener(new ButtonHandler());
      this.add(b);
   }

   private class ButtonHandler implements ActionListener {
      public void actionPerformed(ActionEvent e) {
         System.exit(0);
      }
   }

   public static void main (String [] args) {
      new ClosingWindow().setVisible(true);
   }
}
```

Implementing the Listener Interfaces

A listener class must implement the appropriate listener interface to receive a particular type of event. The java.awt.event package contains 13 listener interfaces. Table 14-1 is a summary of the events and their corresponding listener interfaces.

TABLE 14-1

Events and Their Listener Interfaces

Event	Listener Interface
ActionEvent	ActionListener
AdjustmentEvent	AdjustmentListener
java.awt.AWTEvent (abstract)	AWTEventListener
ComponentEvent	ComponentListener
ContainerEvent	ContainerListener
FocusEvent	FocusListener
InputMethodEvent	InputMethodListener
ItemEvent	ItemListener
KeyEvent	KeyListener
MouseEvent	MouseListener MouseMotionListener
TextEvent	TextListener
WindowEvent	WindowListener

Note that MouseEvent has two corresponding listener interfaces, as we discussed previously.

Each listener interface has one or more methods that must be implemented. Remember, a class that uses an interface must implement *all* methods in that interface. In most cases, the methods in the listener interface determine the event type of the event. For example, MouseListener defines the following methods:

```
public void mouseClicked(MouseEvent e)
public void mousePressed(MouseEvent e)
public void mouseReleased(MouseEvent e)
public void mouseEntered(MouseEvent e)
public void mouseExited(MouseEvent e)
```

These methods correspond to the mouse event types MOUSE_CLICKED, MOUSE_PRESSED, MOUSE_RELEASED, MOUSE_ENTERED, and MOUSE_EXITED, respectively.

FROM THE CLASSROOM

The JDK 1.02 Event Model

It is a good idea to know some of the major differences between how events are handled in the JDK 1.02 and JDK 1.1 for the exam. The methods in 1.02 are currently supported in 1.1 and higher. That is, code written using the 1.02 event handling model will still run on the Java 2 platform. At a future release date, however, it will not be supported. This release date is not yet known, but it would be wise to stop using the 1.02 event model.

The JDK 1.02 uses an *inheritance model* to handle events. Using this method, events are handled by subclassing components so that events may be monitored. The container handles all of the events not handled by its components. You then override methods like action() and handleEvent(). These methods return true or false, depending on whether or not the events were successfully handled. If they were successful, then the processing of the event was complete. If it was not successful (returned false), then the event is sent on for further processing in the objects container.

This process of passing on events if they can not be handled is known as "bubbling up," and results in using up a lot of resources – one of the inherent problems with this model.

Along came the JDK 1.1, which introduced the *event-delegation model* to process events. This model takes the approach that a source object will generate an event that is handled by special classes that are registered to listen for these types of events. As we have seen in this chapter, these special classes, called event listeners, implement one of the java.util.EventListener interfaces, and implement certain methods to process these events.

This new model allows events to be handled by classes that the programmer can select, and not just from those of the component in which the events were generated, which was the case in the 1.1 model.

The event-delegation model is a much more efficient and easier to use model, and should be used over the 1.02 inheritance model.

—*Trent Heintz*

Listener Methods

Table 14-2 summarizes the listener interfaces and their corresponding methods.

To receive a particular type of event, an object must implement the appropriate listener interface and register as an event listener with the event source. The second

TABLE 14-2 Listener Interfaces and Their Methods

Listener Interface	Methods
ActionListener	actionPerformed(ActionEvent e)
AdjustmentListener	adjustmentValueChanged(AdjustmentEvent e)
ComponentListener	componentResized(ComponentEvent e) componentMoved(ComponentEvent e) componentShown(ComponentEvent e) componentHidden(ComponentEvent e)
ContainerListener	componentAdded(ContainerEvent e) componentRemoved(ContainerEvent e)
FocusListener	focusGained(FocusEvent e) focusLost(FocusEvent e)
ItemListener	itemStateChanged(ItemEvent e)
KeyListener	keyTyped(KeyEvent e) keyPressed(KeyEvent e) keyReleased(KeyEvent e)
MouseListener	mouseClicked(MouseEvent e) mousePressed(MouseEvent e) mouseReleased(MouseEvent e) mouseEntered(MouseEvent e) mouseExited(MouseEvent e)
MouseMotionListener	mouseDragged(MouseEvent e) mouseMoved(MouseEvent e)
TextListener	textValueChanged(TextEvent e)
WindowListener	windowActivated(WindowEvent e) windowClosed(WindowEvent e) windowClosing(WindowEvent e) windowDeactivated(WindowEvent e) windowDeiconified(WindowEvent e) windowIconified(WindowEvent e) windowOpened(WindowEvent e)

step is crucial, and it is a classic programmer bug that causes a GUI to be unresponsive to user events.

It is usually a good idea to use the semantic events when possible, because they are typically easier to use and more efficient. For instance, assume you want to know when a user presses a Button component. It is best to implement the ActionListener interface and not the MouseListener interface. This is because only one event will be delivered when the button is pressed. If you implement MouseListener, three events will be delivered, *mouse pressed*, *mouse released*, and *mouse clicked*.

The following is an example of how to implement the ActionListener interface using an inner class. The implementation is then registered with both a Button and a TextField to receive action events.

```
import java.awt.*;
import java.awt.event.*;
public class Foo extends Frame {
   public Foo() {
      final TextField text1 = new TextField();
      final Button button1 = new Button("Select Me!");
      ActionListener l = new ActionListener(){
         public void actionPerformed(ActionEvent e){
            if(e.getSource() == button1){
               System.out.println("Button selected!");
            }else if(e.getSource() == text1){
               String text2=((TextField)e.getSource()).getText();
               String text3=e.getActionCommand();
               System.out.println("ActionEvent text: " + text2);
               System.out.println("TextField text: " + text3);
            }
         }
      };
      button1.addActionListener(l);
      text1.addActionListener(l);

      setLayout(new GridLayout(2,1));
      add(button1);
      add(text1);
      pack();
      show();
   }
   public static void main(String args[]) {
      new Foo();
   }
}
```

The Button fires an action event only when it is selected, and the TextField fires Action events only when the user presses ENTER. Consequently, the number of events being delivered is significantly less than if MouseListener and KeyListener had been implemented.

Note that TextField and Button are declared as final in lines 5 and 6. This is necessary because they are being accessed from within an inner class.

Additionally, two different techniques for obtaining the text entered into the TextField are demonstrated. One uses the getActionCommand() method (line 13) provided by ActionEvent, and the other uses the getSource() method (line 12) provided by EventObject to get a reference to the TextField and query it directly.

EXERCISE 14-2

Window Events

In this exercise, we will implement the WindowListener interface. This will require a Frame that will be the event source. We will register our listener class with the Frame object to handle events generated by it. The object of this exercise is to make our frame close when the close button (usually in the upper-right corner) of the frame is clicked.

1. Create a class that extends Frame and give it any name you want. Make sure you import the java.awt and java.awt.event packages.
2. Create an inner class to handle events from the frame. This class must implement the WindowListener interface, and it must define all seven methods: windowActivated(), windowClosed(), windowClosing(), windowDeactivated(), windowDeiconified(), windowIconified(), and windowOpened().
3. The method we should use to exit our program is windowClosing().
4. Inside the constructor for your frame, place code to set the size of the frame and add a window listener.

The completed code should look like this:

```
import java.awt.*;
import java.awt.event.*;
```

```
class ClosingWindow extends Frame {

    public ClosingWindow() {
        this.setLayout(new FlowLayout());
        this.setSize(300, 300);
        this.addWindowListener(new WindowHandler());
    }

    private class WindowHandler implements WindowListener {
        public void windowActivated(WindowEvent e) {}
        public void windowClosed(WindowEvent e) {}
        public void windowClosing(WindowEvent e) {
            System.exit(0);
        }
        public void windowDeactivated(WindowEvent e) {}
        public void windowDeiconified(WindowEvent e) {}
        public void windowIconified(WindowEvent e) {}
        public void windowOpened(WindowEvent e) {}
    }

    public static void main(String [] args) {
        new ClosingWindow().setVisible(true);
    }
}
```

If there is one thing this exercise demonstrates, it is that it can be a pain to implement all of the methods for a listener class, especially the ones in which you are not interested. The next section will show how this can be simplified.

Using Adapter Classes to Implement Listener Interfaces

You may have noticed that certain listener interfaces, such as MouseListener and WindowListener, have quite a few methods. In many cases, you will be interested in only one method but Java requires you to provide implementations for *all* methods in the listener interface. Of course, you could provide empty implementations for the methods of no interest, but that would be both painful and messy. Enter *adapter classes.*

Adapter classes are classes that implement a particular listener interface with empty implementations. This means that you can subclass an adapter and then override only the methods in which you are interested. The following example uses a MouseAdapter to listen for mouse-clicks that occur on a TextField, and then prints out the location of the mouse cursor at the time of the click.

```
import java.awt.*;
import java.awt.event.*;
public class MouseDemo extends Frame {

   public static class MouseListenerImpl extends MouseAdapter{
      public void mouseClicked(MouseEvent e){
         System.out.println("MouseEvent " + e.paramString() );
      };
   }

   public MouseDemo() {
      TextField text = new TextField();
      text.addMouseListener(new MouseListenerImpl());
      add(text);
      pack();
      show();
   }

   public static void main(String args[]) {
      new MouseDemo();
   }
}
```

It is very common to use an anonymous inner class to specialize an adapter class. The following example uses an anonymous inner class to specialize WindowAdapter to exit an application when the user selects the Close button of the application's frame (Window):

```
import java.awt.*;
import java.awt.event.*;

public class WindowTest{
   public static void main(String[] args){
      WindowListener closeListener = new WindowAdapter(){
         public void windowClosing(WindowEvent e){
            System.exit(0);
         }
      };
      Frame f = new Frame();
```

```
        f.addWindowListener(closeListener);
        f.pack();
        f.show();
    }
}
```

Note that we override *windowClosing()* and not *windowClosed()*. Window closed event types occur only when dispose() is called on a window.

Table 14-3 summarizes the event adapter classes and their corresponding listener interfaces. Note that only listeners with more than one method have listener adapters.

Event Naming Conventions

This section will help you with the memorization of events and event listeners. You may have noticed a naming convention for the AWT events, listeners, and adapters. For each event class there is a corresponding listener interface, and optionally, an event adapter. Additionally, there are methods used to add and remove listeners to the event source (Component). The naming convention is as follows:

Event Class	*event name*Event
Listener Interface	*event name*Listener
Adapter Class	*event name*Adapter
Add Method	add*listenerInterface name*
Remove Method	remove*listenerInterface name*

TABLE 14-3

Adapter Classes and Their Listener Interfaces

Adapter Class	Listener Interface
ComponentAdapter	ComponentListener
ContainerAdapter	ContainerListener
FocusAdapter	FocusListener
KeyAdapter	KeyListener
MouseAdapter	MouseListener
MouseMotionAdapter	MouseMotionListener
WindowAdapter	WindowAdapterListener

Let's use Window events as an example:

Event Class	WindowEvent
Listener Interface	WindowListener
Adapter Class	WindowAdapter
Add Method	addWindowListener
Remove Method	removeWindowListener

Note that there are a couple of exceptions to the naming conventions:

- Mouse Motion Listener corresponds to a MouseEvent, not a MouseMotionEvent.
- PaintEvent has no associated listener interface because it is primarily used to internally serialize paint requests.
- InvocationEvent has no associated listener interface. Invocation events are used to run a piece of code in the AWT event thread using the invoke() and invokeAndWait() methods. This is more of a utility than a part of the AWT event system, so invocation events were not discussed in this chapter.

exam Watch

It is important that you understand the naming conventions for events, but more importantly you should remember the exceptions to the naming conventions.

Now that you have a better understanding of the java.awt package, here are some possible scenario questions and their answers.

SCENARIO & SOLUTION	
What is the primary requirement for an object that wants to receive a certain type of event?	The object must implement the appropriate listener interface.
Which event types provide information about the time the event was generated?	KeyEvent and MouseEvent.
What package contains all of the actual AWT events and listeners?	java.awt.event.
What is the easiest way to create a class that will be a listener without implementing all the other methods you are not interested in?	Use an adapter class such as ContainerAdapter.
How do you get a reference to the event source? Is there more than one way to do this?	Use the getSource() method defined in EventObject. In addition, other event classes provide more specialized versions. Examples are getWindow(), getComponent() , getContainer(), and getItemSelectable().

CERTIFICATION SUMMARY

The Java 2 event model consists of event sources, event objects, and event listeners. Event listeners must first implement the appropriate listener interface and then register themselves as listeners with the event source.

AWT events can be classified as either semantic or low-level. Semantic events are more commonly used than low-level events. The four semantic events are ActionEvent, ItemEvent, TextEvent, and AdjustmentEvent.

Events deliver information to an event listener that tells it more about what happened during the event. Because all events are subclasses of EventObject, the source of the event can be obtained using the EventObject.getSource() method.

Adapter classes provide empty implementations for many of the listener interfaces. This makes it easy to implement a listener interface by subclassing the adapter class and overriding only the desired methods.

✓ TWO-MINUTE DRILL

Here are some of the key points from each certification objective in Chapter 14.

Java Events and Event Listeners

- ❑ The four semantic events are ActionEvent, ItemEvent, TextEvent, and AdjustmentEvent.
- ❑ An object must implement the appropriate listener interface to receive a certain type of event.

The java.awt.event Package

- ❑ AWT events have an integer *event type* associated with them. This type can be accessed using the getID() method defined in AWTEvent.
- ❑ AWT events can be consumed using the protected consume() method defined in AWTEvent. InputEvent subclasses AWTEvent and changes the visibility of consume() to public.
- ❑ Listeners of the Input events (MouseListener, MouseMotionListener, and KeyListener) process their corresponding events before the source component handles them. This allows them to consume the event, effectively hiding it from the source component.
- ❑ MouseEvent has two associated listeners: MouseListener and MouseMotionListener.
- ❑ The following components generate Action events: Button, List, MenuItem, and TextField.
- ❑ Subclasses of TextComponent (TextField and TextArea) generate TextEvents.

- ❑ InputEvent provides the getModifiers() method, which returns the modifier flags for that event. These flags can be tested against public *modifier mask* values defined in InputEvent. The modifier flags represent keys (such as SHIFT or ALT) that were pressed at the time of the input event. InputEvent also provides tester methods for many of these flags. Examples are the isShiftDown() and isAltDown() methods.
- ❑ InputEvent provides the getWhen() method that can be used to get a timestamp representing the time that the event occurred.
- ❑ MouseEvent defines the getClickCount() method to test for double-clicks.
- ❑ MouseEvent provides the following methods to determine the mouse cursor position at the time of the mouse event: getX(), getY(), and getPoint().
- ❑ Adapter classes are provided for many of the listener interfaces. Adapter classes provide empty implementations of all of the methods in a listener interface. It is common practice to use an inner class (usually anonymous) to specialize an event adapter.

SELF TEST

The following questions will help you measure your understanding of the material presented in this chapter. Read all of the choices carefully, as there may be more than one correct answer. Choose all correct answers for each question.

Java Events and Event Listeners

1. Which of the following statements are true of the Java event model? (Choose all that apply.)

   A. An event source can have only one event listener.

   B. An event listener can be of any object type and does not have to extend any other classes or interfaces.

   C. Listeners can be added and removed from event sources.

   D. The listener objects are always notified in the order they were added to the event source.

   E. Event sources can be of any object type and do not have to extend any other classes or interfaces.

The java.awt.event Package

2. Which is the best way to receive events when a Button component is selected?

   A. Create an implementation of ButtonListener and add it as a listener to the Button component by invoking addButtonListener().

   B. Create an implementation of ActionListener and add it as a listener to the Button component by invoking addActionListener().

   C. Subclass ActionAdapter and override the actionPerformed() method. Then, add an instance of the subclass as a listener to the Button component by invoking addActionListener().

   D. Subclass MouseAdapter and override the mouseClicked() method. Then, add an instance of the subclass as a listener to the Button component by invoking addMouseListener().

3. Which of the following events are subclasses of InputEvent? (Choose all that apply.)

   A. MouseEvent

   B. WindowEvent

   C. MouseMotionEvent

   D. KeyEvent

4. Can an object be an event source and an event listener for the same type of event?

A. Yes

B. No

5. If you wanted to ensure that only numeric characters were entered in a TextField component, what is the best approach?

A. Subclass KeyAdapter and implement the keyTyped() method to invoke the consume() method on any event representing a nonnumeric character.

B. Subclass KeyAdapter and implement the keyPressed() method to consume all events.

C. Subclass KeyAdapater and implement the keyTyped() method to invoke setKeyChar(null) on any event representing a nonnumeric character.

D. Subclass KeyEvent and implement the keyTyped() method to consume any event representing a nonnumeric character using the consume() method.

6. Which of the following events are paired with their appropriate listener interfaces? (Choose all that apply.)

A. MouseEvent, MouseListener

B. MouseMotionEvent, MouseListener

C. MouseMotionEvent, MouseMotionListener

D. InputEvent, InputListener

7. Which event classes support the getWhen() method? (Choose all that apply.)

A. MouseEvent

B. WindowEvent

C. ActionEvent

D. KeyEvent

8. How would you determine the time at which a MouseEvent was generated?

A. Implement the MouseListener interface and call System.getCurrentTimeMillis() from within the implemented methods.

B. Invoke the getTime() method on the MouseEvent object.

C. Invoke the getWhen() method defined in the MouseAdapter class.

D. Invoke the getWhen() method on the MouseEvent object.

9. Which of the following event classes are subclasses of ComponentEvent? (Choose all that apply.)

   A. TextEvent

   B. ActionEvent

   C. MouseEvent

   D. WindowEvent

10. A Mouse listener can keep other MouseListeners from receiving a Mouse event by invoking the consume() method on the MouseEvent object.

    A. True

    B. False

11. Which listener interfaces are paired with the appropriate event class?

    A. TextListener, TextFieldEvent

    B. MouseMotionListener, MouseMotionEvent

    C. ActionListener, ActionEvent

    D. KeyListener, KeyPressedEvent

12. Which of the following are valid uses for the flags returned by the getModifiers() method defined in InputEvent? (Choose all that apply.)

    A. Determining which mouse button caused a Mouse event.

    B. Determining whether the ALT key was pressed at the time of a Key event.

    C. Determining whether a Mouse event was caused by a double-click.

    D. Determining whether the SHIFT key was pressed at the time of a Key event.

13. Which listener interface would you implement to determine when components were added to a Panel?

    A. ComponentListener

    B. ContainerListener

    C. ActionListener

    D. InputListener

14. Which of the following is not true about adapter classes?

    A. They implement their corresponding listener interface.

    B. They provide empty implementations for every method in their corresponding interface.

C. They are useful only for interfaces with more than one method.

D. Using an adapter class is more efficient because only the methods that you override are invoked by the event source.

15. Which of the following listener interfaces have an associated adapter class? (Choose all that apply.)

A. KeyListener

B. ItemListener

C. MouseListener

D. ActionListener

E. TextListener

16. Why does it not make sense to have an ActionAdapter class?

A. Because ActionEvent is a low-level event.

B. Because ActionListener is rarely used by developers.

C. Because the ActionListener interface defines only one method.

D. Because ActionListener serves only as a base interface for the other AWT listener interfaces and should not be implemented directly.

17. Which of the following properly implements the mouseClicked() method of MouseListener to print the (x, y) coordinates of a mouse-click? (Choose all that apply.)

A.
```
public void mouseClicked(MouseEvent e){
    Point point = e.getPoint();
    System.out.println("Click at (" + point.x + "," + point.y + ")");
};
```

B.
```
public void mouseClicked(MouseEvent e){
    System.out.println("Click at (" + e.getX() + "," + e.getY() + ")");
};
```

C.
```
public void mouseClicked(MouseEvent e){
System.out.println("Click at (" + e.x + "," + e.y + ")");
};
```

D.
```
public void mouseClicked(MouseEvent e){
int x;
    int y;
    e.translatePoint(x,y);
    System.out.println("Click at (" + x + "," + y + ")");
};
```

18. To enable events for a component, you must first invoke enableEvents() with the appropriate flags.

A. True

B. False

19. Given:

```
1.  import java.awt.*;
2.  import java.awt.event.*;
3.  class X extends Frame implements WindowListener {
4.
5.      public X() {
6.          this.setVisible(true);
7.          this.setSize(300, 300);
8.          this.addWindowListener(this);
9.      }
10.
11.     public void windowClosed(WindowEvent e) {
12.         System.out.println("Program ended.");
13.     }
14.
15.     public static void main(String [] args) {
16.         new X();
17.     }
18. }
```

What is the result of this code?

A. When the user clicks close on the frame, it will output "Program ended."

B. This code will not compile because of line 8.

C. This code will not compile because of line 11.

D. This code will compile if the class is declared abstract and line 16 is removed.

E. None of the above.

20. Given:

```
import java.awt.*;
import java.awt.event.*;
class Y extends Frame {

    public Y() {
        this.setVisible(true);
        this.setSize(300, 300);
```

```
 8.          this.addListener(new WH());
 9.       }
10.
11.       private class WH extends WindowListenerAdapter {
12.          public void windowClosing(WindowEvent e) {
13.             System.out.println("Goodbye.");
14.          }
15.       }
16.
17.       public static void main(String [] args) {
18.          new Y();
19.       }
20.    }
```

Which of the following statements are true? (Choose all that apply.)

A. The program will output "Goodbye" and the Frame will close when a user closes the frame.

B. The program will only output "Goodbye" but the frame will not close when a user attempts to close the frame.

C. There is an error in line 8.

D. There is an error in line 11.

E. There is an error in line 12.

SELF TEST ANSWERS

Java Events and Event Listeners

1. ☑ C and E. C is correct because event sources normally contain methods for adding and removing listeners. E is correct because an event source does not have to be a java.awt.Component class. It can be any type, as long as it has methods for adding listeners and notifying them when an event occurs.
☒ A is incorrect because an event source can have multiple listeners. B is incorrect because all Java event listeners implement the EventListener interface. D is incorrect because the event source can notify listeners in any order it chooses.

The java.awt.event Package

2. ☑ B. Button generates one semantic event, the ActionEvent. You must implement the ActionListener interface and register the implementation as a listener to receive action events through the actionPerformed() method.
☒ A is incorrect because there is no ButtonListener interface defined in the java.awt.event package. C is incorrect because there is no ActionAdapter class defined in the java.awt.event package. D is incorrect because it would be inefficient due to the fact that the implementation of MouseListener would be notified on every Mouse event, not just when the button was activated.

3. ☑ A and D. MouseEvent and KeyEvent are the only subclasses of InputEvent in the java.awt.event package.
☒ B is incorrect because WindowEvent does not subclass InputEvent. C is incorrect because there is no MouseMotionEvent. Remember that there is both a MouseListener and a MouseMotionListener listener interface, but both of these receive MouseEvent objects.

4. ☑ A. Yes. As long as the object implements the appropriate interface and also contains the logic to maintain and notify event listeners, this is fine.
☒ B is incorrect because an object can be an event source and an event listener for the same type of event.

5. ☑ A. Consuming events that represent nonnumeric characters keeps the TextField component from processing the event.
☒ B is incorrect because all events resulting from keys being pressed would be consumed; therefore, no characters could be entered in the TextField component. C is incorrect because

your compiler would complain that it cannot convert null to char. **D** is incorrect because keyTyped() is defined in KeyListener, not KeyEvent.

6. ☑ **A.** MouseEvent is properly paired with MouseListener. Note that MouseEvent could also be properly paired with MouseMotionListener.
☒ **B** and **C** are incorrect because there is no MouseMotionEvent defined in the java.awt.event package. Remember that the methods defined in the MouseMotionListener interface all receive MouseEvents as their parameter. **D** is incorrect because there is no InputListener interface defined in the java.awt.event package. InputEvent simply serves as a base class for MouseEvent and KeyEvent.

7. ☑ **A** and **D.** MouseEvent and KeyEvent both subclass InputEvent and therefore support the getWhen() method.
☒ **B** and **C** are incorrect because WindowEvent and ActionEvent are not subclasses of InputEvent.

8. ☑ **D.** InputEvent defines the getWhen() method that can be used to determine when an event occurred. Because MouseEvent extends InputEvent, MouseEvent also provides this method.
☒ **A** is incorrect because System.getCurrentTimeMillis() will simply return the current time, which is not the time that the event was generated. **B** is incorrect because there is no getTime() method defined in MouseEvent. **C** is incorrect because there is no getWhen() method defined in MouseAdapter. Remember that adapter classes simply implement listener interfaces with empty implementations.

9. ☑ **C** and **D.** MouseEvent is a direct subclass of InputEvent, which is in turn a direct subclass of ComponentEvent. WindowEvent is a direct subclass of ComponentEvent.
☒ **A** and **B** are both incorrect. ActionEvent and TextEvent directly subclass AWTEvent and therefore are not subclasses of ComponentEvent.

10. ☑ **B.** False. Consuming an InputEvent object simply keeps the event source from doing any further processing. This does not keep other listeners from receiving the event.

11. ☑ **C.** ActionListener is the listener interface for ActionEvent objects.
☒ **A, B,** and **D** are incorrect because TextListener, MouseMotionListener, and KeyListener correspond to TextEvent, MouseEvent, and KeyEvent, respectively.

12. ☑ **A, B,** and **D.** InputEvent defines masks for all modifier keys and three mouse buttons. These masks can be bitwise ANDed with the modifier value to test the flags.
☒ **C** is incorrect. To determine the number of mouse-clicks that caused a Mouse event, the getClickCount() method can be invoked on the MouseEvent object.

13. ☑ **B.** Containers such as Panel generate Container events when child components are either added or removed.
☒ **A** is incorrect because Component events are generated only when the Panel's visibility or shape changes, not when its contents are modified. **C** is incorrect because Panel does not generate ActionEvents. **D** is incorrect because there is no InputListener interface defined in the java.awt.event package.

14. ☑ **D.** Just because adapter classes provide an empty implementation for a method does not mean that the event source does not invoke the method.
☒ **A, B,** and **C** are incorrect because they are all true statements about adapter classes.

15. ☑ **A** and **C.** KeyAdapter and MouseAdapter are provided for KeyListener and MouseListener, respectively.
☒ **B, D,** and **E** are all incorrect because no adapter classes are provided for ItemListener, ActionListener, or TextListener.

16. ☑ **C.** ActionListener defines only one method actionPerformed(). It would make no sense to provide an adapter. This holds true for TextEvent and ItemEvent also.
☒ **A** is incorrect on two counts: one is that ActionListener is actually a semantic event, not a low-level event; the other is that it is perfectly acceptable to have an adapter for low-level events. In fact, all adapters provided in the java.awt.event package are for low-level events. **B** is also incorrect. ActionListener is one of the more commonly implemented (if not the most commonly implemented) listener interfaces. **D** is incorrect because ActionListener is intended to be directly implemented.

17. ☑ **A** and **B.** MouseEvent defines two ways of getting the coordinates of the mouse cursor at the time a mouse event was generated: One is to use the getX() and getY() methods to get integer coordinates, and the other is to use getPoint() to get a Point object representing the coordinates.
☒ **C** is incorrect because MouseEvent does not have public fields x and y. **D** is incorrect because translatePoint() modifies the MouseEvent object's coordinates by adding x and y parameters to its existing x and y coordinates.

18. ☑ **B.** False. A component automatically enables a specific event type when the first listener of the appropriate type registers as a listener.

19. ☑ **D.** Any class that implements an interface must implement all declared methods in that interface. The WindowListener interface has seven methods that must be declared. If a class is abstract, however, then it does not need to implement all methods.
☒ **A** is incorrect because the windowClosing() method is used to place code that will close a

frame. **B** is incorrect because it is valid for an event source to add itself as a listener. **C** is incorrect because this is a legal method declaration.

20. ☑ **C** and **D**. **C** is correct because the Window method is called addWindowListener(). **D** is correct because the WindowListener has an adapter called WindowAdapter, not WindowListenerAdapter.
☒ **A** is incorrect because the frame will not close unless the code in windowClosing() contains code to make it close. **B** would be correct if it weren't for the other errors in the code. **E** is incorrect because this is a valid method definition.

15

The java.io Package

CERTIFICATION OBJECTIVES

- 15.01 Navigating a File System
- 15.02 The java.io Hierarchy
- 15.03 Utilizing FileInputStream, FileOutputStream, and RandomAccessFile
- 15.04 Translating between Unicode and Other Character Encodings
- ✓ Two-Minute Drill
- Q&A Self Test

The java.io package is used to read and write data, but it is not limited to disk access. It can be used to read user input from the keyboard, send output to the command line, and send and receive data through a network. Often some of the same classes are used in all three of these operations.

In this chapter, we will cover how to navigate a generic file structure using any operating system; this is important because there are differences between the way UNIX, Windows, and the Macintosh store files. We will go over how to construct input and output objects, and how to use them. We will also learn the hierarchy of classes and interfaces in the java.io package and how they are used with one another.

CERTIFICATION OBJECTIVE 15.01

Navigating a File System

We'll begin this chapter with a relatively simple concept: navigating a file system. The operations used to navigate a file system include the basic UNIX or DOS commands most of us are familiar with, such as changing directories or deleting a file. The File class handles all disk operations of this nature.

A File object is just a representation of either a file or a directory. It is important to remember there is no Directory class; File is used to represent directories. For now, ignore how a file is created to disk. Just keep in mind that a file is *not* created by invoking the File constructor. With that noted, let's take a look at a File constructor:

```
File saveGame = new File("player1.dat");
```

The preceding code has given us a reference to a file on disk called *player1.dat.* The file may or may not actually be present on the disk. Because we did not specify a full path, it will use the current directory as the path. There are actually two kinds of path names that can be specified. The *absolute path* includes the entire directory structure right from the root drive. The *relative path* is the location of the file from the current directory, including any subfolders from the current directory.

exam Watch

A file is not created when we invoke the constructor for the File class. A file is created when we invoke the constructor for FileOutputStream, or invoke the File method createNewFile().

Now that we have a File object, let's try some methods:

```
import java.io.*;
public class Navigate {
   public static void main(String[] args) {
      File saveGame = new File("player1.dat");
      System.out.println(saveGame.getAbsolutePath());
      System.out.println(saveGame.exists());
   }
}
```

Notice the preceding code contains an import statement that allows access to all classes in the java.io package. This code creates a File object and outputs the absolute path of the file. Our program then checks to determine whether the file actually exists. In our case, the file was never created so the output is as follows:

```
C:\Java\SpaceGame\player1.dat
false
```

There are three different constructors for the File class:

- File(String fileName)
- File(String directory, String fileName)
- File(File directory, String fileName)

Notice the third constructor can use a File object to represent a directory instead of a file. A directory is created with the command mkdir(). If you try to create a directory with the same name as an existing file, the operating system will not allow the directory to be created and the method call will return false. Most File methods return a boolean value to indicate whether the disk operation was successful. Let's look at this in some sample code:

```
import java.io.*;
public class Navigate {
   public static void main(String[] args) {
      File saveDir = new File("save");
      System.out.println(saveDir.mkdir());
      File saveGame = new File(saveDir, "player1.dat");
      System.out.println(saveGame.getPath());
      System.out.println(saveDir.isDirectory());
```

```
 9.     }
10.  }
```

For new programmers, line five might look a little odd. Basically it is invoking the method mkdir() in the same line it outputs the boolean return value. Line six initializes another File object called saveGame, which is in the directory *save* as specified in the constructor. Line seven outputs the relative path (as opposed to the absolute path) and line eight uses the method isDirectory() to indicate if this is a file or a directory. The output should look as follows the first time you run it:

```
true
save\player1.dat
true
```

The first true indicates it successfully created the directory. The second true indicates that the File object saveDir is a directory. The second time you run it, the output will be:

```
false
save\player1.dat
true
```

This is because the directory *save* already exists, so the method indicates it was not successful in creating a new directory.

Directory Separators

Different operating systems use different symbols as directory separators. Windows uses a backslash, UNIX uses a forward slash, and the Macintosh uses colons. For this reason, even though we can use a backslash to specify an absolute directory (as in c:\Java), it is more proper to use a system-independent separator. This can be done using the static variable *separator*, which is part of the File class. Examine the following code:

```
import java.io.*;
public class Separator {
   public static void main(String[] args) {
      String folders = "data" + File.separator + "save";
      System.out.println("Creating folder " + folders);
      File dir = new File(folders);
      System.out.println(dir.getAbsolutePath());
   }
}
```

The output for this program will look something like this:

```
Creating folder data\save
C:\Java\Examples\data\save
```

Because I am using Windows, I see backslashes. In actual practice it does not matter which separator you use because Java will automatically convert it to the proper separator for your system. Examine this slightly revised code:

```
import java.io.*;
public class Separator {
    public static void main(String[] args) {
        String folders = "data/save"; //Altered line
        System.out.println("Creating folder " + folders);
        File dir = new File(folders);
        System.out.println(dir.getAbsolutePath());
    }
}
```

I used a forward slash instead of the proper separator variable. Java will still automatically handle this. The output will be something like this:

```
Creating folder data/save
C:\Java\BookTest\data\save
```

Notice that when we use getAbsolutePath(), it gives us the proper Windows system separators. This is part of the platform independence of Java. Keep in mind that if you attempt to use the backslash in a string, Java will think it is an escape character and strange behavior could occur.

Methods of the File Class

There are about 40 methods in the File class, but for the exam you only need to know the major methods for creating, deleting, modifying, and getting information about files. Let's briefly review some of these methods.

- **boolean createNewFile()** Creates a new empty file if the file does not already exist on disk and returns true if successful.
- **boolean delete()** Deletes a file and returns a boolean true value to indicate success.
- **boolean mkdir()** Creates a directory specified by the path name and returns true if successful.

- **boolean renameTo(File destination)** Renames or moves the file and returns true if successful.
- **boolean canRead()** Returns a boolean that indicates whether the operating system will allow the data in this file to be read.
- **boolean canWrite()** Returns a boolean that tells you whether the operating system will allow this file to be modified in any way.
- **boolean exists()** Returns a boolean that indicates whether the file or directory exists.
- **String [] list()** Returns a list of files and directories in the directory denoted by the File object.
- **long lastModified()** Returns a long to represent the number of milliseconds since 00:00:00 GMT, January 1, 1970. This is useful for comparing two files to see which was last modified, and this format is system-independent.
- **String getPath()** Returns the relative path of a file or directory, including the file name.
- **String getAbsolutePath()** Returns the absolute path of a file or directory, including the file name.
- **String getParent()** Returns the parent directory which contains this file, if one is specified. If no parent was specified, it will return null.
- **String getName()** Returns only the name of the file or directory specified by the File object.

EXERCISE 15-1

Navigating the File System

The following exercise will demonstrate how to navigate the file system. We will make a class that creates three files with the names of your favorite authors as the filename. These three files will be stored in a subdirectory called *authors*.

1. Create an object of File to represent your new directory.
2. Invoke the method mkdir() to create the directory.

3. Create three File objects to represent the three files you will create.
4. Invoke the command createNewFile() on all three File objects. Note that you will have to enclose these commands in a try-catch block or throw the IOException out of the main() method.
5. Use the method list() to get an array of Strings representing the filenames, then output them to the screen.

The finished code should look something like this:

```
import java.io.*;
public class Authors {
   public static void main(String[] args) {
      File directory = new File("authors");
      directory.mkdir();
      File name1 = new File(directory, "Doyle");
      File name2 = new File(directory, "Wells");
      File name3 = new File(directory, "Heinlein");
      try {
         name1.createNewFile();
         name2.createNewFile();
         name3.createNewFile();
      } catch(IOException e) {}
      String [] list = directory.list();
      System.out.println("Total files: " + list.length);
      for(int i = 0;i<list.length;i++) {
         System.out.println(list[i]);
      }
   }
}
```

CERTIFICATION OBJECTIVE 15.02

The java.io Hierarchy

The java.io classes are very complex and can be difficult to learn. The myriad of ways they can be used weaves a complex web. Even the basic architecture of the set of classes can be difficult to learn, but this is not to say it is poorly designed. Once you learn the underlying concepts, it can be a very powerful programming tool.

As I mentioned before, the java.io classes are not just for disk input and output, although this is the only function they will ask you about on the exam. The Java designers created the java.io package so it would be easy to input or output many types of data such as Objects, Strings, and bytes with a minimal amount of coding on the part of the programmer. They also designed it to be able to accept input and output from a myriad of sources such as keyboard, network, and disk.

exam Watch

You will only need to know disk input/output for the exam. You are not required to know keyboard or network input/output.

To have this sort of robustness, they created an entire "family tree" of classes and interfaces to do the job. We will start at the top of that tree.

Inputstream and Outputstream Classes

At the top of the java.io class hierarchy are two abstract classes: InputStream and OutputStream, as shown in Figure 15-1. Both of these classes are extended directly from Object. The InputStream and OutputStream classes have some very basic methods for reading and writing bytes only.

There are actually nine methods in InputStream, but some are a little obscure. OutputStream has only five methods. These methods are very basic and deal with reading and writing bit data only. None of these methods need to be learned for the exam.

There are eight known direct subclasses of InputStream. For the exam, you will need to know how to use FileInputStream and subclasses of FilterInputStream. You will also need to know how to use these classes in constructors when chaining InputStreams together. There are six known direct subclasses of OutputStream, but as before, you only need to know how to use FileOutputStream and subclasses of FilterOutputStream for the exam.

FIGURE 15-1

The top of the java.io hierarchy

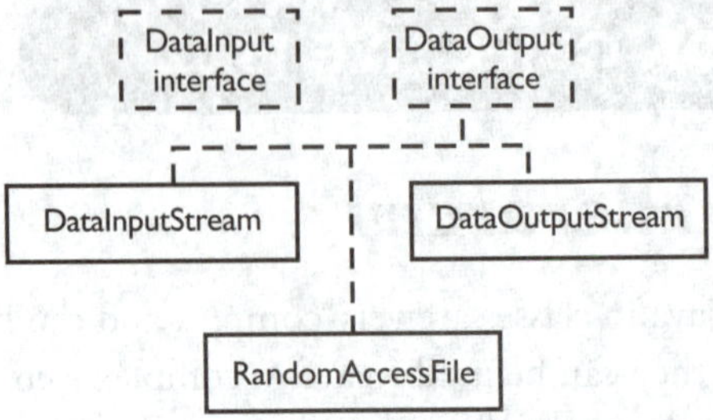

FilterInputStream and FilterOutputStream Classes

Java can handle many types of data such as double, int, and String objects. All of these types of data are processed as streams of bytes at the most basic level. If you look at a dialog box of your Internet connection, it will say something like "204,258 bytes received." Even though you are receiving many different types of data, such as GIFs and text files, the data passes through your computer as streams of bytes.

The classes FilterInputStream and FilterOutputStream are both subclasses of InputStream and OutputStream, respectively. Java uses the analogy that bits of data are like streams of water, and these streams can pass through filters. The stream goes in one end and comes out slightly different on the other end. These classes "filter" the bytes into Strings and other data types and they can also add functionality such as buffering, which we will describe later. Keep in mind, FilterInputStream and FilterOutputStream do not actually provide this functionality; it is the subclasses that provide the functionality.

Let's look at the constructor method for the class FilterOutputStream:

```
public FilterOutputStream(OutputStream out)
```

As you can see, a FilterOutputStream takes an OutputStream as a constructor. Here's where the concept can be difficult to understand: FilterOutputStream extends OutputStream, and it takes an OutputStream object in its constructor. So the question is, how can we make an object of OutputStream if it is abstract? The answer is that any OutputStream object type can be used, and this means all subclasses of OutputStream, such as FileOutputStream. Now let's look at the constructor for FilterInputStream:

```
protected FilterInputStream(InputStream in)
```

This constructor is roughly the same, but notice that it is protected! This means you will not be able to invoke the constructor from your code unless you make your class part of the java.io package. Only other classes in the java.io package will be able to use the constructor.

Subclasses of FilterInputStream

The subclasses of FilterInputStream and FilterOutputStream are the classes that do the real work converting data types. Of all these classes, you only need to be aware of how to use DataInputStream and BufferedInputStream for the exam.

Because these classes all extend FilterOutputStream, they will use an OutputStream in the constructor. The following code shows how we can chain these together for added functionality:

```
DataInputStream in = new DataInputStream (new BufferedInputStream
    (new FileInputStream("test.dat")));
```

FROM THE CLASSROOM

Sources of Input and Output Streams

Although it is not necessary for the exam, it is useful to know how to take data streams from a variety of sources. As we learned, FileInputStream and FileOutputStream are streams from a disk, but what about keyboard and network?

We can grab a keyboard InputStream as follows:

```
InputStream in = System.in;
```

We can output text to the screen using a PrintStream:

```
PrintStream out = System.out;
```

For those familiar with networking, once we have a Socket established with another computer, we can get a stream using the following:

```
InputStream in = socket.getInputStream();
OutputStream out = socket.getOutputStream();
```

Now you can take any of these streams and chain then to a DataInput or DataOutput object:

```
DataOutputStream outData = new DataOutputStream(out);
```

Once this is accomplished, you can easily use the methods of DataOutputStream to write data to the stream. The rest is easy!

—*Trent Heintz*

This line of code gives the input stream the added functionality of being buffered as the data is read from disk, which is much more efficient than reading one byte at a time.

Subclasses of FilterOutputStream

The subclasses of the FilterOutputStream somewhat mirror the subclasses of FilterInputStream in their functionality. Of all these classes, DataOutputStream and BufferedOutputStream are the only FilterOutputStream subclasses you will need to know for the exam.

DataInput and DataOutput Interfaces

Right about now, you are probably wondering when this never-ending chain of classes will end, and when we will actually see some code showing how to read or write data to the disk. Well, I promise it's coming soon.

DataInput and DataOutput objects are responsible for reading and writing the various primitive types of data, as well as some commonly-used data objects. Any class implementing these interfaces will be able to read from a data source or write to it. There are three known classes that implement these interfaces. For the exam, you will need to know all three: DataInputStream, DataOutputStream, and RandomAccessFile, as shown in Figure 15-2.

Like most subclasses of InputStream, DataInputStream uses an argument of type InputStream in the constructor. Likewise, DataOutputStream uses an OutputStream in its constructor.

A *random access file* has the ability to read and write to a file while keeping track of the point at which it is currently located in the file. As you can see in Figure 15-2,

FIGURE 15-2

DataInputStream, DataOutputStream, and RandomAccessFile implement the DataInput and DataOutput interfaces

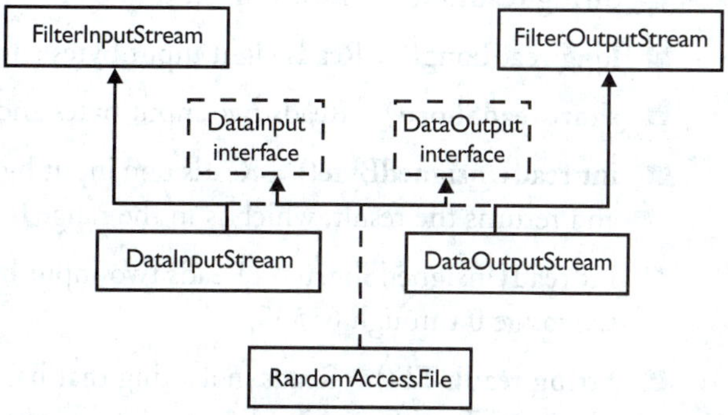

RandomAccessFile implements both the DataInput and DataOutput interfaces. It cannot extend more than one class, however, so instead it *has a* InputStream and OutputStream internally, that is not visible to the application programming interface (API).

Methods of DataInput

There are 15 methods in DataInput, with all but one starting with the prefix *read.* These methods all belong to DataInputStream and RandomAccessFile. It is very easy to figure out what most of these methods would be without being familiar with the actual DataInput class. Just think of the major data types and the methods that would logically be used to read those data types.

- **boolean readBoolean()** Reads one input byte and returns true if that byte is nonzero, false if that byte is zero.
- **byte readByte()** Reads and returns one input byte.
- **char readChar()** Reads an input char and returns the char value.
- **double readDouble()** Reads eight input bytes and returns a double value.
- **float readFloat()** Reads four input bytes and returns a float value.
- **void readFully(byte[] b)** Reads some bytes from an input stream and stores them into the buffer array *b*. The number of bytes is equal to the length of the array object.
- **void readFully(byte[] b, int off, int len)** Reads *len* bytes from an input stream into an array.
- **int readInt()** Reads four input bytes and returns an *int* value.
- **String readLine()** Reads the next line of text from the input stream.
- **long readLong()** Reads eight input bytes and returns a long value.
- **short readShort()** Reads two input bytes and returns a short value.
- **int readUnsignedByte()** Reads one input byte, zero-extends it to type *int*, and returns the result, which is in the range 0 through 255.
- **int readUnsignedShort()** Reads two input bytes and returns an *int* value in the range 0 through 65535.
- **String readUTF()** Reads in a string that has been encoded using a modified Universal Transformation Format-8 (UTF-8) format.

- **int skipBytes(int n)** Makes an attempt to skip over *n* bytes of data from the input stream, discarding the skipped bytes.

Methods of DataOutput

There are 14 write methods in the DataInput interface. All of these are present in the DataOutputStream and RandomAccessFile classes.

- **void write(byte[] b)** Writes all the bytes in array *b* to the output stream.
- **void write(byte[] b, int off, int len)** Writes *len* bytes from array *b*, in order, to the output stream.
- **void write(int b)** Writes the eight low-order bits of the argument *b* to the output stream.
- **void writeBoolean(boolean v)** Writes a boolean value to the output stream.
- **void writeByte(int v)** Writes the eight low-order bits of the argument *v* to the output stream.
- **void writeBytes(String s)** Writes a string to the output stream.
- **void writeChar(int v)** Writes a char value, which is comprised of two bytes, to the output stream.
- **void writeChars(String s)** Writes every character in the string *s* to the output stream in order, two bytes per character.
- **void writeDouble(double v)** Writes a double value, which is comprised of eight bytes, to the output stream.
- **void writeFloat(float v)** Writes a float value, which is comprised of four bytes, to the output stream.
- **void writeInt(int v)** Writes an *int* value, which is comprised of four bytes, to the output stream.
- **void writeLong(long v)** Writes a long value, which is comprised of four bytes, to the output stream.
- **void writeShort(int v)** Writes two bytes to the output stream to represent the value of the argument.
- **void writeUTF(String str)** Writes two bytes of length information to the output stream, followed by the Java-modified UTF representation of every character in the string *s*.

Now, we are finally ready to actually read and write data to the disk drive. This is the crucial part that you must know for the exam.

CERTIFICATION OBJECTIVE 15.03

Utilizing FileInputStream, FileOutputStream, and RandomAccessFile

In this section, we will examine how to use the various file streams to read and write data to disk. This includes using the constructors and methods in FileInputStream, FileOutputStream, and RandomAccessFile. We will also learn to catch IOExceptions when calling certain methods in these classes.

FileInputStream and FileOutputStream Classes

The File Streams are both subclasses of InputStream and OutputStream, as previously shown in Figure 15-1. These classes use a constructor that specifies a file on disk that will be the source of data:

```
FileOutputStream out = new FileOutputStream("player1.dat");
```

It is important to note that by invoking this constructor, we have written a new file to the disk called *player1.dat.* If the file already exists on disk, it will not overwrite it. It also opens the file for output, and, while it is open, no other program will be able to access it for writing. With FileOutputStream, data is always written to the beginning of the file. Any data that was previously in the file will be overwritten completely, even if you just write a single byte of data. There is a second constructor that determines whether the data will be overwritten:

```
FileOutputStream(String name, boolean append)
```

If append is true, it will write at the end of the file, otherwise it will write at the beginning and all the data will be overwritten.

Remember that FileOutputStream extends OutputStream, and the subclasses of FilterOutputStream (such as DataOutputStream) use OutputStreams in their constructors. Now that we have a valid FileOutputStream object called *out*, we can create a FilterOutputStream—in this case, we will use the subclass DataOutputStream:

```
DataOutputStream outStream = new DataOutputStream(out);
```

If you wanted to, instead of using a FileOutputStream, you could also use another FilterOutputStream object in the constructor because FilterOutputStream is a subclass of OutputStream. It would work because the FilterOutputStream must be tied to some actual data source. The following block of code would be perfectly legal (assuming it is programmed to catch or throw an IOException, which we will discuss later):

```
FileOutputStream out = new FileOutputStream("player1.dat");
DataOutputStream outStream1 = new DataOutputStream(out);
DataOutputStream outStream2 = new DataOutputStream(outStream1);
```

Notice outStream2 was constructed using outStream1. This will work fine, even though in reality it is redundant. As the name suggests, data will just filter through each of the filter streams.

Writing Files Using FileOutputStream

Let's review the steps for opening a file on disk and writing to it:

1. Construct a FileOutputStream for writing bytes to a file.
2. Construct a DataOutputStream to write different data types by using the FileOutputStream in the constructor method.
3. Invoke methods of DataOutputStream to write data to the data source.
4. Close the FilterOutputStream.

It is really not that difficult when you get right down to it. Now let's see these steps expanded with some code:

```
import java.io.*;
public class OutputTest {
    public static void main(String[] args) throws IOException {
        FileOutputStream outFile = new FileOutputStream("q.dat");
        DataOutputStream outData = new DataOutputStream(outFile);
```

```
6.          outData.writeUTF("The universe is amazingly big.");
7.          outData.close();
8.      }
9.  }
```

You won't actually see anything happen when you run this code, but you will hear your disk drive "whir" a bit. Analyze the preceding code. Which line of code will end up actually creating the file to disk? The answer is line 4—when the FileOutputStream is constructed. Line 6 uses the method writeUTF(String) to write a string composed of Unicode characters to the DataOutputStream. We will go into Unicode characters more thoroughly later in this chapter.

After running this code, you will notice a file in the directory from which the program was run. If you open it with an editor, you will be able to see the characters that were written to the file. Most likely you will see a space between each character because Java writes 2 bytes of data for each character, so the second byte of data is probably displayed as a space.

on the job

You may wonder why the method close() is used at all because your program seems to run fine without it. The method is used to make sure the computer releases the file when it is done with it. If the file is on a network and you access the file, no one else will be able to access it until you are done with it. To allow someone else to use it, the file must be properly closed using the close() method. Incidentally, the file is automatically released when the program terminates, but this is not considered a clean way to release a file.

EXERCISE 15-2

Using FileOutputStream and DataOutputStream

The following exercise will demonstrate how to write various data types to a file using FileOutputStream and DataOutputStream. Create a file and write to it some of your favorite things as a String, followed by a double to indicate the price tag.

1. Create a FileOutputStream using the file name in the constructor.
2. Create a DataOutputStream for writing different data types.

3. Use the commands writeUTF() to write Strings, and writeDouble() to write the prices.
4. Don't forget to close the file.

```
import java.io.*;
public class WriteData {
   public static void main(String[] args) throws IOException {
      FileOutputStream outFile = new FileOutputStream("favs.dat");
      DataOutputStream outData = new DataOutputStream(outFile);
      String [] favList = {"Explorer", "Cabin", "Athlon PC"};
      double [] priceList = {24999.99, 45000.00, 995.95};
      for(int i=0;i<3;i++) {
         outData.writeUTF(favList[i]);
         outData.writeDouble(priceList[i]);
      }
      outData.close();
   }
}
```

Reading Files Using FileInputStream

The steps for opening an existing file and reading data are very similar to FileOutputStream:

1. Construct a FileInputStream.
2. Construct a DataInputStream by using the FileInputStream in the constructor method.
3. Invoke methods of DataInputStream to read data from the data source.
4. Close the DataInputStream.

Let's examine this with some code. This code will work if you have already run the code in the previous example to create a text file. If not, you will get an IOException because the file does not exist.

```
import java.io.*;
public class InputTest {
```

```
    public static void main(String[] args) throws IOException {
        FileInputStream inFile = new FileInputStream("quote.dat");
        DataInputStream inData = new DataInputStream(inFile);
        String s = inData.readUTF();
        System.out.println(s);
        inData.close();
    }
}
```

Once the FileInputStream constructor is invoked, the file is opened for reading data. All FileInputStream objects begin reading data from the start. The previous example reads a line of Unicode and outputs it to the screen. If all works properly, you should receive the following output:

```
The universe is amazingly big.
```

on the Job

Ever wonder what will happen if you try to read-in a data type different from the one that was written? It will work, but of course in most cases it would be meaningless. For example, imagine we write a sentence to a text file using writeUTF(), then try to read-in the data as all bytes instead of UTF. It will work, and you will see the bytes that represent the individual characters in the file.

EXERCISE 15-3

Reading Data Types From a File Using DataInputStream

The following exercise will demonstrate how to read various data types from a file using DataInputStream. For this exercise, you will be using the file created in Exercise 15-2. The contents of the file should have your favorite things as String data, followed by the price as a double. Try outputting the contents of the file to the screen.

1. Create a FileInputStream with the appropriate file name.
2. Create a DataInputStream using the FileInputStream.
3. Read-in the data using readUTF() and readBoolean().
4. Don't forget to close the file!

The completed code should look something like this:

```
import java.io.*;
public class ReadData {
   public static void main(String[] args) throws IOException {
      FileInputStream inFile = new FileInputStream("favs.dat");
      DataInputStream inData = new DataInputStream(inFile);
      for(int i=0;i<3;i++) {
         System.out.print(inData.readUTF());
         System.out.println(" will cost " + inData.readDouble());
      }
      inData.close();
   }
}
```

Handling IO Exceptions

Up until now, we have largely ignored the IOException by throwing it out of the main() method. IO is often prone to errors, so Java forces us to catch the IOException (or throw it) for any method involved with IO, including constructor methods. For example, the following piece of code will not work:

```
import java.io.*;
public class InputOutput {
   public static void main(String[] args) {
      FileOutputStream file = new FileOutputStream("YabbaDabba.dat");
   }
}
```

If you attempt to compile this code, you will receive the following error:

```
C:\Java\BookTest>javac InputOutput.java
InputOutput.java:4: Exception java.io.FileNotFoundException must be
caught, or it must be declared in the throws clause of this method.
      FileOutputStream file = new FileOutputStream("YabbaDabba.dat");
                                ^
1 error
```

To correct this problem, we could throw the IOException out of the main() method as we saw previously, or we could use one of those try-catch blocks of code. How you decide to handle the exception is entirely up to you:

```
import java.io.*;
public class InputOutput {
   public static void main(String[] args) {
      try {
         FileOutputStream file = new
FileOutputStream("Yabba.dat");
      }
      catch(IOException e) {System.out.println("Error: " + e);}
   }
}
```

Reading and Writing with RandomAccessFile

RandomAccessFile differs from FileInputStream and FileOutputStream in that it can read as well as write to a file once it is opened. In addition, it can read or write to a specified point within the file by using a file pointer. A *file pointer* is a variable of type long that keeps track of where the RandomAccessFile will read or write data within the file.

RandomAccessFile implements both DataInput and DataOutput, so it has all the methods associated with both FilterInputStream and FilterOutputStream combined. It also has the following methods, which are specific to RandomAccessFile:

- **getFilePointer()** Returns the current offset in this file.
- **seek(long)** Sets the file-pointer offset, measured from the beginning of this file, at which the next read or write will occur.

The constructor uses a File or String to represent the file name and another String to indicate whether the file will be read-only or read/write. Examine the following constructor:

```
RandomAccessFile inout = new RandomAccessFile("story.dat", "rw");
```

This line of code will open a file or create one if it is not present already. It will also be able to read or write to that file. To just read from a file, the second argument can be set to "r."

The pointer is an indication of how many bytes into a file the stream is located. The pointer starts at byte 0 when the RandomAccessFile is first instantiated. You can determine where the pointer is by using the method getFilePointer(), and you can set where the pointer should be using the method seek().

Now let's examine some code that will manipulate a random access file. The code will write two pieces of data (in this case, two strings in Unicode text format). It will back up the pointer to where the second string is written, and then overwrite that string with a new one.

```
1.  import java.io.*;
2.  public class InputOutput {
3.      public static void main(String[] args) throws IOException {
4.          RandomAccessFile inout = new RandomAccessFile("story.dat",
5.              "rw");
6.          System.out.println("Pointer is at : " +
7.              inout.getFilePointer());
8.          inout.writeUTF("Spike is a ");
9.          long pointer = inout.getFilePointer();
10.         System.out.println("Pointer is now at : " + pointer);
11.         inout.writeUTF("good dog.");
12.         inout.seek(pointer);
13.         inout.writeUTF("very good dog."); // Overwrites old data
14.         inout.seek(0);
15.         System.out.println(inout.readUTF() + inout.readUTF());
16.         inout.close();
17.     }
18. }
```

This program is somewhat complex. As we can see, line 4 opens a file and creates it if it doesn't already exist. It will be opened with read/write access, as indicated by the string "rw." Lines 6 and 7 use the method getFilePointer() to indicate the position within the file. In this case, the pointer is at the start. Line 8 writes a string of characters in Unicode. Line 9 stores the position of the pointer for later reference (in this case, at point 13). Line 10 writes another block of UTF characters, but then line 12 immediately backtracks to the previously stored position using the method seek(). Line 13 overwrites the data, then *rewinds* to the start using seek() at line 14. It then reads-in the two UTF character blocks. The output is as follows:

```
Pointer is at : 0
Pointer is now at : 13
Spike is a very good dog.
```

Notice the RandomAccessFile object can append data to the end of the file. In contrast, a FileOutputStream overwrites all data that was previously in the file. When you append data to the file, any data that existed after the pointer will be completely overwritten.

It is also worth mentioning that a file written by a FileOutputStream can be read by a RandomAccessFile. The manner in which they store data is identical.

EXERCISE 15-4

Writing and Reading Data Using a Random Access File

The following exercise will demonstrate how to open a random access file, write and read data, then close it. We will make a class that creates a random access file and writes the names of your top three favorite books as a string, followed by the published date (it doesn't matter if you don't know). Then, without closing the file, go back and read-in the name and year of your second-favorite book.

1. Create a RandomAccessFile object, giving it a name in the constructor.
2. For efficiency, you might want to create an array of Strings representing your book titles, and an array of integers for the years.
3. Use the methods writeUTF() and writeInt() to write the titles and years.
4. Go back to the start of the file using seek(), then read-in the first String and integer to get to the second record in the file.
5. Read-in the title and date, and display it on the screen.

Your finished code may look something like this:

```
import java.io.*;
public class RandomAccess {
    public static void main(String[] args) throws IOException {
        RandomAccessFile books = new RandomAccessFile("books.dat", "rw");
        String [] bookList = {"Starship Troopers", "The Hobbit", "The
          Man in the High Castle"};
        int [] yearList = {1959, 1954, 1974};
        for(int i=0; i<3; i++) {
```

```
            books.writeUTF(bookList[i]);
            books.writeInt(yearList[i]);
        }
        books.seek(0);
        books.readUTF();
        books.readInt();
        System.out.println(books.readUTF() + " " + books.readInt());
        books.close();
    }
}
```

An alternate way of moving the pointer to the start of the second record is to store the position of the pointer just before writing the second record. This can be accomplished using the getFilePointer() method.

CERTIFICATION OBJECTIVE 15.04

Translating Between Unicode Text and Other Character Encodings

Up until now, we have been discussing how to read and write the basic data types such as Strings and primitives. In this section, we will be discussing character data only.

Operating systems use many different types of coding schemes to store characters. The characters can be represented by one byte (between 0 and 255), or two bytes (between 0 and 65535), or by other schemes. Byte 0 might represent the *a* character in one encoding scheme, whereas in another it might represent a space. Java is designed to be a platform-independent language, so it uses what is known as Unicode characters. The *Unicode character-encoding* scheme is used by Java to handle character streams.

Your operating system uses its own type of character encoding. For example, Windows uses ISO 8859-1 (also known as ANSI) and Macintosh uses Macintosh Latin-2. There are literally more than one hundred different types of character sets that Java can interpret; for a sampling, see Table 15-1.

TABLE 15-1 A Small Sampling of the Hundreds of Character-Encoding Formats Available

Encoding String	Description
8859_1	ISO Latin-1
8859_2	ISO Latin-2
8859_3	ISO Latin-3
Cp037	USA, Canada (Bilingual, French), Netherlands, Portugal, Brazil, Australia
Cp1046	IBM Open Edition US EBCDIC
Cp850	PC Latin-1
ISO2022CN	ISO 2022 CN, Chinese
MacRoman	Macintosh Roman
UTF8	Standard UTF-8

exam Watch

For the exam, you will only need to know about ISO 8859-1 character encoding, but keep in mind that others exist.

Reader and Writer Classes

To translate these character streams, Java uses Reader and Writer classes. Reader and Writer are both abstract and are extended by InputStreamReader and OutputStreamWriter, respectively.

InputStreamReader

The InputStreamReader class is used for inputting text from a source that is character-encoded. There are two constructors for InputStreamReader. The first constructor specifies only an InputStream, which can be from a file, the keyboard, or some other input source.

```
InputStreamReader keyboardIn = new InputStreamReader(System.in);
```

This constructor uses the default character encoding for your system. For example, if you are using Windows, Java will know to use ISO 8859-1 encoding to read the InputStream.

The second constructor allows you to specify which type of character encoding it will use to read the characters. The following example will input text from a file. In this case, the system does not know what kind of character encoding might have been used to store this text file, so it might be a good idea to specify the type if it did not originate on this system. First, we create an instance of a FileInputStream, as we have seen before:

```
FileInputStream file = new FileInputStream("recipe.txt");
```

Next, we create an instance of InputStreamReader and specify which type of character encoding to use with a string:

```
InputStreamReader inReader = new InputStreamReader(file, "CP037");
```

There are only five methods in InputStreamReader. One is called read(), which reads one single character. It is rather painful for a programmer to read-in a text file one character at a time. For this reason, it is a good idea to chain another type of Reader to make reading and writing easier. BufferedReader is a good one to choose, because it reads a whole line into the buffer, until it encounters a carriage return. The constructor takes a Reader object:

```
BufferedReader inBuffer = new BufferedReader(inReader);
String message = inBuffer.readLine();
```

Let's look at our completed code to read-in a line of text:

```
import java.io.*;
public class ReadData {
   public static void main(String[] args) throws IOException {
      FileInputStream file = new FileInputStream("recipe.txt");
      InputStreamReader inReader = new InputStreamReader(file,
         "CP037");
      BufferedReader inBuffer = new BufferedReader(inReader);
      String message = inBuffer.readLine();
      System.out.println(message);
      inBuffer.close();
   }
}
```

The only class that extends InputStreamReader is FileReader. This is a convenience class that takes a File or String object in the constructor to access a file. It acts exactly like an InputStreamReader, which uses a FileInputStream in the constructor, except that it can be instantiated all at once.

EXERCISE 15-5

Reading and Converting Data Using Character Encoding

The following exercise will demonstrate how to read data from a data source and convert it using a different kind of character encoding. It is called *CrazyKeyboard* because the input will be as your system default (likely ISO 8859-1), but it will attempt to translate it using another character encoding. The result will be some strange symbols when you press ENTER on the keyboard. This program will use System.in instead of a FileInputStream shown previously.

1. Create an InputStream. In this case, DataInputStream will suffice because our InputStream source will use System.in.
2. Create an InputStreamReader using our DataInputStream in the constructor. You can use whatever character-encoding scheme you wish, but if you want to see the odd, garbled characters, make sure you don't use your system default, or you'll see normal text.
3. Create a BufferedReader because we'll be reading one line at a time.
4. Use the method readLine() to gather an entire line of text. Note that you can use the method read() to read-in one character at a time.

   Your program should look something like this when complete:

```
import java.io.*;
public class CrazyKeyboard {
   public static void main(String[] args) throws IOException {
      DataInputStream keyboard = new DataInputStream(System.in);
      InputStreamReader inReader = new InputStreamReader(keyboard,
         "CP037");
      BufferedReader inBuffer = new BufferedReader(inReader);
      while (true) {
         String message = inBuffer.readLine();
         System.out.println(message);
      }
   }
}
```

To terminate this program when it is running, press CTRL-C.

Your command line will echo back characters you type, but when you press ENTER, the program will read the entire line and display it.

OutputStreamWriter

OutputStreamWriter mirrors InputStreamWriter in functionality. If we want to write text to a file, we must first create a FileOutputStream:

```
FileOutputStream fOut = new FileOutputStream("speech.txt");
```

Then we create an OutputStreamWriter using one of the two constructors. If we do not specify the character encoding, it will output the characters using the default encoding for the operating system. In our example, we will specify CP037:

```
OutputStreamWriter outWriter = new OutputStreamWriter(fOut, "CP037");
```

There is only one class that extends OutputStreamWriter and that is FileWriter (similar to FileReader). FileWriter is a convenience class that is the same as using a FileOutputStream with an OutputStreamWriter. The constructor of FileWriter will create a file to disk, if one does not already exist.

For actually writing the data, it is more useful to use PrintWriter than just OutputStreamWriter because of the limited methods for writing characters. PrintWriter allows strings and numbers to be written to the text file:

```
PrintWriter out = new PrintWriter(outWriter);
out.print("The universe ");
out.println("is a very big place.");
```

The final program will look like this:

```
import java.io.*;
public class Writer {
   public static void main(String [] args) throws IOException {
      FileOutputStream fileOut = new
         FileOutputStream("speech.txt");
      OutputStreamWriter outWriter = new
         OutputStreamWriter(fileOut, "CP037");
      PrintWriter out = new PrintWriter(outWriter);
```

```
        out.print("The universe ");
        out.println("is a very big place.");
    }
}
```

Default Encoding Conversion versus Specific Conversion

There are times when you can rely on the default encoding to translate the characters, but there are other times when you must specify the type of encoding to use. It is easy to logically determine whether you must specify a type of encoding. If the input is a file written by the system you are using, or if the input is coming from the keyboard, you can use the default encoding.

If the data is coming externally, either from another computer with a different OS (and the program is not programmed in Java) or an external file, then you must specify what type of character encoding to use.

Now that you have a better idea of file handling, refer to the following Scenario & Solution for some real-world problems that you might encounter. It's up to you to decide which class would be best to use.

SCENARIO & SOLUTION

Which class allows you to open a file and simultaneously read and write data?	RandomAccessFile
Which class is used to output bytes specifically to a file?	FileOutputStream (often chained with DataOutputStream)
Which class can be used to read an ISO 8859-3 file?	InputStreamReader (FileReader is also acceptable. Often chained with BufferedReader.)
Which class would you use to find out to which directory a file belongs?	File
Which class can be used to read double values from a file?	DataInputStream

CERTIFICATION SUMMARY

Everything you need to know about the java.io package for the exam has been presented in this chapter. It can be difficult to digest this material because there are so many interrelated classes in the hierarchy and in constructors. It also doesn't make things any easier with class names that are so similar, such as FileInputStream and FilterInputStream. Everything should fall into place, however, once you have learned some of the key concepts. It helps to use the classes in actual code to become comfortable with the names and usage of these classes.

There are several concepts you must know for the Java exam. Handling the IOException is important. It is also important to know how the various java.io classes are "chained" together with constructors. To understand this concept you will need to know which types of objects are used in each constructor. In other words, you must determine whether the class being used in a constructor is a subclass of the declared type in a constructor.

You will need to know how to use File to navigate a file system. The various methods of File are important to know, as well as how the directory structure is handled.

Finally, you will need to know how to use the various character encodings to read and write character streams. Be sure you understand when to use the default character encoding and when to specify a character encoding in the constructor.

✓ TWO-MINUTE DRILL

Here are some of the key points from each certification objective in Chapter 15.

Navigating a File System

- ❑ The File class is used to create a representation of a file or a directory.
- ❑ The constructor for the File class does not create a new file on disk.

The java.io Hierarchy

- ❑ InputStream and OutputStream are abstract classes at the top of the hierarchy.
- ❑ FilterInputStream and FilterOutputStream are subclasses of InputStream and OutputStream.
- ❑ FilterInputStream and FilterOutputStream add functionality to streams of data.
- ❑ FilterInputStream and FilterOutputStream subclasses use other InputStream and OutputStream classes in their constructors.
- ❑ FileInputStream and FileOutputStream are subclasses of InputStream and OutputStream on a different branch from FilterInputStream and FilterOutputStream.

Utilizing FileInputStream, FileOutputStream, and RandomAccessFile

- ❑ A file is created on disk when the constructor is run for a FileOutputStream.
- ❑ RandomAccessFile can both read and write data. It also keeps track of data with a file pointer.
- ❑ You can specify whether a RandomAccessFile is read/write or read-only using the strings *rw* and *r* respectively in the constructor.
- ❑ IOException errors must be caught or thrown when using any methods that access a data stream. This includes the constructor methods for FileOutputStream and FileInputStream.

Translating between Unicode and Other Character Encodings

- ❑ Unicode character encoding is the scheme used by Java.
- ❑ Windows uses ISO 8859-1 character encoding.
- ❑ InputStreamReader is used to read text characters from a source that may be encoded.
- ❑ OutputStreamWriter is used to write text characters to a destination using encoding.
- ❑ BufferedReader is often chained with InputStreamReader to read text streams.
- ❑ PrintWriter is often chained with OutputStreamWriter to write text streams.
- ❑ You may need to specify a character-encoding scheme when data is coming from an external source. If data is coming from your operating system, the default encoding should be used.

SELF TEST

The following questions will help you measure your understanding of the material presented in this chapter. Read all of the choices carefully, as there may be more than one correct answer. Choose all correct answers for each question.

Navigating a File System

1. Which of the following File class constructors are valid? (Choose all that apply.)

   A. File a = new File(new File("data") , "map.dat");

   B. File b = new File("map.dat");

   C. File c = new File("map.dat", "rw");

   D. File d = new File("map.dat", "r");

   E. File e = new File("data", "map.dat");

2. Which of the following classes allow you to create a new file to disk? (Choose all that apply.)

   A. File

   B. RandomAccessFile

   C. FileInputStream

   D. FilterInputStream

   E. FileWriter

3. Which of the following classes allow you to delete a file?

   A. FileOutputStream

   B. FileInputStream

   C. File

   D. FilterInputStream

   E. DataOutputStream

   F. RandomAccessFile

The java.io Hierarchy

4. Which of the following object types are valid constructor parameters for FilterOutputStream? (Choose all that apply.)

   A. File

   B. Nothing

   C. String

   D. FileOutputStream

   E. DataOutputStream

   F. FilterOutputStream

5. Which of the following object types may be used as a parameter of a FileOutputStream constructor? (Choose all that apply.)

   A. File

   B. No arguments

   C. String

   D. FileOutputStream

   E. DataOutputStream

   F. FilterOutputStream

6. Which of the following object types are valid parameters for the constructor of DataInputStream?

   A. File

   B. Nothing

   C. String

   D. FileOutputStream

   E. DataOutputStream

   F. FilterInputStream

Utilizing FileInputStream, FileOutputStream, and RandomAccessFile

7. Given:

```
import java.io.*;
 public class Minerals {
    DataOutputStream dataOut;
    public void openFile() throws IOException {
       File out = new File("geology_map.dat");
       dataOut = new DataOutputStream(out);
    }
 }
```

What will happen if you attempt to compile this class and call the openFile() method?

A. It won't compile because there is no try-catch block.

B. The class will compile, but when the program is run the file will not be created because the filename is longer than eight characters.

C. The class won't compile because there is a problem with the File constructor.

D. The class won't compile because there is a problem with the DataOutputStream constructor.

E. The class will compile and the code will create a file called "geology_map.dat" (if this does not already exist), which will be 0 bytes in size.

8. Given:

```
import java.io.*;
 public class WriteData {
    public static void main(String[] args) {
       try {
          File employee = new File("Joe.dat");
       } catch (IOException e) {
          System.out.println("Error: " + e);
       }
    }
 }
```

What is the result of this program?

A. The class will compile, but an error will occur when it is run.

B. The class will not run or compile.

C. The class will compile and run fine, and a file will be created called "Joe.dat."

D. The class will compile and run fine, but no file will be created.

E. None of the above.

9. Given:

```
import java.io.*;
public class ReadEmployee {
    public static void main(String[] args) {
        File employee = new File("Joe.dat");
        FileInputStream in = new FileInputStream(employee);
    }
}
```

What will happen when you attempt to compile and run this code?

A. The class will compile, but an error will occur when it is run.

B. The class will not run or compile.

C. The class will compile and run fine, and a file will be created called "Joe.dat."

D. The class will compile and run fine, but no file will be created.

E. None of the above.

10. Given:

```
import java.io.*;
public class WriteData {
    public static void main(String[] args) {
        File employee = new File("Joe.dat");
        try {
            FileOutputStream out = new FileOutputStream(employee);
            DataOutputStream outData = new DataOutputStream(out);
            outData.writeString("James Dickey");
            outData.writeInt(34);
        } catch (IOException e) {
            System.out.println("Error: " + e);
        }
    }
}
```

What is the result of this code?

A. The class will compile, but an error will occur when it is run.

B. The class will not run or compile.

C. The class will compile and run fine, and a file will be created called "Joe.dat."

D. The class will compile and run fine, but no file will be created.

E. None of the above.

11. Given:

```
import java.io.*;
public class Test {
    public static void main(String[] args) throws IOException {
        FileOutputStream outFile = new FileOutputStream("year.dat");
        DataOutputStream outData = new DataOutputStream(outFile);
        outData.writeInt(1066);
        outData.close();
    }
}
```

Assume there is a file on the disk called "year.dat" that resides in the current directory. What is the result of this code?

A. The file will not compile.

B. The file will compile, but will generate an error when run.

C. The class will run and overwrite the file called "year.dat," then it will write the integer 1066 to the file.

D. The class will run, but it will not overwrite the existing file called "year.dat." It will then overwrite all data in the file and replace it with the integer 1066.

E. The class will run, but it will not overwrite the existing file called "year.dat." It will then append the integer 1066 to the end of the existing file.

12. Which of the following constructors are valid for the RandomAccessFile class? (Choose all that apply.)

A. RandomAccessFile a = new RandomAccessFile("cards.txt", "wr");

B. RandomAccessFile b = new RandomAccessFile("cards.txt", "r");

C. RandomAccessFile c = new RandomAccessFile(new File("cards"));

D. RandomAccessFile d = new RandomAccessFile("cards.txt", "w");

E. DataInput e = new RandomAccessFile("cards.txt", "r");

13. Given:

```
import java.io.*;
public class Random {
    public static void main(String[] args) throws IOException {
        RandomAccessFile inout = new RandomAccessFile("story.dat",
            "rw");
        inout.seek(inout.length() - 1);
        inout.close();
```

```
8.     }
9.  }
```

At what position will the pointer be set after line 5?

A. Just before the very last byte in the file.

B. Just after the very last byte in the file.

C. At the beginning of the file.

14. Given:

```
import java.io.*;
public class Inventory {
   public static void main(String[] args) throws IOException {
      FileInputStream inFile = new FileInputStream("surplus.dat");
      DataInputStream inData = new DataInputStream(inFile);
      String s = inData.readUTF();
      System.out.println(s);
      inData.close();
   }
}
```

Assume there is a file in the current directory called "surplus.dat" that contains a string of Unicode characters. What will happen if you attempt to compile and run this block of code?

A. The file will not compile.

B. The file will compile, but the class will generate an error when run.

C. The class will run and overwrite the file called "surplus.dat" and then it will overwrite all data in the file.

D. The class will run and read-in the first line of UTF characters as a string, then display it on the screen.

E. The class will run and read-in every line of UTF characters in the file, then display it on the screen.

Translating between Unicode and Other Character Encodings

15. You are using a Windows system to write some code that will read text characters from a file called inventory.dat. Which of the following lines of code will create an object we can use to read characters that use ISO 8859-1 character encoding? Assume the variable *file* represents a FileInputStream. (Choose all that apply.)

A. InputStreamReader a = new InputStreamReader(file, "CP037");

B. InputStreamReader b = new InputStreamReader(file);

C. InputStreamReader c = new InputStreamReader(file, "8859_1");

D. FileReader d = new FileReader("inventory.dat");

E. FileReader d = new FileReader(file);

16. Given:

```
public class Inventory {
    public static void main(String[] args) throws IOException {
        FileInputStream inS = new FileInputStream("surplus.dat");
        InputStreamReader inR = new InputStreamReader(inS);
        BufferedReader inBuffer = new BufferedReader(inR);
        String message = inBuffer.readLine();
        System.out.println(message);
        inBuffer.close();
    }
}
```

Assume this code will be executed in a Windows environment, and there is a file in the current directory called "surplus.dat" that contains a string of characters in the default character encoding. What will happen if you attempt to compile and run the following block of code?

A. The file will not compile due to something within the method main().

B. The file will not compile for some other reason.

C. The file will compile, but the class will generate an error when run.

D. The class will run and read-in the first line of text.

17. For a project you are working on you need to write characters to a data stream using a Macintosh character encoding. You would like to be able to write large strings of text, as opposed to one character at a time. You have already created a FileOutputStream and need to chain it to some other objects. Which of the following classes would you chain together to accomplish this? (Choose all that apply.)

A. DataOutputStream

B. BufferedOutputStream

C. PrintWriter

D. FileInputStream

E. OutputStreamWriter

18. In which of the following scenarios would you use the default character encoding when using a stream of characters? (Choose all that apply.)

A. Reading a text file that was created on your system (and not written using UTF).

B. Reading a text file from a file that originated on a different operating system.

C. Reading-in a stream of characters being generated from a network stream from a computer using a different operating system

D. Reading-in a stream of characters from your keyboard.

19. Given:

```
import java.io.*;
 public class Writer {
    public static void main(String [] args) throws IOException {
       FileOutputStream fOut = new FileOutputStream("p.txt");
       OutputStreamWriter outWriter = new OutputStreamWriter(fOut);
       PrintWriter out = new PrintWriter(outWriter);
       out.print("You are almost done.");
    }
}
```

What will this class accomplish when it is compiled and run?

A. The file will not compile due to something within the method main().

B. The file will not compile for some other reason.

C. The file will compile, but the class will generate an error when run.

D. The class will run and read-in the first line of text.

E. The class will run and write a line of text in the same character encoding your operating system uses.

F. The class will run and write a line of text in some other character encoding.

20. You are using a Linux PC to develop an application for Linux. In which of the following scenarios would you use a specific character encoding when using a stream of characters? (Choose all that apply.)

A. Reading-in a file that was created on your system (and not written using UTF).

B. Reading-in a text file from a file from another operating system.

C. Writing characters to a file that will be used for a Macintosh computer.

D. Reading-in a stream of characters coming from a keyboard on another operating system through the network.

SELF TEST ANSWERS

Navigating a File System

1. ☑ A, B, and E. A is legal because there is a constructor that takes a File object as a directory and a string as the file name. B is legal because there is a constructor that takes only a string for a filename. E is legal because there is a constructor that takes a string for a directory and a string for the file name.
   ☒ C and D are incorrect because these constructors would apply only to the RandomAccessFile class.

2. ☑ A, B, and E. A is correct because File can create a file with the createNewfile() method. B and E will create a file when the constructor is invoked.
   ☒ C is incorrect because an InputStream only reads data, and to write or create a file you need to use an OutputStream. D is incorrect primarily because Filter Streams are used for generic data streams, not for file streams only.

3. ☑ C. File is the only class that can delete a file from disk using the delete() method.
   ☒ A, B, D, E, and F are all incorrect. A, B, and F are specifically used with files, but they do not have the proper method to delete a file. D and E are used with generic streams and are not specifically used for disk accessing.

The java.io Hierarchy

4. ☑ D, E, and F. Any class that is a subclass of OutputStream can be used in the constructor for FilterOutputStream.
   ☒ A, B, and C are incorrect because none of these are OutputStream objects.

5. ☑ A and C. A is legal because there is a constructor that takes a File object as a file representation. C is legal because there is also a constructor that takes a string for a filename.
   ☒ B, D, E, and F are incorrect. B is incorrect because there is no default constructor method with zero arguments. D, E, and F are incorrect because there is no constructor that takes OutputStream classes as a parameter.

6. ☑ F. Any class that is a subclass of InputStream can be used in the constructor for DataInputStream.
   ☒ A, B, C, D, and E are incorrect. A, C, D, and E are not subclasses of InputStream. B is incorrect because there is no default no-argument constructor.

Utilizing FileInputStream, FileOutputStream, and RandomAccessFile

7. ☑ D. It is correct because a DataOutputStream uses an OutputStream in the constructor. In our example, it is using a File, and File is not a subclass of OutputStream. The program should probably use a FileOutputStream in the DataOutputStream constructor.
☒ A, B, C, and E are incorrect. A is incorrect because the IOException is correctly handled by throwing it out of the method openFile(). B is incorrect because there is no limitation of eight characters on the size of a filename. C is incorrect because the File constructor is fine. E is incorrect because there was no FileOutputStream constructor invoked.

8. ☑ B. The class will not compile because there is no possibility of an exception being thrown in the statement that creates a File object. It is illegal to use a try-catch block of code when no exception may be thrown.
☒ A, C, D, and E are all incorrect because the class will not compile, so we don't even get as far as running the program.

9. ☑ B. The class will not compile properly. The statement that constructs a FileInputStream must be surrounded by a try-catch block, or the IOException (FileNotFoundException) must be thrown out of the main() method.
☒ A, C, D, and E are incorrect because the class will not compile, so we don't even get as far as running the program.

10. ☑ B. It will not work because of the line that attempts to write the string. There is no method called writeString() in DataOutputStream. The actual method is called writeChars() or writeUTF().
☒ A, C, D, and E are incorrect because the program never actually compiles, so it can't be run.

11. ☑ D. If the existing file already exists, the class will not overwrite it. When writing data with DataOutputStream, the data is written to the beginning of the file and overwrites all data previously stored.
☒ A, B, C, and E are all incorrect. A and B are incorrect because the code is valid and no compiler errors could be generated here. C is incorrect because if a file already exists it will not be overwritten. E is incorrect because data is not appended to the end of the file.

12. ☑ B and E. B is legal because there is a constructor to take a String representing a file name, and a String representing read or read-write ("r" or "rw"). E is legal, even though it is a little tricky. RandomAccessFile implements DataInput (and DataOutput), therefore you can declare it as an object of type DataInput.

☒ A, C, and D are all incorrect. A is incorrect because the string "wr" is invalid. To indicate read-write access, use "rw." C is incorrect because there must be a String indicating read-only or read-write access. D is incorrect because there is no mode of write-only.

13. ☑ A. The method length() returns the total number of bytes. By using length - 1, it positions the pointer not quite at the end of the file, (1 byte from the end to be exact).
☒ B and C are both incorrect. B is incorrect as explained previously. If we used inout.seek(inout.length()), it would put the pointer right at the end of the file. C is just plain incorrect.

14. ☑ D. The program opens a file called "surplus.dat," then chains the FileInputStream to a DataInputStream. It then reads one line of Unicode characters and outputs it to the screen.
☒ A, B, C, and E are all incorrect. A and B are incorrect because, with the given information in the question, this file will compile and generate no errors when the class is run. C is incorrect because the class is reading data, not writing it. E is incorrect because the method readUTF() will read only one line of Unicode text, not the whole file.

Translating between Unicode and Other Character Encodings

15. ☑ B, C, and D. B is correct because one of the InputStreamReader constructors uses only an InputStream object in the constructor. This constructor uses default encoding, which on a Windows system is ISO 8859-1. C is correct because the other constructor uses an InputStream object and a string representing the type of encoding to use. In this case, the question asked for ISO 8859-1 encoding, so the string "8859_1" is appropriate. D is correct because the FileReader class is used for convenience, and does the same thing as an InputStreamReader associated with a file.
☒ A and E are both incorrect. A is incorrect because this constructor uses some character encoding other than ISO 8859-1. E is incorrect because the other constructor for FileReader uses a File as an argument. The question specified that *file* represents a FileInputStream.

16. ☑ B. Everything about this class is fine except for the missing line that imports the java.io classes. Remember to be very thorough when analyzing code examples on the exam!
☒ A, C, and D are incorrect. A is incorrect because everything in the main method works fine, assuming the import java.io command is used. C and D are incorrect because the class will not get as far as compiling.

17. ☑ C and E. C is correct because the PrintWriter is used to write different data objects as text. E is correct because an OutputStreamWriter actually handles the character encoding. OutputStreamWriter would be used in the PrintWriter constructor.

☒ A, B, and D are all incorrect. **A** is incorrect because a DataOutputStream is good for writing different types of data, but it does not do character encoding. **B** is incorrect because this class adds functionality to buffer data before writing it, which we do not really need here. A BufferedWriter would accomplish this if we were worried about efficiency when writing. **D** is incorrect because an input class serves no purpose here.

18. ☑ **A** and **D**. **A** is correct because the file would have been stored using your system default character encoding (unless UTF was used). **D** is correct because your keyboard will output characters in your system default.
☒ **B** and **C** are both incorrect. **B** is incorrect because a file from another operating system is likely to be in a specific character encoding. **C** is incorrect because the stream of characters will be character encoded in something else, unless it uses UTF.

19. ☑ **E**. The OutputStreamWriter uses no specific encoding, so it will use the default character encoding for the operating system.
☒ **A**, **B**, **C**, **D**, and **F** are incorrect. **A** and **B** are incorrect because the file compiles without errors. **C** is incorrect because there is nothing indicated that will cause an error at runtime. **D** is incorrect because the class will output text, not read it in. **F** is incorrect because no specific character encoding is used.

20. ☑ **B**, **C**, and **D**. **B** is correct because you would have to specify the character encoding if it came from another operating system. **C** is correct because the file would need to be written using Macintosh character encoding. **D** is correct; because it is from another operating system, it will need to be read with a specific character encoding.
☒ **A** is incorrect because default encoding could be used.

JAVA™

SUN CERTIFIED PROGRAMMER®

A

About the CD

This CD-ROM contains the CertTrainer software. CertTrainer comes complete with ExamSim, Skill Assessment tests, and the e-book(electronic version of the book). CertTrainer is easy to install on any Windows 98/NT/2000 computer and must be installed to access these features. You may, however, browse the e-book directly from the CD without installation.

Installing CertTrainer

If your computer CD-ROM drive is configured to autorun, the CD-ROM will automatically start up upon inserting the disk. From the opening screen you may either browse the e-book or install CertTrainer by pressing the *Install Now* button. This will begin the installation process and create a program group named CertTrainer. To run CertTrainer use START | PROGRAMS | CERTTRAINER.

System Requirements

CertTrainer requires Windows 98 or higher and Internet Explorer 4.0 or above and 600 MB of hard disk space for full installation.

CertTrainer

CertTrainer provides a complete review of each exam objective, organized by chapter. You should read each objective summary and make certain that you understand it before proceeding to the SkillAssessor. If you still need more practice on the concepts of any objective, use the "In Depth" button to link to the corresponding section from the Study Guide.

Once you have completed the review(s) and feel comfortable with the material, launch the SkillAssessor quiz to test your grasp of each objective. Once you complete the quiz, you will be presented with your score for that chapter.

ExamSim

As its name implies, ExamSim provides you with a simulation of the actual exam. The number of questions, the type of questions, and the time allowed are intended to be an accurate representation of the exam environment. Figure A-1 shows the screen you will see when you are ready to begin ExamSim.

FIGURE A-1 The ExamSim opening page

When you launch ExamSim, a digital clock display will appear in the upper left-hand corner of your screen. The clock will continue to count down to zero unless you choose to end the exam before the time expires.

Saving Scores as Cookies

Your ExamSim score is stored as a browser cookie. If you've configured your browser to accept cookies, your score will be stored in a file named *History*. If your browser is not configured to accept cookies, you cannot permanently save your scores. If you delete this History cookie, the scores will be deleted permanently.

E-Book

The entire contents of the Study Guide are provided in HTML form, as shown in Figure A-2. Although the files are optimized for Internet Explorer, they can also be viewed with other browsers, including Netscape.

FIGURE A-2

Study Guide contents in HTML format

Help

A help file is provided through a help button on the main CertTrainer screen in the lower right hand corner.

Upgrading

A button is provided on the main ExamSim screen for upgrades. This button will take you to www.syngress.com, where you can download any available upgrades.

B

About the Web Site

At Access.Globalknowledge, the premier online information source for IT professionals (http://access.globalknowledge.com), you'll enter a Global Knowledge information portal designed to inform, educate, and update visitors on issues regarding IT and IT education.

Get *What* You Want *When* You Want It

At the Access.Globalknowledge site, you can

- Choose personalized technology articles related to your interests. Access a news article, a review, or a tutorial, customized to what you want to see, regularly throughout the week.
- Continue your education, in between Global courses, by taking advantage of chat sessions with other users or instructors. Get the tips, tricks, and advice that you need today!
- Make your point in the Access.Globalknowledge community by participating in threaded discussion groups related to technologies and certification.
- Get instant course information at your fingertips. Customized course calendars show you the courses you want, and when and where you want them.
- Obtain the resources you need with online tools, trivia, skills assessment, and more!

All this and more is available now on the Web at http://access.globalknowledge.com. Visit today!